Gender Oppression and Globalization

Gender Oppression and Globalization

CHALLENGES FOR SOCIAL WORK

Janet L. Finn
Tonya Evette Perry
Sharvari Karandikar
EDITORS

Council on Social Work Education
Alexandria, Virginia

Library of Congress Cataloging-in-Publication Data

Gender oppression and globalization : challenges for social work / edited by Janet L. Finn, Tonya E. Perry, and Sharvari Karandikar.
     pages cm
  Includes bibliographical references and index.
  ISBN 978-0-87293-136-7 (alk. paper)
  1. Women's rights. 2. Sex discrimination against women. 3. Sexism.
  4. Globalization. I. Finn, Janet L., 1956-II. Perry, Tonya E. III. Karandikar, Sharvari.

  HQ1236.G461535 2013
  305.42—dc23

                              2013035265

Printed in the United States of America on acid-free paper that meets the American National Standards Institute Z39-48 standard.

Council on Social Work Education, Inc.
1701 Duke Street, Suite 200
Alexandria, VA 22314-3457
www.cswe.org

Cover art: "Unity" ©Monica Stewart. Reprinted with permission of the artist.

Contents

CONTENTS

CONTENTS

Foreword

JAN M. IVERY, former co-chair
ROBERTA S. PEARLMUTTER, co-chair

CSWE Council on the Role and Status of Women
in Social Work Education

This book represents a synergy among a conversation started at a Council on Social Work Education (CSWE) Annual Program Meeting (APM), an "unconference," and a commitment of members of the CSWE Council on the Role and Status of Women in Social Work Education (the Women's Council), and CSWE to produce a publication focused on issues related to women and girls in a global and social justice context. In other words, a "perfect storm" of events and activities contributed to this book.

The Women's Council is a council of the CSWE Commission on Diversity and Social and Economic Justice. The charge of the Women's Council is to

1. carry major responsibility for CSWE's development of curriculum materials related to women's issues in social work education;
2. identify procedures within academe and social work education that impede full participation of women;
3. recommend to the CSWE Board of Directors policy statements or development or modifications of internal policy;
4. assist in coordinating activities related to women at all levels of social work education; and
5. stimulate new programs and activities.

As part of this charge, members of the Women's Council organize informational sessions (called Connect Sessions) at each APM in addition to participating in other presentation formats to advance feminist knowledge in social work theory, research, practice, policy, and education. The Women's Council also sponsors activities such as the Mentor Recognition Fund and the Feminist Scholar Award at the annual Networking Breakfast to honor scholars and mentors who have advanced feminist scholarship as well as networking and connecting with the next generation of feminist scholars.

In 2007 three members the Women's Council—Janet Finn, Patricia O'Brien, and Izumi Sakamoto—presented "Social Work Educators' Explorations of Globalization and Women's Oppression: Problems and Possibilities" at the APM. These women organized the session, developed the content, and presented material that stimulated and excited the participants. Feminist views of gender oppression and globalization elicited a rich and dynamic conversation. At the 2008 APM these women, along with Kara Mileski, facilitated the session Gender-Based Oppression and Globalization: Critical Pedagogy and Practice as a follow-up to the themes proposed in the 2007 discussion. After reviewing the feedback and themes from these presentations, the Women's Council committed itself to disseminating the knowledge shared and generated from these meetings into a publication to address the issues of women and girls within social work education from a global perspective.

Participants wanted more: more conversation, dialogue, opportunities to share narratives, experiences, and emotions. "Go-Glo" (short for gender oppresion and globalization) became an Initiative Group of the Women's Council, and new members Sharvari Karandikar and Tonya Perry joined this Women's Council work group. Also that year the corporate Board of Directors of *Affilia* began discussions at an APM Think Tank about hosting a conference on feminism in social work. In 2009 that group hosted a meeting in San Antonio, TX, to discuss the conference idea; members of Go-Glo participated, focusing again on extending and deepening the conversation about gender oppression and globalization.

Eighteen months later, *Affilia's* Unsettling Feminisms "unconference" presented significant opportunity to further enrich the dialogue, include additional voices, and connect feminist and womanist experiences across many locales, populations, and issues. Members of the Women's Council participated, Go-Glo presented, and its members shared their voices on other topics as well. Patricia O'Brien, representing Jane Adams College of Social Work in Chicago and then co-chair of the Women's Council, served as host. The idea of producing a book emerged from the work of Go-Glo, the "unconference," and the Women's Council task group on feminist scholarship, research, and publication.

Julia Watkins, at that time executive director of CSWE, encouraged the editors to submit a book prospectus to CSWE Press and in spring 2011, immediately following the Chicago meeting, Finn, Karandikar, and Perry issued a call for papers. The editors solicited contributions from a diverse community of critical gender scholars that addressed the intersectionality of racism, sexism, heterosexism, and other forms of oppression and structural violence reflective of the lived experiences of women and girls. Instead of focusing only on empirical research, the editors sought contributions that spoke to the personal, political, and historical dimensions of gender-based oppression and globalization as a way to probe possibilities for social change in both pedagogy and practice. This book addresses the absence of critical analysis of gender-based oppression and globalization in the social work literature.

The book is not intended to provide direct answers to questions about gender-based oppression. Instead, it has been organized to use lived experiences to illustrate the complexity of gender-based oppression in the global context. It will help students grapple with the social constructions of gender and power in the global context by providing empirical research and reflexive essays that challenge students to ask themselves the "why" and "how" questions associated with the conditions that promote gender-based oppression and to suggest strategies that might be used to address these forms of oppression. Focusing on the intersection of gender-based oppression and globalization advances both theory and practice in social work education.

A colleague, preparing to teach a women and social work course, commented that no book based in social work had been written about women's experiences for more than 15 years. We believe that this book recognizes the complexities of women's lives and work; it acknowledges the connections between culture, gender, and oppression within a global context. It addresses questions we care about and acknowledges that we must seek and find or create responses. It will become the book of choice for our colleague and, we hope, for many others who teach about the experiences of women.

The steadfast work of Go-Glo members and CSWE's support of the project have been essential. We deeply appreciate their efforts in providing a forum for feminist scholars to share their diverse perspectives on this topic.

Acknowledgments

This book came to fruition with the help of many individuals, groups, and institutions. Initial ideas for a project on gender oppression and globalization were nurtured in conversations among members of the CSWE Council on the Role and Status of Women in Social Work Education. The Women's Council, as it is also known, is charged with the development of educational resources relevant to women's issues in social work education. Beginning in the spring of 2007, members of the scholarship work group of the Women's Council launched a discussion about gender oppression and globalization and the challenges and opportunities for social work education. The Women's Council sponsored a think tank session at CSWE's Annual Program Meeting (APM) in fall 2007 and a special session at the 2008 APM to broaden the conversation. Growing interest in the topic among social work educators encouraged members of the Women's Council to translate the vision of a book project into a concrete plan of action.

With background research underway, we issued a call for chapters in early 2011. The Unsettling Feminisms (un)conference, held at the University of Illinois–Chicago in May 2011, provided a venue for promotion of the book project and for making connections with potential contributors. By fall 2011 we had a talented cadre of authors committed to sharing their diverse and dynamic scholarship on gender oppression, globalization, and the challenges for social work.

We thank Jeane Anastas, Elizabeth Hutchison, Jan Ivery, Rosa Jimenez-Vasquez, Patricia O'Brien, Izumi Sakamoto, Susan Sarnoff, the members of the scholarship work group, for their insights into the development of this project. We are also grateful for the leadership of Marci Lazzari, Catherine Collins, Patricia O'Brien, Jan Ivery, Pam Kovacs, and Sue Perlmutter, who served as cochairs of the Women's Council during the time this book was in development. We extend our heartfelt thanks to former CSWE Executive Director Julia Watkins for her unflagging support of this project. Thanks to Elizabeth Simon and publications staff at CSWE Press for their critical and creative work in bringing this book to fruition and to the anonymous reviewers whose insightful feedback enriched the final product.

We also offer our individual acknowledgements. *Janet Finn:* I would like to thank the students in my "Social Work in a Global Context" and "Women and Social Action in the Americas" courses. They have challenged and inspired me, and our rich discussions have pushed me to further examine the questions addressed in this book. I thank my mother, Barbara Howard Finn, who has shown me the power of women's strength and resilience in so many ways over the years. I offer a special thanks to my husband, Dave Ames, for his support, good humor, and belief in the power of words to create change.

Tonya Perry: I give thanks to God, the creator and sustainer of the universe, for revealing my gifts and guiding me along a path of divine purpose, of which this project is a manifestation. I gratefully acknowledge Dr. Curtis Martin, dean of Alabama A & M University's School of Education, Humanities, and Behavioral Sciences, for his leadership. I am particularly indebted to the faculty and staff of the Department of Social Work, Psychology & Counseling for their encouragement of my contributions toward the development of this important work. I would like to extend a very special thanks to my departmental chair, Dr. Edith C. Fraser, for being a model of servant leadership and a vigorous supporter of my scholarship. There are no words to convey my gratitude to my parents, CSM (RET) Joshua and Demathraus Perry, without whom I would not be; their unconditional love and unending support have inspired and sustained me. I am eternally grateful to my cherished family, friends, and mentors, who have taught, loved, and supported me throughout my journey. Finally, I extend special thanks to my partner, Colin J. Mitchell, for loving me and keeping me balanced.

Sharvari Karandikar: I would like to thank Dr. Janet Finn, Dr. Tonya Perry, and Dr. Patricia O'Brien for recommending me as one of the editors of this book and guiding me throughout this process. I also wish to thank Dr. Tom Gregoire, dean of the College of Social Work, Ohio State University, for his continued support and encouragement for my research and development. I owe a big thank-you to my family—my husband Kumar and my dearest son Vishnu—for being so supportive and caring; without them this would not have been possible.

Introduction

Conceptualizing Gender Oppression, Globalization, and the Implications for Social Work

JANET L. FINN, TONYA E. PERRY, AND SHARVARI KARANDIKAR

Each day social workers confront the plights of women in a globalizing world. Women make up two thirds of the world's illiterate adults. Every 90 seconds a woman dies in pregnancy or childbirth. Violence threatens the safety and well-being of millions of women each day. It is conservatively estimated that three million women and girls are trafficked into the global sex trade each year. Women still earn only 75 cents for every dollar men earn. Seventy percent of the 1.2 billion people living in poverty around the world are female (Global Fund for Women, 2012; Population Reference Bureau, 2011; UNESCO, 2005; UN Women, 2011; United Nations, 2010; United Nations Population Fund [UNFPA], 2005; Women's Environment and Development Organization [WEDO], 2006).

At the same time, women are working individually and collectively to challenge and change these fundamental inequities. They are linking local and transnational efforts in honoring the voices, respecting the dignity, and championing the rights of women in the context of globalization. Social workers have key roles to play here as well. As part of an initiative launched by the Council on the Role and Status of Women in Social Work Education, an advisory group to the Council on Social Work Education (CSWE), the editors sought to bring questions of gender oppression and globalization front and center for social workers. We solicited participation from scholars in social work and related fields whose work addresses the intersection of gender oppression and globalization in concrete, specific, and diverse ways. This book is the result of their remarkable efforts, and it provides insight, direction, and possibilities for social work engagement at this intersection.

Gender Oppression and Globalization: Challenges for Social Work critically explores the mutually shaping relationship between globalization and gender oppression and considers the implications for social work. Contributors engage in critical feminist inquiry regarding the well-being of women and girls in the context of globalization and its many reverberations. We consider globalization as a feminist issue and focus on the status of women and girls, their vulnerabilities and resilience, the forms and mechanisms of oppression shaping their lives, and possibilities for social work action. We contend that without constant vigilance we are at risk of losing ground regarding the safety and status of women and girls in the face of increasing global inequality, militarization, and marketization of social life. We have a responsibility to prepare social workers to engage in critical thought and action that will inform and transform practice related to gender oppression in the complex context of globalization.

Miriam Dinerman (2003) and Fariyal Ross-Sheriff (2007), as past and current editors of *Affilia: Journal of Women and Social Work*, have named globalization as a women's issue and called for critical, systematic social work engagement with its processes and effects. To date, however, social work scholars and educators have paid limited attention to the profound intersection of globalization and gender oppression. Several social work scholars have addressed ways forces of globalization are connected to changes and challenges in domestic social policies and practices (Dominelli, 1999, 2010; Ferguson, Lavalette, & Whitmore, 2005; Healy, 2002; Ife, 2000; Karger, 2005; Midgely, 2007; Reisch, 1998). Some have addressed specific ways globalization matters to social work and have called for increased social work knowledge regarding histories of empire and colonialism, debt crisis, and structural adjustment policies and practices (Polack, 2004). Some have called for the infusion of global perspectives into the articulation of social work values and ethics (Link, 1999). Some have advocated for a human rights perspective as the foundation for social work and the starting place for advocating for women's rights (Mapp, 2008; Reichert, 2003). Others have engaged in debates over the risks and benefits of globalization and considered the relevance for social justice, global health, and human rights (Bywaters, McLeod, & Napier, 2009; Dominelli, 2002, 2008, 2010; Ferguson et al., 2005; Mapp, 2008; Midgley, 2004; Payne & Askeland, 2008; Polack, 2004; Rossiter, 2005; van Wormer, 2005).

However, there has been limited analysis of gender and gendered identities in relationship to globalization and little discussion in the social work literature of the ways globalizing forces shape our understandings of women's experiences and the policies and practices affecting women's everyday lives. Further, limited attention has been given to the creative and critical ways women on the ground are coming together, making their voices heard, and taking individual and collective action to resist and transform the diverse forms of oppression shaping their lives. This book explores these questions through critical analyses and case studies that are geared for student, practitioner, and activist audiences and that offer theoretical frames, personal accounts, practical examples, and hands-on possibilities to inform and transform thought and action.

CSWE (2008) challenges the profession to take a global perspective in its quest for social and economic justice, promotion of human rights, elimination of poverty, and enhancement of quality of life for all. Further, pressing issues of survival that confront so many women, their families, and communities cannot be understood or addressed without a critical grasp of the larger historical, political, economic, and social forces that shape local experience and the challenges for social justice therein (Abram, Slosar, & Walls, 2005; Adams, Dominelli, & Payne, 2005; Allan, Pease, & Briskman, 2003; Blundo, 2006; Lyons, 1999; Pease & Fook, 1999; Rossiter, 2005). Students and teachers alike face a daunting task as we try to translate these mandates into concrete learning and practice experiences that enable us to think and act critically and proactively, not only to understand but to begin to dismantle the multiple forms and forces of oppression shaping women's lives. To be prepared for 21st-century challenges, social workers need concrete, grounded examples of the complex intersections of globalization in the lives of women and girls, a critical theoretical understanding of those intersections and their relationship to gender oppression, and creative strategies for education and action that promote women's rights, human dignity, and social justice locally and globally. *Gender Oppression and Globalization: Challenges for Social Work* tackles these complex questions. In this volume a diverse community of critical gender scholars addresses theoretical, political, and practical questions regarding the relationship and response of social work education to gender oppression and globalization.

In this introduction we provide readers with an overview of the concepts of globalization and gender oppression. We probe what globalization means and why it matters in understanding forms and mechanisms of oppression. We then turn to the concept of gender oppression and provide readers with a brief summary of current data on the status of women and girls globally. We examine the relationship between globalization and gender oppression and explore globalization as a feminist issue. Finally, we consider contributions of critical race, feminist, and womanist theories and practice in understanding and in changing the conditions of women's lives, and we demonstrate the relevance of these issues for social work practice in the 21st century.

What Is Globalization and Why Does It Matter to Social Work?

Globalization is a complex and contested concept. In general, globalization refers to complicated transnational political and economic processes that have (a) restructured relations and alignments of nations and regions of the world; (b) stimulated new linkages, flows, and disruptions of people, ideas, cultures, and politics; and (c) contributed to shifting patterns of migration, forms of labor, and relations of power and inequality (Appadurai, 2002; Cole & Durham, 2007; Giddens, 1999; Harvey, 1989; Hoogvelt, 1997; Mapp, 2008). Frequently, the economic aspects of globalization are emphasized in its definition. For example, *Merriam-Webster's* defines *globalization* (n.d.) as "the development of an increasingly integrated global economy marked especially by free trade, free flow of capital, and the tapping of cheaper foreign labor markets." The International Labour Organization (ILO; Dejardin, 2008, p. 1) describes globalization as encompassing the "dynamic processes of international trade and finance that interconnect and increasingly integrate national economies." Chandra Mohanty (2006) encourages us to look beyond the neutral language of economic globalization to name and recognize the pervasive power of corporate globalization. She draws insight from writer and activist Arundhati Roy, who describes the combined power of the "check book and the cruise missile" (Mohanty, 2006, p. 8), which is the pairing of economic control and militarized force, as key tools of corporate-led globalization.

Some writers have identified the potential of globalizing forces that create opportunities for technological advance, open space for cross-border communication, and promote the engagement and exchange of ideas, people, and resources on a scale previously unimaginable (Friedman, 1999; Held & McGrew, 2003; Stiglitz, 2007). Such possibilities for compression of time and distance hold potential for enhancing global consciousness and building a truly global society. Less optimistic perspectives have pointed to the rising rates of poverty, unemployment, and inequality; acceleration of social and environmental degradation; growing transnational corporate power; and increasing violence and militarization that have gone hand in hand with globalization (Cohn & Enloe, 2003; Harvey, 1989; Held & McGrew, 2003: Korten, 2001; Piven & Cloward, 1997; Scholte, 2008; Stiglitz, 2002). As Bigelow and Peterson (2002) assert, globalization is associated with increased economic inequality, lower real wages, and greater labor insecurity.

Some writers contend that globalization is a distinct new phase of social, economic, and political development marked by fundamental transformations of human experiences of and relationship to time and space (Appadurai, 2002; Giddens, 1999; Harvey, 1989). Thomas Friedman (1999), for example, defines globalization as the

> inexorable integration of markets, nation–states, and technologies to a degree never witnessed before—in a way that is enabling individuals, corporations, and nation–states to reach around the world farther, faster, deeper, and cheaper than ever before . . . [and] the spread of free-market capitalism to virtually every corner of the world. (pp. 7–8)

Others argue there is nothing new about globalization. Rather, we are currently witnessing the latest manifestation of long-term social, political, and economic processes with roots in transcontinental practices of trade, conquest, colonialism, and empire building of long duration (Cooper, 2001). Bigelow and Peterson (2002), for example, describe the crushing debt crises experienced by many countries in the wake of economic globalization as the *new colonialism* of the late 20th and early 21st centuries. Some scholars link processes of globalization to the spread of cultures of surveillance, control, and militarism, and point to the increasing militarization of everyday life as a troubling feature of contemporary globalization (Enloe, 2004; Mohanty, 2003, 2006; Sudbury, 2005). And some suggest that what we are witnessing at present is a rapid globalization of the economy without an accompanying globalization of citizenship, thus leaving basic human rights and dignity in jeopardy (Ife, 2000). As Moghadam (1998) contends, the globalization of capital has resulted in the massive expansion of markets and technologies. At the same time it has also exacerbated existing economic and social inequalities in and among regions of the world. Those inequalities play out along numerous intersecting axes, including gender (Johnston-Anumonwo & Doane, 2011; Munck, 2005).

Unprecedented pressures for economic growth have pushed demands on ecosystems and intensified competition between the rich and the poor for scarce resources. The global reorganization of labor has resulted in creating new social subjects, including *flexible* workers employed part-time for no or few benefits or labor protections, *displaced* workers whose jobs have been made obsolete by new technologies or replaced by lower-wage workers in another part of the globe, and *migrant* workers who leave family and community behind in search of paid work beyond local or national borders (Bair, 2010; Cabezas, Reese, & Waller, 2007; Chang, 2000; Dominelli, 1999, 2010; Harvey, 1989; Hondagneu-Sotelo, 2003; Ife, 2001; Korten, 2001; Ross-Sheriff, 2011.

An understanding of globalization calls for an understanding of neoliberalism, its underlying economic logic and driving ideology (Piven & Cloward, 1997; Scholte, 2008). It is a logic of "market rule on a global scale" (McMichael, 2000, p. 149). According to David Harvey (2005), a basic assumption of neoliberalism is that human well-being can best be advanced through the widest spread of a market economy and application of entrepreneurial skills. A neoliberal economic model seeks to expand the reach and frequency of market transactions into all arenas of social life. Neoliberal approaches champion the direct privatization of government services and see the only legitimate role of the state as keeping markets open and unfettered (Jurik, 2006). As Cabezas and colleagues (2007) write, neoliberalism

> privileges the expansion of the "free" (without regulation and tariff) market and the global integration of economies. It proposes the abolition of government intervention in economic matters and radical cutbacks in social services, including education, health care, housing, agricultural subsidies, and nutrition. (p. 6)

An understanding of neoliberal logic and practice is key for social work. Fundamentally, a neoliberal approach calls for dismantling a social safety net. Instead, private enterprise and individual initiative are viewed as the means to creating wealth, eliminating poverty, and improving human welfare. Market-based competition is touted as a virtue, and many of the social institutions that have been central to social work, such as social insurance, welfare, public education, and social services, are seen as costly, unnecessary, and outdated. In fact, such institutions may well be viewed as obstacles to maximizing economic growth and output (Ferguson et al., 2005; Reese, 2007). As Michael Reisch (2006, p. 69) states, through the workings of economic globalization, market values take precedence over the values and goals of social well-being and welfare provisioning. The consequences can be devastating, especially for people who have already experienced social exclusion and economic marginalization.

The logic of neoliberalism has become widely accepted as economic common sense over the past few decades. Governments worldwide, either voluntarily or under pressure because of debt crises, have undertaken reforms to reduce taxation; cut back state support to education, social services, and social insurance; and dismantle labor and environmental protections. Neoliberal approaches have called for the replacement of social responsibility for support and protections with privatized alternatives. A number of social work scholars have critically examined the implications of globalization and neoliberalism for social work and social welfare. They have addressed the relationship of neoliberalism to issues of poverty, immigration, welfare, reform, health care, labor, and the environment. And they have considered ways neoliberal policies and practices fit into existing social hierarchies of race, gender, class, age, citizenship, and (dis)ability and threaten the already precarious life circumstances of vulnerable groups and individuals (Dominelli, 2002, 2008, 2010; Ferguson et al., 2005; Hick, Fook, & Pozzuto, 2005; Ife, 2000; Jurik, 2006; Kilty & Segal, 2006; Polack, 2004; Reese, 2007; Reisch, 2006; Schram, 2006; Sparr, 1994).

A relevant example of the workings of neoliberal economic logic can be seen in the embrace of welfare reform in the United States at the end of 20th century (Kilty & Segal, 2006; Reese, 2007). Proponents of welfare reform argued that a new welfare discipline was needed to end poor people's dependency on the state for basic economic survival. Welfare programs dating from the New Deal, premised on the notion that poor citizens were entitled to basic economic support, were dismantled in the 1990s and replaced with time-limited, work-based programs. Participants could receive a minimal amount of public assistance in exchange for labor at less than minimum wage. Individual states could set their own limits on the number of months of lifetime eligibility for assistance, with a federal maximum set at 60 months (Hays, 2004; Kilty & Segal, 2006)

The success of welfare reform was measured in terms of the numbers of people no longer receiving welfare assistance rather than the numbers of people no longer living in poverty. Failure was seen in terms of individual deficits rather than the structure of the economy or rates of unemployment. Although many participants did work, they seldom received sufficient wages, hours, or benefits to rise out of poverty. Poor women, in particular poor women of color and their children, were especially hard hit by the effects of these policies (Abramovitz, 2006; Morgen, Acker, Wieght, & Gonzales, 2006). Now, more than 15 years after the celebration of these neoliberal reforms, poverty rates are on the rise, unemployment rates are high, and more and more families are at risk of losing their homes as well as their jobs as a result of shifts in the global economy (Miles & Fowler, 2006; Nichols, 2012). At the same time, this neoliberal model of welfare reform has been touted as a success and exported abroad to be duplicated in other countries (Reese, 2007). For example, Ellen Reese has powerfully depicted the ways Wisconsin's model of welfare reform was aggressively promoted throughout Europe by conservative think tanks and international circuits of policy makers at a time when the European Union faced declining economies, aging populations, major changes in industry and manufacturing, internationalization of finance, growing deficits, and budget constraints. However, the discourse of welfare reform ignored these structural problems and aimed antiwelfare rhetoric at already vulnerable and marginalized populations, including immigrants, minority youths, and single mothers (Reese, 2007, pp. 87–89).

What Is Oppression and Why Does It Matter to Social Work?

Social workers are charged with the responsibility of confronting oppression and working to eliminate the forms and mechanisms of oppression that constrain the lives and life chances of individuals and groups. Given that the issue of oppression is central to our work, it is essential that we have a critical grasp of the concept. *Oppression* may be defined as the unjust exercise of power or authority by one group over another. It may involve silencing of voice, denial of access to resources, or the use of direct forms of violence (Finn & Jacobson, 2008, p. 39; Van Soest & Garcia, 2003; Young, 1990). Oppression, quite literally, describes how some members of a society are pressed down by others in overt and covert ways. It may play out through practices of sexism, racism, ageism, classism, colonialism, and ableism, to name a few.

Dorothy Van Soest and Betty Garcia (2003) have identified the following key elements that are common to all forms of oppression:

- Oppression bestows power and advantage on certain people who are regarded as the "norm" against whom others are judged (e.g. White, male, heterosexual).
- Oppressions are maintained by ideologies of superiority or inferiority and by threat (and reality) of both individual and institutional forms of violence.
- Oppressions are institutionalized in societal norms, laws, policies, and practice.
- Oppression works to maintain the invisibility of those oppressed. (p. 35)

Further, Van Soest and Garcia identify racism as a form of oppression that is deeply entrenched in the United States. They argue that a critical awareness of racism as a complex interplay of institutional, sociopolitical, interpersonal, economic, and psychological processes is essential to understanding the forms and mechanisms of oppression (p. 33).

Institutionalized oppression refers to the systematic mistreatment of members of particular social identity groups or of those labeled by dominant groups as *different*. It plays out through the workings of social institutions—such as the legal, education, health, and welfare systems—in ways that exclude, deny, disadvantage, or otherwise violate the dignity and rights of people because of their social group identity or label. We bear witness to the results of institutional oppression in multiple arenas, such as the overrepresentation of people of color in the criminal justice system; underrepresentation of women, especially women of color, in legislative bodies; and the denial of basic civil rights to people who identify as gay, lesbian, bisexual, or transgender.

Critical race and feminist theorist Patricia Hill Collins (2000) challenges what she terms "additive" (p. 18) models of oppression and argues instead for the need to understand interlocking systems of oppression. Hill Collins calls for inclusive thinking about the ways forms and practices of oppression, such as sexism, racism, classism, heterosexism, and ageism, work together in mutually reinforcing ways that produce complex matrices of domination. She writes,

In addition to being structured along axes such as race, gender, and social class, the matrix of domination is structured on several levels.

People experience and resist oppression on three levels: the level of personal biography; the group or community level of the cultural context created by race, class, and gender; and the systemic level of social institutions. Black feminist thought emphasizes all three levels as sites of domination and as potential sites of resistance. (p. 227)

Black feminist thought, including Hill Collins' (2000) construct of interlocking oppressions, has contributed significantly to the expanding knowledge base concerning oppression. This literature includes a large body of work produced by critical race theorists, which we address later in our discussion.

Activist scholars such as feminist philosopher Iris Marion Young have also provided concrete frameworks for examining ways forces of racism, gender oppression, and other forms of oppression manifest themselves in people's everyday lives. For example, Young (1990) develops the concept of oppression in terms of five *faces* through which oppression plays out in people's everyday lives. According to Young's model, the five faces of oppression are exploitation, marginalization, powerlessness, cultural imperialism, and violence. Exploitation is the process through which the paid or unpaid labors of one group are denied social and economic value as they contribute to the betterment of a more privileged group, as exemplified in the unpaid care-giving that constitutes much of "women's work." Marginalization is the process of creating second-class citizens by denying members of some groups the right to full social, economic, or political participation in society. Powerlessness entails denial of access to resources and to the right to participate in decision making that affects one's life. Cultural imperialism involves the imposition of a dominant group's worldview and meaning system on subordinated groups, thus rendering the group invisible or marked as different and therefore deviant. Violence refers to structural violence and direct personal violence directed at members of oppressed groups. Such violence is often accompanied by a high level of tolerance among members of the dominant group. According to Young, multiple faces may work in concert, contributing to mutually reinforcing forms and practices of oppression. When we speak of gender oppression in this context, we refer to forms and practices of exclusion, denial, silencing, disempowerment, and violence one may be subjected to because of one's gendered identity. Gender can be understood as the social meanings given to identification as male and female in a particular cultural, political, and historical context, and the accompanying social roles, attributes, and characteristics associated with the spectrum of masculinities and femininities. Societal notions about gender shape understandings of sex roles and sexual identity as well as understandings and expectations of men's and women's capacities, responsibilities, and limits. Although concepts of gender are socially constructed, they operate in ways that reinforce deeply embedded assumptions regarding presumably natural differences (Ortner, 1996).

On the surface, the concept of gender seems simple and straightforward. But once we scratch the surface we see the complexities. We are socialized from birth in powerful ways to think about what it means to be male or female, so that arbitrary ideas about differences simply go without saying and become taken for granted over time. The very notion of a binary difference of male versus female is one of those taken-for-granted ideas (Foss, 2012). In addressing issues of gender and gender oppression here we are considering how dominant societal and cultural assumptions regarding gendered identities and relations become embedded in social institutions, relations, and practices and how they work to silence, subordinate, and disempower. As we come to recognize the faces of gender oppression, we become better equipped to challenge them.

In sum, we consider gender not as a single axis of difference but as part of a complex matrix of social identity and experience. In the following section we introduce readers to some key aspects of the forms and consequences of oppression in the lives of women and girls globally. We then turn to a more in-depth look at the contributions of critical race, feminist, and womanist thought in understanding and addressing gender oppression in the context of globalization.

Considering Gender Oppression in a Global Context

As the statistics in the opening paragraph indicate, women carry an unequal burden of poverty and illiteracy around the world. Although some progress has been made in terms of girls' access to primary education, the gender gap persists. Girls are still less likely to go to school than boys (United Nations, 2010). In the least developed countries, fewer than half the girls remain enrolled in school at the secondary level (WEDO, 2006). Women are the poorest of the poor. Women and children make up two thirds of the world's one billion people living on less than a dollar a day (WEDO, 2006). Although women are responsible for 60% to 80% of the world's food production and perform more than two thirds of the work hours in the world, they only earn 10% of the world's income and own only 1% of world property (WEDO, 2006). The unpaid, often invisible, work done by women adds up to an estimated $11 trillion per year (Broad, 2002). Yet, the hours and the value of much of the labor of women, especially care work, simply go unnoticed.

Women and girls continue to be victims of systematic violence on a global scale. The World Health Organization (2005) reports that one in five women is likely to be a victim of rape. The mass rape of women and girls is broadly used as a weapon of war (Kristof & WuDunn, 2009). For example, a UN report claims that 90% of women and girls over age 3 were sexually abused in parts of Liberia during civil war (Kristof & WuDunn, 2009). Women and girls also make up approximately 80% of people who are trafficked across borders for labor exploitation each year, the majority forced into the commercial sex trade (UNFPA, 2005).

Women suffer health consequences of gender inequality. Although women are responsible for the majority of care for others, their own health is too often neglected. More than half a million women die in childbirth each year, the majority in poor countries. Women's limited decision-making opportunities in households and nations limit their rights to reproductive justice. Increased incidence of AIDS and HIV among women reflects their limited power in terms of sexual consent and condom use. Likewise, limited educational opportunities further constrain women's autonomy and power in negotiating sexual relations and reproductive rights (UN Women, 2011).

Processes of economic globalization in recent years have had particular consequences in the lives of women (Sparr, 1994). For example, according to a report published by the ILO, there has been a growing trend toward outsourcing, cross-border, and overseas production, and "export zone" production since the 1980s (Dejardin, 2008, p. 1). Women make up the "overwhelming majority" of workers in the labor-intensive, export-oriented industries in developing countries. And they tend to be concentrated in the most vulnerable jobs in the global system of production, such as agribusiness and care work (Dejardin, 2008, p. 1). Women's work in the global economy tends to be characterized by insecure, low-wage labor in poor working conditions (Wright, 2006). Working women are concentrated in the low end of what has become known as global supply chains. In effect, this expanding global system of production has served to replicate and reinforce gender inequalities, leaving women workers ever more vulnerable (Bair, 2010; Dejardin, 2008).

The global financial crises of the past few years have exacerbated gender inequalities and women's vulnerability. As the UN Commission on the Status of Women (2009) reported, these financial and economic crises have had gender-specific effects and placed a disproportionate burden on women, especially poor, migrant, minority women. Women are often the first to be laid off. Cuts in public expenditures place an undue burden on women, who are then expected to take up the slack through their unpaid labors in the so-called care economy. And those in the informal sectors of the economy, such as street vendors and domestic workers, where women's labor is concentrated, have been particularly hard hit by global economic recessions (UN Commission on the Status of Women, 2009).

The significant role of women in the global economy, as well as their gendered vulnerability, is illustrated by the concept of global care chains, a term coined by Arlie Hochschild (2000) to describe the "series of links between people across the globe based on the paid or unpaid work of caring" (Hochschild, 2009, p. 1). According to Amaia Perez Orozco (2009) global care chains are

> networks of transnational dimensions that are formed for the purpose of maintaining daily life. These networks are comprised of households which transfer their caregiving tasks from one to another on the basis of power axes, such as gender, ethnicity, social class, and place of origin. (p. 4)

A global care chain might consist of an employed upper-middle-class woman in a more developed country hiring a woman from a less developed country to do child care work and other domestic labor. The migrating caregiver then turns to her own daughter or mother to provide care work at home while she travels abroad for employment. Women constitute the majority of workers in these global care chains.

Women are pushed and pulled into global care chain migration. Poverty, low wages, and unemployment in their home countries, desire to expand their social and economic opportunities, and hopes of improving the lives and life chances of their families draw women in. Women then use their relatively better economic position abroad to provide support for their families. At a global level, women migrants send about the same amount of funds in remittances to their home countries as do men. However, women earn less overall than men and thus send a higher proportion of their income than do men. Women are more likely than men to send remittances regularly and over a longer period of time. They tend to send smaller sums more often, which means they have to pay more in transfer fees. Whereas men most often send remittances to their wives, women migrants are more likely to send remittances to women who are responsible for caring for their children (Fudge, 2010; International Organization for Migration, n.d.; Ramirez, Dominguez, & Morais, 2005; Ross-Sheriff, 2011; United Nations-International Research and Training Institute for the Advancement of Women, 2008).

The United Nations, through its Commission on the Status of Women, annual human development reports, the UN Women annual reports (2011, 2012), and the UN World's Women report (2010), has been drawing attention to the costs and consequences of gender inequality. Giving attention to the gendering of globalization through analysis of the feminization of labor and patterned practices of global care chains has been a key aspect of the work. UN reports on women's health, political participation, economic participation, human rights, education, activism, and status vis-à-vis Millennium Development Goals have documented the areas of progress and ongoing challenges. For example, the Human Development Report (UN Development Programme, 2011) noted that the distribution of income had worsened at the country level in much of the world, thus leaving poor women ever more vulnerable on multiple fronts.

The 2011 HDR specifically addressed issues of environmental sustainability and described how gender inequalities are exacerbated by environmental damage and degradation. Women bear a disproportionate burden of environmental degradation given their responsibilities for subsistence, such as maintaining crops for family consumption and collecting firewood and water. In 2010 the HDR introduced a new measure, the Index of Gender Inequality, in an effort to more closely monitor and adequately respond to the range of issues affecting women's well-being globally. The index combines measures of (a) maternal mortality, (b) adolescent fertility rates, (c) numbers of seats in congress/parliament held by women, (d) percentage of population with at least a secondary education, (e) labor force participation rate, and (f) a combined measure of reproductive health based on access to and use of contraception, prenatal care, births attended by a trained health care provider, and fertility rate. It is an attempt to encapsulate a more integrated assessment of the multifaceted nature of gender inequality and thus provide guidance for more coordinated, multidimensional courses of action.

In recent years systematic efforts on a global scale have been made to recognize and address the persistence of gender oppression and inequality. For example, the United Nations has called for action to

- •Protect and empower women living in conflict regions
- •Promote women's political decision making
- •Strengthen the political will to end violence against women
- •Enhance women's economic power and autonomy
- •Involve women as key players in national development planning and budgeting
- •Confront use of rape as an act of war
- •Actively engage women in all aspects of peace building (United Nations, 2010; United Nations Development Fund for Women, 2010; United Nations Human Development Programme, 2010; UN Women, 2011, 2012; UNFPA, 2010).

These efforts are important for addressing and improving the status of women globally.

Questions of gender oppression and the possibilities of concrete local actions for change have also been brought to popular consciousness by investigative journalists. For example, Nicholas Kristof and Sheryl WuDunn's book, *Half the Sky: Turning Women's Oppression Into Opportunity Worldwide* (2009), has brought detailed accounts of women's struggles against violence, oppression, exclusion, and inequality to mass audiences and provided concrete examples of women's grounded action for change and possibilities for support and solidarity. Their work has been gaining attention among social work educators and students, sparking dialogue and debate. Although their book does not provide a critical framework of analysis of gender oppression and globalization, the individual and deeply personal accounts they document provide graphic evidence of the pervasiveness of violence and exploitation in women's lives and of courageous action for change against the odds.

Through the specific contributions of critical race, feminist, and womanist thinkers; grounded activists; and committed allies, efforts to combat gender oppression locally and globally have gained traction. And it is through their efforts that a more critical understanding of the complex relationship between gender oppression and globalization has been brought to light. We turn now to key contributions that have guided our thinking in producing this book.

Contributions of Critical Race, Feminist, and Womanist Thought in Addressing Globalization and Gender Oppression

A growing body of scholarship brings a critical perspective to bear in trying to understand, unravel, and resist the processes and consequences of economic globalization that jeopardize the rights, dignity, and well-being of vulnerable individuals and groups, with particular attention to women. This scholarship has been undertaken by feminist and womanist scholars who bring critical race theory (CRT) to bear in their work, by feminist scholars who have interrogated the discourses and practices of international development over the past 50 years, and by feminist scholars within and beyond social work who have closely examined questions of women's labor, rights, well-being, and power in the context of globalization. In this section we provide a brief overview of CRT and ways it has shaped and been shaped by feminist thought and practice. We then turn to some of the contributions of feminists who have brought critical race/feminist thought and practice to bear in addressing gender oppression in the context of international development and globalization. Their work has shaped our thinking and fueled our desire to engage a broader social work audience in tackling these complex issues.

CRT. CRT is an interdisciplinary theoretical framework concerned with the relationships of race, racism, and power (Crenshaw, Gotanda, Peller, & Thomas, 1995; Delgado & Stefancic, 2001). Because it is focused not only on illuminating the dynamic interplay of race, racism, and power but also on the questioning and transformation of these sociopolitical constructs and structures, CRT has been most appropriately framed as a movement. "The critical race theory movement is a collection of activists and scholars interested in studying and transforming the dynamics of race, racism, and power" (Delgado & Stefancic, 2012, p. 3). At its core, the CRT movement is concerned with eliminating racism with the ultimate goal of eliminating all forms of oppression (Crenshaw et al., 1995).

Central assumptions of CRT are that (a) racism is a central feature of American society, an assumption that severely undermines notions of color blindness and neutrality; (b) racism has a utilitarian function in that it advances the material interests of White elites and the psychic interests of working-class Whites; (c) race is a social construct rather than a biological reality; (d) identity cannot be reduced to race but is intersectional in nature; and (e) because of their unique histories and experiences of oppression, people of color have a "presumed competence" to speak about race and racism (Delgado & Stefancic, 2012, p. 10).

The CRT movement has been greatly influenced by a number of philosophers, thinkers, and revolutionaries, such as Michel Foucault, Jacques Derrida, Sojourner Truth, Frederick Douglass, and Cesar Chavez. The CRT movement draws heavily on two of its predecessors—critical legal studies and radical feminism—and it has been greatly informed by two movements that preceded it, the Black Power and Chicano movements of the 1960s and 1970s. The influences of these disciplines and movements on CRT are reflected in various understandings central to CRT such as legal indeterminacy and skepticism of triumphalist history borrowed from critical legal studies as well as CRT's emphasis on group empowerment and redressing historical wrongs borrowed from the civil rights movement. Perhaps most relevant to our discussion here are the ways feminism has contributed to the CRT movement. Feminism's framing of the intersections of power and the social construction of roles as well as illuminating the invisible, insidious nature of oppression are central assumptions underlying CRT (Crenshaw et al., 1995; Delgado & Stefancic, 2012).

The inception of the CRT movement extends to the 1970s when many lawyers, legal scholars, and activists recognized that the civil rights gains of the 1960s were being challenged and that the energy captured during that era was becoming stagnant. In the summer of 1989 a nucleus of pioneering activist scholars, such as Derrick Bell, the late Alan Freeman, Richard Delgado, and a number of other like-minded people, convened near Madison, Wisconsin, to exchange ideas, theories, and strategies to understand and combat racism, particularly the subtler forms of racism that appeared to be escalating (Crenshaw et al., 1995; Delgado & Stefancic, 2012).

Since 1989 the CRT movement has galvanized a broad array of interdisciplinary scholars, students, and activists to engage in meaningful related scholarship. Although CRT pioneers Richard Delgado and Derrick Bell, the intellectual father of the CRT movement, continue to be active in the movement, the CRT literature has been significantly expanded in the past two decades by an interdisciplinary cadre of contemporary scholars. Among this cadre are Kimberle Crenshaw, Angela Harris, Charles Lawrence, Mari Matsuda, Patricia Williams, Neil Gotanda, Mitu Gulati, Jerry Kang, Eric Yamamoto, Ian Haney Lopez, Laura Gomez, Margaret Montoya, Juan Perea, Francisco Valdes, Cheryl Harris, and Angela Owuachi-Willig (Delgado & Stefancic, 2012).

Although the beginnings of CRT are deeply entrenched in law, a number of disciplines have embraced CRT. Scholars in education, social work, political science, sociology, and women's studies have applied a CRT perspective to examine issues of concern (Dixon & Rousseau, 2005; Howard-Hamilton, 2003; Lavia, 2007). The CRT movement is highly consistent with social work in that it provides a vehicle for understanding and responding to issues related to race, power, and racism in our attempt to promote social justice (Razack & Jeffrey, 2002). An emerging body of literature uses CRT to interrogate social work education, teaching, and practice (Abrams & Moio, 2009; Razack, 2009; Razack & Jeffrey, 2002). For example, Razack (2009) challenges social workers engaged in international education and practice to be mindful of the ways privilege and oppression play out in classroom and practice settings and to be consistent in efforts to localize the global.

In the context of this book CRT provides a useful tool for examining gendered patterns of oppression wherever they exist. Through the lens of CRT we are compelled, for example, to conceptualize global gender oppression as a function of the realities of hypercapitalism, which in turn has emerged in specific historical and cultural contexts. CRT also supports our recognition that women who are experiencing oppression in their daily lives are indeed vessels of expert knowledge. Further, CRT compels us to question our own sense of neutrality and objectivity as we seek to understand gendered patterns of oppression, attempt to articulate strategies to combat it, and engage in antioppressive practice. Finally, CRT teaches us that our work to end gender oppression is linked to the overarching goal of ending all forms of oppression to attain social justice for all people.

Womanism. Consistent with other activist paradigms that recognize the intersectional nature of gender oppression and the various ways it presents itself in the lives of women is womanism:

a social change perspective rooted in Black women's and other women of color's everyday experiences and everyday methods of problem solving in everyday spaces, extended to the problem of ending all forms of oppression for all people, restoring the balance between people and the environment/nature and reconciling human life with the spiritual dimension. (Phillips, 2006, p. xx)

Whereas some argue that womanism is a special kind of feminism, others contend that despite its shared focus on eliminating gender oppression, the historically unique circumstances of Black womanhood in which womanism is so deeply rooted distinguishes it from feminism (Davis, 1983; Duran, 2010; Phillips, 2006; Steady, 1987; Walker, 1983). At its core womanism is concerned with (a) the struggle for liberation of all people, (b) the recognition of the ordinariness of oppression as it is expressed in the daily lives of those who experience it, (c) interconnectedness, (d) the transcendental nature of being, and (e) the pursuit of collective well-being of the universal community through social transformation (Phillips, 2006). Since Alice Walker's (1983) published expression of womanism, it has been adopted, critiqued, and expanded on by multidisciplined scholars across the globe (e.g., Carlton-LaNey, 1997; Duran, 2010; Hudson-Weems, 1993; Mikell, 1995; Ogunyemi, 1985).

The global presence of womanism is particularly apparent on the African continent, which has been argued by some to be the home of very feminist ideals, including West African–derived, woman-centered conceptualizations of self-determination and self-agency (Davis, 1983; Oyewumi, 2003; Steady, 1987). Womanism's global presence has fueled notable gender-related activism and program development in Africa. Duran (2010) asserts that womanism is "a driving force behind much of the activity of many West African cultures, including their current work with NGO's" (p. 171). Womanism is thus a dynamic activist paradigm advancing international gender discourse and empowerment.

Critiques of international development. Another critical theoretical direction informing our thinking about gender oppression and globalization stems from the work of feminist scholars and activists who began to question the absence of attention to women as international development programs expanded in the post–World War II era. These scholars critiqued the theories and policies guiding dominant development practices and challenged the invisibility of women therein (see Drolet, 2010, for a concise overview). Over time they called for the integration of women in development processes, critiqued Western models and assumptions embedded in those processes, critically examined the constructions of gender that have informed international development, and explored the relationship between dominant development approaches and the ongoing oppression of women (Beneria, 2003; Beneria & Sen, 1981; Boserup, 1970; Moghadam, 1998).

For example, since the 1970s Cynthia Enloe, a feminist scholar and professor of political science and international development studies, has trained her gaze on questions of gender in the context of globalization. Through her studies in international political conflict and the global spread of militarization, Enloe came to critical feminist consciousness as she began to ask "where are the women?" In a 2003 conversation published in *Signs*, Enloe describes her experience of learning about patriarchy and incorporating critical analysis of patriarchy in her work. When she first heard the term, she thought, "Oh no, not patriarchy, I don't know what it is and I don't talk that way!" (Cohn & Enloe, 2003, p. 1191). However, through her studies of militarization and its effect on women's lives she learned to name patriarchy, give examples of how it works, and recognize it as a tool for understanding the workings of power. Enloe describes the importance of confronting patriarchy:

> It means you have to ask about the daily operations of both masculinity and femininity in relationship to each other. It is not men-on-top that makes something patriarchal. It's men who are recognized and claim a certain form of masculinity, for the sake of being more valued, more "serious," and "the protectors of/and controllers of those people who are less masculine" that makes any organization, any community, any society patriarchal. It's never automatic; it's rarely self-perpetuating. It takes daily tending. It takes decisions—even if those are masked as "tradition." It relies on many women finding patriarchal relationships comfortable, sometimes rewarding. And you and I in our own work have found women who would much rather not rock the patriarchal boat—often for good reasons. Patriarchal structures and cultures have proved to be so adaptable! (Cohn & Enloe, 2003, p. 1191)

Enloe (2000a, 2004) recognized the importance of listening to women and the stories of their everyday lives to understand the ways processes of globalization are gendered and how they play out in diverse local contexts. She has described the violating effects on women's lives of the globalization of U.S. military presence and challenged the assumptions of military response to political conflict as "self-evident" (Cohn & Enloe, 2003, pp. 1, 203). And she has called attention to the workings of masculinity and femininity in organizational contexts engaged in the processes and effects of globalization, such as the United Nations, World Bank, and international aid organizations. Her work has furthered critical understanding of globalization as a phenomenon that is not gender neutral (Cohn & Enloe, 2003; Enloe, 2000a, 2004, 2007).

Julia Drolet (2010) has critically examined the development paradigms promoted by institutions such as the World Bank and the U.S. Agency for International Development (USAID) and the ways women and gender have been considered by these entities. Paying particular attention to microenterprise schemes that target women, Drolet (drawing from Rankin) contends that these institutions promote a model of "financial self-sustainability" that constructs poor women as rational economic actors, and thus the "onus for development falls squarely on their shoulders releasing the state from considerable civic obligation" (p. 218). In so doing, Drolet argues, the overall neoliberal agenda remains intact with concerns about poverty alleviation merely inserted therein.

Similarly, Ananya Roy (2007) has critically deconstructed what she terms the "gender order of global poverty management" and the construction of "Third World Woman" (pp. 28–29). Roy considers how development capital flows through institutions such as the World Bank and USAID in ways that produce the third world woman, who is tasked with the responsibility for poverty alleviation through microenterprise. Women, so constructed, become reduced to efficient units of development work. Further, she argues, even as the alleviation of poverty has become ever more closely linked to finance capital and corporate interests, the image of the Third World Woman remains a constant presence. Roy writes, "She is a fetish, a magical object. This is 'in her name'" (p. 35). The work of these scholars raises important questions regarding constructions of gender and *otherness* that shape the ideologies, policies, and practices of international development organizations.

Transnational and global feminisms. Insights of CRT and critiques of international development and the expanse of global capitalism have come together in the contributions of scholars and activists who define themselves as transnational or global feminists (Waller & Marcos, 2005). For example, Chandra Talpade Mohanty (1991) is a transnational feminist theorist, writer, and activist who has been broadly recognized for her ground-breaking essay "Under Western Eyes,"[2] in which she challenged the ways White Western feminists had constructed a homogeneous image of the third world woman as *other*, a passive, vulnerable victim of oppression. Mohanty's work, in effect, linked critical race and feminist theory. She argued that (White) Western feminists had failed to recognize the complexity, diversity, and agency of women of the Global South. She has called for a fundamental rethinking of a transnational feminist political project, grounded in recognition of and respect for difference and a critique of global capitalism as the bases to build solidarity and engage in collective resistance to oppressive forces variously shaping and constraining women's lives globally (Mohanty, 1991, 2003). Mohanty contends that transnational feminist work must be attentive to the "micropolitics of context, subjectivity, and struggle, as well as to the macropolitics of global economic and political systems and processes" (Mohanty, 2003, p. 501). She argues forcefully that globalization matters to women. Mohanty (2006) writes:

> The argument I am making here is very simple: imperialism, militarization, and globalization all traffic in women's bodies, women's labor, and ideologies of masculinity/femininity, heteronormativity, racism, and nationalism to consolidate and reproduce power and domination. Thus, it is anti-racist, anti-imperialist, anti-capitalist, multiply gendered feminist praxis that can provide the ground for dismantling empire and re-envisioning just, humane, and secure homespaces for marginalized communities globally. (p. 9)

Myra Marx Ferree and Aili Mari Tripp (2006), editors of *Global Feminism: Transnational Women's Activism, Organizing, and Human Rights,* have taken a grassroots focus in examining localized contexts of women's struggles for dignity, personhood, and power; their intersections with transnational forces; and the challenges and possibilities of transnational women's activism and rights claims. Their work speaks broadly of feminist mobilization in the context of transnationalism. In their edited volume, *The Wages of Empire: Neoliberal Policies, Repression, and Women's Poverty*, Cabezas and colleagues (2007, pp. 6–8) argue that neoliberalism, the economic logic behind globalization, which privileges the expansion of the free market at the expense of state support of social services, education, and health care, is a feminist issue. They challenge the bulk of scholarship on globalization that has been done in gender-neutral terms and highlight feminist approaches that examine the "intersecting politics of gender, race, and class in the ideologies and consequences of imperial globalization" (p. 8). Their work, based on case studies of women's grounded experiences in diverse national and cultural contexts, documents the effects of neoliberal policies and practices on women's lives; illustrates the multiple burdens women bear as workers, caregivers, and community builders; and makes explicit connections among globalization, military repression, and the exploitation of women. Such studies exemplify scholarship that can inform and transform social work education and practice. They have expanded our thinking about constraints, contradictions, and possibilities for transformation.

Feminist scholars in social work have also drawn attention to the need for critical inquiry into the particular and localized contexts in which globalizing forces and systemic inequalities insinuate themselves in women's everyday lives (Mehrotra, 2010; Mitra, 2011; Moosa-Mitha & Ross-Sheriff, 2010). These scholars point to increasingly globalized class and racial disparities, structured inequalities of power that distort gender identities, and the silencing of marginalized voices as key problems that social workers have a responsibility to address (Gringeri & Roche, 2010; Mehrotra, 2010). They call for critical reflexivity in which we recognize our own subjectivities and consider the relations of power in which social work knowledge and practice are intertwined. They challenge social workers to question binary thinking and to consider the complex and intersecting forms and relations of power and oppression shaping women's lives. They call for inquiry and practice that is informed and inspired by critical race, postcolonial, womanist, and, more recently, transnational feminist thought (Dill-Thornton & Zambrana, 2009; Hill Collins, 2000; Lyons, 2006; Mohanty, 1991, 2003; Weir, 2008). As Moosa-Mitha and Ross-Sheriff (2010) state:

> Transnational feminism extends its analysis to include a critique of
> global processes that result in inequities, such as global capitalism and
> militarism, that transverse the boundaries of nation states and expose

the complicity of colonizing patriarchal state practices wherever they occur. (p. 107)

These critical perspectives inform our understanding of historical and contemporary forces of capitalism, imperialism, colonialism, racism, militarism, and migration that shape the particular contexts of women's lives, serving as constraints and catalysts for action. These and other critical race, feminist, and womanist scholars call for close critical examination of the ways processes and consequences of globalization are gendered, how they manifest themselves in women's everyday lives, how they intersect within complex matrices of oppression, and how we can engage in practices of resistance, solidarity, and social justice action at the local level and beyond (see, for example, Chang, 2000; Hochschild & Ehrenreich, 2004; Hondagneu-Sotelo, 2007; Naples & Desai, 2002; Ong, 1985; Spivak, 1996).

In sum, *Gender Oppression and Globalization: Challenges for Social Work* is grounded in critical race, feminist, and womanist thought and informed by cutting-edge scholarship within and beyond social work. It responds to recent calls for engaged social work inquiry into the relationship among a changing global order; relations of power; constructions and negotiations of social identities; interlocking systems of oppression; and possibilities for liberatory practice (Finn & Jacobson, 2008; Gringeri & Roche, 2010; Kemp & Brandwien, 2010; Mehrotra, 2010; Samuels & Ross-Sheriff, 2008). The editors offer this volume as a catalyst for dialogue and action within and beyond social work. We do not pretend to offer an exhaustive overview of women's global experiences of gender oppression and activism. We recognize that our collective effort is at best partial. We have not, for example, addressed the complex histories of women's struggles and activisms in the Arab world, nor have we brought accounts of indigenous women's histories and actions to bear. Rather, we have sought to create an opening for further engagement that reflects part of the rich tapestry of research and action related to gender oppression in the context of globalization.

Contributions to This Volume

The contributors bring a range of critical perspectives to bear in illuminating forms and processes of oppression, resistance, liberation, and solidarity, and in considering innovative directions for social work education and practice in the United States and elsewhere. Through case studies, field research, and personal reflections on practice, contributors examine the intersectionality of racism, sexism, heterosexism, and other forms of oppression and structural violence reflective of the experiences of women and girls. They speak about the personal as well as political and historical dimensions of gender-based oppression and globalization, and probe possibilities for transformative pedagogy and practice. They attend to the effects of globalization in the lives of women and girls and in the operations of systems of care and control in the United States and abroad as well as the border-crossing connections of globalization and gender oppression. They raise questions about binary notions of gender, consider ways gendered oppression shapes men's experiences and relations, and call for action by men and women together to challenge oppressive policies and practices.

Contributors explore these connections through careful analyses of key issues such as migration policies; incarceration practices; movements of people, images, and messages across borders; and the marketing of gender, sexuality, and labor. They consider ways histories and policies of militarization, colonialism, and industrial development continue to configure gendered identities and relations and women's lived experiences. They explore the infiltration of neoliberal policies and practices into the lives of vulnerable women and the forms of resistance, power, and organization women have marshaled in response. They bring critical theories of oppositional consciousness to bear in understanding intersecting forms of oppression and in challenging dominant social work thought and practice. The contributors situate themselves in relation to their work and provide connections between their personal stories and the larger politics and history of gender oppression and globalization. Finally, the contributors address implications for social work knowledge and practice and provide practical, hands-on teaching/learning applications to provoke further thought and action.

We have divided the book into six sections, reflecting a process of engagement with issues of gender oppression and globalization that moves readers from accounts of on-the-ground realities and opportunities for consciousness-raising to explorations of critical theory, policy analysis, grassroots activism, and transformational teaching and learning. However, the issues addressed are interwoven, and we encourage readers to consider the chapters as parts of a larger tapestry rather than points on a linear progression. Each chapter concludes with a series of discussion questions or teaching-learning activities to create further opportunity for critical dialogue and engagement with these challenging issues.

Part 1, "Bearing Witness and Building Consciousness," introduces readers to the everyday realities of gender oppression as experienced by women and men engaged in sex work in the context of global capitalism and offers a popular education approach to understanding sex trafficking as a component of human trafficking. In Chapter 1, "False Promises of the Big City," Sharvari Karandikar and Lindsay Gezinski present a tell-it-like-it-is account of people living on the streets of Kamathipura, Asia's largest red-light area, in Mumbai, India, as a context for understanding globalization and gender oppression. The authors present narratives of two female sex workers and two male intimate partners of sex workers from Kamathipura. The narratives highlight negative effects of globalization leading to economic, social, political, and legal vulnerabilities of females and males living in Kamathipura. In the broader societal context, men and women were identified as victims of globalization in their own right. However, analysis of their interpersonal relations from a gendered lens reveals additional victimization of female sex workers. With a rapidly changing Indian economy and structural changes in and around the city of Mumbai, this chapter provides a window into the marginalization and oppression of female sex workers.

In Chapter 2, "Developing a Critical Understanding of Human Trafficking," Maria Beatriz Alvarez and Edward Alessi take a popular education approach to explore the issue of human trafficking in the context of globalization. The authors present a critical examination of the discourses and practices of human trafficking in the context of globalization and labor exploitation, consider issues of gender therein, and differentiate human trafficking from sex trafficking. They propose a broader framework that conceptualizes human trafficking as a form of labor exploitation linked to globalized market economies and armed conflict. The authors contend that this framework not only helps social workers identify and assist trafficked people, it also highlights the profession's role in addressing the social, economic, and gender disparities that create conditions of vulnerability. The authors introduce readers to the philosophy and methodology of popular education and the Theatre of the Oppressed as a means of understanding how such disparities make people vulnerable to exploitation, and they consider clinical and political issues relevant to social work. These chapters set the stage for the more intimate accounts contained in Part 2.

In Part 2, "Courageous Voices," readers encounter more intimate spaces of this nexus of globalization and gender oppression—theaters of performance poetry, cells of a women's prison, and the meeting room of a Harlem social service agency. In each of these contexts, courageous voices talk back to violent and violating forces and images and offer unique insights into the possibilities of "globalization from below" (Brecher, Costello, & Smith, 2000, p. ix). In Chapter 3, "'There Is Life Here,'" Sarah Carnahan offers theoretical insights into the trauma borne of gender oppression and brings readers in as the audience to poet voices publicly naming and restorying trauma. Carnahan brings a framework of critical trauma theory to bear in exploring the ways performance poetry can provide an alternative space where women are able to express themselves and heal from multiple forms of trauma and oppression. Carnahan foregrounds the ways trauma is not isolated to individuals but also ruptures from systems of oppression, exploitative globalization, and war or conflict, sending ripples through communities, nations, and generations. Performance poems by Suheir Hammad and Ani DiFranco, which offer microcosms of the differential effects of trauma, globalization, and warfare, are explored in linking theory and practice.

In Chapter 4 Carol Jacobsen takes readers inside prisons where growing numbers of women are confined in the shadow of global capitalism. Jacobsen addresses the possibilities for "breaching the fence" to work for justice and human rights with incarcerated women. She offers a global perspective on women's incarceration and makes connections between the systemic abuses of women in prisons and other forms of gendered violence, violation, and oppression shaping many women's everyday lives. She describes the criminalization of women's lives and massive expansion of the prison industrial complex that coincided with the globalization of capital in the 1980s. Jacobsen, an artist, educator, and director of the Michigan Women's Justice & Clemency Project, engages students, social workers, educators, attorneys, and other citizens as critical allies advocating with and for women prisoners. Drawing from her experiences as a filmmaker, educator, and organizer, Jacobsen brings grounded research and grassroots activism to bear in telling a story of resistance and hope for incarcerated women. She blends theories and practices of social work, legal advocacy, and creative political activism to empower women as they challenge gender injustice in prisons.

In Chapter 5 Tonisha Taylor bravely voices a critique of the hypersexualized media constructions of Black women that circulate globally, and she engages young women themselves as critics and change agents. She explores the global circulation of these media portrayals and explores how they are perceived, internalized, and resisted by young Black girls. As Taylor says, with the pervasiveness of hip-hop and the subsequent rise of "video vixens," internalization of what is considered desirable for women in the urban community occurs as early as grade school. This problem is further augmented by the globalization of media messages, with stereotypical displays of Black women broadcast via various platforms (i.e., television, radio, Internet, print ads). There is great pressure to conform to these images, leading young girls to invest an incredible amount of time, energy, and money into their appearance. Taylor explores how increasingly globalized media messages, with stereotypical displays of Black women, are shaping girls' experiences and identities, and how, in turn, negative effects can be minimized. She describes her experience of using culturally relevant pedagogy for consciousness-raising group work with the young Black women of Sisterlink, a Harlem-based social service agency as a strategy of resistance and healthy, proactive image building.

Part 3, "Critical Theory and Practice," addresses the power of womanist thought and Chicana feminism in shaping the researchers, their research efforts, and practice possibilities for engaging complex questions of gender oppression and globalization. As HIV/AIDS continues to devastate the lives of Ghanaian women, the need for greater insight into their HIV/AIDS-related knowledge and behaviors becomes more urgent. In Chapter 6, "Pounding the Yam," Tonya Perry and Jeongah Kim examine the intersection of gendered aspects of globalization with the HIV/AIDS-related knowledge and behaviors of young Ghanaian market women. Based on a World Health Organization survey of 138 young women in Accra, Ghana, Perry and Kim critically examine the ways globalization has contributed to the economic deprivation of the masses of Ghanaian women, thereby influencing the significant micro-level choices they make in their daily lives regarding HIV/AIDS-related risk and protective behaviors. The authors argue that the ability of Ghanaian women to exercise agency over their bodies is being compromised by their displacement as low-wage earners in the informal economy. They further illustrate how the gendered livelihoods of the masses of Ghanaian women are historically rooted in the processes of colonization, globalization, neoliberalism, and the accompanying structural adjustments. Their cross-sectional study of HIIV/AIDS-related knowledge and behaviors of Ghanaian women deepens our contextualized understanding of their vulnerability to HIV/AIDS.

In Chapter 7, "Chicana Feminisms, Intersectionality, and Social Work," Leticia Villarreal Sosa and Ali Moore address Chicana feminisms, intersectionality theory, and borderlands theory in understanding the relationship of gender oppression and globalization. They show how a Chicana feminist perspective can help shift the way social workers understand Chicanas and Chicanos and other marginalized groups. The authors draw on theories of oppositional consciousness among U.S. third world feminists as a framework for thought and practice with men and women encountering intersections of race, class, and gender in an increasingly globalized world. The authors present a theoretical model developed by Villarreal Sosa that accounts for the social and historical context and intersectionality of social identity. This chapter also explores how this model can be applied to social work research and practice with Mexican youths in Chicago as well as with youths in Dar es Salaam, Tanzania. Through the use of case studies, the authors discuss the incorporation of men in gender empowerment work and research. Finally Villarreal Sosa and Moore address the importance of self-reflection and awareness of one's own intersectionality of social identity and social location of privilege or oppression in social work research and practice.

In Part 4, "Policies and Practice," contributors offer historical and contemporary critiques of social policy related to gender and globalization through the lenses of transnational feminism and intersectionality. In Chapter 8 Jeongah Kim probes questions of gender and globalization in South Korea from a transnational feminist perspective. Kim examines the status of women and work and gender equity policy in South Korea in the context of globalization. She explores the gendered effects of globalization and governmental responses to it using a feminist lens. Kim first considers the embedded history of gender inequality in relation to culturally determined gender ideologies in Confucianism. She takes a historic view of globalization in South Korea and examines the ways a female-intensive labor force met the country's demands for economic growth starting in the early 1960s. She then considers gender-equity policies that have been enacted over the past two decades and explores their effects on women's lives. Kim argues that despite their tremendous contributions to the nation's economy, women workers have not received full and equal access to and participation in all facets of the labor market. Attention to the dynamic interplay among globalization, culture, gender, and policy may offer significant guidance toward implementing transformative strategies aimed at achieving gender equity.

In Chapter 9, "Immigration and Intersectionality," Bharati Sethi and Olena Hankivsky examine tensions in contemporary Canadian immigration policy when issues of gender and globalization collide. Drawing from a community-based research project with new immigrants in Canada's rural-urban community, Sethi and Hankivsky examine gendered aspects of immigration policies and human capital discourse in the context of current neoliberal policies and recent changes to the Canadian Immigration and Refugee Protection Act. Using a case example from the research project, the authors show how women's subordinate position in migration can create economic, political, and social barriers to their resettlement and negatively affect their health. The authors address a neglected space in social work literature regarding immigration, gender, and health care policies, and discuss the implications for visible minority women. Drawing on intersectionality theory, they demonstrate how gender intersects with sexual identity, social class, immigration status, geographical area, ability, and other characteristics to render migrant women's social location one of great vulnerability. Further, the case example shows how certain groups such as gays and lesbians are further marginalized because of the interplay between their sexual orientation, culture, and immigration status.

In Part 5, "From Grassroots to Global Action," the contributors start with women's grassroots efforts to confront powerful forces of globalization in their home communities and move to broader implications. In Chapter 10, "Here's My Heart," Susan Chandler draws on the expertise of women workers in Las Vegas casinos as they critique and respond to corporate globalization, and she invites readers to join their cause. Chandler explores the narratives of the immigrant women who make up the core of the 60,000-member-strong Las Vegas Culinary Union. She offers an inside, women-focused look into corporate gaming, on the one hand, and the world of the workers who make it run, on the other. Chandler traces the transformation of maids, cocktail waitresses, laundry workers, and cooks as they came to realize through collective action that they were far more than arms that worked. She locates their narratives in the broader context of globalization, critically examining Las Vegas as a global tourist destination where gendered patterns of labor migration play out, where neoliberal policies and practices are felt in people's everyday lives, and where a few global corporations wield tremendous political and economic power. The author addresses why conditions of labor should be of interest to social workers, explores the power and possibility of grassroots organizations to counter the oppressive forces of globalization, and calls social workers to action for social and economic justice.

In Chapter 11, "To Be Poor, Hungry, and Rural," Quenette Walton and Patricia O'Brien learn from the expertise of community women in Nicaragua, whose own learning and lived realities have been shaped by the violence of globalized capital interests over time. They explore women's struggles as well as the ways they are organizing resistance and action to confront the consequences of globalization. The authors examine the intersection of sustainable food development, globalization, and neoliberal policies in the lives of women locally and globally through a case study of the experiences of women residing in rural Tola Rivas, Nicaragua. They address globalization and neoliberalism in relation to access to healthy and affordable food and the well-being of women, the ways Nicaraguan women's experiences have been trivialized, and the implications of failed economic growth in the community. Their case study highlights the ways women collectively resist oppressive forces, drawing on their revolutionary history while using local strategies for developing access to nutritious food for their families. The authors draw attention to issues of resistance and strategies for developing access to quality and sustainable food, and they discuss how social workers can engage in effective community practice, locally and globally. The chapter promotes critical dialogue on the economic and political forces of market competition and free trade that affect access to healthy and sustainable food for nurturing human life.

Part 6, "Pedagogy and Practice," brings readers full circle through an exploration of the strategies for and reflections on teaching and learning about gender oppression and globalization in the classroom and beyond. In Chapter 12 Janet Finn and Kara Mileski explore questions of globalization and gender oppression in the context of social work education. Informed by feminist theory and principles of popular education, the authors share the process and outcomes of their ongoing critical dialogue about the challenges, possibilities, and necessity of teaching and learning about the intersections of globalization and gender oppression. The authors use the Just Practice perspective, a social justice framework, to examine questions of meaning, power, history, context, and the possibility for critical pedagogy (Finn & Jacobson, 2008). They provide teaching–learning examples and hands-on resources to engage students in addressing the intersections of globalization and gender oppression in the classroom context and beyond.

Izumi Sakamoto addresses her experience of designing and teaching a course on globalization and gender-based oppression for MSW students and explores critical consciousness in international and transnational contexts in Chapter 13, "Critical Consciousness in International Contexts." From 2005 to 2009 Sakamoto taught a course titled Globalization and Transnationalism: Social Work Responses Locally and Globally. She addresses challenges she has faced in the classroom, assignments that have helped students grapple with those challenges, and student creativity in the process. Sakamoto examines assumptions that students (often Canadian born, White, middle-class) frequently hold regarding women of the Global South as oppressed in authoritative and patriarchal societies. She proposes strategies for raising consciousness about students' privileges associated with being in the Global North and what they take for granted as "good" and "universal." Further she explores the experiences, perspectives, and contributions of students who are immigrants from the Global South. In negotiating the complex and sensitive themes in the classroom, Sakamoto pays close attention to whiteness by helping students see what has been taken for granted and by protecting minoritized students who may experience spiritual and emotional harm by witnessing whiteness demonstrated by their peers.

In Chapter 14, Finn, Perry, and Karandikar draw together common threads and reflect on lessons learned from this rich and diverse collection. The editors address the challenges faced by social work educators, students, and practitioners as they confront the complex intersection of globalization and gender oppression. They show how the conceptual frames, strategies for analysis, lessons in critical reflection, and practice possibilities put forth in these chapters not only inform social work thought and practice but also hold transformative potential for social workers and the profession.

Notes

1. For an insightful overview of the gender and development literature and issues, see Drolet, 2010.

2. See Mohanty (2002) for an important discussion of the concepts third world; Global South, Global North; and alternative language such as *one-third world, two-thirds world*.

References

Abram, F., Slosar, J., & Walls, R. (2005). Reverse mission: A model for international social work education and transformative intra-national practice. *International Social Work, 48*(2), 161–176.

Abramovitz, M. (2006). Neither accidental nor simply mean-spirited: The context for welfare reform. In K. Kelty & E. Segal (Eds.), *The promise of welfare reform* (pp. 23–38). Binghamton, NY: Haworth Press.

Abrams, L., & Moio, J. (2009). Critical race theory and the cultural competence dilemma in social work education. *Journal of Social Work Education, 45,* 245–261.

Adams, R., Dominelli, L., & Payne, M. (Eds.). (2005). *Social work futures: Crossing boundaries and transforming practice.* New York, NY: Palgrave/MacMillan.

Allan, J., Pease, B., & Briskman, L. (Eds.). (2003). *Critical social work: An introduction to theories and practices.* Crows Nest, New South Wales, Australia: Allen & Unwin.

Appadurai, A. (2002). (Ed.). *Globalization.* Durham, NC: Duke University Press.

Bair, J. (2010). On difference and capital: Gender and the globalization of production. *Signs: Journal of Women in Culture and Society, 36*(1), 203–226.

Beneria, L. (2003). *Gender, development and globalization.* London, UK: Routledge.

Beneria, L., & Sen, G. (1981). Accumulation, reproduction and women's role in economic development: Boserup revisited. *Signs: Journal of Women in Culture and Society, 7*(2), 279–298.

Bigelow, B., & B. Peterson (2002). *Rethinking globalization: Teaching for justice in an unjust world.* Milwaukee, WI: Rethinking Schools Press.

Blundo, R. (2006). Shifting our habits of mind: Learning to practice from a strengths perspective. In D. Saleeby (Ed.), *The strengths perspective in social work practice* (4th ed., pp. 24–25). Boston, MA: Pearson.

Boserup, E. (1970. *Women's role in economic development.* London, UK: Allen & Unwin.

Brecher, J., Costello, T. & Smith, B. (2000). *Globalization from below: The power of solidarity.* Cambridge, MA: South End Press.

Broad, R. (2002). (ed.). *Global backlash: Citizens initiatives for a just world economy.* Oxford, UK: Rowman and Littlefield.

Bywaters, P., McLeod, E., & Napier, L. (2009). *Social work and global health inequalities: Practice and policy developments.* Chicago, IL: University of Chicago Press.

Cabezas, A., Reese, E., & Waller, M. (2007). *The wages of empire: Neoliberal policies, repression, and women's poverty.* Boulder, CO: Paradigm.

Carlton-LaNey, I. (1997). Elizabeth Ross Haynes: An African American reformer of womanist consciousness, 1908–1940. *Social Work, 42,* 573–583.

Chang, G. (2000). *Disposable domestics: Immigrant women workers in the global economy.* Boston, MA: South End Press.

Cohn, C., & C. Enloe (2003). A conversation with Cynthia Enloe: Feminists look at masculinity and the men who wage war. *Signs: Journal of Women in Culture and Society, 28,* 1187–1207.

Cole, J., & Durham, D. (Eds.). (2007).*Generations and globalization: Youth, age, and family in the new world economy.* Bloomington, IN: Indiana University Press.

Cooper, F. (2001). What is the concept of globalization good for? An African historian's perspective. *African Affairs 100*(399), 189–213.

Council on Social Work Education. (2008). *Educational policy and accreditation standards.* Retrieved from http://www.cswe.org/File.aspx?id=41861

Crenshaw, K., Gotanda, N., Peller, G., & Thomas, K. (Eds.), (1995). *Critical race theory: The key writings that formed the movement.* New York, NY: The New Press.

Davis, A. (1983). *Women, race, and class.* New York, NY: Vintage.

Dejardin, A. (2008, September). *Gender dimensions of globalization.* Paper presented at the meeting of the International Labour Organization, Geneva, Switzerland.

Delgado, R., & Stefancic, J. (2001). *Critical race theory: An introduction.* New York, NY: New York University Press.

INTRODUCTION

Delgado, R., & J. Stefancic, J. (2012). *Critical race theory: An introduction.* (2nd ed.). New York, NY: New York University Press.

Dill-Thornton, B., & Zambrana, X. (Eds.). (2009). *Emerging intersections: Race, class, and gender in theory, policy, and practice.* New Brunswick, NJ: Rutgers University Press.

Dinerman, M. (2003). Globalization as a women's issue. *Affilia; Journal of Women and Social Work, 18*(2): 114–117.

Dixon, A. D., & Rousseau, C. K. (2005). And we are still not saved: Critical race theory in education ten years later. *Race, Ethnicity and Education, 8*(1), 7–27.

Dominelli, L. (1999). Neo-liberalism, social exclusion and welfare clients in a global economy. *International Journal of Social Welfare, 8*(1), 14–22.

Dominelli, L. (2002). *Anti-oppressive social work theory and practice.* London, UK: Macmillan.

Dominelli, L. (2008). *Anti-racist social work* (3rd ed.). London, UK: Palgrave MacMillan.

Dominelli, L. (2010). *Social work in a globalizing world.* Cambridge, UK: Polity Press.

Drolet, J. (2010). Feminist perspectives in development: Implications for women and microcredit. *Affilia: Journal of Women and Social Work, 25*(3), 212–225.

Duran, J. (2010). African NGOs and womanism: Microcredit and self-help. *Journal of African American Studies, 14*(2), 171–180.

Enloe, C. (2000a). *Bananas, beaches, and bases: Making feminist sense of international politics.* Berkeley, CA: University of California Press.

Enloe, C. (2000b). *Maneuvers: The international politics of militarizing women's lives.* Berkeley, CA: University of California Press.

Enloe, C. (2004). *The curious feminist: Searching for women in the new age of empire.* Berkeley, CA: University of California Press.

Enloe, C. (2007). *Globalization and militarism: Feminists make the link.* Berkeley, CA: University of California Press.

Ferguson, I., Lavalette, M., & Whitmore, E. (2005). *Globalisation, global justice, and social work.* New York, NY: Routledge.

Ferree, M., & Tripp, A. (2006) *Global feminism: Transnational women's activism, organizing, and human rights.* New York, NY: New York University Press.

Finn, J., & Jacobson, M. (2008). *Just practice: A social justice approach to social work* (2nd ed.). Peosta, IA: Eddie Bowers.

Foss, S. (2012). *Gender stories: Negotiating identity in a binary world.* Long Grove, IL: Waveland Press.

Friedman, T. (1999). *The lexus and the olive tree.* New York, NY: Farrar, Straus, & Giroux.

Fudge, J. (2010, May). *Global care chains: Transnational migrant care workers.* Paper presented at the meeting of the International Association of Laws Schools Conference on Labour Law and Labour Market in the New World Economy, Milan, Italy.

Giddens. A. (1999). *Runaway world: How globalization is reshaping our lives.* London, UK: Profile Books.

Globalization. (n.d.) In *Merriam-Webster's online dictionary.* Retrieved from http://www.merriam-webster.com/dictionary/globalization.

Global Fund for Women. (2012). *Status of women fact sheet.* Retrieved from http://www.globalfundforwomen.org/impact/media-center/fact-sheets/status-of-women-fact-sheet

Gringeri, C., & Roche, S. (2010). Beyond the binary: Critical feminisms in social work. *Affilia: Journal of Women and Social Work, 25*, 337–340.

Harvey, D. (1989). *The condition of postmodernity.* Cambridge, MA: Blackwell.

Harvey, D. (2005). *A brief history of neoliberalism.* New York, NY: Oxford University Press.

Hays, S. (2004). *Flat broke with children*. New York, NY: Oxford University Press.

Healy, K. (2002). Managing human services in a market environment: What role for social workers? *British Journal of Social Work, 32*, 527–540.

Held, D., & McGrew, A. (2003). *The global transformation reader*. Cambridge,UK: Polity Press.

Hick. S., Fook, J., & Pozzuto, R. (2005). *Social work: A critical turn*. Toronto, Canada: Thompson.

Hill Collins, P. (2000). *Black feminist thought: Knowledge, consciousness, and the politics of empowerment*. New York, NY: Unwin Hyman.

Hochschild, A. (2000). Global care chains and emotional surplus value. In W. Hutton & Anthony Giddens (Eds.), *On the edge: Living with global capitalism* (pp. 130–146). London, UK: Jonathon Cape.

Hochschild, A. (2009). Love and gold. *Scholar and Feminist Online 8*(1), 1–6. Retrieved from http://sfon line.barnard.edu/work/hochschild_01.htm

Hochschild, A., & Ehrenreich, B. (2004). *Global woman: Nannies, maids and sex workers in the new economy*. New York, NY: MacMillan.

Hondagneu-Sotelo, P. (2003). *Gender and U.S. migration: Contemporary trends*. Berkeley, CA: University of California Press.

Hondagneu-Sotelo, P. (2007). *Domestica: Immigrant workers cleaning and caring in the shadow of capital*. Berkeley, CA: University of California Press.

Hoogvelt, A. (1997). *Globalization and the postcolonial world*. Baltimore, MD: Johns Hopkins University Press.

Howard-Hamilton, M. (2003). Theoretical frameworks for African American women. *New Directions for Student Services, 104*, 19–27.

Hudson-Weems, C. (1993). *Africana womanism: Reclaiming ourselves*. Troy, MI: Bedford.

Ife, J. (2000). Localized needs and a globalized economy: Bridging the gap with social work practice. *Canadian Social Work, 2*(1), 50–64.

Ife, J. (2001). *Human rights and social work: Towards rights-based practice*. Cambridge, UK: Cambridge University Press.

International Organization for Migration (IOM) (n.d.). *Gender, migration, and remittances*. [IOM Info Sheet 51-10]. Retrieved from http://www.iom.int/jahia/webdav/site/myjahiasite/shared/shared/mainsite/published_docs/brochures_and_info_sheets/Gender-migration-remittances-infosheet.pdf

Johnston-Anumonwo, I., & Doane, D. (2011). Globalization, economic crisis and Africa's informal economy women workers. *Singapore Journal of Tropical Geography, 32*, 8–21.

Jurik, N. (2006). Microenterprise development, welfare reform, and the contradictions of new privatization. In K. Kelty & E. Segal (Eds.), *The promise of welfare reform* (pp. 121–132). Binghamton, NY: Haworth Press.

Karger, H. (2005). *Shortchanged: Life and debt in the fringe economy*. San Francisco, CA: Berrett-Koehler.

Kemp, S., & Brandwein, R. (2010). Feminisms and social work in the United States: An intertwined history. *Affilia: Journal of Women and Social Work, 25*, 341–364.

Kilty, K., & Segal, E. (2006). (Eds.). *The promise of welfare reform*. Binghamton, NY: Haworth Press.

Korten, D. (2001). *When corporations rule the world*. (2nd ed.). West Hartford, CN: Kumarian Press.

Kristof, N., & WuDunn, S. (2009). *Half the sky: Turning women's oppression into opportunity worldwide*. New York, NY: Vintage.

Lavia, J. (2007). Repositioning pedagogies and postcolonialism: Theories, contradictions and possibilities. *International Journal of Inclusive Education, 11*(3), 283–300.

Link, R. (1999). Infusing global perspectives into social work values and ethics. In C. Ramanathan & R. Link (Eds.), *All our futures: Social work practice in a global era* (pp. 69–93). Belmont, CA: Wadsworth.

Lyons, K. (1999). *International social work: Themes and perspectives.* Brookfield, VT: Ashgate.

Lyons, K. (2006). Globalization and social work: International and local implications. *British Journal of Social Work, 36,* 365–380.

Mapp, S. (2008). *Human rights and social justice in a global perspective.* New York, NY: Oxford University Press.

McMichael, P. (2000). *Development and social change: A global perspective.* Thousand Oaks, CA: Pine Forge Press

Mehrotra, G. (2010) Toward a continuum of intersectionality theorizing for feminist social work scholarship. *Affilia: Journal of Women and Social Work, 25,* 417–430.

Midgley, J. (2004). *Lessons from abroad: Adapting international social welfare innovations.* Washington, DC: NASW Press.

Midgley, J. (2007). Perspectives on globalization, social justice and welfare. *Journal of Sociology & Social Welfare, 34*(2), 17–36.

Mikell, G. (1995). African feminism: Toward a new politics of representation. *Feminist Studies, 21*(2), 405–425.

Miles, B., & Fowler, P. (2006). Changing the face of homelessness: Welfare reform's impact on homeless families. In K. Kilty & E. Segal (Eds.) *The promise of welfare reform* (pp. 143–154). Binghamton, NY: Haworth Press.

Mitra, A. (2011). To be or not to be a feminist in India. *Affilia: Journal of Women and Social Work, 26*(20), 182–200.

Moghadam, V. (1998). Feminisms and development. *Gender and History, 10,* 590–597.

Mohanty, C. (1991). Under Western eyes: Feminist scholarship and colonial discourses. In C. Mohanty, A. Russo, & L. Torres (Eds.), *Third world women and the politics of feminism* (pp. 1–47). Bloomington, IN: Indiana University Press.

Mohanty, C. (2002). "Under Western eyes" revisited: Feminist solidarity through anti-capitalist struggles. *Signs: Journal of Women in Culture and Society, 28,* 500–535.

Mohanty, C. (2003). *Feminism without borders: Decolonizing theory, practicing solidarity.* Durham, NC: Duke University Press.

Mohanty, C. (2006). U.S. empire and the project of women's studies: Stories of citizenship, complicity, and dissent. *Gender, Place, and Culture, 13*(1), 7–20.

Moosa-Mitha, M., & Ross-Sheriff, F. (2010). Transnational social work and lessons learned from transnational feminism. *Affilia: Journal of Women and Social Work, 25*(2), 105–109.

Morgen, S., Acker, J., Wieght, J., & Gonzales, L. (2006). Living economic restructuring at the bottom. Welfare restructuring and low-wage work. In K. Kelty & E. Segal (Eds.), *The promise of welfare reform* (pp. 81–96). Binghamton, NY: Haworth Press.

Munck, R. (2005). *Globalization and social exclusion: A transformationalist perspective.* Bloomfield, CT: Kumarian Press.

Naples, N., & Desai, M. (2002). *Women's activism and globalization: Linking local struggles and transnational politics.* New York, NY: Routledge.

Nichols, A. (2012). *Poverty in the United States.* Retrieved from http://www.urban.org/publications/412653.html

Ogunyemi, C. (1985). Womanism: The dynamics of the contemporary Black female novel in English. *Signs: Journal of Women in Culture and Society, 11*(1), 63–80.

Ong, A. (1985). *Spirits of resistance and capitalist discipline: Factory women in Malaysia.* Albany, NY: SUNY Press.

I

Orozco, A. (2009). *Global care chains* (Working Paper No. 2, Gender, Migration, and Development Series). Santo Domingo, Dominican Republic: United Nations Research and Training Institute for the Advancement of Women.

Ortner, S. (1996). *Making gender: The politics and erotics of culture.* Boston, MA: Beacon Press.

Oyewumi, O. (2003). Feminism, sisterhood, and other foreign relations. In Oyeronke, O. (Ed.), *African women and Feminism: Reflecting on the politics of sisterhood* (pp. 1–24). Trenton, NJ: Africa World Press.

Payne, M., & Askeland, G. (2008). *Globalization and international social work: Postmodern change and challenge.* Burlington, VT: Ashgate.

Pease, B., & Fook, J. (Eds.). (1999). *Transforming social work practice: Postmodern critical perspectives.* New York, NY: Routledge.

Phillips, L. (2006). *The womanist reader.* New York, NY: Routledge.

Piven, F. F., & Cloward, R. (1997). *The breaking of the American social compact.* New York, NY: Free Press.

Polack, R. (2004). Social justice and the global economy: New challenges for social work in the 21st century. *Social Work, 49*(2), 281–290.

Population Reference Bureau. (2011). *The world's women and girls 2011 data sheet.* Washington, DC: Author.

Ramirez, C., Dominguez, M. G., & Morais, J. M. (2005). *Crossing borders: Gender, remittances, and development.* New York, NY: United Nations Entity for Gender Equality and the Empowerment of Women.

Razack, N. (2009). Decolonizing the pedagogy and practice of international social work. *International Social Work, 52*(1), 9–21.

Razack, N., & Jeffery, D. (2002). Critical race discourse and tenets for social work. *Canadian Social Work Review, 19*(2), 257–271.

Reichert, E. (2003). *Social work and human rights: A foundation for policy and practice.* New York, NY: Columbia University Press.

Reese, E. (2007). Politicians, think tanks, and the global promotion of the "Wisconsin Model" of welfare reform. In A. Cabezas, E. Reese, & M. Waller (Eds.) *The wages of empire: Neoliberal policies, repression, and women's poverty* (pp. 86–97). Boulder, CO: Paradigm Press.

Reisch, M. (1998). *Economic globalization and the future of the welfare state.* Ann Arbor, MI: University of Michigan School of Social Work.

Reisch, M. (2006). Welfare reform and the transformation of the U.S. welfare state. In K. Kelty & E. Segal (Eds.), *The promise of welfare reform* (p. 69–80). Binghamton, NY: Haworth Press.

Rossiter, A. (2005). Where in the world are we? Notes on the need for a social work response to global power. In S. Hick, J. Fook, & R. Pozzuto (Eds.), *Social work: A critical turn* (pp. 189–202). Toronto, Canada: Thompson Educational.

Ross-Sheriff, F. (2007). Globalization as a women's issue revisited. *Affilia: Journal of Women and Social Work, 22*(2), 133–137.

Ross-Sheriff, F. (2011). Global migration and gender. *Affilia: Journal of Women and Social Work, 26*(3), 233–238.

Roy, A. (2007). In her name: The gender order of global poverty management. In A. Cabezas, E. Reese, & M. Waller (Eds.), *The wages of empire: Neoliberal policies, repression, and women's poverty* (pp. 28–39). Boulder, CO: Paradigm.

Samuels, G., & Ross-Sheriff, F. (2008). Identity, oppression, and power: Feminisms and intersectionality theory. *Affilia: Journal of Women and Social Work, 23*(1), 5–11.

Scholte, J. (2008). *Globalization: A critical introduction.* London, UK: MacMillan.

Schram, S. (2006). The old black magic? Welfare reform and the new politics of racial implication. In K. Kelty & E. Segal (Eds.), *The promise of welfare reform* (pp. 223–236). Binghamton, NY: Haworth Press.

Sparr, P. (Ed.) (1994). *Mortgaging women's lives. Feminist critiques of structural adjustment.* London, UK: Zed Press.

Spivak, G. (1996). Diasporas old and new: Women in the transnational world. *Textual Practice, 10*(2), 245–269.

Steady, F. (1987). African feminism: An overview. In R. Terborg-Penn & A. Benton Rushing (Eds.), *Women in Africa and the African diaspora* (pp. 3–24). Washington, DC: Howard University Press.

Stiglitz, J. (2002). *Globalization and its discontents.* New York, NY: Norton.

Stiglitz, J. (2007). *Making globalization work.* New York, NY: Norton.

Sudbury, J. (Ed.). (2005). *Global lockdown: Race, gender, and the prison industrial complex.* New York, NY: Routledge.

United Nations Commission on the Status of Women. (2009). Fifty-third Session, Item 3(b). Gender perspectives of the financial crisis. [E/CN.6/2009/CRP.7]. New York, NY: United Nations.

United Nations, Department of Economic and Social Affairs. (2010). *The world's women, 2010: Trends and statistics.* New York, NY: Author.

United Nations Development Fund for Women. (2010). *UNIFEM annual report, 2009–10.* New York, NY: United Nations.

United Nations Development Programme. (2011). *Human development report 2011.* New York, NY: United Nations.

United Nations Human Development Programme. (2010). *Human development report 2010.* New York, NY: United Nations.

United Nations International Research and Training Institute for the Advancement of Women. (UN-IN-STRAW). (2008). *UN-INSTRAW annual report, 2007-2008.* New York, NY: United Nations.

United Nations Population Fund (UNFPA). (2005). *UNFPA state of the world's population.* New York, NY: United Nations.

United Nations Population Fund (UNFPA). (2010). *UNFPA state of the world's population.* New York, NY: United Nations.

UN Women. (2011). *Annual report, 2010–2011.* New York, NY: United Nations.

Van Soest, D., & Garcia, B. (2003). *Diversity education for social justice: Mastering teaching skills.* Alexandria, VA: Council on Social Work Education.

van Wormer, K. (2005). Concepts for contemporary social work: Globalization, oppression social exclusions, human rights, etc. *Social Work and Society, 3*(1), 1–9.

Walker, A. (1983). *Womanist.* San Diego, CA: Harcourt Brace Jovanovich.

Waller, M., & Marcos, S. (Eds.) (2005). *Dialogue and difference: Feminisms challenge globalization.* New York, NY: Palgrave.

Weir, A. (2008). Global feminism and transformative identity politics. *Hypatia, 23*, 110–133.

Women's Environment and Development Organization. (2006). *Data on the status of women worldwide.* Retrieved from http://www.wedo.org/wp-content/uploads/data-on-the-status-of-women-worldwide-_2_.pdf

Wright, M. (2006). *Disposable women and other myths of global capitalism.* New York, NY: Routledge.

Young. I. M. (1990). *Justice and the politics of difference.* Princeton, NJ: Princeton University Press.

Part 1

BEARING WITNESS AND BUILDING CONSCIOUSNESS

CHAPTER 1

False Promises of the Big City

Understanding Globalization and Gender Oppression Among People Living on the Streets of the Kamathipura Red-Light Area in Mumbai, India

SHARVARI KARANDIKAR AND LINDSAY GEZINSKI

The idea for this chapter emerged in the summer of 2010. The authors were collecting data on sex-trafficked victims' health-based vulnerabilities, and it involved about 90 days of fieldwork in the Kamathipura red-light area of Mumbai, India. During the first week of our field visit, as we were walking toward Kamathipura, we noticed three new and unusual development projects. Only 20 steps away from brothels was a huge shopping mall, a McDonald's, and a 38-floor high-rise building overlooking the red-light area. This high-rise was being constructed in the exact location where a nongovernmental organization (NGO) used to be, and where Sharvari once worked as a social worker. This construction was a result of the demolition of parts of Kamathipura that were inhabited by sex workers. The obvious questions that came to our minds were: Where did the women go? What happened to the NGO office? What are the authorities planning to do about such construction almost encroaching on the space that for the past 200 years has been occupied by the sex industry? The other thought that crossed our minds was, how will this development affect the women and children and the local businesses? Will it benefit the women in any way? Will they be forced into other safer professions, or will they be forced into the margins even more? Will they have better incomes and healthier sanitation options? Will they have better health care, and will their children be ensured schooling?

With these questions in mind, we set out to understand globalization and how it has affected the lives of women and men living in Kamathipura. In this chapter we start out by introducing the concept of globalization and its overall effects on the Indian economy. Then, we set the stage by a historical, social, and political context of Kamathipura, Asia's oldest and largest red-light area. We then present narratives of two female sex workers and two male intimate partners of sex workers from Kamathipura. The narratives highlight their experiences related to the backlash of globalization in India. We further analyze the narratives through a gendered lens and compare females and males on the basis of the existing social, economic, political, and legal context of Kamathipura.

Understanding Globalization and Gender Oppression

India has pursued economic liberalization of policy since the mid-1980s, opening its economy to the global market in the early 1990s (Ganguly-Scrase, 2003). In July of 1991, India implemented the New Economic Policy of 1991, a set of market-friendly reforms advocated by the World Bank and the International Monetary Fund for countries in the Global South (Upadhyay, 2000). The New Economic Policy effectively devalued the rupee and reduced public investment and expenditure, and it increased interest rates, imports, and foreign investments. Opinions vary regarding the effects of globalization on the Indian population, specifically pertaining to gender equity.

According to Nayar (2006), India has benefited in the areas of economic growth, industrial growth, and competitiveness of business in the global economy. Further, Nayar claims that globalization has led to fewer economic crises and a decline in poverty. Others have claimed that women occupy a higher social status in the era of globalization, as there is a greater acceptance of single women and women who postpone marriage to fulfill career aspirations (Madhok & Raj, 2011). Moreover, the middle class has grown, benefitting most from the structural adjustment reforms (Deshpande 1998; Ganguly-Scrase, 2003; Lakha, 1999). For instance, middle-class women in urban areas have greater access to higher education and are pursuing careers in fields such as engineering, management, and computer science (Madhok & Raj, 2011).

4

However, structural adjustment policies have negatively affected the most vulnerable populations in India. The wages of the poor, who constitute three quarters of the population, have remained virtually stagnant (Basu & Thomas, 2009). Globalization has resulted in the transition from a primarily agrarian society to an industrialized, market-driven society (Banerjee, 2003). For example, privatization policies and agricultural technologies have disintegrated rural communities, resulting in decreased employment for women and an increase in legal and illegal migration within India and to other countries (Banerjee, 2003; Grey, 2005). Increased urbanization in combination with few job opportunities in the formal sector for women increases poverty (Upadhyay, 2000). As a result, women may look for work in the informal sector, including sex work. Additionally, globalization may open up opportunities for trafficking especially in rural areas (Banerjee, 2003). Thus, the view of women as commodities has increased as a result of globalization. Globalization in many ways changed the lives of people in rural India. Migration to urban cities such as Mumbai drastically increased in 1990. However, there was minimal improvement in literacy levels. The population continued to increase, but the government did not speed up infrastructure development to complement the increasing population demands.

Though Mumbai offered solutions for low-wage job opportunities, the quality of life for immigrants remained poor. Men and women who migrated to Mumbai in the late 1980s and early 1990s lived on day-to-day subsistence and were unable to benefit from the overall economic development in the city. Migrant populations mingled with the local poor and started settling down in low-income areas. The slum area in Mumbai increased exponentially, and the quality of life suffered. Thus, the backlash of globalization was felt by the marginalized people who remained poor and lived in unhealthy situations. Globalization also brought along health concerns, including HIV/AIDS among immigrant workers who visited red-light areas such as Kamathipura and were identified as a high-risk population for contracting and spreading HIV infections.

Kamathipura gained importance in the public eye in the early 1980s when the first case of HIV in India was detected in a sex worker. Suddenly, sex workers gained a lot of attention, but most of this was in form of stigmatization, ridicule, and criticism for spreading the HIV infection to the "normal population." Kamathipura was never talked about in the mainstream media before this time period. Ironically, Kamathipura existed as a red-light district in Mumbai since the early 1800s when it was established by the British for the entertainment of their troops. After the British left India in 1947, the red-light area was taken over by local brothel keepers and sex workers. Over the years, Kamathipura expanded and is now considered to be a necessary social evil (Menen, 2007). Kamathipura is populated by about 5,000 sex workers—male, female, and transgender, either brothel based or street based (Committed Communities Development Trust staff, personal communication, May 10, 2007). Kamathipura is also one of the most rundown areas in the city of Mumbai. Each of the 13 lanes in Kamathipura is crowded with small huts, tea stalls, shops, lodges, pawn shops, restaurants, and brothels. The brothels have tiny rooms separated from one another by thin curtains and are rented out to sex workers on an hourly basis. These rooms are cheap; it costs anywhere from 20 to 100 rupees (about US$2) to use the rooms. More than 40% of sex workers in Kamathipura are homeless (Menen, 2007). They live on the streets, the footpaths, and on the pavements. Their belongings fit in a small plastic bag that they carry with them everywhere they go. At night, they stand on the same street and solicit sex. When they get clients, they rent a brothel room for a certain amount of time and pay a share of their earnings to the brothel keeper. Apart from sex workers, female and male brothel keepers, pimps, clients, husbands, and partners of sex workers are also seen on the streets of Kamathipura. Sex work is the primary business in the area and is an income-generating industry for those directly and indirectly involved in it. From sex workers, brothel owners, shopkeepers, restaurants owners, hotel and bar owners to pimps, clients, and the police, sex work is a money-making business.

A majority of the residents of Kamathipura are migrants from other states of India and from neighboring countries such as Nepal and Bangladesh. Once introduced to the sex industry, they do not return to their native places (Frederick, 2000). Almost 90% of the people living in Kamathipura have some sexually transmitted infection at any given point in time (Gangoli, 2006), and 70% are estimated to be HIV positive (Menen, 2007). The people living in Kamathipura belong to the lowest socioeconomic stratum of Indian society; they are below the poverty line and cannot afford to live in any other location in the city. Kamathipura provides them with cheap accommodation, food, drink, and drugs. There are numerous dance bars, movie theaters, and gambling halls in the area for entertainment. No one ever protests against the deplorable situation. People in Kamathipura live in silence and accept their clandestine existence. People here are infamous in the outside world and do not belong to the glitter and glory of the city of Mumbai. Their existence is confined to the margins of society, to the 13 lanes of Kamathipura. The anonymity of these lanes helps them forget their unfortunate past. No matter how harsh and dangerous, they all live here, finding acceptance in the apathy of Kamathipura. Their dignity, which is often questioned by the outside world, is not contested in Kamathipura. It is safe amid its dangers. However, Kamathipura has undergone several changes in the past decade. The government and private contractors and builders are trying hard to obtain property in and around Kamathipura to develop high-rise residential buildings and offices as well as shopping malls and movie theaters. Eating establishments such as McDonald's and KFC are now open in the vicinity. Although this is seen as a welcome change by some, it's not an ideal situation for the residents of Kamathipura. They are still living in poverty and find it difficult to make ends meet. Sex workers suffer the most, as they are arrested more frequently and have been pushed into unfamiliar and dangerous areas to solicit sex. This has reduced social work intervention in the area, and social workers are finding it extremely difficult to locate sex workers.

Methods and Purpose of the Present Study

The authors collected data during the summer of 2010 when Kamathipura was experiencing structural changes. The purpose of this research was to understand the lives of the men and women living in Kamathipura and to understand how globalization and recent changes in Kamathipura are affecting them. Four respondents, two female sex workers and two male intimate partners, were interviewed using an in-depth interviewing method. Each interview session lasted about 1 hour, and each respondent was interviewed in four sessions. The interviews were open ended, and the respondents were asked to narrate their life stories. All the interviews were conducted in Hindi and were audiotaped. For the purpose of analysis, each interview was transcribed and translated into English. Each interview was written in the form of a narrative.

The following section contains four narratives, which capture, in essence, the structural poverty and victimization described by the respondents. Although each narrative speaks for itself, the reader cannot help but notice similar themes across the four. The purpose of the chapter is to (a) explore similarities between respondents in the existing social, economic, political, and legal context of Kamathipura, and (b) analyze these realities in the light of gender. Males and females had several similar experiences of poverty and disparity; however, when gender is used as a lens for analysis, women seemed more vulnerable compared with men.

The Narratives

The following narratives tell the story of men and women residing in Kamathipura. Ratna and Manisha are female sex workers, and Aslam and Ramesh identify themselves as intimate partners of sex workers. The narratives are in the respondents' own language with its crudeness and colloquialisms. Modification to make the sentences grammatically correct was deliberately avoided, except for clarity.

RATNA

I am a sex worker for the past 19 or maybe 20 years. I am not sure. My mother died during my birth, and when I was 3 months old, my father passed away. I lived with my two older sisters in a small village on the Maharashtra-Karnataka border and worked in a field. None of us sisters went to school. We never had enough to eat and had to work for very long hours on the field. We were poor, and when you are poor everyone takes advantage of you. I think I was around 11 years old, 2 months after my first menstrual period. One evening as I was on my way back home my landowner's son called out to me. He was with three other men. They started taking off my saree, and even before I could say or do anything they had started molesting me. That night I was gang-raped in the farm in which I worked by the landowner's son and his friends. I did not understand what was going on and did not even know how to fight back with those men. All that I remember now is that I was in pain. There was blood all over my saree and I was crying and shouting for help. No one came to my rescue. I went home the next morning and told my sisters about the incident. They were scared and advised not to tell anybody about what had happened. I was asked to keep quiet and forget about the incident. Though it was not possible for me to forget what had happened, I did not say anything with the fear of losing our wages. The next day when I went to the field I was asked to leave. I had lost my job. I decided not to go back home. I did not want to be a burden for my sisters. I was wandering in the village in search of a job and was determined to return home only after getting another job. After 4 days I met a man who promised me a job in the big city [Mumbai]. He sold me in a brothel in Kamathipura for Rs20,000.

Life here has also been so difficult. I married a man who was my client. He was a taxi driver but a lazy one. After we got married he left his job. He started "helping" me with clients but that was hardly any help. He would take away my money and force me to take clients. I had become his money-making machine. During my first pregnancy, I was detected HIV positive. I started taking help from organizations here, but he never went to the doctor. He died a few years back. Now I am living with another man. He is worse. He beats me a lot. He is also a pimp and that too a famous one in the area. What bad luck! He follows me to the brothels and keeps track of my time. He drinks a lot, gets angry, and beats me when I take slightly longer time with a particular client. He checks my underwear to see if I had sex with any man without his permission. I am nine months pregnant, this is my third baby, but he thinks the child is not his. What can I say? He beats me all the time so I left the room. I live on the pavement now. All these men destroyed my life. Now I have HIV, they say even a drop of my blood can destroy someone's life. How did I get so much power?

We are not the real culprits. No sex worker should be blamed for HIV, because if it was only sex workers how come the "good women" are dying of AIDS too? It's all because of the men who sleep with many women and they infect everyone. Men should be told about condoms, not women because men have to use condoms not women! Women work hard, but they are still arrested. The clients, pimps, our own husbands, and even the police beat us. I don't understand this. Why are we arrested? We are poor and hungry. We don't have money to take a bath even. Why doesn't anyone talk about all this? They don't give us ration cards; we don't get any services from the government. [The Indian government uses ration cards to distribute subsidized food.] Why are we so ignored? I don't know! The police also take money from us. Every time to pay Rs 1,200 fine is just impossible. I have taken loans to pay them and it's on high interest. I don't know what to do about this life.

There is just one difference between you and me. I was born in a wrong family and you were born in a right family. If God had done the reverse, I would be interviewing you and you would be living my life as an orphan, a sex worker who was raped, widowed, and detected HIV positive! Nothing worse can happen now.

MANISHA

I am from Mumbai. My parents died in a road accident when I was 8 years old. I have no siblings, and I have always lived on the roadside. Even when my parents were alive we lived on pavements near Sandhurst Road [an area in South Mumbai] and after their death too I lived on the roads. I was introduced to sex work when I was 11 years old by other girls in the vicinity. As I had no income and nothing to eat, I used to beg for money and food on the traffic signals. Some of my friends were earning very well in red-light areas, and one of them asked me if I was interested. She took me to a *gharwalli* [brothel owner] in Kamathipura, and the gharwalli readily agreed to keep me. The gharwalli promised to give me food, clothes, and a place to stay and told me that I would have to have sex with men in return and earn money. She told me that she would have a share in the money I earned but promised that the money will be more than sufficient for me to look after myself. I was only 11 years old at that time, but I think I was more mature than my age. After living on the road for my entire life I was not scared of anything. Many men had tried to touch me when I was growing up. I was not raped, but one night when I think I was around 10 years old, one man was trying to take off my clothes. I could feel something on my body; I woke up and started screaming. The man was naked and was trying to undress me. I screamed with fright, and my neighbors gathered and drove the man away. When the gharwalli made an offer to me I thought about the decision to start sex work. I chose to get into the profession and thought to myself that rather than getting raped on the roads I would at least get some money out of the same work.

I am here for 12 years. I married a man and we have six children, of which two are mine and four are from my *admi's* [partner's] first marriage. My admi's name was Raja. He died a month ago. Raja was a drug addict, and he committed suicide. He was heavily drugged when this incident took place. Raja did not force me to do sex work, but he suspected that I earned from sex work and followed me everywhere. He did not have any source of income, and I started selling used electronic goods (secondhand) in the local market to earn and support our family. Raja would accompany me to work and kept an eye on my actions. I did not like his attitude, and I was not used to any monitoring right from childhood. When I was with Raja I tried to stay away from sex work as much as possible. However, when I had nothing to eat and when Raja would be absolutely out of consciousness due to drugs and alcohol, I had to go for sex work in desperation. I did not tell him about it and tried to save that money with the social workers in the organization.

On the day when Raja committed suicide we had a very big argument in the morning. Raja wanted some money to buy drugs, and I refused to give him money. He got angry and as always started beating me up. This incident happened in front of our children. When Raja started beating me I tried to beat him back. He kicked me, pushed me on the ground, and stood on my chest. He kicked my stomach and spit on me several times. He pulled my hair and dragged me on the road. I was scared, I was crying and screaming for help but everyone thought it's just one of our regular fights and no one interfered. I escaped and took refuge at Prerana center [a drop-in center run by a social work organization]. Raja thought that I had gone into sex work again, and he started searching for me in the red-light area. He didn't find me there and got angry. He poured a bottle of kerosene on his body and started shouting that if I don't get out of my brothel he would burn himself. Just as he was going to light the matchstick, people from the neighborhood stopped him and took him to the police station. Some of my friends came to the Prerana center to call me. I went to the police station and spoke to the police officer. When Raja saw me at the police station he started verbally abusing me again; the police got angry and started scolding him. Raja took off the matchstick from his pocket and lit himself on fire. He ran outside the building into the police station compound and even though the police tried to save him, within no time he was unconscious. We tried to admit him to the hospital but Raja did not survive this accident.

I don't even know if I am sad about his death. After he passed away I was in a state of shock for almost 5 days. I was shocked not so much about his death but more about how he died. I saw it in front of my eyes. I saw how drugs had made him wild, and even though I was angry at him I could not see him suffer.

You should take a walk in the inner lanes of the red-light area and corridors of brothel houses. You would see women lazing during the daytime because they have worked and stayed awake for the whole night. Men are seen sitting outside on the corridors playing cards or smoking *beedis* [a hand-made, low-cost roll of tobacco wrapped in dried leaves, an alternative to cigarettes]. Some women would be cooking or dropping children off to schools and day-care centers as men do not work in the red-light areas. If you look more closely you will see women crying over their ill fate. Some are beaten up and tortured, some are ill, some have bruises and swollen muscles, but I think they are all scared to die, and that's why keep on living. There is no place for women. The police don't protect us. They are our worst enemies. They drive us away and abuse and beat us like dogs. I have to borrow money from the money lenders to give them [as a bribe] for releasing me. They should protect us, and our work should be recognized, but what to do in a red-light area, there is sadness all around. All men in red-light area depend on woman's money, and yet the woman is powerless.

ASLAM

I am 25 years old. I never attended school. I was born in Bihar [a state in north India], and our family was very poor. When I was 8 years old, my uncle brought me to Mumbai. I was taken to Dharavi [Asia's largest slum district] and sold to a *zari* [embroidery] factory owner. Instead of a pencil to read and write, I was given a needle to work with. I was taught to embroider and stitch. I learned zari work as a child. I got some money and needed all of it to survive. Every day I was locked into the factory with other children so that we would not run away. We worked almost 14 hours every day.

For 10 years I worked in the zari factory in Dharavi. Though I lived in Mumbai all along I had never left the Dharavi slum area. When I was 18, I decided to move out. Some friends brought me to Kamathipura. I had heard about the area and was fascinated about going to sex workers. But I never imagined that going to Kamathipura would be a one-way ticket for me.

I started going to sex workers. In the first 1 week of living in Kamathipura's brothels with different women, I was ripped off my savings of Rs1,000. I had no money left. But the temptation was very bad. It was like lure; the women, the music, alcohol, hashish, I was so high. I was in trance and all this was new to me. I could beg, borrow, or steal; I could do anything to live in pleasure. I decided to stay in Kamathipura. But the excitement was over in a few months. My reality was stark. I was poor, homeless, unemployed, and uneducated. No woman would entertain me without money. I had gotten addicted, and drugs and alcohol also required money. I started borrowing, and there were debts. Life is not as easy as it should be. I found a job in a zari factory in Kamathipura. I still work there. But this is not such a big factory, and the wages are very less. We are 10–11 of us and hardly make enough money to survive.

I have been in this area for the past 6 years or so. I have managed to survive. I still have a good time. There are problems, but this life is better than my life in Dharavi. I also have a woman now. I live with her. We have been together for 2 years and have two children. She was pregnant, so we got married. I don't think it is wrong. I am doing good work by accepting her. These women are so helpless. They are even more helpless than I was. I can understand the reason why they come to sex work. Though I want her to stop, I can't do anything. We depend on each other. Our children will be without food if she stops working. I dream of getting her out of the area. I am sure my dream will come true. I try to buy lottery tickets. Someday God will be kind and I will win *lakhs* [hundreds of thousands] of rupees just like that. Unless there is any miracle, I won't be helped. All of us are victims of circumstances. Our poverty and desperation drives us to this area. Our family background is very bad. We have nothing, and in that nothingness we all search for survival. When you don't get food to eat, you have to steal or solicit, what's the difference? The government does nothing for us. They have given up. So many people live here on the streets.

What are you asking about violence? Violence among us is nothing compared to what the world has done to us. No I don't beat her every day. I am very jealous of her clients. Why do they get so much of her time? She is busy at odd hours. I can't have her when I want. These are my problems with her profession. That's why I don't want her to be a sex worker. She gets beaten up, but what can I do? We are poor and helpless. I have to allow her to work. She will stop if I tell her, but I can't tell her to stop. When I get enough money I will not let her work. I will treat her like a queen but not yet. Now she has to work. She is not doing wrong. This work should be legal. I will go for it! The police here need to be arrested. Sex work is not wrong. They also know that but they still arrest. They are so cruel. I hate them. They take bribes also. Go and talk to them and they will tell you.

Authors' note: Aslam's childhood resembles the reality of thousands of children in India who are trafficked into Mumbai to work as child laborers under extremely difficult conditions. With barely enough food to survive, most of their childhood is spent in learning embroidery work. The living conditions of these laborers are deplorable; there is no access to safe drinking water or sanitation, and even food is scarcely available. The finished goods are expensive designer clothes exported to foreign countries by rich factory owners. For the businesses that employ these children, the profits are enormous, and the investment is the bare minimum. Hence, child labor is another major social problem faced by India and other developing countries.

RAMESH

I was born here in Kamathipura in a local hospital. I am 25 years old. I have lived here for all my life. I have three brothers and one sister. My mother was a sex worker, so we were all born and raised here. My mother was poor and she had to work and send money home. She was alone as our father abandoned her. She had to do sex work to feed us. As a child, I took help from different organizations in Kamathipura. I have attended day- and night-care shelters, boarding schools, but nothing worked. They all tried to get me out of this area, but I still live here. My mother tried to educate me, but I studied only till second grade. I was never interested in studies. I spent my childhood on the streets of Kamathipura, and I saw and heard all that they say children should not know about at a young age. I saw a lot of things, sex work, and the way they do business, how Mother would be beaten up at times. I saw poverty and experienced hunger and a lot of frustration. My childhood was filled with such experiences. Now at 25, I hate this area, but I still prefer to live here. Where else can I fit in?

I have married a woman here who is also a sex worker and am taking care of her and her two children [from her previous marriage]. I don't work regularly, but when I do, I get Rs150 per day. Till 6 months ago I was a thief, a robber. I would steal money from clients or from anyone in the area. I would cut people's bags or even pick pockets. However, I became a thief also because of the bad influence over me. It was not my fault. The circumstances made me a thief. Now that I don't steal I can tell you openly who I was. I stopped stealing 6 months ago. I stopped because my wife brought her children here and in them I saw myself. If they see me doing bad things, they will also become like me. I don't wish for anyone to have similar fate as mine.

How I became a thief is also a story. When I was about 18, I fell in love with a minor girl. She was newly sold into Kamathipura. We were planning to elope and get married. The police got information that her brothel had a minor girl and so they conducted a raid in the brothel. When they conducted the raid, I was with her so they arrested both of us. I told them that I was in love with the girl, but they didn't believe in me. They filed a false complaint of robbery in my name and called me a thief. After getting out of the jail I was so angry. I started stealing and actually became a thief. Now the police here know that I am a thief. They arrest me all the time. I have not been a thief for the past 6 months, but the police still arrest me.

I met my current wife 3 years back, and we have been living together since. When I met her she was new to the place. She was crying a lot because she was cheated to come here. I took pity on her. I showed sympathy, and as I started talking and meeting her more I felt some attraction toward her. I forced her at first to make me her client and told her that I loved her. She was very reluctant as she didn't like sex work at all. But I was so persistent that she gave in finally and became mine. I explained to her the rules of this business and how life in Kamathipura is. I taught her how to do sex work, how to call and attract customers. I helped her get some clients and pay back her dues to her brothel owner. Eventually she also understood the importance of having a man to support a woman in this area, and she agreed to live with me.

The biggest problem in this area is of women. The women do this work for money. They do work because in the village there is no other option to earn. Women have to come here and sell sex. It's the easiest thing to do, and sex work is important because if it's not there, women in good families will be at risk of being raped. So these women are not wrong, but still the police arrest them very often. Every time they arrest, the woman has to pay a fine of Rs1,200, and only then she is released. Most women are afraid of the police. In my opinion sex work should be legal. The police should stop arresting women randomly. The women should be allowed to do sex work. I have seen this area since my childhood. I lived here because of my mother who was a sex worker, and now I am living here because my wife is a sex worker. I drink a lot. I drink every day. I eat, drink, and sleep. I have no friends and nothing to look forward to. Stealing would give me a kick, but I have stopped that too. Now I am bored so I drink more. I was drinking before you came here, and I will drink soon after the interview. Why should I be ashamed? I can say this openly. I drink in my own room. I don't go anywhere. I don't talk with anyone these days. I used to take drugs, but now I have stopped so I just drink a lot. I like to be high on something.

My life has been so depressing that I have to live with alcohol. As a child, I lived on the road or in some organization's day and night shelter. My mother took me from one organization to the other. I went to a different school every time. We were very poor, and my mother tried to take care of us. I had so many siblings that she could not care for all of us together. I have gone to different hostels, organizations, night schools, et cetera, but I was a bad student so I never studied. I got into bad habits as a child. I saw so much crime that I became a thief myself. In my sadness I drink. I am not responsible. I don't work, earn. I even spend my wife's money on drinks. My wife works hard. I am now trying to understand her side and understand that she has to work. Now I am helping her to work. If a client does not give the promised amount to her I beat him instead of beating her. No one else will help us. I have wanted to get a ration card, but they don't give me. They ask for thousands of papers. I can't even read, where am I going to get them the papers from?

In this area men beat women a lot. Some do that because they want money. Some drink and beat a lot. However, men should think like I thought. They should think that a woman is also a worker or a laborer. She is a machine that can produce money. In this society men are unemployed. I am also unemployed and have been jobless for so long, I am lazy and unskilled. Sex work is a job and is quick money. That's what I think. I don't know what women think. It does not matter what they like. It's at least a job. They have work. Men like me don't. This is Mumbai; here you have to work to live.

Emerging Themes

Although each narrative presented here is unique, some similar sentiments are expressed across all four. The critical themes that emerged from the four narratives are presented in the following two sections, which explain the globalized context of Kamathipura and situate the vulnerabilities of its key players. Similarities in males and females are analyzed in each section, followed by an analysis through a gendered lens that helps with understanding the differences in the realities of males and females. In the context of Kamathipura, though the realities of males and females converge at one level, there are differences. These differences indicate additional vulnerabilities of female sex workers. Their struggle for survival is challenged even further because they are women in the predominantly male-dominated culture of Kamathipura. Gender is an important construct in the realities of Kamathipura residents and is discussed in each section.

ANALYSIS OF THE SOCIOECONOMIC CONTEXT OF KAMATHIPURA

The social and economic realities of the respondents illustrate their vulnerability and marginalization. They talked about a family history of poverty and deprivation. The respondents belong to poor families; they do not have an education or any other skills. Two of them come from rural families in India where income-generating opportunities are minimal. All of them belong to castes traditionally considered as low caste, and consequently ill treatment and denial of basic rights is a common experience among them. From living in extreme poverty and hunger to homelessness and forced child labor, their experiences are stark. Thus, their entry in Kamathipura occurred out of their need to survive. This need was defined as destiny by Ratna and choice by Manisha. Ratna described her childhood as painful. She was orphaned, raped, and trafficked into sex work. Entering sex work was certainly not a choice for her; she was drawn into it by what she described as her destiny. Manisha, on the other hand, chose sex work as her profession. Like Ratna, she was also orphaned during her childhood. She was homeless for the most part of her life, and given the options she had for herself, she decided on sex work. She says, "I chose to get into the profession and thought to myself that rather than getting raped on the roads I would at least get some money out of the same work."

The men in the group also reported choosing Kamathipura over other options. In the case of Aslam, the choice was between Asia's largest red-light area (Kamathipura) and Asia's largest slum area (Dharavi). Aslam had spent his entire childhood working as a bonded laborer in a factory in Dharavi. For him, Kamathipura offered freedom from the bondage. The same sense of freedom was experienced by Ramesh, who was born and raised in Kamathipura. Even after being taken away, Ramesh considered Kamathipura as his home. He was never comfortable outside of that setting. He says, "I hate this area but I still prefer to live here. Where else can I fit in?"

Although the educated and the rich in India have a variety of professions and destinations to choose from, the people on the margins do not have such opportunities. Given the limited options, respondents in this study entered and continued to live in Kamathipura. However, life in Kamathipura did not change their economic and social status. The booming sex industry and the marked geographical change in Kamathipura's surroundings did not bring in different income-generating opportunities to these men and women. They remained poor, hungry, and homeless, often living on the streets. They continued to struggle just as they did in their early life. Basic amenities such as food, clothing, and shelter are not available to them.

The Gendered Lens Although poverty was common to all four respondents, it was seen in conjunction with severe violence in the lives of the two female sex workers. Ratna described her life in Kamathipura as "difficult." She described multiple abusive relationships with clients who turned into partners and pimps. She opted to live on the pavement to escape the violence from her current partner/pimp. Ratna questioned her life and expressed her anger at the males who abused her. She said, "Women work hard, but they are still arrested. The clients, pimps, our own husbands, and even the police beat us. I don't understand this. Why are we arrested? We are poor and hungry. We don't have money to take a bath even. Why doesn't anyone talk about all this?"

Manisha, also a victim of violence, echoed similar sentiments. She complained about the men in her life and even the police, who had beaten and tortured her. She acknowledged that even though sex workers earned a living, and men were unemployed and depended on women, women still ended up powerless and abused. The preceding analysis indicates the difficulties of sex workers to survive as females in a primarily male-dominated society. Even as primary providers for their families, the women do not have the power to make decisions. They are exploited by their own partners, and in the existing poverty, the additional coercion and violence are unbearable.

Male partners, on the other hand, acknowledged violence toward women and their hardships but accepted them as part of sex workers' lives. The males' personal identities as "victims" were so overwhelming that they failed to acknowledge the victimization of women. Aslam said that violence between him and his sex worker partner was "nothing compared to what the world has done" to them. Ramesh also blamed his own vulnerabilities and did not think about the violence he perpetrated on his partner. He considered sex work to be a boon that had helped him survive.

The two sex workers described their violent intimate relationships with sadness. They talked about severe physical and mental outcomes of violence. Sex workers identified themselves as victims of violence, but the male partners did not identify themselves as perpetrators. For the male partners, the term *perpetrators of violence* was not applicable to their intimate relationships. In the context of poverty, illiteracy, unemployment, and hunger, male partners identified themselves as victims and not perpetrators. Though male partners interviewed for this research were victims of the existing structural poverty and deprivation, their perpetration of violence against female sex workers cannot be ignored. Analysis of violence and victimization through a gendered lens indicates a more pervasive and intense victimization of women in Kamathipura.

ANALYSIS OF THE POLITICAL AND
LEGAL CONTEXT OF SEX WORK

The political viewpoint on sex work in India is moralistic. The same law that applies to trafficking is followed in cases of sex work, because there is no separate law for sex work in India. Under the Immoral Trafficking and Prevention Act of 1956, any activity associated with sex work is considered a criminal offense. Soliciting sex is considered to be a crime; standing on public property to solicit sex is a crime, and so is living on the income of sex workers. Keeping and managing brothels is also a crime, and none of the brothels in India are legal.

There is a lot of discussion and debate on the law and its punitive nature. The first point of contention is the grouping of trafficking and sex work into the same law, which thereby considers trafficking and sex work to be the same. Victims of trafficking have no protection, and they are arrested by the police. If the police suspect that the woman who is arrested is a minor, they report her to the antitrafficking squad. She is kept in an observation home and eventually sent back to her hometown or village. However, if the woman arrested is not a minor, she is asked to pay a minimum fine of Rs1,200 (about $30). Once the fine is paid, she is released and free to leave. Ratna and Manisha both talked about their fear of the police. In describing her experience with the police in Kamathipura, Manisha said, "The police don't protect us. They are our worst enemies. They drive us away and abuse and beat us like dogs."

The male partners also talked about police atrocities and arrests. Aslam expressed his anger at the police in Kamathipura and complained about getting arrested. He said, "The police here are so cruel. They beat me for drinking, doing drugs, roaming on the streets. I hate them. Their round-ups are useless. They take bribes also." Ramesh also expressed his anger and frustration at the criminal nature of sex work. He acknowledged his dependence on sex work as a profession and demanded its legalization so that female sex workers could work freely. Both of the female sex workers and their male partners said there is nothing wrong with sex work and that instead of getting arrested by the police in the area, sex workers should be protected.

The Gendered Lens Though all the four respondents expressed similar views on the existing political context of sex work and demanded its legalization, the reasons for such a demand were different. Ratna and Manisha talked about how sex work was important to them and their families. Their demand for legalization came out of their personal experiences with the police and the lack of protection from violence. Male partners also acknowledged violence from the police and demanded legal status for sex workers. However, their reasons for demanding the legalization of sex work were different compared with those of the female sex workers. Male partners wanted legalization so their sex worker partners could solicit freely and make more money. Aslam and Ramesh were both unemployed and depended on their partners for day-to-day income. They talked about their helplessness and unemployment and considered sex workers to be fortunate to have a source of income. They wanted their partners to continue with sex work to earn a living.

Apart from this, Ramesh referred to sex work as "quick and easy money" and talked about how in Kamathipura women are like "a machine that can produce money." By calling sex workers machines, Ramesh objectifies female sex workers. He also disregarded the effort that his sex worker partner was making to earn a living. For him, sexual intercourse seemed to be easy for women, a common patriarchal belief, where men believe that women do not have to exert any effort during sexual intercourse. Male force and aggression during sexual intercourse are seen as their hard work and contribution to the experience, whereas female emotions and experiences are ignored. Females are believed to be passive and receptive during sexual intercourse, thereby making it easy for them. Apart from this, Ramesh added that sex workers are needed in the society "to protect women from good families from being raped." They acknowledged the popular patriarchal belief about sex work—that it is an inevitable social evil, necessary to satisfy uncontrollable male sexuality.

The reasons given by male partners for legalization of sex work were based on their past experiences. They considered sex work to be important for their personal and financial needs and disregarded the choices and the needs of the female sex workers in continuing with the profession. They also believed that sex work is easy and a quick way to make money, and they supported the patriarchal notion that males have uncontrollable sexual needs that can be satisfied by female sex workers.

Although males and females suffer the consequences of the punitive law on sex work enforced in Kamathipura, female sex workers reported more direct and severe penalties. Female sex workers were arrested more frequently compared with male clients, pimps, and partners (Kamathipura police staff member, personal communication, May 12, 2007). Ratna talked about her difficulty in paying fines to the police for her release, and Manisha and Ratna both talked about borrowing money from money lenders to give to the police. Aslam and Ramesh also reported being arrested in police roundups, but they did not have to pay any fine for their release. The men who are arrested in the area are detained for a few hours, warned, and released. Because they are never caught "due to intention of soliciting sex," as stated in the law, they are arrested on grounds of suspicion of pimping or receiving services from a sex worker. Because they are arrested merely on the basis of suspicion, the men find it easier to stay away from the police (Kamathipura police staff member, personal communication, May 12, 2007).

Sex workers however, complained that their access to help from police was curtailed because of the law. They did not feel comfortable approaching the police to seek protection from violence because of the fear of being identified and arrested. Female sex workers, as victims of violence in Kamathipura, have no legal help and protection.

Discussion

This chapter provides evidence that structural adjustment policies have negatively affected the most vulnerable populations in India. Although the narratives in this chapter have very different beginnings, each person has been similarly affected by globalization. As previously stated, India has undergone a transition from a primarily agrarian society to an industrialized one as a result of globalization. Ratna and Aslam migrated from rural areas to Mumbai. Ratna was trafficked and sold to a brothel, and Aslam was trafficked for the purpose of labor in the Dharavi slums. With the advent of globalization, Ratna and Aslam became profitable commodities for others. Moreover, globalization's negative effect on employment prospects for the poor led each of these individuals to engage in illegal activity. Ratna and Manisha continue to engage in sex work; Aslam and Ramesh have engaged in factory work, theft, and pimping. The case studies highlight some of the similarities between males and females in the context of Kamathipura. Analyses of the four narratives indicated economic, social, political, and legal vulnerabilities of females and males in Kamathipura. The four respondents lived in poverty and did not receive benefits from any welfare plans and programs that other Indian citizens living below the poverty line receive. They were unable to obtain proof of residence, birth certificates, voter identification cards, and bank accounts because of their "illegal existence." Without any form of identification, the respondents found it difficult to approach government offices including public hospitals for medical aid. This is true not only for the respondents in this study but also for the majority of the other residents of Kamathipura who receive help from local social work organizations to access government offices (Prerana Resource Center staff member, personal communication, May 16, 2007).

Through their narratives, the respondents described their struggles for survival. Sex work is their sole source of income, and they wanted safety and security within the profession. Additionally, female sex workers suffer severe consequences of male domination and patriarchy in Kamathipura. Female sex workers are physically, sexually, and financially exploited on a regular basis, and such exploitation is not reported to the law-enforcing authorities. Sex workers' demands for safety in sex work still remain unanswered, and the societal consciousness and political will is against them. Their "immoral" and "illegal" status impairs their social visibility, and they live on the fringes of society (Menen, 2007).

The four narratives provide a unique and in-depth understanding of the lives of people in Kamathipura. In the broader societal context, males and females can be identified as victims in their own right. However, analysis of their interpersonal relations from the perspective of a gendered lens indicates additional victimization of females. The respondents lived in the same environment and converged at some level in their lives. They echoed similar concerns and issues about their day-to-day lives and identified with one another. However, the same respondents diverged on the basis of gender. Males were seen to be more aggressive and exploitative, and females were victimized and abused.

Conclusion

The preceding analysis offers several implications for social work practice, policy, and research. We conclude by highlighting some of these implications.

PRACTICE IMPLICATIONS

The preceding discussion highlights the lack of implementation of social welfare programs in Kamathipura. The respondents do not have access to ration cards and other economic benefits that are provided by the government. The poverty-alleviation programs and low-income housing provision programs available among other marginalized sections of Indian society are not implemented in Kamathipura. Social workers can advocate for implementation of such programs and lobby with the government to make provisions for vocational training and employment opportunities for unemployed people in the area.

The preceding discussion also highlights the patriarchal perceptions of male intimate partners toward female sex workers. These findings indicate a need for gender sensitization workshops for male intimate partners to break their patriarchal myths. Prior research on sex workers has indicated that inclusion of males may be effective in combating violence against female sex workers (Monto, 2004). Apart from that, couples interventions and counseling support may also be useful in combating violence (Committed Communities Development Trust staff member, personal communication, May 13, 2007).

POLICY IMPLICATIONS

The discussion indicates sex workers' discontent about the criminal nature of sex work. Sex workers demand protection in the profession and ask for police help instead of police harassment. For the female sex workers in Kamathipura, sex work is the sole source of income. The findings from the narratives indicate a need for decriminalization of sex work. The criminal aspects in the red-light area, such as violence from male clients, pimps, and partners, can be reported to the police and action can be taken. Criminalizing the profession has pushed sex workers to the margins of society. Sex workers do not report violence to the police for fear of being identified as involved in prostitution. Contemporary Indian feminist organizations are arguing in favor of decriminalization and sex workers' rights (Jana, 2007; Seshu, 2007). The findings of this study may be important to those lobbying for sex workers' rights.

RESEARCH IMPLICATIONS

The findings indicate a lack of employment opportunities for males in Kamathipura. Further research on reasons for unemployment, barriers to employment, educational and occupational aspirations of people in Kamathipura, and availability of resources and work opportunities in the area might be useful. Apart from that, research on perceptions of other male stakeholders in Kamathipura such as clients and the police about violence and sex work can also be conducted.

There are numerous social work organizations in Kamathipura; however, most of these organizations provide services in terms of HIV care, support, and prevention for sex workers and child care services for sex workers' children. None of the organizations in Kamathipura work with males specifically on violence prevention. For future research, there is a need for geographically mapping interventions in Kamathipura and understanding the different services that are made available to sex workers and stakeholders. Gaps in interventions should be identified, and research should inform newer, more innovative interventions in the area that are unique and nonrepetitive.

Discussion Questions

1. What are the benefits and disadvantages of globalization in India discussed in this chapter? What other benefits and disadvantages do you foresee that are not discussed in the chapter?
2. How does globalization cut across gender and socioeconomic class differently? For example, how does globalization affect women and men differently? How does globalization affect the poor and wealthy differently?
3. Discuss the levels of globalization: individual, community (e.g., Kamathipura), national, transnational. How do the narratives exhibit the mul-

tiple layers of globalization? How do these layers interact? For instance, how does globalization at the national level affect the individual?

4. Do you believe that gender-based violence is a symptom of globalization? Or is gender-based violence simply a result of individual actions? Explain.

5. How would the participants situate themselves in the globalization debate? For example, would the participants be pro- or antiglobalization? How would the authors situate themselves in the globalization debate?

References

Banerjee, U. D. (2003). Globalization and its links to migration and trafficking: The crisis in India, Nepal and Bangladesh. *Canadian Woman Studies, 22*(3/4), 124–130.

Basu, R., & Thomas, M. D. (2009). Exploring women's daily lives and participation in the informal labour market in Mumbai, India. *Gender & Development, 17*(2), 231–242.

Deshpande, S. (1998). After culture: Renewed agendas for the political economy of India. *Culture Dynamics, 10*(2), 147–169.

Frederick, J. (2000). *Fallen angels: The sex workers of South Asia.* New Delhi, India: Luster Press.

Gangoli, G. (2006). *Silence hurt and choice: Attitudes to prostitution in India and the West.* London, UK: London School of Economics.

Ganguly-Scrase, R. (2003). Paradoxes of globalization, liberalization, and gender equality: The world-views of the lower middle class in West Bengal, India. *Gender & Society, 17*(4), 544–566.

Grey, M. (2005). Dalit women and the struggle for justice in a world of global capitalism. *Feminist Theology, 14*(1), 127–149.

Jana, S. (2007). *About Durbar Mahila Samanwaya Committee.* Retrieved from http://www.durbar. org/html/profile.asp

Lakha, S. (1999). The state, globalization, and Indian middle class identity. In M. Pinches (Ed.), *Culture and Privilege in Capitalist Asia* (pp. 252–276). New York, NY: Routledge.

Madhok, B., & Raj, S. J. (2011). Globalization, higher education, and women in urban India: A development ethics approach. *Journal of Third World Studies, 28*(1), 141–154.

Menen, R. (2007). *Karma sutra: Essays from the margin.* Newbury Park, CA: SAGE.

Monto, M. A. (2004). Female prostitution, customers, and violence. *Violence Against Women, 10*(2), 160–188.

National Commission for Protection of Child Rights. (n.d.). *The Immoral Traffic (Prevention) Act.* Retrieved from ncpcr.gov.in/Acts/Immoral_Traffic_Prevention_Act_(ITPA)_1956.pdf

Nayar, B. R. (2006). *India's globalization: Evaluating the economic consequences.* Washington, DC: East-West Center Washington.

Seshu, M. (2007). *Prostitute, sex worker, woman in prostitution and sex work: The tyranny of terminology.* Retrieved from http://www.sangram.org/info4_1.aspx

Upadhyay, U. D. (2000). India's new economic policy of 1991 and its impact on women poverty and AIDS. *Feminist Economics, 6*(3), 105–122.

CHAPTER 2

Developing a Critical Understanding of Human Trafficking

A Primer for Social Workers

MARIA BEATRIZ ALVAREZ AND EDWARD J. ALESSI

People don't want to realize that someone is suffering. We are the ones that picked the food that someone is bringing to the table. They look at a tomato, it looks fresh and good, so they eat it, but they don't see the sweat, the exploitation.

—Martinez, tomato picker, trafficked to Florida (Woolf, 2003)

We provide this chapter as a primer for social workers about the growing and widespread phenomenon of human trafficking and include the following:
- The principles of the social work profession and their application to human trafficking
- How each of us came to be concerned about the issue
- Key terms and concepts, especially concerning human trafficking as a phenomenon of growing concern in a globalized market economy and in light of constructions of femininities and masculinities
- Relevant policies and research
- Recommendations for research and practice
- Critical consciousness exercises

The Principles of Social Work

Since its inception as a distinct discipline, the social work profession has had an enduring commitment to social justice. Jane Addams (1910) referred to social justice as a unifying value shared by charity and settlement workers, and that same commitment to social justice has been reaffirmed in the National Association of Social Workers' (NASW, 1999) *Code of Ethics* and in the Council for Social Work Education's (CSWE, 2008) *Educational Policy and Accreditation Standards.* Social work scholars have discussed the meaning of social justice as the unifying value of the profession (Wakefield, 1988a, 1988b) and the challenges that social workers face putting that principle into practice in a socially unjust world (Caputo, 2002; Polack, 2004; Reisch, 2002).

This discussion about the correspondence of social work principles and practice becomes especially important when confronting human trafficking, because in a society ruled by market-based economics, vulnerable populations are treated as fungible commodities in a volatile marketplace. Indeed, human trafficking is a human rights violation and a global public health issue (Goździak & Bump, 2008; Laczko & Goździak, 2005). It entails the transportation and enslavement of human beings for financial gain. Thus, it is crucial that social workers have a critical understanding of human trafficking to guide their interventions at the micro-, mezzo-, and macrolevels.

Maria Beatriz's Story

The profession's commitment to social justice attracted me to study social work in the United States after having studied philosophy in Argentina and engaged in *popular education* in the inner-city and the rural areas of the country. For me, popular education meant the pedagogy of the oppressed of Paulo Freire. What drew me to Freire's work was his commitment to developing the critical consciousness of people who are socially, politically, and economically marginalized so that they can critique and act on their conditions. Freire believed that the development of one's critical consciousness leads to an in-depth understanding of the world, its relationships of power, and its social and political contradictions. This understanding, allied with concrete and collective actions, can liberate learners from internalized oppressions and allow them to become active agents of social change.

My interest in social justice and popular education started when I was an adolescent growing up in Buenos Aires during the years of the "dirty war." El Proceso, as it was known, was a campaign of state-sponsored terrorism carried out by the military to protect the interests of the wealthy by labeling all political resistance to their regime as Communist and then brutally eradicating it. (It is estimated that more than 20,000 people "disappeared" between 1976 and 1983.[1])

During this period of military repression I witnessed on a daily basis the devastating effects of an unequal distribution of wealth at the local and regional levels. For example, Buenos Aires, a center of economic, social, and political power, attracted migrant workers from poorer provinces and neighboring countries seeking a better livelihood for themselves and their families. These migrant workers often settled on the periphery of the big city, establishing their homes in large shantytowns, or *villas miserias,* often living in crowded conditions, lacking running water, sewage facilities, and electricity. I taught literacy during my high school years in one of these shantytowns located in the margins of one of the most affluent suburbs in Buenos Aires while carrying around a copy of Freire's (1970) *Pedagogy of the Oppressed,* a book considered dangerous by the military regime.

Seeking to understand these social inequalities and relationships of power, I became interested in "core–periphery" and "center-and-margin" relationships, in part because of my growing familiarity with liberation theology, which tries to ally political and ethical concerns through a mandate to practice a preference for the poor. This means, in short, to base social action on the teachings of Jesus Christ and narratives told about his actions with the marginalized and the powerful people of his time. But most of all this theology is based on the idea of Jesus having been born on the periphery of the Roman Empire, which is interpreted as liberation coming from the margins. Core-periphery and center-and-margin are dialectical relationships that imply perceptions and exercise of power. Liberation theology assumes that social change comes from mobilizing the transformational forces among the oppressed, whose position in the periphery allows them to critically understand their role in the totality, free themselves from internalized oppressions, and become agents of social change. Thus, at the age of 16 I found myself putting into practice a Freire-style popular education informed by the morality of liberation theology in a time of political repression, working with people living on the margins in a city that itself, although at the core of Argentina, was on the periphery of the Global North (for more on the Global North and South, see Kacowicz, 2007; Reuveny & Thompson, 2007), thus shaping my critical consciousness in a way that hooks (2000) beautifully describes:

> Living as we did—on the edge—we developed a particular way of seeing reality. We looked both from the outside in and from the inside out. We focused our attention on the center as well as on the margin. We understood both. . . . Our survival depended on an ongoing public awareness of the separation between margin and center and the ongoing private acknowledgement that we were a necessary, vital part of that whole. (p. xvi)

The critical consciousness developed through my earlier life experiences also informed my social work practice, mostly with immigrants from around the world, but particularly with people from Latin American countries. I heard their stories of struggle and resiliency. Some of them, including children, traveled for months in hazardous conditions, often in the night, led by *coyotes*, hoping to arrive in a land that upheld the promise of the livelihoods denied to them in their native countries.[2]

My desire to understand and overcome the global structural inequalities that affect people's access to employment, education, health, safety, political stability, human well-being, and peace led me to research the experiences of immigrants and refugees, particularly the experiences of women in post-conflict areas and their movement into the labor market. Labor migration and human trafficking are so closely interconnected that research on the former ineluctably led me to investigate the latter.

Edward's Story

Unlike Maria Beatriz, my interest in social justice emerged through my clinical work in mental health settings. After I completed my master's degree in social work, I had a very narrow understanding of the concept. I was under the impression that social workers only engaged in social justice pursuits if they linked clients to concrete services, helped them access entitlements or public benefits, or focused on macro level or policy-based interventions. I did not see how the pursuit of social justice was connected to my job as a clinical social worker in a hospital-based outpatient psychiatry clinic where my primary function was performing psychiatric assessment and conducting individual and group psychotherapy. Although the majority of my clients identified as racial/ethnic minorities and lived in communities affected by unemployment, poverty, and violence, I still questioned how conducting psychotherapy with this population was a social justice pursuit aligned with the organizing values of the social work profession. I soon realized that this question was not a new one; in fact, it has sparked considerable debate among the profession for a very long time (see Epple, 2007; Specht & Courtney, 1994; Swenson, 1998; Wakefield, 1988a, 1988b).

During my doctoral studies in clinical social work, I started to gain clarity regarding this issue. My confusion stemmed from the way I conceptualized social justice: It was much too narrow. Social justice pursuits are not limited to engaging in social reform or helping clients access economic resources. According to Wakefield (1988a, 1998b), providing psychotherapy to clients deprived of primary psychological goods such as self-respect, self-esteem, and self-confidence is also a social justice pursuit. These psychological goods are necessary for promoting self-efficacy, sustaining healthy relationships, and navigating complex organizational and social systems. Thus, helping clients obtain primary psychological goods through psychotherapy ensures minimal levels of distributive justice (Wakefield, 1998a). Most of my clients were deprived of primary psychological goods from early ages, as extreme social stressors contributed to trauma, poverty, neglect, and dissolution of family and social support networks.

My goal of trying to understand social justice in broad terms led to my interest in studying human trafficking. The profession's focus on sex trafficking was much too narrow and as a result ignored the plight of numerous people forced to work in a variety of areas (Alvarez & Alessi, 2012). Furthermore, the use of the metanarrative that views all trafficked people as helpless victims also limits the profession's efforts to help people affected by trafficking. For social justice pursuits to be effective at the micro-, mezzo-, and macro levels, social workers should understand the historical and social antecedents of the problem as a way to advocate for structural changes to address the detrimental conditions that leave individuals vulnerable to human trafficking. Social workers must also be aware of the severe psychological trauma that may result from being a victim of human trafficking, regardless of the area where one is forced to work (International Organization for Migration [IOM], 2009).

To infuse the profession's core social justice values into the policy and clinical interventions aimed at helping people affected by trafficking, we believe it is essential for social workers to develop a critical understanding of how globalized market economies can promote conditions of vulnerability to trafficking, how ideas of gender are constituted through trafficking, and how trafficking shapes gendered experiences and relations. Our overview will, at times, be a bit tangled because of the competing agendas and vocabularies at play, but a useful vocabulary that will lead to an equally useful set of practices will emerge.

What Is Human Trafficking?

Human trafficking is not a self-evident term. Its meaning depends on who selects the people to include in the term, a selection based on research, beliefs, morality, and a whole host of other factors, which then subsequently affect the statistics reported on the number of people being trafficked, the policies that flow from that analysis, and how these policies are enforced (see McDonald, 2004; Ray, 2006; and Weitzer, 2007).

Also involved in defining this central term are the opinions of the "trafficked" themselves, because not all of them consider themselves victimized by their traffickers or see themselves as enslaved by their conditions. In addition, the lines between states of being, such as those that fall between being smuggled and being trafficked, shift depending on changes in a multitude of intertwined elements (Kapur, 2005; Kempadoo 2005).

Therefore, before we present some of the current research on human trafficking to demonstrate where people are in their understanding of the term, we would like you to do a short thought experiment about defining the term for yourself, perhaps in a dialogue with somebody you trust, a kind of dialogue that Paolo Freire might use to get people to think outside their usual intellectual boxes.

1. Think of your community, in whichever way you would like to define it. Who is in? Who is out? How is membership defined? Is this a homogenous or a diverse community? Why homogeneous? Why diverse?

2. What are the relationships of power in this community? Who holds more power? Why? How is power defined?

3. Are there prostitutes or sex workers in your community? Does it make a difference if they are called prostitutes or sex workers? What kind of difference and why?

4. Where are prostitutes/sex workers located (socially, not geographically) in your community: at the center, on the margins, and so on? Why are they there?

5. Are there domestic workers in your community? Where are they located in the community? Why?

6. Are there agricultural workers in your community? Where are they located in the community? Why?

7. You may apply the same set of questions to different labor sectors: production, construction, mining, tanning industries, hospitality services, and so forth.

8. Does gender play a role in the transactions that take place in your community? How?

9. Does globalization play a role in these transactions? How?

10. Do people want to stay in or leave this community? Why?

11. How does this community understand what it means to be human? Do the transactions in the community foster human development? How?

12. Does your community know about human trafficking? Are human trafficking and sex trafficking differentiated? How?

13. Does your community consider itself affected by human trafficking? How?

14. Has your community taken any action against trafficking? What actions if any? Why?

If you found yourself making shifts, positive or negative, in how you think and speak as you answered these questions, then you have begun to use what Freire (1974) called *critical consciousness* to make yourself aware of the overt and covert assumptions in our language and points of view about the world.

This short exercise will also help you be more aware of how the definition of the term *human trafficking* (as often happens with many other definitions) can shift depending on your worldview, feelings, moral principles, beliefs—in short, who you are in the world.

And if it is difficult for a single person or small group to formulate a clear, steady understanding of the term, think how much more difficult it is when societies, governments, and economies become involved in understanding and defining the term. Let's take a brief look at some of those debates.

Shifting Perspectives Over the Term *Human Trafficking*

At the international level, two main opposing viewpoints, drawn from work by feminists (which we will discuss later), played a major role in the definition of human trafficking. These two positions reached a compromise during the United Nations Convention against Transnational Crime in Palermo, Italy, by defining human trafficking according to three key elements:

1. The act—what is done: "recruitment, transportation, transfer, harbouring, or receipt of persons"
2. The means—how it is done: "threat or use of force, coercion, abduction, fraud, deception, abuse of power or vulnerability, or giving payments or benefits to a person in control of the victim"
3. The purpose—why it is done: "exploitation, which includes exploiting the prostitution of others, sexual exploitation, forced labour, slavery, or similar practices and the removal of organs" (United Nations Office on Drugs and Crime [UNODC], 2000, art. 3).

The UN definition (2000) specifies that when the person exploited is a minor, defined as a person younger than 18 years of age, the means are irrelevant, because a minor has not yet reached the age of consent. Children are at particular risk for human trafficking; they can be trafficked for sexual and labor exploitation, begging, organ harvesting, and domestic servitude.

The UN definition, also known as the Palermo Protocol, is the most cited in research, policy, and practice, though it is often interpreted differently at the operational level.[3] Some of these interpretations can be summarized in the following four frameworks that emphasize distinct aspects of human trafficking:

1. The morality framework, rooted in the antiprostitution campaigns in the 19th century, links antitrafficking efforts with the abolition of prostitution. This framework focuses mainly on trafficking for prostitution,

ignoring other forms of trafficking or even other forms of sexual enslavement, such as forced marriages or domestic servitude.

2. The radical feminist framework, linked with the Violence Against Women Movement, sees trafficking as another manifestation of the violation of women's rights in a patriarchal society. This framework tends to focus on the victimization of women who are seen as the deceived prey of traffickers and ignores that on some level these women have a choice (or agency) as migrant workers. It also ignores the enslavement of men who are trafficked into labor or sexual exploitation. Radical feminists see prostitution as exploitation and do not consider the consent of the victim to be relevant. The morality and the radical feminist frameworks are often used in media depictions of trafficking.[4]

3. The law enforcement framework, represented by the Palermo Protocol, which was drafted during an international convention against transnational crime, is the most favored by governments that see trafficking as a law enforcement issue with a mandate to prosecute the offenders and protect the victims. It focuses mainly on combating international crime and illegal immigration. This framework tends to overlook the trafficking situations that occur within national borders, and the protection of the victims often depends on their cooperation in the prosecution of the traffickers.

4. The labor migration framework is more comprehensive than the preceding ones because it recognizes the structural factors in a global economy that push people to migrate in search of employment and thus render them more vulnerable to trafficking. However, this framework also assumes that the structural inequalities that push people to leave are permanent, and it focuses on the protection of the rights of migrant workers at the expense of delving into the root causes of trafficking (Alvarez & Alessi, 2012; Ray, 2006).

One thing these four frameworks have in common is that they all conceptualize human trafficking ex post facto, that is, at the time of or after the trafficker takes control over the trafficked victim, at the expense of examining the root causes of trafficking (Ray, 2006). This is important to note, because although each of these frameworks offers an important insight into the problem, they stop where we want to begin our analysis, which is with the conditions, the root causes, the ab initio rather than the ex post, that set up the conditions that propel people (especially women) into an often desperate search for the means to sustain a dignified life.

How We Understand Human Trafficking

Our understanding of the term *human trafficking* has four components: economics, gender, a focus on root causes, and the agency of victims.

We believe human trafficking is best understood as an economic outcome of globalization, conceptualized as an array of "processes that entail intensified global interconnectedness (and subsequent changes in local livelihoods), via the mobility of culture, capital, information, resistance, technologies, production, people, commodities, images, and ideologies" (Gunewardena & Kingsolver, 2007, p. 7).

We define this economic globalization as the integration of the economies of nation–states into a borderless capitalist market, mediated by institutions (such as the World Trade Organization) that ensure that capital flows along the paths of least resistance while blocking anything that threatens capital's movements and profits, be it labor rights, environmental concerns, or social welfare systems (see Fotopoulos, 2001). From this perspective, people become commodities traded in and through markets, in essence no different than other commodities such as cars, food, or clothing.

Second, we agree with Horgan (2001) and Gunewardena and Kingsolver (2007) that economic globalization also needs to be analyzed as a gendered process, where interpretations of what is feminine and what is masculine are active elements in the exchanges between capital and labor. That last statement may seem unusual because it is not something that is readily apparent to people, but let us offer an example that demonstrates what we mean.

Since the 1970s the International Monetary Fund has mandated structural adjustment policies (SAP) requiring governments to open their economies to international trade and financial flows as a condition for receiving loans. These SAPs usually force governments to implement austerity measures, such as cutting back on services and selling off nationalized industries to private corporations. However, these austerity measures do not affect everyone equally. As research has shown, the austerity measures implemented by the borrowing countries tend predominantly to affect women, and the multinational corporations given entry into countries' economies through the SAPs prefer women workers, who are seen as more likely to accept less desirable working conditions and pay (Pyle, 2001). Thus, the corporations use social constructions of gender to their advantage (Pyle, 2002). In this way, seemingly impersonal and rational processes create situations that have severe gender effects.

Third, we also believe that understanding human trafficking in the context of gendered economic globalization gives us a better analytical opportunity to investigate and address its root causes, what Ray (2006) calls the "underlying factors such as discrimination against women, lack of education, lack of access to resources, and poverty, including feminization of poverty" (p. 925). Without investigating the conditions that render people, predominantly women, vulnerable to trafficking, "if the conditions that foster trafficking continue to exist, traffickers will merely have to change their strategies and forms of exploitation to stay a step ahead of law enforcement" (p. 925).

Fourth, we disagree with the central image proposed by certain antislavery and antitrafficking campaigns that present trafficked people as innocent victims who need to be rescued from the traffickers and reunited with their communities of origin. This metaphor of a victim subject not only fails to recognize the agency, however constrained, of illegalized migrants who have been trafficked to work in a variety of areas, but more importantly it diverts attention from "understand[ing] how processes of capitalist globalization and the consequent effects of dislocation and dispersal shape the mobility of illegalized migrants" (Kapur, 2002; Sharma, 2005, p. 88) and the globalized capitalist practices that deprive workers of their livelihoods in the first place. We agree with Sharma (2005) that victim subject rhetoric operates as a "moral panic" (p. 89), which justifies the use of regressive practices to enforce immigration control.

Of course, different people have different views on the costs and benefits of globalization, but there is neither the time nor space here to analyze in depth the economic and political debates between neoliberal and radical theorists, and their concerns are really not necessary to understand that one indisputable result of economic globalization is that capital's geographical unmooring to pursue profit anywhere has created an analogous unmooring of the labor capital needs to generate those profits, which often has a strong gender bias built into it.[5]

A vast number of people move internally and internationally in search of employment and a better livelihood, which in turn can render them more vulnerable to labor exploitation and abuse.[6]

A Resting Point

Before we move on, we would like to take a moment to summarize where we are. We anchor our understanding of the term *human trafficking* in the economic globalization of capital. This process has created labor markets that have drawn in millions of people who are, by a variety of capitalist practices, deprived of a chance of earning a livelihood where they live. This movement of millions of people has a gender bias to it, because women are disproportionately affected by the dislocations caused by economic globalization. But rather than treat them as victims who need to be saved, we propose instead that a focus on the root causes that have made them vulnerable in the first place will be more helpful in eradicating the situation. Our intention in presenting this perspective, as we stated at the beginning of this chapter, is to help social workers become more informed about the situation of human trafficking, so they can identify trafficked people and provide them with appropriate services.

In our next section we delve into some important distinctions that need to be made about migration, smuggling, and trafficking.

Gendered Migration, Smuggling, and Trafficking

As with most things pertaining to this area of study, the migrations induced by globalization have spurred positive and negative outcomes. For instance, many immigrants who provide low-wage labor in the Global North send remittances to the Global South, supporting the economies of poor countries and providing social welfare that these countries cannot or do not provide (Kapur, 2005). For example, in 2010 the World Bank (2011) estimated that $325 billion in remittances went to the Global South.

Although from an economic perspective remittances are often presented as gender neutral, they are in fact the result of intricate processes of negotiations in which gender dynamics play an important function that cannot be dissociated from women's economic and social roles (Ramirez, Garcia Dominguez, & Miguez Morais, 2005). According to the United Nations International Research and Training Institute for the Advancement of Women (2007), the global percentage of female migration remained fairly stable, only increasing 2 points from 1960 to 2007 (47% to 49%). However, how women have migrated has changed: More women migrate alone rather than with relatives, searching for jobs to support their families back home and with the expectation that they will self-sacrifice for the well-being of their families. Consequently, women who migrate alone are also exposed to gender discrimination and are at greater risk of being exploited in sex and labor trafficking (United Nations Department of Economic and Social Affairs, 2004).

Of course, as these tremendous flows of people have generated income for their home countries, they have also incentivized, inadvertently and deliberately, a pervasive and profitable transnational business in smuggling and trafficking the humans swept up in these great migrations, often abetted by immigration policies and discriminatory attitudes designed to keep people out but that only make them vulnerable to exploitation. An example of where immigration policies unintentionally created an opportunity for organized transnational crime was the deportation of about 20,000 foreign-born but U.S.-raised felons to Central America. Some deportees were members of two Los Angeles gangs, the MS-13 and MS-8, with very few ties to their countries of origin. In 10 years MS-13 became pan-Hispanic and not only expanded operations into human smuggling and trafficking but also established partnerships with the Mexican drug cartels (Koslowski, 2011).

There are, of course, distinctions between smuggling and trafficking that social workers should be aware of. From a law enforcement perspective, the United Nations Office on Drugs and Crime (UNODC, 2000) established three key definitional differences between smuggling and trafficking: consent, transnationality, and exploitation. Smuggling requires transnational border crossing, whereas trafficking may happen within the confines of the same state. Smuggled immigrants generally give consent to be smuggled; in contrast, the victims of trafficking have not consented, or if they have, between the departure and destination points they were deceived by the traffickers and subjected to slavelike conditions. In addition, the commercial transaction between the smuggler and the migrant ends after crossing the border, whereas trafficking entails ongoing exploitation of the victim for the profit of the trafficker.

However, in practice, smuggling migrants for labor purposes may be difficult to distinguish from trafficking for labor exploitation, because the two conditions lie on a continuum without clear transition points that signal when one condition has morphed into the other. First, the traffickers may also act as smugglers and use the same routes for trafficking and smuggling; second, the smuggled migrants may become trafficked while in transit; and, finally, the conditions during the smuggling process may be so abusive that it would be difficult to believe that the smuggled migrant gave consent.

Debt bonds are another example of the blurred boundaries between smuggling and trafficking: A smuggled migrant may have already paid the trafficker for being smuggled but is told that during transit more expenses were accumulated, which the migrant has to pay with his or her own labor and is therefore forced to work for the trafficker in the destination country. Sometimes a person with the so-called debt bond may be moved from one location to another to accumulate more "debt" and justify the bondage.

For example, a woman may consent to being smuggled to work as a waitress in a foreign country, or she may even willingly hire a smuggler to facilitate the border crossing to work in the sex industry abroad. In the transit process she becomes enslaved by the trafficker who seizes her documents, restricts her mobility, subjects her to threats to herself and her family, and forces her to work without pay. In fact, the woman in our example becomes a victim of trafficking at some point during transit or at the point of destination, whereas during the earlier phases she could be seen as an illegal immigrant being smuggled and thus committing a crime herself. The fear of being arrested for a crime may be used by the trafficker as a way of controlling her and may deter her from seeking help. As Ditmore (2005) points out, "Trafficking in persons defines a victim of crime rather than an agent, while smuggling necessarily implicates the person who has engaged the services of a smuggler" (p. 109). Additionally, the ex post facto nature of trafficking as a crime and the difficulties in establishing the intent of the trafficker during the recruitment phase illustrate some of the challenges in identifying and dealing with human trafficking (Sanghera, 2005).

For the purposes of this chapter, though, although it is important to understand the distinctions between the terms *trafficking* and *smuggling*, in reality, we are most concerned about the consequences of any sort of enforced peonage, whether that happens through being trafficked or smuggled, in which a person's time, body, and spirit have been exploited by others seeking to profit from his or her vulnerabilities and desires.

How This Relates to Policy

In the section "Shifting Perspectives Over the Term *Human Trafficking*," we mentioned that the UN definition of trafficking, which is the most used in policy and research, represented a compromise between two opposing feminist views on trafficking and prostitution.

Let's consider in more detail how this affects making policy, which in turn affects how social workers have to deal with the ways these policies are applied and the consequences for actual human beings. On the one hand, the Human Rights Network, a coalition of radical feminists and Christian right lobbyists, maintains that prostitution is immoral and is a representation of the oppressive patriarchal society that treats women as commodities.[7] This group proposed the criminalization of prostitution and advocated that in the definition of trafficking, all forms of sex work should be considered exploitation and the consent of the victim irrelevant (Ditmore, 2005).

On the other hand, groups such as the Human Rights Caucus (Ditmore, 2005) proposed that sex workers are *workers*, and as workers they have agency (that is, some measure of power, as in defining how and where they work) and should not be considered victims, as this definition robs them of their power to make choices.[8] Caucus members believed that sex trafficking should be defined by the working conditions and not the type of work. They further proposed that "legal recognition [be given] to the sex industry" as a category of work and that recognition include "other human rights protections such as witness protection and health care" (Ditmore, 2005, p. 111). Though they acknowledged the existence of abuses in the sex industry, they also believed that the criminalization of sex work would render sex workers less visible and more vulnerable to such abuses:

> These conflicting agendas—a criminalization perspective versus a human rights perspective—played themselves out fully in shaping trafficking policies in the United States. Perhaps the most prominent example of how the ideological debates on trafficking influence policy decisions can be seen in the United States with the Victims of Trafficking and Violence Protection Act of 2000, enacted under President Bill Clinton and reauthorized under President George W. Bush in 2003, whose addenda put a stronger focus on sex trafficking and obscured the distinctions between smuggling people to work in the sex industry and sex trafficking. (Trafficking Victims Protection Act [TVPA], 2003)

During the congressional hearings prior to the enactment of the TVPA, numerous groups from a wide spectrum of interests and political positions testified on their understanding of human trafficking. Although these groups agreed in several areas—the need for prevention, protection, and prosecution (also known as the three Ps) to combat trafficking; the criminalization of the traffickers; and the recognition of trafficked people as victims—they held divergent views on the distinctions between sex labor, prostitution, and forced prostitution as forms of sex trafficking (Stolz, 2007). Many groups used the press as their battleground to debate their views on trafficking, and some accused the Clinton administration of weakening international laws against prostitution and pornography (Bennet & Colson, 2000; Blomquist, 2000; Shenon, 2000; Strode, 2000).

Although the U.S. House of Representatives and the Senate passed the Victims of Trafficking and Violence Protection Act and President Clinton signed the bill on October 28, 2000, the hearings continued between 2001 and 2005 because the reauthorizations of 2003 and 2005 gave lobbyists the opportunity to raise new issues (Stolz, 2007; Trafficking Victims Protection Reauthorization Act, 2003; Trafficking Victims Protection Reauthorization Act, 2005; Victims of Trafficking and Violence Protection Act, 2000). In 2003 the reauthorization of the act included, along with other amendments, "a restriction on the awarding of grant funding for programs and organizations for the protection of and assistance to victims. Specifically, no grant funds were to be used to promote, support, or advocate the legalization of prostitution" (Stoltz, 2007, p. 321).

Furthermore, the U.S. National Institute of Justice requires that any applicant for research funding on trafficking in human beings must certify that it does not "promote, support, or advocate the legalization or practice of prostitution" (U.S. National Institute of Justice, 2007, p. 4). Likewise, the U.S. Agency for International Development [USAID] (2003) does not fund international organizations that fight the spread of AIDS unless they have a policy explicitly opposing prostitution and sex trafficking.

The TVPA antiprostitution pledge was maintained during the reauthorizations of 2005 and 2008 (Trafficking Victims Protection Reauthorization Act, 2005; William Wilberforce Trafficking Victims Protection Reauthorization

Act, [TVPRA] 2008). Anticipating the 2012 TVPRA reauthorization, human rights advocates called on President Barack Obama's administration to protect the rights of sex workers who suffer violence and discrimination and to change federal policies that conflate sex work with trafficking: "Revoke 'anti-prostitution pledge' requirements for U.S. Global AIDS recipients and anti-trafficking funds, which significantly reduce the capacity of organizations seeking to decrease harm against sex workers" (Lerum, Saunders, Barlin, Wahab, & Swift, 2011, p. 3).

Where All This Brings Us as Social Workers

Although methodological and theoretical problems as well as ideological debates have made the collection of reliable data and the production of accurate statistics difficult (Goździak & Bump, 2008; Laczko & Goździak, 2005), it is estimated that worldwide between 4 and 27 million individuals have been victims of trafficking or forced labor at any given time (U.S. Department of State, 2007). It is quite likely that any social worker, during his or her career, will encounter a number of these people. Therefore, it is important to be able to recognize the hallmarks of being trafficked, in great measure because they can be easily overlooked or attributed to other conditions.

Despite the methodological limitations available, research indicates by and large that "abuse, deprivation and stress-filled or terrifying circumstances are all hallmarks of human trafficking" (UNODC, 2009, p. 15). One constraint in the research has been that the majority of the information on the health and mental health needs of trafficked people originates in studies of victims receiving post trafficked services (UNODC, 2008), which in most instances focused on women and girls trafficked for sexual exploitation (Goździak & Bump, 2008).

Notwithstanding these limitations, the evidence suggests trafficked persons experience similar psychological reactions to those of torture victims. Zimmerman and colleagues (Zimmerman et al,, 2003; Zimmerman, Hossain, Yun, Roche, Morison, & Watts, 2006a, 2006b) conducted a survey of women entering posttrafficking services in Europe and found that many of the participants suffered from emotional and cognitive impairments similar to those found in torture victims. Such impairments included peritraumatic dissociation, disturbing and upsetting memories, hyperarousal, intrusive thoughts, recurrent nightmares, helplessness, irritability, difficulty concentrating, depression, and anxiety. The acuteness of the cognitive impairments affected the women's ability to make decisions about their safety, diminished their credibility in the criminal investigations and immigration proceedings, and increased their risk of further traumatization. The severity of the posttraumatic symptoms did not decrease until nearly 90 days after the women began receiving services. One of Zimmerman and colleagues' recommendations was to have a waiting period before members of law enforcement interview victims of trafficking. However, this waiting period, based on the mental health needs of the victim, may be at odds with the expectations of law enforcement personnel to gather time-sensitive evidence against the traffickers.

Similar to traumatized asylum seekers and torture victims, trafficked people have suffered many losses: family, home, belongings, social roles, customs, and livelihood. In some cases the cumulative effect of these losses is experienced as a loss of "personal identity and . . . a loss of continuity and self-sameness" (Droždek & Wilson, 2004, p. 244). As a result, asylum seekers and torture victims share with trafficked people the experience of having been subjected to uncontrollable and unpredictable stress, which has been linked to prolonged posttraumatic stress symptoms (Basoğlu & Mineka, 1992). Thus, the services for trafficked people should be based on "good practices used for victims of domestic violence, sexual assault, and torture, and for immigrants and refugees" (Zimmerman et al., 2008, p. 4).

Moreover, depending on the type of work trafficked individuals are forced to perform, they can present with health problems such as malnutrition, dehydration, respiratory problems, high blood pressure, skin infections, accidental injuries, hypothermia, frostbite, pelvic inflammatory disease, vaginal fistulas, sexually transmitted infections, or unsafe abortions, to name a few (IOM, 2009).

Often trafficking victims come in contact with health care providers while they are still controlled by the trafficker, and social workers in settings such as emergency rooms, health clinics, and women's health services may play a pivotal role in the identification and assistance of trafficked people.

For example, a man who arrives at an emergency room with dehydration, respiratory problems, high blood pressure, and skin infections, and also reports working in agriculture could be a victim of trafficking. Or a woman who seeks medical treatment because of an accidental injury, who appears guarded and anxious, and who is under the watchful company of a "boyfriend" or "family relative" playing the role of protector, could also be identified as a victim of domestic servitude or sex trafficking. Or a teenager who has a skin infection after getting a tattoo and tells the pediatric nurse in the emergency room that her adult companion is her father or her mother could be a runaway teen who is being prostituted by the pseudo-relative and has gotten a tattoo of that person's name as a form of branding used by traffickers as a way of control.[9]

Social workers who come into contact with trafficked individuals need to understand that trafficked people may not be ready to leave their exploitative situation out of fear of retaliation from the traffickers, threats made against their family members, pressure to pay their debt bonds, fear of immigration or law enforcement officials, confusion about their status as trafficking victims, loss of their decision-making capacity because of trauma, and in some cases, out of loyalty to the trafficker.

When interviewing people suspected of trafficking, it is best to use a trauma-informed approach, making it a priority to instill a sense of safety and hope, speaking with clients privately and using language interpreters when necessary, being mindful that whoever accompanies the client as a "friend," "relative," or "co-worker" could, in fact, be the trafficker.[10]

Because research on the efficacy of assistance and treatment services specifically for trafficked people is limited (Goździak & Bump, 2008), social workers providing treatment can draw on effective mental health treatments for torture victims, asylum seekers, and refugees with posttraumatic stress disorder, anxiety, and depression (Drożdek & Wilson, 2004; Foa et al., 2005; Neuner, Shcauer, Klaschik, Karunakara, & Elbert, 2004; Paunovic & Öst, 2001; Turkovic, Hovens, & Gregurek, 2004; van der Kolk, 1996; van der Veer & van Waning, 2004), and for victims of sexual assault and intimate partner violence (Echeburua, de Corral, Zubizarreta, & Sarasua, 1996; Foa, Rothbaum, Riggs, & Murdock, 1991; Kubany et al., 2004; Resick, Jordan, Girelli, Hutter, & Marhoefer-Dvorak, 1988; Resick, Nishith, Weaver, Astin, & Feuer, 2002). The main treatment model used in these outcome studies was cognitive-behavioral therapy, which has been recommended by the International Society for Traumatic Stress Studies for the treatment of posttraumatic symptoms (Resick, et al., 2007), such as the ones reported by trafficked people seen in post-trafficked services (Zimmerman et al., 2003).

Conclusion

We try to offer in this primer for social workers what a primer usually offers: instructive information immediately applicable, buttressed by a detailed sketch of the research and debate underlying our assertions and recommendations.

First, it is important to us to shift the perspective on human trafficking from the moral/ideological and law enforcement one to a focus on human rights, which the conventions following the Palermo Protocol began to acknowledge (Sanghera, 2005). For us, understanding human trafficking as a human rights violation opens up space for a discussion about the vulnerabilities to trafficking fostered by the unequal distribution of wealth on a global scale, which is the perspective we ultimately believe provides the best understanding of the problem and the best source of solutions to it. This is applicable to sex trafficking as well, which is a form of human trafficking. Failing to understand sex trafficking in such a context may result in inappropriate or insufficient prevention and intervention efforts and less inclusive policies that do not address the root causes of the problem or that discriminate against certain groups.[11]

Second, it is important to develop knowledge of the experiences, struggles, and survival strategies of trafficked people grounded in their own realities rather than by the agendas of particular political positions or interest groups. In this regard, participatory methods such as participatory action research or feminist participatory action research (see Brydon-Miller, Maguire, McIntyre, 2004; Boontinand, 2005), informed by the tenets of popular education, will help social workers engage with trafficked people in a shared process of discovery and understanding of the root causes of trafficking, and communally decide which actions to take to implement social change and shape social policy.

Third, we try to provide an all-too-brief compilation of signs and markers of a person being trafficked that social workers can use to assess the situation and provide appropriate interventions, advocacy, and referrals.

Finally, we offer the following set of exercises to complement the thought experiment at the beginning of this chapter to help people to continue sensitizing and shifting their thoughts about this issue. We hope you find this information useful, and we look forward to opening a dialogue about this pervasive and insidious practice.

Group Exercises

EXERCISE 1

1. Read the four excerpts beginning on p. 47.
2. Do an Internet search of the term *modern-day slavery* and review the websites that adopt this definition to refer to human trafficking.
3. Gather in small groups and choose a facilitator whose role is to assist the group with the dialogue, stimulating the discussion by probing the social, economic, cultural, political, and historical roots of the problem and helping the group reflect on its own power dynamics.

We suggest some of these questions as a start, but others can be added as needed:

- What are some of the key arguments for describing human trafficking as modern-day slavery?
- What are the arguments against?
- How would you define and describe human trafficking?
- What are some examples of human trafficking in your community, state, province, or country?
- What, if any, forms of action and advocacy are at work to protect victims?
- What actions might you take to further these efforts?
- How does a critical understanding of gender inform your thinking about the practice of human trafficking?
- How might you develop a popular education approach to raise consciousness in your community regarding the reality and extent of human trafficking?

EXCERPTS

Most Americans' idea of slavery comes right out of *Roots*. . . . The slavery plaguing America today takes a different form, but make no mistake, it is real slavery. Whereas the law sanctioned slavery in the 1800s, today it is illegal. . . . An average slave in 1850 might have cost the equivalent of $40,000 in modern money, but today's slave can be bought for a few hundred dollars. Lower cost makes the modern slave easily affordable, but it also makes him or her a disposable commodity. . . . No form of slavery, past or present, is not horrific; however, today's slavery is one of the most diabolical strains to emerge in the thousands of years in which humans have been enslaving their fellows (Bales & Soodalter, 2009, pp. 5–6)

"Slavery" is often used to name instances of trafficking. . . . However, despite the violent and brutal history that the term invokes, most researchers in the field of contemporary trafficking, even those who wish to incite moral indignation, acknowledge that the debt-bondage, indentureship, and hyperexploitative contractual arrangements are the most common forms of contemporary forced labor forces. . . . The distinction between different labor regimes is important here, for whereas slavery is premised on property relations. . . . debt-bondage, indentureship, and forced labor are lodged in contractual, wage relations and principles of free labor power and its market exchange value. . . . "slavery-like practices" is a term preferred by anti-trafficking researches and activists who wish to carefully signal the commonalities and distinctions between legal enslavement, and forced, waged labor. (Kempadoo, 2005, pp. xix–xx)

People get away with enslaving village girls for the same reason that people got away with enslaving blacks two hundred years ago: The victims are perceived as discounted humans. . . . The tools to crush modern day slavery exist, but the political will is lacking. . . . We're not arguing that Westerners should take up this cause because it's the fault of the West; Western men do not play a central role in prostitution in most poor countries. . . . So this is not a case where we in the West have a responsibility to lead because we're the source of the problem. Rather, we single out the West, even though we're peripheral to the slavery, because our action is necessary to overcome a horrific evil. (Kristoff & WuDunn, 2010, pp. 24–25)

In countries with widespread trafficking we favor a law enforcement strategy. . . . "It's pretty doable", says Gary Haugen, who runs the International Justice Mission. "You don't have to arrest everybody. You just have to get enough that it sends a ripple effect and changes the calculations." . . . Many liberals and feminists are taken aback by the big stick approach we advocate, arguing that it just drives sex establishments underground. . . . It's true that the crackdown in Mumbai drove some brothels underground. . . . But the crackdown also made prostitution less profitable for brothel owners, and so the price of a girls bought or sold among Mumbai's brothels tumbled. Thus traffickers instead began shipping young flesh to Kolkata, where they could get a better price. That suggests that there is now less trafficking into Mumbai, which represents at least some success. (Kristoff & Wu-Dunn, 2010, pp. 26–31)

EXERCISE 2

1. Create a poster, a skit, a poem, a song, or a human sculpture that addresses the themes and debates in this chapter.
2. Develop and pose a series of "But why?" questions that could bring to light some of the reasons a person leaves his or her home community and country and enters the path of global migration.

EXERCISE 3

1. Watch *Last Rescue in Siam* available from http://www.youtube.com/watch?v=70rPAxLFFKU. This is a 10-minute movie made by sex workers in silent-movie style.
2. Discuss the arguments presented in the film.
3. Engage in a discussion about prostitution as a moral or economic issue, asking "But why?" questions.

EXERCISE 4: (*LAST RESCUE IN SIAM* CONTINUED)

1. Talk about alternatives and action. Pose this question to your group: What can we do about it?
2. Develop an action project.

Notes

1. For more on the dirty war, see Lewis (2002). I also recommend films such as *The Official Story* by Luis Puenzo (1985), *Night of the Pencils* by Hector Olivera (1986), or *Funny Dirty Little War*, also by Hector Olivera (1983).

2. Coyote, slang for the person who smuggles other people across the border, comes from the Nahuatl word *cóyotl* (American jackal or prairie wolf), perhaps used because the coyote is known for speed, cunning, and fierceness. On the international smuggling of children, see Uehling (2008).

3. To address the differences in operational indicators that were negatively affecting research and practice, the International Labor Organization (2009) and the European Commission set up an expert group to design indicators and tools to assess human trafficking. The consultants used the Delphi methodology and proposed 67 indicators that can be accessed at http://www.ilo.org/forcedlabour.

4. In the last decade an increasing number of cinematic productions have portrayed human trafficking in a variety of film genres including documentaries such as *The Day My God Died* (Levine, 2003), *Sex Slaves* (Bienstock, 2006), or *Hummingbird* (Mosher, 2007); full-length crime drama films such as *Holly* (Collmer, 2006), *Eastern Promises* (Webster & Lantos, 2007), *Trade* (Amritraj, 2007), or *Taken* (Hoarau, 2008); and television miniseries thrillers, such as *Human Trafficking* (Doyle & Dominick, 2004).

5. For example, Immanuel Wallerstein (1995) disapproves of the liberal claims that "the liberal state—reformist, legalist, and somewhat libertarian—was the only state that could guarantee freedom. And for the relatively small group whose freedom is safeguarded this was perhaps true. But unfortunately that group always remained a minority perpetually enroute to becoming everyone" (p. 2). See also Paul Farmer's (2003) critique of the U.S. notion of being a liberal in the introduction to his book *Pathologies of Power: Health, Human Rights, and the New War on the Poor.*

6. According to the IOM (2011), in 2010 it was estimated that encompassing international and internal migration, nearly a billion people were migrants, that is, 124 million migrated internationally and 740 million internally.

7. The Human Rights Network includes international organizations such as the Coalition Against Trafficking Women, the International Human Rights Federation, the International Abolitionist Federation, Soroptimist International, Equality Now, and the European Women's Lobby.

8. The Human Rights Caucus includes the Asian Women's Human Rights Council, the International Human Rights Law Group, the Global Alliance Against Trafficking Women, and the Women in Law and Development in Africa.

9. In 2011 the National Tattoo Association formed a partnership with the Polaris Project, an antitrafficking organization, to provide training to tattoo artists to help them recognize the signs of human trafficking and prevent the use of tattoos for branding.

10. Based on the IOM (2009) handbook for health care providers, the Polaris Project designed a human trafficking comprehensive assessment tool, available from http://www.polarisproject.org/.

11. For example, 100 fishermen from Thailand were trafficked to work in international waters and were kept in captivity for 3 years. They were deprived of proper food and water, and as a result 39 men died of malnutrition. Those who returned had severe health and mental health problems; however, they were not considered victims of human trafficking because at the time, the Thailand Social Devel-

opment and Human Security Ministry only included women and children as target groups for human trafficking (Bhumiprabhas, 2007).

References

Addams, J. (1910). Charity and social justice. *The Survey, 24*(11), 441–449. Retrieved from http:// tigger.uic.edu/htbin/cgiwrap/bin/urbanexp/main.cgi?file=new/show_doc_search.ptt&doc= 726

Alvarez, M. B., & Alessi, E. (2012). Human trafficking is more than sex trafficking and prostitution: Implications for social work. *Affilia: Journal of Women and Social Work, 27*(2), 142–152.

Amritraj, A., et al. (Producers), & Kreuzpaintner, M. (Director). (2007). *Trade* [Motion Picture]. Germany/ United States: Roadside Attractions.

Bales, K. & Soodalter, R. (2009). *The slave next door: Human trafficking and slavery in America today*. Berkeley, CA: University of California Press.

Basoğlu, M., & Mineka, S. (1992). The role of uncontrollable and unpredictable stress in post-traumatic stress responses in torture survivors. In M. Basoğlu (Ed.), *Torture and its consequences: Current treatment approaches* (pp. 182–228). New York, NY: Cambridge University Press.

Bennett, W. J., & Colson C. W. (2000, January 10). The Clintons shrug at sex trafficking. *Wall Street Journal*, p. A26.

Bhumiprabhas, S. (2007, May 14). The misery of male slavery, *The Nation* (Thailand). Retrieved from http://www.nationmultimedia.com/2007/05/14/headlines/headlines_30034148.php

Bienstock, R. (Producer and director). (2006). *Sex slaves*. [DVD]. Canada: Canadian Broadcasting Corp. Available from http://www.pbs.org/wgbh/pages/frontline/slaves/

Blomquist, B. (2000, January 8). Hooker's panel puts the first lady on the spot. *New York Post*, p. 6.

Boontinand, J. (2005). Feminist participatory action research in the Mekong Region. In K. Kempadoo, J. Sanghera, & B. Pattanaik (Eds.), *Trafficking and prostitution reconsidered: New perspectives on migration, sex work, and human rights*. (pp. 175–197). Boulder, CO: Paradigm.

Brydon-Miller, N., Maquire, P., & McIntyre, A. (2004). *Traveling companions: Feminism, teaching, and action research*. Westport, CT. Praeger.

Caputo, R. (2002). Social justice, the ethics of care, and market economies. *Families in Society, 83*, 355–364.

Collmer, A. (Producer) & Mosher, G. (Director). (2006). *Holly* [Motion picture]. United States: Priority Films.

Council on Social Work Education. (2004). *Educational policy and accreditation standards*. Retrieved from http://www.cswe.org/File.aspx?id=13780

Ditmore, M. (2005). Trafficking in lives: How ideology shapes policy. In K. Kempadoo, J. Sanghera, & B. Pattanaik (Eds.), *Trafficking and prostitution reconsidered: New perspectives on migration, sex work, and human rights* (pp. 107–126). Boulder, CO: Paradigm.

Doyle, C., & Dominik, A. (Writers), & Duguay, C. (Director). (2004). *Human trafficking* [Television miniseries]. United States: Lifetime Entertainment Network.

Droždek B., & Wilson, J. (2004). Uncovering: Trauma-focused treatment techniques with asylum seekers. In J. Wilson & B. Droždek (Eds.), *Broken spirits: the treatment of traumatized asylum seekers, refugees, war and torture victims* (pp. 243–276). New York, NY: Brunner-Routledge.

Echeburua, E., de Corral, P., Zubizarreta, I., & Sarasua, B. (1996) Treatment of acute posttraumatic stress disorder in rape victims: An experimental study. *Journal of Anxiety Disorders, 10*(3), 185–199.

Epple, D. M. (2007). Inter and intra professional social work differences: Social work's challenge. *Clinical Social Work Journal, 35*(4), 267–276.

Farmer, P. (2003). *Pathologies of power: Health, human rights, and the new war on the poor.* Berkley, CA: University of California Press.

Foa, E. B., Dancu, C. V., Hembree, E. A., Jaycox, L. H., Meadows, E. A., & Street, G. P., & Yadin, E. (2005). Randomized trial of prolonged exposure for posttraumatic stress disorder, and their combination with and without cognitive restructuring: Outcome at academic and community clinics. *Journal of Consulting and Clinical Psychology, 73*(5), 95.

Foa, E. B., Rothbaum, B., Riggs, D., & Murdock, T. (1991). Treatment of posttraumatic stress disorder in rape victims: A comparison between cognitive-behavioral procedures and counseling. *Journal of Consulting and Clinical Psychology, 59*(5), 715–723.

Fotopoulos, T. (2001). Globalization: The reformist left and the anti-globalization "movement." *Democracy & Nature: The International Journal of Inclusive Democracy, 7*(2), pp. 233-280. Retrieved from http://democracynature.org/vol7/takis_globalisation.htm

Freire, P. (1970). *Pedagogy of the oppressed,* New York, NY: Herder and Herder.

Freire, P. (1974). *Education for critical consciousness.* New York, NY: Continuum.Freire, P. (1998). *Pedagogy of freedom.* Lanham. MD: Rowman & Littlefield.

Goździak, E. M., & Bump, M. N. (2008). *Data and research on human trafficking: Bibliography of research-based literature.* Retrieved from http://humansecuritygateway.com/documents/ISIM_HumanTrafficking_Bibliography.pdf

Gunewardena, N., & Kingsolver, A. (2007) Introduction. In N. Gunewardena & Ann Kingsolver (Eds.), *The gender of globalization: Women navigating cultural and economic marginalities.* Santa Fe, NM: School for Advance Research Press.

hooks, b. (2000). *Feminist theory: From margin to center.* (2nd. ed.) Cambridge, MA: South End Press.

Hoarau, D. (Producer) & Morel, P. (Director). (2008). *Taken* [Motion Picture]. France: Europa Corp.

Horgan, G. (2001). How does globalization affect women? *International Socialism Journal, 92.* Retrieved from http://pubs.socialistreviewindex.org.uk/isj92/horgan.htm

International Labour Organization. (2009). *The cost of coercion: Global report under the follow-up to the ILO Declaration on Fundamental Principles and Rights at Work.* Retrieved from http://www.ilo.org/global/topics/forced-labour/publications/WCMS_106268/lang--eng/index.htm

International Organization for Migration. (2009). *Caring for trafficked persons: Guidance for health providers.* Retrieved from http://publications.iom.int/bookstore/free/CT_Handbook.pdf

International Organization for Migration. (2011). *World migration report.* Retrieved from http://publications.iom.int/bookstore/free/WMR2011_English.pdf

Kacowicz, A. M. (2007). Globalization, poverty, and the north–south divide. *International Studies Review, 9,* 565–580.

Kapur, R. (2002). The tragedy of victimization rhetoric: Resurrecting the "native" subject in the international/post-colonial feminist legal politics. *Harvard Human Rights Journal, 15,* 1–37.

Kapur, R. (2005). Cross-border movements and the law: Renegotiating the boundaries of difference. In K. Kempadoo, J. Sanghera, & B. Pattanaik (Eds.), Trafficking and prostitution reconsidered: New perspectives on migration, sex work, and human rights (pp. 25–41). Boulder, CO: Paradigm.

Kempadoo, K. (2005). Introduction: From moral panic to global justice: Changing perspectives on trafficking. In K. Kempadoo, J. Sanghera, & B. Pattanaik (Eds.), *Trafficking and prostitution reconsidered: New perspectives on migration, sex work, and human rights.* (pp. vii–xxxiv). Boulder, CO: Paradigm.

Koslowski, R. (2011). Economic globalization, human smuggling, and global governance. In D. Kyle & R. Koslowski (Eds.), *Global human smuggling: Comparative perspectives* (pp. 60–84). Baltimore, MD: John Hopkins University Press.

Kristoff, N. D., & WuDunn, S. (2010). *Half the Sky: Turning oppression into opportunity for wormen worldwide.* New York, NY: Random House.

Kubany, E. S., Hill, E. E., Owens, J. A., lannce-Spenser, C., McCraig, M. A., & Tremayne, K. J. (2004). Cognitive trauma therapy for battered women with PTSD (CTT-BW). *Journal of Consulting and Clinical Psychology, 72*(1), 3–18.

Laczko F., & Goździak, E. (2005). Data and research on human trafficking: A global survey. *International Migration, 43*(1/2), 5–16. Retrieved from http://www.iom.int/jahia/Jahia/cache/offonce/pid /1674?entryId=7996

Lerum, K., Saunders, P., Barlin, D., Wahab, S. & Swift, J. (2011). *Reducing violence against sex workers: What are the policy options?* Retrieved from http://faculty.washington.edu/lerum/Policy%20 Brief%20FINAL.pdf

Lewis, P. H. (2002). *Guerrillas and generals: The dirty war in Argentina.* Westport, CT: Praeger.

Levine, A. (Producer, director). (2003). *The day my god died* [Documentary film]. United States: Andrew Levine Productions. Retrieved from http://www.thedaymygoddied.com/contact.php

Mayo, P. (2004). *Liberating praxis: Paulo Freire's legacy for radical education and politics.* Westport, Praeger Publishers.

McDonald, W. (2004). Traffic counts, symbols & agendas: A critique of the campaign against trafficking of human beings. *International Review of Victimology, 11*(1), 143–176.

Mosher, H. (Producer, director). (2007). *Hummingbird* [DVD]. Available from http://watchdocu men-tary.org/watch/hummingbird-video_58ffc0023.html

National Association of Social Workers. (2008). *Code of ethics.* Retrieved from http://www.naswdc. org/pubs/code/code.asp

Neuner, F., Schauer, M., Klaschick, C., Karunakara, U., & Elbert, T. (2004). A comparison of narrative exposure therapy, supportive counseling, and psychoeducation for treating posttraumatic stress disorder in an African refugee settlement. *Journal of Consulting and Clinical Psychology, 72,* 579–587.

Olivera, H. (Director). (1983). *No habrá más penas ni olvidos.* [Funny dirty little war]. [Motion picture]. Argentina: Aries Cinematográfica.

Olivera, H. (Director). (1986). *La noche de los lápices.* [Night of the pencils].[Motion picture]. Argentina: Aries Cinematográfica.

Paunovic, N., & Öst, L. G. (2001). Cognitive-behavior therapy versus exposure therapy in the treatment of PTSD in refugees. *Behavior Research and Therapy, 39,* 1183–1197.

Polack, R. J. (2004). Social justice and the global economy: New challenges for social work in the 21st century. *Social Work, 49,* 281–290.

Puenzo, L. (Director). (1985). *The official story* [Motion picture]. Argentina: Almi Pictures, Koch Lorber Films.

Pyle, J. (2001). Sex, maids, and export processing: Risk and reasons for gendered global production networks. *International Journal of Politics, Culture, and Society, 5*(1), 55–76.

Pyle, J. (2002). *How globalization fosters gendered labor networks and trafficking.* Paper presented at the annual Globalization and Trafficking Conference, Honolulu, Hawaii. Retrieved from http://www.hawaii.edu/global/projects_activities/Trafficking/Pyle.doc

Ramirez, C., Garcia Dominguez, M., & Miguez Morais, J. (2005). *Crossing borders: remittances, gender and development.* Retrieved from http://www.un-instraw.org

Ray, N. (2006). Looking at trafficking through a new lens. *Cardozo Journal of Law & Gender, 12*(3), 909–929

Reisch, M. (2002). Defining social justice in a socially unjust world. *Families in Society, 83,* 343–354.

Resick, P. A., Jordan, C. G., Girelli, S. A., Hutter, C. K., & Marhoeder-Dvorak, S. (1988). A comparative outcome study of behavioral group therapy for sexual assault victims. *Behavior Therapy, 19*(3), 385–401.

Resick, P. A., Monson, C. M., & Gutner, C. (2007). Psychosocial treatments for PTSD. In M. J. Friedman, T. M. Keane, & P. A. Resick (Eds.), *Handbook of PTSD: Science and practice* (pp. 330–358). New York, NY: Guilford Press

Resick, P. A., Nishith, P., Weaver, T.L., Astin, M.C. & Feuer, C.A. (2002). A comparison of cognitive-processing therapy with prolonged exposure and a waiting condition for the treatment of chronic posttraumatic stress disorder in female rape victims. *Journal of Consult Clinical Psychology, 70,* 867–879.

Reuveny, R., & Thompson, W. (2007). The North-South divide and international studies: A symposium. *International Studies Review, 9,* 556–564.

Sanghera, J. (2005). Unpacking the trafficking discourse. In K. Kempadoo, J. Sanghera, & B. Pattanaik (Eds.), *Trafficking and prostitution reconsidered: New perspectives on migration, sex work, and human rights* (pp. 3–24) Boulder, CO: Paradigm.

Sharma, N. (2005). Anti-trafficking rhetoric and the making of a global apartheid. *National Women's Studies Association Journal, 17*(3), 88–111.

Shenon, P. (2000, January 13). Feminist coalition protests U.S. stance on sex trafficking. *New York Times,* p. A5.

Specht, H., & Courtney, M. E. (1994). *Unfaithful angels.* New York, NY: The Free Press.

Stolz, B. A. (2007). Interpreting the U.S. human trafficking debate through the lens of symbolic politics. *Law & Policy, 29*(2), 311–388.

Strode, T. (2000, January 10). Land, others ask White House to reverse on sex trafficking. *Baptist Press.* Retrieved from http://assets.baptiststandard.com/archived/2000/2_2/pages/exploitation.html

Swenson, C. R. (1998). Clinical social work's contribution to a social justice perspective. *Social Work, 43,* 527–535.

Trafficking Victims Protection Reauthorization Act, Pub. L. No. 108-193, 117 (2005). http://www.legal momentum.org/assets/pdfs/tvpra-senate-house-passed-p.pdfStat.2875

Turkovic, S., Hovens, J. E., & Gregurek, R. (2004). Strengthening psychological health in war victims and refugees. In J. Wilson & B. Drožděk (Eds.), *Broken spirits: the treatment of traumatized asylum seekers, refugees, war and torture victims* (pp. 221–242). New York, NY: Brunner-Routledge.

Uehling, G. L. (2008). The international smuggling of children: Coyotes, snakeheads, and the politics of compassion. *Anthropological Quarterly, 81,* 833–871.

United Nations Department of Economic and Social Affairs. (2004). *Survey on role of women in development: Women and international migration.* Retrieved from http://www.un.org/womenwatch/daw/public/WorldSurvey2004-Women&Migration.pdf

United Nations International Research and Training Institute for the Advancement of Women (2007). *Feminization of migration.* Retrieved from http://ebookbrowse.com/feminization-of-migration-instraw-pdf-d36699597

United Nations Office on Drugs and Crime (UNODC). (2000). *Protocol against the smuggling of migrants by land, sea and air, supplementing the United Nations convention against transnational organized crime.* Retrieved from http://www.uncjin.org/Documents/Conventions/dcatoc/final _documents_2/convention_smug_eng.pdf

United Nations Office on Drugs and Crime (UNODC). (2008). *An introduction to human trafficking: Vulnerability, impact, and action.* Retrieved from http://www.ungift.org/docs/ungift/pdf/knowledge/background_paper.pdf

United Nations Office on Drugs and Crime (UNODC). (2009). *Global report on trafficking in persons.* Retrieved from http://www.unodc.org/documents/human-trafficking/Global_Report_on_TIP. pdf

U.S. Agency for International Development. (2003). *Trafficking in persons: The USAID strategy for response.* Retrieved from http://www.usaid.gov/

U.S. Department of State. (2007). *Trafficking in persons report.* Retrieved from http://www.state. gov/g/tip/rls/tiprpt/2007/82799.htm

U.S. National Institute of Justice. (2007). *Solicitation: Trafficking in human beings research and comprehensive literature review* (NIJ Publication No. 2007-1582). Retrieved from http://www. ncjrs.gov/pdffiles1/nij/sl000796.pdf

van der Kolk, B. A. (1996). A general approach to treatment of posttraumatic stress disorder. In B. A. van del Kolk, A. C. McFarlane, & L. Weisaeth (Eds.), *Traumatic stress: The effects of overwhelming experience on mind, body, and society* (pp. 417–440). New York, NY: Guilford Press.

van der Veer, G. & van Waning, A. (2004). Creating a safe therapeutic sanctuary. In J. Wilson & B. Droždek (Eds.), *Broken spirits: the treatment of traumatized asylum seekers, refugees, war and torture victims* (pp. 187–220). New York, NY: Brunner-Routledge.

Victims of Trafficking and Violence Protection Act. (2000). Pub. L. 106–386. Retrieved from http:// www.uscis.gov/ilink/docView/PUBLAW/HTML/PUBLAW/0-0-0-22532.html

Wakefield, J. (1988a). Psychotherapy, distributive justice, and social work, Part 1: Distributive justice as a conceptual framework for social work. *Social Service Review, 62*(2), 187–210.

Wakefield, J. (1988b). Psychotherapy, distributive justice, and social work, Part 2: Psychotherapy and the pursuit of justice. *Social Service Review, 62*(3), 353–382.

Wallerstein, I. (1995). *After liberalism.* New York, NY: The New Press.

Webster, P., & Lantos, R. (Producers), & Cronenberg, D. (Director). (2007). *Eastern promises* [Motion picture]. United States and Canada: Serendipity Point Films.

Weitzer, R. (2007). The social construction of sex trafficking: Ideology and institutionalization of a moral crusade. *Politics & Society, 35*, 447–475. doi:10.1177/0032329207304319

William Wilberforce Trafficking Victims Protection Reauthorization Act. 122 Stat. 5044 (2008). Retrieved from http://www.uscis.gov/USCIS/Laws/Memoranda/2010/William%20Wilberforce%20TVPR Act%20of%202008%20July%20212010.pdf

Woolf, A. (Director). (2003). Dying to leave [Television series episode]. In *Wide Angle,* New York, NY: WNET.

World Bank. (2011). *Migration and remittances factbook 2011.* Retrieved from http://siteresources .worldbank.org/INTLAC/Resources/Factbook2011-Ebook.pdf

Zimmerman, C., Hossain, M., Yun, K., Roche, B., Morison, L., & Watts, C. (2006a). *Stolen smiles: The physical and psychological health consequences of women and adolescents trafficked in Europe.* London School of Hygiene and Tropical Medicine. Retrieved from http://www.peacewomen.org /portal_resources_resource.php?id=515

Zimmerman, C., Hossain, M., Yun, K., Roche, B., Morison, L., & Watts, C. (2006b). *Stolen Smiles: A summary report on the physical and psychological health consequences of women and adolescents trafficked in Europe. London School of Hygiene and Tropical Medicine.* Retrieved from http://www.lshtm.ac.uk/hpu/docs/StolenSmiles.pdf

Zimmerman, Hossain, M., Yun, K., Gajdadziev, V., Guzun, N., Tchomarova, M., . . . Watts, C. (2008). The health of trafficked women: A survey of women entering posttrafficking services in Europe. *American Journal of Public Health, 98*(1), 55–59.

Zimmerman, C., Yun, K., Shvab, I., Watts, C., Trappolin, L., Treppete, M., . . . Regan, L. (2003). *The health and consequences of trafficking in women and adolescents: Findings from a European study.* London, UK: London School of Hygiene and Tropical Medicine.

Part 2

COURAGEOUS VOICES

CHAPTER 3

"There Is Life Here"

An Examination of Trauma, Globalization, and Conflict in Women's Performance Poetry

SARAH CARNAHAN

I am a Quaker social worker/activist/scholar who is committed to nonviolence, social justice, and living empathically. People are often surprised to find that my research focuses on global violent conflict and its effects on women. Indeed, at times I am surprised to find myself here. And the circuitous route that brought me to this place—this place that resides in the tensions between conflict and peacemaking, connection and disconnection, empathy and distance, coherence and rupture, theory and lived lives—can be difficult to track.

My journey began with what seemed like separate interests: my commitment to nonviolent, antiwar feminist activism and study, and my participation in the spoken word community in my hometown of Portland, Maine. My initial entry point into performance poetry was through the work of radical queer feminist poet Alix Olson (2008). As I dove more deeply into performance poetry as an area of academic feminist inquiry while studying for my MSW at Ohio State, I discovered the poetry of Suheir Hammad, which still frequently moves me to tears, even after countless engagements with her work. Now working on my PhD in women's, gender, and sexuality studies as well as completing my clinical MSW at Ohio State, I have begun looking at this poetry through the lens of critical trauma theory, which challenges me to see the trauma caused by globalized conflict not only as rupture that destroys but also as rupture that has the power to connect. And this is where I now find myself.

Rupturing the Stories We Tell: Feminist Narrative Theory

My work of bringing together critical trauma theory and women's narratives of globalized conflict has been influenced by feminist autobiographical theorists who reject the notion of a stable, coherent self as incompatible with women's diverse experiences and development. Indeed, this idea of a "separate and unique selfhood" (Friedman, 1998, p. 72) is so endemic to Western philosophical and psychological thought that it often goes unnoticed and unquestioned in many fields, including autobiographical studies and social work. As Susan Standford Friedman writes, "Psychoanalytic models of the autobiographical self remain fundamentally individualistic because the healthy ego is defined in terms of its ability to separate itself from others" (p. 73). One feminist autobiographical theorist who rejects the notion of a stable, individuated self is Leigh Gilmore (1994), whose work focuses on the importance of what she terms the autobiographics in women's life writing:

> I offer the term *autobiographics* to describe those elements of self-representation which are not bound by a philosophical definition of the self derived from Augustine, not content with the literary history of autobiography, those elements that instead mark a location in a text where self-invention, self-discovery, and self-representation emerge within the technologies of autobiography. . . . Autobiographics, as a description of self-representation and as a reading practice, is concerned with interruptions and eruptions, with resistance and contradiction as strategies of self-representation. (p. 42)

Key to Gilmore's theorizing of women's self-representation is not only the fact that this self-representation is not simply a clean case in which one will come to "know thyself" (as Augustine charged) and narrate that self fully and coherently, but also that women's autobiographical self-representations are *intentional*. In other words, women who produce life narratives do so thoughtfully, making choices about how and what they represent, including the choice to represent themselves and their experiences in nonlinear fashions. For Gilmore, women's life writings often stray from traditional narrative formats to strategically convey elements of their identities or experiences to represent an autobiographical "*I* that contrasts with the *I* in the traditional . . . forms or epistemologies" (Gilmore, 1994, p. 43). These traditional forms and epistemologies have historically been rooted in men's experiences, men's theories of identity (that is, men's theories of men's and women's identity and identity development), and men's life writings; for example, many theories of development, such as psychoanalytic theory and Erikson's stages, are based exclusively on men's developmental narratives and experience. Narratives that eschew traditional bounds, such as blogs, performed narratives, and cowritten narratives, have become an important space in which women can construct, co-construct, collaborate, and interact across and through identities in the globalized world.

From the Ground, Up: Defining Our Terms

Like the sites of discomfort in traditional theories of selfhood and the possibility for opening up linear trajectories that are found in feminist narrative theory, trauma and traumatic events also rupture stability, chronology, and the ways in which we made meaning *before*. In *Precarious Life: The Powers of Mourning and Violence*, Judith Butler (2006) argues that if there is one commonality that spans human existence, it is our shared vulnerability to injury and mortality:

> The body implies mortality, vulnerability, agency: the skin and the flesh expose us to the gaze of others, but also to touch, and to violence, and bodies put us at risk of becoming the agency and instrument of all these as well. (p. 26)

Though one's social identity and location (i.e., where one is positioned in society in terms of one's levels of social privilege or marginalization) can have an effect on the likelihood that one will experience trauma, no one can completely escape inherent human vulnerability. As Janoff-Bulman states, "Victims are threatening to non-victims, for they are manifestations of a malevolent universe rather than a benevolent one" (as cited in Brown 2008, p. 99). The vulnerability that is inherent in human existence, coupled with the unpredictability of many traumatic events, leaves everyone open to the possibility of trauma; no wonder that in our cultural discourse we often understate, pathologize, and distance trauma.

Yet what if we broaden our conceptualizations of trauma? Whose identities, bodies, communities, experiences, utterances, and cultures are effaced when the discursive and clinical gaze of trauma is fixed on individual pathology and direct experience? Cultural competence is one of the defining characteristics of ethical social work practice; we are ethically bound to work diligently to increase our understanding of how culture has an effect on experience, and we are expected to take that into account in our work with clients. However, contemporary notions of trauma and posttraumatic stress disorder (PTSD) often do not take into account the ways culture and identity affect people's vulnerability to trauma as well as their experience of trauma and its effects. Laura S. Brown (2008) addresses this shortcoming in the introduction to her book *Cultural Competence in Trauma Therapy: Beyond the Flashback* when she writes, "To date, few of the excellent psychotherapeutic models that have been developed for working with trauma survivors have intentionally taken into account this diversity and complexity of human identity and experience as it informs the encounter with trauma," and she astutely points out that culturally specific therapeutic interventions for trauma in "special populations" generally do not expand into the practice of trauma treatment providers (pp. 7–8).

The emerging interdisciplinary field of critical trauma theory seeks to challenge and encourage those involved in trauma studies to examine the ways the vulnerability to, and the experience of, trauma is mediated by issues of identity (i.e., gender, race, sexuality, class), social location, oppression, and geographical location. In her chapter "Trauma Ongoing," Ann Cvetkovich (2003) pushes for a theory that would consider "trauma as depathologized and demedicalized in favor of cultural responses that can address it as a collective, and not just an individual, phenomenon" (p. 60). In grappling with questions of community, identity, collectivity, and societal systems and structures, critical trauma theory can be used to liberate our understandings of trauma from individualistic pathology-based discourses, which often only increase marginalization and isolation, and thus run the risk of compounding trauma. For example, in his book *Crazy Like Us: The Globalization of the American Psyche*, Ethan Watters (2010) recounts the influx of Western trauma therapists after a tsunami in 2004 caused widespread damage in Indonesia. These therapists employed treatment protocols from their home locations, treating trauma as individual mental health diagnoses to be resolved in treatment that often includes taking a break from the community and day-to-day responsibilities. As he states,

> This is a common patter of mental health healing in the West: take a sick leave from the stresses in your life in order to heal. If, however, the social difficulties are the primary symptom of distress, taking time

away from one's duties and social roles to pursue something like individual counseling may actually exacerbate the problem. (p. 93)

At the same time, in Sri Lanka people found strength and healing within
their extremely resilient communities. In situations like this standard trauma
treatment that individualizes symptoms can run the risk of retraumatizing those
whom therapists hoped to help (Watters 2010, p. 87–88, 93).

Furthermore, in engaging with critical trauma theory we must also be willing and equipped to be self-reflexive. In other words, we must continually ask
ourselves the same questions we ask of others. For example, self-reflexive practice
means that if we are critical of the ways other societies are oppressive to women,
we must be rigorous in examining how our own culture is oppressive to women.
This is crucial to critical trauma theory, because we need to be aware of our own
social locations, our own engagements with or our experiences of trauma, and
the ways our work and even our very identity dynamically interact with societal
structures and systems that resist or reinforce cultural and individual trauma.
This is not easy to do, especially as we may find that we are survivors or perpetrators of trauma. As Watkins and Shulman (2008) write in *Toward Psychologies
of Liberation*, "As members or descendants of members of groups that have either experienced or perpetrated injustice and violence, many of us are faced
with comprehending these consequences" (pp. 81–82). Whether one is a victim
or perpetrator of violence—or both—self-reflexivity is a necessary first step in
seeing how trauma affects our own lives, and thus how we might heal from and
intervene in systems that perpetuate it.

My own conceptualization of trauma has been influenced by the clinical
understandings of trauma (i.e., American Psychiatric Association, 2000; clinical
practice journals) as well as by scholars from many fields, such as those referred
to throughout this chapter, whose work delves into the realm of critical trauma
theory. In developing a working definition for trauma in my work, I had a number of primary concerns. My definition of trauma needs to pay homage to the
weightiness of trauma, its effects on bodies, lives, identities, places and spaces,
and the ways people move through and perform in the world. Yet, at the same
time, trauma and trauma survivors are burdened with unwarranted stigma,
which can be reinforced by our definitions of trauma if we are not careful. Although I do think that those who have experienced trauma are often indelibly

changed through the experience, trauma is not always already totalizing. I have tried to offer a definition that acknowledges that trauma alters but does not define a person. Further complicating my definition is the fact that trauma is multidimensional, as it interfaces with human beings and cultures in all their complexities; trauma is individual and also cultural, historical, and transgenerational (many scholars in Holocaust and indigenous studies, such as Michael Rothberg and Aaron Denham, have done insightful work about transgenerational trauma). I aimed to create an inclusive definition of trauma, recognizing that trauma can result from a series of small events, or as is more traditionally the focus of clinical literature, a large event; trauma can also be linked to historical events or an event seen or experienced vicariously. I have struggled to create a working definition of trauma that is clear and tangible yet also takes into account the fluid and dynamic nature of trauma and its effects. Keeping those concerns in mind, I define trauma as a destabilizing and distressing experience or string of experiences that exceed one's ability to make sense of and comprehend the event or events that have been experienced. Traumatic events may be experienced directly (e.g., physical/emotional abuse) or indirectly (e.g., seeing a natural disaster unfold through media outlets) and may be experienced on an individual (e.g., sexual assault) or shared (e.g., war, genocide, racism) level. Traumatic events rupture one's sense of self and also one's sense of safety, stability, agency, and belonging in one's body or one's world. Trauma refers not only to the rupturing events, but also to their aftereffects, which may include psychologically, emotionally, and corporeally reexperiencing the events; having trouble being present in the here and now; experiencing acute or generalized fear about the events and the possibility of the events reoccurring; and feeling acutely distant or removed from oneself, those around oneself, or from one's community or society.

Catharsis, Unspeakability, and the Subaltern

As noted by Judith Herman (1997) and Diana Taylor (2006), one characteristic often cited as emblematic of trauma is its unspeakability. The experience of a traumatic event defies one's sense-making capacities; it confounds the subject's ability to place the event or events within a logical and socially acceptable framework. The traumatic event cannot be reasoned with in terms of cause and effect. In the opening of her seminal work, *Trauma and Recovery*, Judith Herman

(1997) brings to the forefront the unspeakable nature of trauma: "The psychological distress symptoms of traumatized people simultaneously call attention to the existence of an unspeakable secret and deflect attention from it" (p. 1). Herman defines the unspeakable as "certain violations of the social compact [that] are too terrible to utter aloud" (p. 1). This unspeakability that appears and reappears in clinical and theoretical literature as a hallmark of trauma has long been a focal point of the healing process.

Originally outlined and defined by Freud, the idea of catharsis has been considered instrumental, if not mandatory, in the process of healing from trauma; indeed, this was the basis of Freud's "talking cure" (Breuer & Freud, 1957). Freud believed that women's symptoms of hysteria were rooted in the unspeakability of traumatic events. Because hysterical women were unable to speak about the traumas they were victims of (often sexual abuse), the emotions of these experiences remained trapped in their bodies, manifesting themselves in the physical and psychological symptoms of hysteria. Thus, catharsis (the verbal reconstruction and repeated telling of a traumatic event) developed as a means of treating hysteria and, later, trauma. Freud believed not only that catharsis could release the emotions that had built up in the body of the traumatized individual but that repeated narrations of previously unspeakable trauma could give the traumatized patient a sense of mastery over the trauma; the patient would no longer be an object living under the control of the unspeakable (Herman 1997, p. 12; Littrell 2009, p. 301).

This therapeutic focus on recounting a traumatic event as a means to master the emotions that have overcome the traumatized person is still very present in contemporary clinical practice. For example, in an article for the *Clinical Social Work Journal*, Nancy L. Beckerman and Jennifer Pass (2008) write that in terms of trauma and PTSD, "Exposure therapy . . . has proven the most effective of the cognitive behavioral treatments" (p. 257). Often part of this exposure therapy includes narrating a traumatic event (or events) repeatedly to desensitize a person to the story and loosen the emotional grip that the past trauma continues to have. Judith Herman (1997) points out that this narrative model has been used with combat veterans since before PTSD was used as a diagnosis for veterans (pp. 25–27). It is theorized that speaking the trauma repeatedly and desensitizing a person to the story and the images, memories, and places that are associated with the traumatic event or events will help a person to heal and move on. Herman notes that this "cathartic culture" (p. 172) has become so ingrained in popular consciousness that trauma survivors sometimes will plunge into the details of their traumas before they are ready, because that is so commonly understood as the way to heal. Mastery of one's trauma implies that healing from trauma has an end point when a person will feel as though she has regained control of the traumatic event. A person has healed when she or he can exert control over the trauma narrative, and perhaps by extension, the memory and aftereffects of the traumatic event or events; this dovetails with the idea of development as a linear process with an end point being an individuated person.

This idea of mastery and an endpoint to healing that emphasizes a particular means and trajectory of healing does not offer alternatives for diverse trauma survivors whose trauma and healing might be marked by difference. The idea of feminist narrative therapy and restorying one's experience in a way that illuminates the workings of patriarchy and oppression is applicable here to a certain extent (Lee, 1997). However, it is complicated by holistic, critical notions of trauma that include transgenerational and cultural trauma as opposed to being located in an individual's experience. Likewise, though narrative therapy is also being used in traumatized communities as a means of restorying an experience (Horsely, 2007), the public narratives at the center of this chapter intentionally stretch beyond the bounds of ethnic/cultural communities and are meant not only to restory a community's trauma and resilience but also to challenge viewers, listeners, and readers to critically examine their own place in global systems of trauma. Thus, although narrative therapy has interesting intersections with the trauma narratives at the center of my analysis, it does not adequately address the trauma or means of telling that are drawn in by critical trauma theory.

In contrast, critical trauma theory suggests that neither trauma nor healing from trauma is this simple, as trauma leaves a trace in the body and psyche, continually revisiting the person who has experienced it. Laura S. Brown (2008) describes the multifaceted symptoms and aftereffects of trauma. "For many individuals trauma manifests in the body as well as the psyche. . . . Trauma has biological, psychological, psychosocial, and existential sequelae, and no one component of this multifaceted picture of distress can be understood in isolation from the rest" (p. 64). Furthermore, trauma resides not only in the traumatized individual's body and psyche but can also be shared and passed on to community and family members, as when stories, deaths, and losses are passed down through generations as in the previously mentioned work of Holocaust and indigenous studies scholars. Given these complexities of trauma and the ways one's identity and social location can affect one's experience and understanding of trauma, it seems a bit simple to assume there is an end point to healing in which the traumatic experience and its aftereffects are resolved or mastered through a prescribed mode of speaking the unspeakable.

Given critical trauma theory's charge to be attentive to social location, identity, and culture, and in considering how social marginalization and oppression can exacerbate or make a person more vulnerable to trauma, we must ask ourselves who is excluded in the therapeutic prescription of telling and retelling a linear construction of a trauma narrative as a means of healing? For example, if the idea of a linear narrative that mimics developmental models resulting in an individuated adult is based in Western men's experience, can a woman ever be considered healed from trauma? Likewise, if the individualized method of trauma treatment and narrative healing does not apply to cultures that stress community, how do we avoid further marginalization and traumatization in working with people in these cultures? I argue that theories like critical trauma theory, which are clearly influenced by postmodern and postcolonial theories, can expand our notions of trauma and trauma healing

Gayatri Spivak is one of the most well-known postcolonial scholars, and much of her work focuses on what is known as the *subaltern subject*, or those who are most marginalized in global society. Frequently, third world women have been used to epitomize the subaltern subject. In perhaps her most well-known and frequently cited work, Spivak (1988) asks, "Can the Subaltern Speak?" As postmodernism's theories of fragmented, changeable identity have been woven into postcolonial and subaltern studies, the identity of the subaltern subject has become more fluid. This fluidity, I believe, allows us to look at the ways the expectations placed on trauma narratives can negatively affect those who have been marginalized or isolated by the unspeakability of trauma and, furthermore, may be doubly marginalized because of social location or identity. In her chapter, Spivak concludes, "The subaltern as female cannot be heard or read. . . . The subaltern cannot speak. . . . Representation has not withered away" (p. 308). Representation, in this sense, refers to the myriad ways one's identity is portrayed in society, for example, through the news, the media, public discourse, political debates, and such. According to Spivak, the subaltern woman is always preceded by a representation of herself—not to be confused with a representation *by* herself—therefore, her voice is always already displaced by that representation, regardless of the fact that it likely does not portray her lived experience. Thus, she cannot speak.

However, what if we take up the challenge posted by critical trauma theory to open up modes of self-representation, trauma, and healing? What if we problematize the expectation for a certain type of trauma narrative? Clinical social worker Laura Wrenn (2003) critiques the presumption that a singular mode of speaking trauma is the best means of understanding and healing from trauma.

> The positivist model has led to a narrowing of understanding dynamics that are crucial to trauma research and treatment: those of the murky world of interpretation, meaning, and unconscious. . . . Unless we understand the underlying meaning of the client's report, we will never gain access to the cognitive representation of experience and understand why painful early objects continue to persist. . . . Above all else, the client is the author of his/her own life. (pp. 126, 136)

Perhaps if we displace the expectation for a certain kind of trauma narrative (i.e., the linear, reconstructed, individual, multiply recounted story of the event) as a means to a certain kind of healing (mastery, desensitization), we might allow for people who have experienced trauma to act as agents in their own speaking—a speaking that is not bound by genre or a certain kind of clinical performance, but a speaking that is determined by the speaker.

Trauma and Performance

Diana Taylor writes extensively about the overlap between trauma and performance. For Taylor (2006), the connection between performance and trauma is found in the embodied repetition of both:

> Trauma and posttraumatic stress particularly make themselves felt on and through the body long after the initial blow has passed. Trauma returns with its emotional punch, through involuntary behaviors, flash-backs, and nightmares. The past revisits, full force, as present.

The repeat characterizes trauma, which is always reexperienced viscerally, as a constant state of again-ness. (p. 52)

Similarly, repetition is a key aspect of performance. In his article "What Is Performance?" Richard Schechner (2002) also stresses this repetition that is inherent in performance. Schechner claims that all human social behavior can be studied as performance because "every action, no matter how small or encompassing, consists of twice-behaved behaviors" (p. 23). We are constantly performing, as our own actions mimic the behaviors of others or are repeats of our own behavior, so in that way, our behavior is rehearsed. However, "performances are made from bits of restored behavior, but every performance is different from any other" (p. 23). In line with Schechner's acknowledgment of performance as repeated and unique, Taylor (2003) asserts that "trauma, like performance, is characterized by the nature of 'its repeats'" *and* trauma and performance are both "always in situ. Each intervenes in the individual/political/social body at a particular moment and reflects specific tensions" (p.167). Thus, the telling and the embodiment of trauma and performance may be looked at as repetition and as a unique, singular narration.

Furthermore, the increasingly acknowledged transmissibility of trauma (Denham, 2008; Fassin & Rechtman, 2009; Rothberg, 2009; Watkins & Shulman, 2008) across generations, communities, bodies, and identities means that performance holds not only the potential to narrate trauma in ways that are nonhegemonic and perhaps more available for diverse narrative expressions, but the public performance of trauma can also create a visceral connection between the subject performing the trauma, and the audience members hearing the trauma narration. In the next section, I briefly touch on the work of Suheir Hammad and Ani DiFranco as examples of trauma performance in the wake of September 11, 2001.

Embodying Marginalization, Performing September 11, 2001

Suheir Hammad is a Palestinian American performance poet who was born in a refugee camp in Amman, Jordan. Her parents were 1948 Palestinian exiles who left the country during the 1948 Arab-Israeli war. From there, her family moved to Beirut, Lebanon, before immigrating to Brooklyn in 1978 when

Hammad was 5 years old. Hammad went to Hunter College and has remained in New York since (Khan, 2009). As a poet, Hammad's work often centers on the images of Arab Americans in the post–September 11 context. The poem *first writing since* (2001) charts her personal experiences immediately following the attacks and explores greater global and social contexts surrounding this event and its subsequent ramifications. The poem is quite likely the most widely circulated of Hammad's writing, and it has been published in numerous journals and anthologies since September 11. Hammad (2002) also performed an abbreviated version of *first writing since* on the second season of *Russell Simmons Presents Def Poetry Jam*, and the recording of that performance is now widely available on YouTube.

In *first writing since*, Hammad (2001) draws on critical trauma theory's understanding of trauma as communal. She narrates the experience of September 11 not only on an individual level but also as it has affected the Muslim community in the United States, and even more broadly as it has resulted in a ripple effect of trauma globally. E. Ann Kaplan (2005) writes that "cultural context should not be excluded from trauma research, for it determines how symptoms are experienced and expressed. . . . cultures too may be traumatized" (p. 68). This cultural- and community-level trauma is very viscerally reflected in Hammad's (2002) poem:

> please god, after the second plane please, don't let it be anyone
> who looks like my brothers . . . one more person ask me if i knew the
>   hijackers.
> one more motherfucker ask me what navy my brother is in.
> one more person assume no arabs or muslims were killed.
> one more person assume they know me, or that i represent a people.
> or that a people represent an evil. or that evil is as simple as a flag and
>   words on a page.[1]

The traces of cultural and community trauma are clearly evident in Hammad's (2002) performance. Not only does Hammad perform the trauma of September 11 as an individual New Yorker, but she also performs the trauma as a member of the Arab American community. For Hammad, the trauma of September 11 cannot be separated from her social location, as she grapples simultaneously with the invisibility and denial of Arab victims of September 11 and the assumption that members of her cultural community are always, already perpetrators, never grievable victims. Thus, Hammad's individual experience of the trauma of September 11 is further ruptured by the assumptions, oppressions, and prejudices that have permeated the dominant cultural discourse since September 11.

Furthermore, because Hammad (2002) performs her poem, her very body and identity do not allow the reader to separate herself or himself from societal systems that create trauma through uncritical individualizing and pathologizing. Hammad's physical presence as an Arab American woman provokes the reader to consider the ways identity and social location are implicated in the experiences and performances of trauma. Hammad's physical presence and her Palestinian American Muslim identity also work to distance the majority of audience members who do not share her social location, to reassert that the very fact that living in a globalized world means that nations are undeniably linked and systems of power, imperialism, and warfare affect subjects and citizens differentially. Hammad's body does not allow her audience the privilege of ignoring the ways race, class, gender, and location mediate the traumas of war, globalization, and systematic oppression. Not only is the audience viscerally confronted with the differential experiences of trauma, but the words Hammad performs reinforce this message that is transmitted through her body: "i know for sure who will pay./in the world, it will be women, mostly colored and poor. women will have to bury children and support themselves through grief" (Hammad, 2002). In narrating her trauma not only as an individual U.S. citizen coping with the event and the aftermath of September 11, Hammad's embodied performance forces her audience to come to terms with its own experiences of cultural and societal trauma, not only as subjects who may be traumatized, but also as subjects who may be implicated in reproducing trauma.

Writing from a very different social location from Hammad's, Ani Di-Franco is a White bisexual singer, songwriter, and poet originally from Buffalo, New York, and is now based in New Orleans. However, DiFranco considers herself a "traveler," because she tours frequently (Righteous Babe Records, 2013). DiFranco is well-known for her explicitly political, left-leaning feminist politics, and her views come through strongly in her lyrics. Early in her career, she decided to "use her voice and her guitar as honestly and unflinchingly as she could, writing and playing songs that came straight from her own experience, her boundless imagination, her sharp wit, and her ever-more-nuanced understanding of how the world works" (Righteous Babe Records, 2013). DiFranco was based in New York City for the first 15 years of her career and was living there when the events of September 11, 2001, took place. Her poem "Self-Evident" was written shortly after September 11, and a recording of it can be found on her live CD set, *So Much Shouting, So Much Laughter* (DiFranco, 2002). Though there is no video of her performing the poem, the audio recording allows the listener to hear the audience's reaction to her words, and, interestingly, a number of people have made YouTube videos to accompany the poem.

Whereas Hammad's (2002) reaction to "people saying this was bound to happen let's/not forget u.s. transgressions" was "hold up, i live here, these are my friends and fam," DiFranco could be easily cast off as falling into the category of people who use the traumatic rupture of September 11 to highlight U.S. transgressions inside the country and globally. She describes

a morning beatific
in its indian summer breeze
on the day that america
fell to its knees
after strutting around for a century
without saying thank you
or please. (DiFranco, 2002)

However, like Hammad, DiFranco portrays communal trauma, as she places herself as a witness to and a member of a traumatized community of New Yorkers. Just as Hammad (2002) includes herself in lost community members when she says that it was "me in those buildings," DiFranco (2002) states, "we were all on time for work that day/we all boarded that plane for to fly/and then while the fires were raging/we all climbed up on the windowsill/and then we all held hands/and jumped into the sky." In the next stanza DiFranco describes her own experience of the event: "the exodus uptown by foot and motorcar/looked more like war than anything i've seen so far," and records the experiences of others in her community of New Yorkers who fill the streets with "stories" of "sudden twists and near misses/and soon every open bar is crammed to the rafters/with tales of narrowly averted disasters" whose trauma is embedded in societal trauma, as "as all over the country/folks just shake their heads." As a

New Yorker who is also openly critical of U.S. politics and practices, arguably to a more explicit extent than Hammad, DiFranco's performance highlights the embodied tension of being a member of a traumatized national community while also critically examining how that same community perpetuates local and global oppression and conflict.

In her description of September 11, DiFranco (2002) highlights the unspeakability of traumatic events as she recalls media coverage in which "every jackass newscaster was struck dumb and stumbling/over 'oh my god' and 'this is unbelievable' and on and on." DiFranco uses this traumatic rupturing of conventional discourses and frameworks of meaning to draw attention to global and national subjects whose trauma does not typically make it into the frame of hegemonic discourse and media coverage,[2] as she proposes

a toast to all the folks who live in palestine
afghanistan
iraq
el salvador . . . to the folks living on the pine ridge reservation
under the stone cold gaze of mt. rushmore
to all those nurses and doctors
who daily provide women with a choice
who stand down a threat the size of oklahoma city
just to listen to a young woman's voice . . . to all the folks on death row
    right now
awaiting the executioner's guillotine
who are shackled there with dread and can only escape into their heads
to find peace in the form of a dream.

From this point, DiFranco's (2002) poem largely focuses on "countless crimes against humanity" committed by the U.S. nationally and globally, bringing marginalized subjects and frequently denied global politics into the frame.

When considering these poems by Hammad and DiFranco, we must remain mindful not only of the similarities but also of the differences in their social locations. Violent international conflict that uproots and shatters one's sense of home was part of Hammad's life from her birth as the child of refugee parents in Lebanon. Although it is clear that DiFranco resides outside of and is unflinchingly critical of mainstream U.S. society and politics, she has not

73

experienced the trauma of refugees who are made homeless by systems of globalized capitalism, violence, and oppression. As I continue to examine these poems in my work, I cannot help but wonder how the trauma of dislocation and loss of citizenship versus the privilege of stable citizenship in a society that dominates globalized systems might account for the different articulations and criticisms of these poets who embody and perform the unspeakably tense space of being a member of a traumatized community that is also complicit in the creation and perpetuation of globalized trauma and conflict.

Finally, when taking a critical trauma approach, it is crucial to be attentive to more than just the pathological or rupturing aspects of traumatic events. Rather, we must also be mindful of the resilience of individuals and communities in the face of rupturing traumatic events. Hammad's (2001) *first writing since* ends with the lines:

anyone hearing this is breathing, maybe hurtin', but breathing for sure.
and if there is any light to come, it will
shine from the eyes of those who look
for peace and justice after the rubble
and rhetoric are cleared and the
phoenix has risen.
affirm life.
affirm life.
we got to carry each other now.
you are either with life, or against it.
affirm life.

Hammad does not give her audience the opportunity to cast her off as a singularly traumatized Palestinian nor a traumatized New Yorker. Rather, her public testimony challenges her audience to see the resilience and conviction of someone whose identity resides at the intersection of multiple traumas and erasures and to act on their responsibility to foster growth and promote justice in the wake of trauma.

Implications for Feminist Social Work Praxis

Allowing critical trauma theory to intersect with clinical notions of trauma takes an already stunningly complex and weighty concept and further complicates it by insisting that those engaging with notions and experiences of trauma consider "how culture, context, and identity can render an experience traumatic" (Brown, 2008, p. 95). To acknowledge and be self-reflexive about our own stake in and experience of trauma not only as possible victims and survivors but also as social actors who are, to varying degrees, complicit in globalized systematic oppressions that have the ability to create and compound traumatic experiences can be daunting, to say the least. However, it is only through this dislocation of trauma from isolated individual pathology that we might hope to gain the insight and knowledge necessary to aid in the dynamic and ongoing process of articulating and healing from trauma along with the dismantling of oppressive systems that create and exacerbate traumatic events. Finally, in examining the intersections of trauma and performance, feminist clinical social workers can help create a therapeutic space that is collaborative and nonhierarchical, values that are core to feminist therapeutic practice (Ballou, Hill, & West, 2008, p. 145). In a therapeutic space that promotes collaboration, rather than diagnosis or professional expertise, speaking of trauma may take many different formats, and continuous healing and agency might be found in embracing narratives that are nonlinear, culturally located, self-determined, and performed through whatever means the subject chooses.

Social Work Teaching Possibilities

1. Present printed copies of the poems to students for initial discussion, followed by an audio- or videorecording of the poets' performances. Discuss the ways the different presentations of the poem affect the students' reception and understanding, also considering how the poets' voices, bodies, and identities in the performances affect their interpretations of the poems.

2. Hold an in-class, noncompetitive poetry slam/reading. Encourage students to write their own poems about their experiences and social identities or choose poems that speak to them to share with their classmates. Allow time to reflect on the poems and on the act of embodied sharing and performance.

3. Invite class members to find or compose short essays, poems, or lyrics that capture for them a critical voice speaking to the meaning and power of trauma. Invite in-class performance readings followed by small-group

discussions of the embodied experiences of being a performer and being a member of the audience present at the performance.

Notes

1. Unless otherwise noted, poems quoted in this chapter are from the performed version.

2. I am drawing on Judith Butler's (2010) theory that "cultural modes of regulating affective ethical dispositions through a selective and differential framing of violence" creates a situation in which "certain lives do not qualify as lives or are, from the start, not conceivable as lives within certain epistemological frames" and therefore "these lives are never lived nor lost in the full sense" (p. 1).

References

American Psychiatric Association. (2000). *Diagnostic and statistical manual of mental disorders*. Washington, DC: Author.

Ballou, M. B., Hill, M., & West, C. M. (2008). *Feminist therapy theory and practice: A contemporary perspective*. New York, NY: Springer.

Beckerman, N. L., & Pass, J. (2008). After the assault: Cognitive trauma therapy with a single event trauma survivor. *Clinical Social Work Journal, 36*(3), 255–263.

Breuer, J., & Freud, S. (1957). *Studies on hysteria* (J. Strachey, Trans.). New York, NY: Basic Books.

Brown, L. S. (2008). *Cultural competence in trauma therapy: Beyond the flashback*. Washington, DC: American Psychological Association.

Butler, J. (2010). *Frames of war: When is life grievable?* New York, NY: Verso.

Butler, J. P. (2006). *Precarious life: The powers of mourning and violence*. London, UK: Verso.

Cvetkovich, A. (2003). Trauma ongoing. In Judith Greenberg (Ed.), *Trauma at home: After 9/11* (pp. 117–123). Lincoln: University of Nebraska.

Denham, A. R. (2008). Rethinking historical trauma: Narratives of resilience. *Transcultural Psychiatry, 45*(3), 391–414. doi: 10.1177/1363461508094673

DiFranco, A. (2002). Self-evident. On *So much shouting, so much laughter* [CD]. Buffalo, NY: Righteous Babe Records.

Fassin, D., & Rechtman, R. (2009). *The empire of trauma: An inquiry into the condition of victimhood*. Princeton, NJ: Princeton University Press.

Friedman, S. S. (1998). Women's autobiographical selves: Theory and practice. In S. Smith & J. Watson (Eds.), *Women, autobiography, theory* (pp. 72–82). Madison, WI: University of Wisconsin Press.

Gilmore, L. (1994). *Autobiographics: A feminist theory of women's self-representation*. Ithaca, NY: Cornell University Press.

Hammad, S. (2001). First writing since. *Middle East Report 221*, 2–3.

Hammad, S., (Writer) & Simmons, R., (Producer). (2002). First writing since [Television epidsode]. In R. Simmons (Producer), *Russell Simmons presents def poetry jam*. New York, NY: Home Box Office. Retrieved from http://www.youtube.com/watch?v=d24Q7qts4pA

Herman, J. L. (1997). *Trauma and recovery: The aftermath of violence—from domestic abuse to political terror*. New York, NY: Basic.

Horsely, K. (2007). Storytelling, conflict and diversity. *Community Development Journal, 42*(2), 265–269.

Khan, R. (2009). Suheir Hammad. [Television episode]. In *One-on-one*. Doha, Quatar: Al Jazeera Media Network.

Kaplan, A. E. (2005). *Trauma culture: The politics of terror and loss in media and literature*. New Brunswick, NJ: Rutgers University Press.

Lee, J. (1997). Women re-authoring their lives through feminist narrative therapy. *Women & Therapy, 20*(3), 1–22. doi: 10.1300/J015v20n03_01

Littrell, J. (2009). Expression of emotion: When it causes trauma and when it helps." *Journal of Evidence-Based Social Work, 6*(3), 300–320.

Olson, A. (2013). *About Alix*. Retrieved from http://www.alixolson.com/about/

Righteous Babe Records. (2013). *Ani DiFranco: Biography*. Retrieved from http://www.righteousbabe.com/ani/bio.asp

Rothberg, M. (2009). *Multidirectional memory: Remembering the Holocaust in the age of decolonization*. Stanford, CA: Stanford University Press.

Schechner, R. (2002). *Performance studies: An introduction*. London, UK: Routledge.

Spivak, G. (1988). Can the subaltern speak? In C. Nelson & L. Grossberg (Eds.), *Marxism and the interpretation of culture* (pp. 271–313). Urbana: University of Illinois Press.

Taylor, D. (2003). *The archive and the repertoire: Performing cultural memory in the Americas*. Durham, NC: Duke University Press.

Taylor, D. (2006). DNA of performance: Political hauntology. In D. Sommer (Ed.), *Cultural agency in the Americas* (pp. 52–81). Durham, NC: Duke University Press.

Watkins, M., & Shulman, H. (2008). *Toward psychologies of liberation*. New York, NY: Palgrave Macmillan.

Watters, E. (2010). *Crazy like us: The globalization of the American psyche*. New York, NY: The Free Press.

Wrenn, L. J. (2003). Trauma: Conscious and unconscious meaning. *Clinical Social Work Journal, 31*(2), 123–137.

CHAPTER 4

Breaching the Fence

Claiming Justice and Human Rights
With Incarcerated Women

CAROL JACOBSEN

In this chapter I critically examine the incarceration of women worldwide, considering histories of abuse, experiences of poverty, mental illness, and racism, unequal treatment by the law, gendered modes of punishment, and systemic abuses in prisons that shape women's experiences. I explore the criminalization of women's lives and the massive expansion of the prison industrial complex that coincided with the globalization of capital in the 1980s. Drawing on my roles as artist, educator, and director of the Michigan Women's Justice & Clemency Project, I discuss grassroots strategies for students, social workers, educators, attorneys, and other citizens to forge alliances with women prisoners and resist the injustice of women's criminalization and the dehumanization of their lives by the prison system. I combine an analysis of issues of representation and research relating to women's criminal processing and incarceration with a discussion of my experiences as a filmmaker, grassroots organizer, and teacher. I draw on theories and practices of social work, legal advocacy, and creative political activism to empower incarcerated and nonincarcerated women in affecting public policy and social change.

Global Incarceration of Women

Of the estimated 500,000 women incarcerated worldwide, almost one half are in prisons in the United States (American Civil Liberties Union, 2013; Carson & Sabol, 2012; Greene, Frost, & Pranis, 2006). Most of them are serving time for nonviolent poverty- or abuse-induced crimes. The institutionalized disparities and discrimination inherent in most criminal legal systems globally have produced a prison population that is racially imbalanced, educationally and economically disadvantaged, and suffering from high rates of mental illness as well as histories of abuse (Bloom, Owen, & Covington, 2003; Human Rights Watch, 2013). In addition, prisons are packed; education, programs, and health care are abysmal; and human rights are shockingly disregarded. For incarcerated women the critical implications of all these problems are intensified (Bloom et al., 2003; Sudbury, 2002). As Angela Y Davis (1998) notes:

> Considering the fact that as many as half of all women are assaulted by their husbands or partners, combined with dramatically rising numbers of women sentenced to prison, it may be argued that women in general are subjected to a far greater magnitude of punishment than men. (p. 344)

Research has shown that women's lawbreaking differs radically from men's in that it is largely produced by social and individual domination, victimization, prejudice, and abuse (Atwood, 2000; Bloom et al., 2003; U.S. Department of Justice, 1996). In many countries women are selectively punished and imprisoned for having sex outside marriage, for reporting rape, for failing to have a male family member to protect them, or to flush out male relatives hiding from authorities (Human Rights Watch, 1995). In addition, huge numbers of women would not be incarcerated at all if they were men because of gender-based crimes such as prostitution, checks written with insufficient funds to support children whose fathers are not held accountable by the law, and crimes committed by or under duress or threat of death from abusive male codefendants (Bloom et al., 2003; Davis, 1998). Such unequal treatment by the law worldwide has wrongfully incarcerated thousands of women whose actions, including murder, were for their own survival (Atwood, 2000; Bloom et al., 2003; Buel, 2003; Chesney-Lind, 1997; Davis & Shaylor, 2001; Schneider, 2000; Sudbury, 2002). Despite the promise of nations that signed the Universal Declaration of Human Rights and its covenants to protect the rights of all humans, gender-based violence, murders, and incarceration continue to be legitimized by state, social, and corporate structures around the world through their refusal to devote critical resources to end this crisis (Amnesty International, 2004).

Clemency and the Battered Women's Movement

For prisoners who seek redress after unfair trials, excessive sentencing, or denial of equal rights, clemency represents the last hope for justice. As a power vested in the head of state, awarding clemency allows for the remission of criminal sentences after conviction through pardon, commutation, reprieve, or amnesty. Unfortunately, in the United States clemency has declined in use because of exploitation by opponents of those who exercised it as it was originally intended, an obligation of office that serves as a vital function in the system of checks and balances, or because it has sometimes been granted opportunistically as a form of favoritism (Love, 2010). Nevertheless, in the past few decades clemency has raised new and crucial legal questions about racial and gender discrimination in the capital punishment of primarily Black defendants and in the life or long sentences for women who acted in self-defense against abusers.

In December 1990, when Governor Richard Celeste of Ohio granted clemency to 25 women prisoners who were convicted of killing their abusers, his act (which was prompted by a coalition of feminist activists and attorneys led by his wife, Dagmar Celeste) gave a boost to all of us who were participating in the emerging battered women's movement in the United States and abroad (Gagné, 1998; McColgan, 1993). At the time I was living in London, where I was working and protesting with the Southall Black Sisters outside Holloway Prison and the Home Office in London on behalf of freedom for Kiranjit Ahluwalia and Sara Thornton, two battered women who killed their abusers. The progress and ultimate success of that campaign gave me hope that we could accomplish the same thing in the United States. And, indeed, advocates have enacted changes in the law and in law enforcement, and gained the release of battered women prisoners in many states since then (Gagné, 1998; McColgan, 1993; Schneider, 2000). Unfortunately, at the same time the pandemics of violence against women, the wrongful convictions of women who defend themselves, and the human rights abuses of incarcerated women have not diminished.

Acts of Survival From Public Protest to Private Sex Work

My interest in issues of women's decriminalization and human rights is rooted in personal experience and a political desire to activate my artistic practice through feminist theory. Shortly after I left graduate school in the early 1980s,

I was living in Europe for the first time when I encountered feminist activism on an international scale (Jacobsen, 1986). I traveled with a friend to Greenham Common Women's Peace Camp outside the North Atlantic Treaty Organization base near London, where we met women who had come from all over the world to protest the buildup of nuclear weapons and the international war machine. The women tunneled under, crawled over, and cut through the perimeter fence on the military base. They blocked convoys and painted airplanes. They wrote articles and published books. And they were arrested for disturbing the peace and disorderly conduct. At their trials, the protestors shrieked with laughter, sang songs, and mocked the British court system, white wigs and all. As I watched the spectacles in the courtrooms, I was struck by the connection between my own and so many other women's experiences globally—rape, abortion, battering, prostitution, lesbian identity, voicing opposition—that were silenced by social norms and punished by the state.

After I returned to the United States, I was drawn to the courts again. I wanted to see who was being arrested for disturbing the peace here. It was prostitutes. The number of sex workers criminalized in Detroit annually, more than 800, seems to have changed very little over the past 25 years despite the massive exodus of Detroit's population during that period (Trent, 2006). As Julie Pearl's (1987) early groundbreaking study demonstrated, arresting prostitutes remains an easy way for police to boost their arrest records at taxpayers' expense. Recently, a glimmer of hope appeared in the form of a pioneering court project in Detroit led by District Judge Leonia Lloyd. Her program assists street prostitutes through abuse counseling, drug treatment, job training, and expunging of arrest records on completion of the program's steps, which last from 93 days (the sentence for soliciting for prostitution or related charges) to 1 year (Hunt, 2007). Projects such as this intervene in the abuse-to-prison pipeline and represent a significant step toward decriminalizing women's acts of survival.

The grassroots films I made with street prostitutes in Detroit during those years only deepened my commitment to issues of women's criminalization, and in 1989 I was invited by a prisoner rights activist to make a film with women in Huron Valley Women's Prison. Once inside, I was hooked. First, I was shocked by the crushing mind-set of cruelty that dominated the institution and the human beings, "the docile bodies," (Foucault, 1995, p. 137) locked within "a mechanism of 'punishment-reproduction'" (p. 278); and second, I was stunned to discover who the so-called murderers are in our women's prisons. Many, if not most, had broken the law to save their own lives. At 17, I too broke the law to escape an abusive marriage by having an illegal abortion. I was lucky I had friends and family to help and hide me from my stalker and from the law until I could pick up my life, return to school, move on.

Because I grew up in the shadow of the world's largest walled prison in Jackson, Michigan, I also became alarmed when I realized we were all living in the shadow of a prison. The changes in our public policies toward crime and punishment began in the 1980s when the rise of global capitalism made large populations of working people dispensable (Hallinan, 2001). What Susan Faludi (1991) called the decade of "backlash" (p. 12) was a period of relapse, of thwarting the strides made by the liberation movements of the 1960s and 1970s. Exploiting public fears and unemployment rates, self-interested politicians and corporate media produced a war on drugs and crime that became a war on women and people of color, despite the decreasing crime levels and the human cost (Alexander, 2010; Chesney-Lind, 1997; Faludi, 1991; Hallinan, 2001; Quester, 2007; Sudbury, 2002). Government funds were funneled into the toxic prison industry, and jobs, services, and contracts were sold to the public as a solution for the (manufactured) problem of crime and the (real) problem of an absconding corporate economy. People in the United States who were laid off from the auto, technology, clothing, and other industries were easily maneuvered into building new, bigger institutions and expanding the accompanying slave-labor force (Elk & Sloan, 2011). Davis and Shaylor (2001) dubbed the effect of prison profiteering at the expense of human misery "the penal equivalent of ambulance chasing" (p. 5). African American men were caught in the dragnet, but women, who were incarcerated at a rate more than double that of men from 1985 to 2007 despite their minor roles as accessories to male co-defendants' crimes, became the easiest targets for drug-, poverty-, and abuse-related arrests around the world (Alexander, 2010; Davis, 2005; Davis & Shaylor, 2001).

Keys to the Prison

Inaccessible and invisible to most people, prisons are closed systems situated on the margins of our landscapes and our minds. As such, they have become warehouses for the sexualized and racialized abuse and domination of human beings

(Amnesty International, 1999; Bloom et al., 2003; Human Rights Watch, 1998; Kupers, 2010). As Angela Davis (2003, pp. 22–29) noted in her examination of the historical links between U.S. slavery and the early penitentiary system (for example, when she points to the similarities between prison regulations and the Slave Codes and compares human conditions under slavery with the prison punishments of isolation, abuse, and hard labor), prisons are fundamentally obsolete extensions of colonial and domestic servitude.

The keys to *breaking into* prison, or *breaching the fence*, are persistence, education, and collaboration with other advocates. Because I was initially brought inside by another advocate to make a film with women prisoners, I was able to build lasting trust and friendships. However, my filming ended in the mid-1990s when Michigan governor John Engler issued a ban on virtually all visitors except Bible readers, lawyers, and a limited number of nuclear family members or friends. The few programs and college classes that existed were cancelled, and media contacts and recording devices were prohibited. The ban was a reaction to the investigations of sexual and other abuses in women's prisons by Amnesty International (1999), Human Rights Watch (1998), the U.S. Justice Department (1996), and the UN Commission on Human Rights (1996), and to the lawsuits filed by courageous women prisoners (*Neal et al. v. Michigan Department of Corrections et al.*, 1996; *Nunn et al. v. Michigan Department of Corrections et al.*, 1993). Amnesty International (1999) and Human Rights Watch (1998) both named Michigan as one of the worst prison systems for women in the United States because of sexual assaults by guards and retaliation and medical neglect by the system.

By the time the ban went into effect, I was working inside the prison with women in my role as director of the Michigan Women's Justice & Clemency Project, an all-volunteer grassroots effort founded by a former prisoner. Together with volunteer attorneys, students, and other citizens, we assisted women prisoners who acted in self-defense against their abusers in their bids for freedom, and we worked for the human rights of all women incarcerated in Michigan. I was taking students and volunteers with me one at a time on each visit to collect files and gather legal research for motions, appeals, clemency petitions, and parole support. Visits were always difficult because prison rules are harsh and constantly changing, and because visitors are treated as being guilty by association with prisoners. Walking into the lobby, we learned to expect excuses for the endless delays. Either the officer on duty could not find our letter (sent in advance to the warden listing our identification details, the reason for our visit, and specific prisoners we wished to see), or the lien clearance was not logged in, or the computer was down, or the prisoner could not be located, and so on and so forth. If the delay lasted for more than an hour, the shift would change, the prisoner count would begin, a lockdown might be called, or some other reason arose to keep us waiting. Sometimes we were turned away entirely: The warden was gone that day, the computer was not working, one of us was not wearing the proper clothing (e.g., skirt not long enough, collar not high enough, improper bra, whereas male visitors were not required to wear equivalent clothes; shorts were acceptable, no jock straps required, etc.). When we finally got inside, we entered a locked glass cage for pat downs; clearance by the metal detector; examination of shoes, feet, hair, mouth and ears; and shuffling of paperwork. As legal visitors, we were usually granted, on request, the benefit of a private office off the visiting room where we spent several hours with each woman.

Some students who accompanied me had worked briefly with women in jails or in forensic centers or courtrooms, so they were able to put those experiences together with the prison visits. In many ways, visits constitute a foundation (as well as a piling on of frustrations) to build the determination to work toward a different social/political/legal system.

Public Education and Advocating for Women's Decarceration

The first time I taught a women's studies seminar with graduate students in social work I felt I had been given a gift. As an art professor, teaching primarily photography, video, and activist art classes, I was thrilled to work with a group of students who were advanced in their education about feminist issues of domestic violence and were hungry to engage with the subject of women's criminalization, my own field of research and practice.

Our successes in the Michigan Women's Justice & Clemency Project had been modest. In 1998–99, we freed two women through motions in court who were serving life sentences for killing their abusers (Jacobsen, 2008; Lyon, Hughes, & Thomas, 2001), and through the years we testified at public and parole hearings; gave workshops, lectures, and panels inside and outside the prisons; held rallies, public screenings, and other events; built media contacts and wrote letters to editors and to the parole board; and advocated with judges, legislators, and other policy makers. We also protested ongoing human rights violations in the women's prisons, in particular, the practice of four-point chaining and other atrocities committed against women in segregation units (Jacobsen, 2000). Perhaps our best accomplishment has been in our public education efforts and in sharing hope with women on both sides of the fence to collectively resist the injustices of women's criminalization and the dehumanization of their incarceration. We sent hundreds of students and volunteers out into the world with a commitment to challenging public policy by working for feminist justice and change; and we formed partnerships with women inside to carry their drafted legislation and bids for freedom forward to those in power. Still, our dozens of clemency petitions for battered women prisoners had all been flatly denied.

In January 2007 Governor Jennifer Granholm began her final term in office, and we realized that this was an opportunity to press harder on her to act. As a former prosecutor, she would not be inclined to second-guess lawful convictions and grant clemencies. But as a Democrat, she might be liberal enough to do it. As a woman, she would not want to appear "soft on crime." But her experience might give her compassion for survivors of domestic violence. Finally, since she was not facing reelection, she had less to fear from the political backlash that has paralyzed American politicians' fair and open exercise of the clemency power for decades (Love, 2010).

Social work students had volunteered with the Clemency Project from the beginning, but starting in that summer of 2007, I decided to issue a call only for social work graduate students to participate in a special women's studies seminar. Focusing on theories and practices of social work (which the students taught me something about!), legal advocacy, and creative political activism, our aim was to increase pressure on the governor to grant clemency for battered women prisoners over the next few years. We would continue to organize rallies and public events to gain media coverage, but we would step up our legislative efforts and media contacts through letters to editors and op-ed pieces. At one point, I bought expensive tickets to an event that allowed me 5 minutes' face time with the governor. She praised the project's efforts with the tired platitude, "Just keep up the great work." But the remark reminded us that she would not take the risk (she had hopes of moving up the political ladder) without sufficient public support. And so we proceeded to contact more judges, visit more legislators, and widen our efforts with others, including reporters who might be able to access the governor and help us generate broader public support. I did not have all these strategies in mind at the time, but they evolved as I was able to work with these small, motivated cohorts of social work students who rotated through my seminars and traveled with me to prisons and courthouses across the state over the next several years.

Self-Defense and Women's Unequal Treatment by the Law

Of the approximately 12,000 women who are serving time for murder in U.S. state prisons, it is estimated that one third killed an intimate male partner, most of them in response to violence, and many more were convicted of murder that was committed by their abusers (Browne, 1987; Campbell et al., 2003; Carson & Sabol, 2012; Schneider, 2000; Snell, 1994). Attempts have been made to address women's experiences through laws on provocation, loss of control, and battered woman's syndrome in countries such as the United States, Canada, Australia, South Africa, and in Europe (Ramsey, 2010; Rozenberg, 2010; Walker, 1979). However, most of these laws have proved inadequate or even harmful to women defendants who were forced to kill their abusers (Belknap, 2001; Nourse, 2001; Ramsey, 2010). Battered woman's syndrome is a concept that was first defined by forensic psychologist Leonore Walker (1979) in her book, *The Battered Woman*. She described a cycle of violence characterized by three recurrent phases: (1) a tension-building stage consisting of minor abuse, (2) an acute battering stage consisting of uncontrollable explosions of brutal violence, and (3) a respite stage that includes loving behavior and pleas for forgiveness from the batterer. Walker argued that a woman who is caught in this cycle is living with constant fear that translates into a state of learned helplessness. She narrows her focus to techniques of survival rather than escape because she knows that her abuser will kill her if she leaves.

Feminists have criticized Walker's theory for a number of reasons: (a) it tends to pathologize women who are beaten; (b) it engenders stereotypes of women as helpless victims; (c) it implies a single model, which excludes most women; and (d) it ignores the many strategies women use for their own survival, from placating abusers to leaving to calling police to fighting back. Perhaps most important, the theory diverts attention from the failure of law enforcement and the courts to provide equal protection to women and instead converges with society's tendency to blame women for their own abuse. Most scholars agree that gender inequality rather than a psychological classification is the underlying reason for violence against women globally and must form the framework for battered women's defense (Belknap, 2001; Bloom, et al., 2003, Gagné, 1998; Schneider, 2000).

In general, the law of self-defense has been recognized and incorporated into legal systems around the world, including the UN charter, which recognizes the "inherent right of individual or collective self-defence" (Charter of the United Nations, n.d., chapter 7, art. 51). In the United States and many European nations, self-defense laws require a person's honest or reasonable belief that the danger of bodily harm is imminent and that force is necessary. However, the ways the laws are interpreted are gender biased and fail to work for women (Bloom, et al., 2003; Gillespie, 1989; Schneider, 2000). For example, scholars have found the following:

1. The honest or reasonable belief is generally interpreted from a *reasonable male* perspective because women's actions are typically viewed as unreasonable rather than understood in the context of women's experiences, particularly battered women's (Belknap, 2001; Chesney-Lind, 1997; Schneider, 2000).

2. *Imminence* is generally defined as a single, brief confrontation (two men fighting in a bar, for example), which does not reflect woman abuse, since battering is not characterized by a single episode (Maguigan, 1991). As Cynthia Gillespie (1989) argues, "In circumstances like these, it is not at all an exaggeration to say that the threat of death or serious injury is always imminent" (p. 68).

3. The bodily harm requirement assumes that people are of equivalent size and strength and punishes women who use an object or weapon to protect themselves against male abusers who can easily overpower them (Belknap, 2007; Gillespie, 1989).

4. The necessity of force is based on the notion of proportionality of response and the assumption that a person should leave before needing to respond. Virtually every Western country has adopted the requirement of proportionality in its law on self-defense, although there has been some global revolt based on the popular belief that people should

be allowed to defend themselves when the law fails to protect them against aggressors (Lerner, 2006). In most of the United States, the law does not require retreat from an attack, especially in one's own home. Therefore, the condemnation of a battered woman that is embedded in the question, "Why didn't she leave?" attests to the failure of courts to make this legal point understood and ignores the large body of evidence showing that women do leave despite the fact that they are in the greatest danger of being killed when they leave (Browne, 1987; Mahoney, 1991).

Many scholars agree that the greatest obstacle for women defendants is the state itself through its individual judges, prosecutors, defense attorneys, and jurors, who all persistently refuse to follow the law (Belknap, 2007; Bloom et al., 2003; Buel, 2003; Coker, 2001; Maguigan, 1991; Quester, 2007; Schneider, 2000). Failing to provide equal protection to women who are assaulted, overcharging women who defend themselves, hiding or ignoring exculpatory evidence in battered women's cases, ridiculing or disbelieving women's abuse, and denying women their right to expert testimony in court are a few of the most common examples of state violence against women (Quester, 2007; Schneider, 2000). In *People v. Nancy Seaman* (2007), for example, jurors simply chose to ignore substantial evidence of abuse when they convicted Seaman of first-degree murder in the death of her violent husband. After the trial, one juror stated, "She was not a meek, howling woman waiting for the next beating." (Brasier, 2005, p. A1). The judge, who belatedly recognized the jury's (and his own) error, amended the conviction to second-degree murder. But the prosecutor appealed it and the first-degree murder conviction was reinstated.

For women of color the difficulties are compounded. Sharon Allard and other scholars have shown how insidiously common stereotypes and media representations work against Black women by showing them as typically large, sexually aggressive, and hostile (Allard, 1991; Ammons, 1995; Sudbury, 2002). In *People v. Juanita Thomas* (1983), for example, the defendant, an African American woman, was convicted of first-degree murder by an all-White jury despite overwhelming evidence of a self-defense struggle and documentation of more than 100 calls to police. Exculpatory evidence mysteriously disappeared before trial, and the prosecutor's shocking justification for pursuing the case was that the defense "never really gave us *a profile* of a battered spouse" (emphasis added) (Gave, 1980). As Renee Callahan (1994) asked, with no little irony, "Will the 'Real' Battered Woman Please Stand Up?"

In *People v. Quiana Kenisha Lovett* (2012) the defense attorney refused to present the history of abuse. The case involved a classic, face-to-face struggle between the woman and her boyfriend, who had her backed against the wall in a choke hold, something he had done to her before. Photographs taken by her mother after the incident (Detroit police did not photograph her injuries) showed bruises on the woman's face, jaw, and neck. She testified that at that point she could not breathe and reached around, grabbed a paring knife, and stabbed her abuser one time in self-defense. When he collapsed, she was devastated, performed CPR, and confessed to police without an attorney. "Confessing" without an attorney is all too common and is ultimately disastrous for battered women who kill their abusers. Often in a state of shock and horrified or unable to believe that the abuser is dead, they are easily manipulated by police through intimidation, feigned sympathy, and false promises. At the trial, the defense attorney's failure to educate himself about women's responses to domestic violence was catastrophic. He argued self-defense without presenting evidence of past abuse or expert testimony. Quiana Lovett was convicted of second-degree murder. Prior to sentencing, the judge received documentation of the abuse from the defendant's family and supporters, including a past police report. He indicated his regret, stating, "I didn't know until we got into this post-trial stage about . . . the battering" (*People v. Quiana Lovett*, sentencing transcript, at 23). Nevertheless, he failed to take the abuse into account and sentenced her to 16 years in prison.

In a similar case involving a woman's face-to-face struggle with her abuser a Detroit judge blatantly broke the law when she denied the defendant's request for an expert witness in battering, ruling that such evidence was "common knowledge" and, therefore, unnecessary to explain the woman's actions (*People v. Lekisha Danielle Hines*, 2011 Court of Appeals Opinion, at 6). The woman was convicted of second-degree murder and sentenced to 25 years in prison. In 2012 her case was overturned on appeal because of the judge's error, and she pled to manslaughter rather than face the same judge in a second trial. She was sentenced to 7 years in prison (she will serve all 7 years because in Michigan there are no early paroles or reductions in sentences for good behavior).

Most feminist legal scholars and litigators oppose differential handling of women's cases that subjects them to unequal treatment by the law, but they also oppose models of formal equality, because those are grounded in male experience, which often becomes "equality with a vengeance" (Chesney-Lind & Pollock-Bryne, 1995; Schneider, 2000). The claim that gender-neutral laws and interpretations provide equal protection becomes gender discrimination in practice (Dragiewicz & Lindgren, 2009). As Carol Smart (1989) and others (e.g., Quester, 2007) have warned, legal standards alone will also not guarantee equality, since the law remains in the hands of individuals and agencies far removed from the values and politics of the global women's movement.

Instead, changes in international and local laws are needed that work together with public education to incorporate gender in ways that embody women's physical differences and women's range of experiences as well as address the pervasive and socially constructed problems of gender discrimination and abuse (Belknap, 2001; Bloom, et al., 2003; Coker, 2001; Maguigan, 1991; Nourse, 2001; Quester, 2007; Schneider, 2000). An international effort that contains an agenda for systemic legal change to end discrimination against women based on the principle of equality can be found in the Convention on the Elimination of All Forms of Discrimination Against Women, which was adopted in 1979 by the UN General Assembly and ratified by 187 countries, but it has not been signed by the United States.

The Women's Studies Seminars for Graduate Students in Social Work

From 2007 through 2010 the women's studies summer seminars for graduate students in social work took place weekly or sometimes biweekly. The meetings revolved around case discussions, fieldwork reports, and research assignments. Students were given several of my films to introduce them to the women's versions of their cases, which rarely had been heard in court (Jacobsen, 1994, 1997, 2000). We scheduled our prison visits and research trips to courthouses, wrote letters to editors and legislators, and did filing and other clerical work. Some group projects varied. For example, one summer we split among us all the cases of women on death row in the United States. Students did research, and then we wrote letters to the governors, news media, legislators, and judges in those states giving our reasons for opposing the women's death sentences. Students also did some of the planning for the annual rally and other events, although much of that organizing was carried out by volunteers and undergraduate students in my fall classes.

Outside the seminars, each student accompanied me one at a time on two or three prison trips to meet with women prisoners during the semester. On other days, they traveled with me in small groups to courthouses where we pored over case files and wrote summaries on the spot. On their own, they conducted research on cases in newspaper archives and articles in scholarly journals. Since many students had contacts with other nonprofits on and off campus, they served as liaisons for the Clemency Project. And occasionally, students were able to attend trials or clemency hearings of battered women. At the end of each summer, they submitted a log of their completed research and activities.

For individual trips to the prison, each student was given case information in advance and briefed on the way. They wrote letters of support to the parole board for every woman they met, and sometimes they did follow-up research for women, such as sending lists of resources or updates on legislation. We usually met with two women in an afternoon, and our notes went into the women's files for incorporation into their clemency petitions or packages for the parole board. Our discussions centered around details of the women's cases and accomplishments in prison, but they were also opportunities for the women to talk about the past abuse and their experience in prison. Unlike male prisoners, most women have few visitors, and many have none at all. We saw both women who had been involved with the project for years and those who were new to the project. We also met with women who were held in the segregation unit and in what is called the mental unit, or Level 4. Prisoners can be sent to segregation or assigned to Level 4 for any reason by any officer at any time. For example, if a prisoner argues with an officer or with another prisoner, it can mean an assault ticket that sends her to segregation. Or if a prisoner is seen touching someone it can be cause for a sexual misconduct ticket. It is not unusual for a misconduct ticket to be manufactured out of thin air by an officer out of retaliation, a grudge, or to side with another officer. Occasionally, a prisoner will request a brief stay in segregation for protection from a guard or another prisoner. In segregation, prisoners are locked away from the general population in 6 x 9 cells, alone 23 hours a day, without human contact, and with little opportunity for exercise or programs. They are fed through slots in the door and denied visits, telephone calls, books, television, and other materials. They can be held for months, years, or decades in this unit. One woman we visited had been locked in segregation for eight months until the woman in the next cell hanged herself. The woman cried frantically that she would do the same thing if the warden did not let her out into the general population. She was then placed in Level 4, where she was locked down 22 hours a day and later was returned to segregation. Another woman told us she has spent 6 years bouncing from Level 4 to segregation and back. Both women have been four pointed (laid flat, sometimes naked, on a thin mattress atop a cement slab and shackled at wrists and ankles to large eye screws in the concrete), which can be ordered by a guard for any prisoner for periods of days or weeks. Often it is retaliatory, but the official rationale is "not for punishment, but for protection," and "for [her] own good" (Jacobsen, 2000). One courageous woman, Jamie Whitcomb, sued the state for torture and won her case in a jury trial after spending most of her 4-year sentence in segregation and flat on her back for months, chained to a slab (*Whitcomb v. Sizemore et al.*, 1996). We found that because we visited women who were being held in segregation the guards often backed off from harassing them, at least for a time, knowing that someone was keeping watch and reporting abuse. At other times, women were harassed even more for talking to us. Many times prisoners in segregation had to meet with us through a thick glass window, which blocked communication entirely. We could often see the mental and physical deterioration on women's faces and bodies after months of isolation in these cells. It was often difficult to debrief on our drive home after these heartbreaking visits. We wrote reports on the atrocities and sent them to governors, legislators, judges, investigators, and human and civil rights organizations.

For our major group project each summer we usually made three trips to the state capital. Students scheduled meetings with six to eight senators or representatives (or their aides) for each trip. Often, we seized opportunities to meet with additional legislators we met in offices, hallways, or elevators. We presented a file to each one containing a list of documents that doubled as our agenda for the meeting: a list of the women we represented with a summary of their cases; a list of women murdered by husbands or boyfriends in a single year in the state of Michigan (to demonstrate that the women we represented were more likely to have been murdered than survivors); drafts of legislation on changing sentencing guidelines for battered women defendants written by our attorneys; drafts of legislation written by women prisoners; examples of legislation in other states, such as the habeas law in California allowing women whose cases are linked to battering to apply for parole; information about torture in the segregation unit; Clemency Project brochures; and current bills we were supporting (e.g., for reinstatement of credits for good behavior, against life sentences for juveniles).

Clemencies for Battered Women in Michigan Prisons, 2008–2010

During her final years in office, between 2008 and 2010, Governor Jennifer Granholm granted 28 clemencies to women and 147 to men (*State of Michigan Journal*, 2010). About 2,000 applications were submitted during those last few years. Only 10 clemencies were granted to women convicted of serious crimes (murder or conspiracy), whereas the remaining 18 went to women who had minor drug and probation offenses or terminal medical cases. All but 1 of the 10 clemencies for women convicted of serious crimes went to aiders and abettors of male codefendants who actually committed the crimes. The one exception was a factually innocent woman who was supported by the federal court and represented by the University of Michigan Law School. During the same time, the parole board released five women from parolable life sentences, all of whom were also aiders and abettors. Such releases of "lifers" by the parole board were an anomaly. For decades, the Michigan parole board had held prisoners long past their release dates and refused to release any prisoner serving a parolable life sentence, in opposition to the law (Louisell, 2003).

Although they were politically safe and painfully few in number, the releases that were granted during that period were remarkable in a state that had long been known for its harsh sentencing practices and for spending a larger percentage of its general budget on corrections than any other state in the United States (see Sigritz, 2007, p. 60).

The Michigan Women's Justice & Clemency Project represented more than 40 women for clemency or parole during that period. About half of them were serving life sentences. Only four women were among the 10 who were granted clemency from serious crimes (although we also supported two women who submitted their own successful clemency petitions), and two of the four received paroles (we also supported one more who submitted her own successful bid for parole). The women we represented who were granted clemency or parole from life sentences during that period were

•Linda Hamilton, murder 1, life. In 1976 Linda's husband assaulted her, raped her 4-year-old daughter, held her and the children hostage, and then stalked them when they escaped. She filed complaints with police and doctors but nothing was done to protect her or her children. Linda's trial judge testified at her commutation hearing (at age 93, he arrived aided by a walker with former governor and Mrs. William Milliken, our staunchest supporters in the Clemency Project), stating he did not have all the facts at her bench trial and this was the only time he ever requested a commutation in a case. Linda was granted clemency in 2009.

•Doreen Washington, murder 1, conspiracy, life. Doreen's violent husband set her on fire and beat her and the children constantly. Police would not take her complaints when she went to the police station. Her foster son shot her husband to protect the family. Doreen served 20 years. She had support from her trial judge and was granted clemency in 2008.

•Minnie Boose, murder 1, life. Minnie hired an acquaintance to kill her abusive husband and served 29 years. She received clemency in 2009.

•Levonne Roberts, murder 1, life. Levonne was terrorized by her violent boyfriend, and after he killed a man she immediately reported it to police. Nevertheless, she was convicted of first-degree murder along with her boyfriend and served 25 years. She was granted clemency in 2009.

•Barbara Anderson, murder 2, life. She served almost 20 years for the death of her violent husband, who was killed by a friend. Detroit police threatened her and screamed at her, threw chairs, and finally terrorized her into "confessing." The victim's family fully supported her release from the beginning because they knew she was violently abused. Barbara was paroled from her life sentence in 2009.

•Mildred Perry, murder 2, conspiracy, life. Mildred was convicted in the 1979 death of her abusive husband who beat and terrorized her throughout their marriage. She told her story to a psychic, who hired a killer. The psychic was never prosecuted; the killer served 12 years. Millie received parole in 2008 after serving 29 years.

Although we celebrated every woman's release, we mourned the lost opportunity for many more who deserved their freedom but remained in prison.

Conclusion

Over the years it has been disheartening to see women unjustly prosecuted, tried, and sentenced for acting in their own defense against abusers when police, prosecutors, courts, and social systems failed to provide them with equal protection. Although granting clemency to women who committed crimes for their own survival may not change the criminal processing system, it does serve to publicly challenge legalized discrimination and communicate the need for feminist change. Without it, there is no hope for justice for those who are unfairly sentenced to life in prison.

In the end, it was undoubtedly our friends and supporters in policy making, media, and other positions close to the governor (legislators, judges, ministers, and especially former Governor Milliken) who had the greatest influence on the governor's action. Our small focused groups of graduate students in social work were crucial to our ability to place greater pressure on those in power as well as to research and file clemency petitions, produce public rallies and events, and expand our media coverage—all of which provided a climate of public support and sympathy for battered women's (and other prisoners') releases.

Going in and out of the women's prisons in Michigan for more than two decades, we have seen the culture of the women's prisons become more inhuman and the physical condition of women's incarceration deteriorate as they struggled to survive in jammed-together, vermin-infested cubicles and cages. We have known a number of women who died, some by their own hand, others from medical neglect. Harsh, punitive sentencing has caused severely overcrowded women's prisons nationally and globally, while cutbacks in food, medical care, programs, and facilities have produced gnawing hunger and physical and mental health crises inside (Atwood, 2000; Davis, 1998; Davis & Shaylor, 2001). Top-down, ossified attitudes in the name of "security" became convenient cover-ups for a demented regime of cruelty (Cusac, 2009; Davis, 2005). Prisoner suicides and suicide attempts have increased dramatically in recent years, especially in Michigan, and especially among young, mentally ill, and lesbian women who are the most often targeted for harassment and assault by officers. Investigators and consultants who advocate for improved conditions in prisons are ignored by officials even when they suggest only minor solutions to a system that Angela Davis (2005), Michelle Alexander (2010), Ann-Marie Cusac (2009), and others have identified as obsolete and broken beyond repair.

Feminist perspectives that provide a critical awareness about the ways so-called gender-blind and neutral laws are bigoted and destructive also reveal how the criminal/legal/penal system functions within the larger logic of global capitalism to produce gender inequality, violence against women, increasing rates of women's incarceration, and punitive public policies. More important, they offer a radical solution through the abolition of the international prison industry and a profound respect for the human and civil rights of all the world's citizens—that is, the right to food, housing, health care, education, compassionate care for the disabled and mentally ill, and freedom from wrongful imprisonment, torture, and war—that will create a world we can now only imagine.

Suggestions for Class Exercises and Assignments

Invite students to work in pairs or teams to

1. Find state, national, and global data and statistics on women's lawbreaking and incarceration.

2. Learn about the status of women in prison in their state or region. For example, the number of women incarcerated, reasons for incarceration and lengths of sentences, number of women incarcerated for convictions related to defending themselves against abuse, existence and publications of advocacy organizations, special court or jail programs for sex workers, domestic violence shelters, and survivor programs.

3. Research model legislation, protocols, and landmark lawsuits regarding violence against women, gender inequality, and processing of women by the legal system.

4. Research news articles on women's criminal cases and go to county clerks' offices to study the public records and case files, or send freedom of information act requests to police departments for reports on particular criminal cases.

5. Conduct teach-ins or speak-outs or other public events to present and share data and stories and invite advocates, columnists, scholars, activists, legislators, and so on to speak and learn about the issues.

References

Alexander, M. (2010). *The new Jim Crow: Mass incarceration in the age of colorblindness.* New York, NY: The New Press.

Allard, S. (1991). Rethinking the battered woman syndrome: A Black feminist perspective. *UCLA Women's Law Journal, 1*(1), 191–207.

American Civil Liberties Union. (2013) *Women in Prison.* Retrieved from http://www.aclu.org/prisoners-rights/women-prison

Ammons, L. A. (1995.) Mules, madonnas, babies, bathwater, racial imagery and stereotypes: The African-American woman and the battered woman syndrome, *Wisconsin Law Review, 5,* 1003–1080.

Amnesty International. (1999). *Not part of my sentence: Violations of the human rights of women in custody.* Washington, DC: Author.

Amnesty International. (2004). *Amnesty international launches global campaign to stop violence against women.* Retrieved from http://www.amnesty.org.uk/news_details.asp?NewsID=15231

Atwood, J. E. (2000). *Too much time: Women in prison.* London, UK: Phaidon Press.

Belknap, J. (2001). *The invisible woman: Gender, crime, and justice.* (3rd ed.). Belmont, CA: Thomson/Wadsworth.

Bloom, B., Owen, B., & Covington, S. (2003). *Research, practice, and guiding principles for women offenders: Gender-responsive strategies.* Washington, DC: U.S. Department of Justice, National Institute of Corrections.

Brasier, L. L. (2005, January 25). Seaman jury rejects battered wife claim. *Detroit Free Press,* p. A1.

Browne, A. (1987). *When battered women kill.* New York, NY: The Free Press.

Buel, S. M. (2003). Effective assistance of counsel for battered women defendants: A normative construct. *Harvard Women's Law Journal, 26,* 217–350.

Callahan, R. (1994). Will the "real" battered woman please stand up? In search of a realistic legal definition of battered woman syndrome. *American University Journal of Gender, Social Policy & the Law, 3*(1), 117–152.

Campbell, J. C., Webster, D., Koziol-McLain, J., Block, C. R., Campbell, D., Curry, M. A., . . . & Wilt, S. A. (2003). Assessing risk factors for intimate partner homicides. *National Institute of Justice Journal, 250,* 18.

Carson, E. A., & Sabol, W. J. (2012). *Prisoners in 2011.* Washington, DC: Bureau of Justice Statistics.

Charter of the United Nations. (n.d.). *Chapter VII: Actions with respect to threats to the peace, breaches of the peace, and acts of aggression.* Retrieved from http://www.un.org/en/documents/charter/chapter7.shtml

Chesney-Lind, M., & Pasko, L. J. (1997). *The female offender: Girls, women, and crime.* Thousand Oaks, CA: SAGE.

Chesney-Lind, M., & Pollock-Byrne, J. (1995). Women's prisons: Equality with a vengeance. In A. Merlo & J. Pollock (Eds.), *Women, law and social control* (pp. 155–175). Boston, MA: Allyn & Bacon.

Coker, D. (2001). Crime control and feminist law reform in domestic violence law: A critical review. *Buffalo Criminal Law Review, 4,* 801–860.

Cusac, A. M. (2009). *Cruel and unusual: The culture of punishment in America.* New Haven, CT: Yale University Press.

Davis, A. Y. (1998). Public imprisonment and private violence: Reflections on the hidden punishment of women. *New England Journal on Criminal and Civil Confinement, 24,* 339–351.

Davis, A. Y. (2003). *Are prisons obsolete?* New York, NY: Seven Stories Press.

Davis, A. Y., & Shaylor, C. (2001). Race, gender, and the prison industrial complex in California and beyond. *Meridians: Feminism, race, transnationalism, 2*(1), 1–25.

Dragiewicz, M., & Lindgren, Y. (2009). The gendered nature of domestic violence: Statistical data for lawyers considering equal protection analysis. *American University Journal of Gender, Social Policy, & the Law, 17,* 229–260.

Elk, M., & Sloan, B. (2011, August 1). The hidden history of ALEC and prison labor. *Nation*, p. 1. Retrieved from http://www.thenation.com/article/162478/hidden-history-alec-and-prison-labor#

Faludi, S. (1991). *Backlash: The undeclared war against American women*. New York, NY: Crown.

Foucault, M. (1995). *Discipline and punish: The birth of the prison* (2nd ed.). New York, NY: Random House.

Gagné, P. (1998). *Battered women's justice: The movement for clemency and the politics of self-defense*. New York, NY: Twayne.

Gave, K. (1980, June 17). Professor says Thomas too timid to plan murder. *Lansing State Journal*, B-1.

Gillespie, C. (1989). *Justifiable homicide: Battered women, self-defense, and the law*. Columbus, OH: Ohio State University Press.

Greene, J., Frost, N., & Pranis, K. (2006). *The punitiveness report: Hard hit: The growth in the imprisonment of women, 1977–2004*. New York, NY: Women's Prison Association.

Hallinan, J. T. (2001). *Going up the river: Travels in a prison nation*. New York, NY: Random House.

Human Rights Watch. (1995). *The Human Rights Watch global report on women's human rights*. New York, NY: Author.

Human Rights Watch. (1998). *Nowhere to hide: Retaliation against women in Michigan state prisons*. *Human Rights Watch, 10*(2). Retrieved from http://www.hrw.org/reports98/women/

Human Rights Watch. (2013). *World report 2012*. Retrieved from http://www.hrw.org/world-report-2012

Hunt, A. (2007, March 16) A fresh start: A Wayne County rehabilitation program is giving women caught in a cycle of drugs and prostitution a way out. *Detroit Free Press*.

Jacobsen, C. (1986). The creative politics of Greenham Common Women's Peace Camp. *Heresies: Journal of Women in Art and Politics, 20*, 60–65.

Jacobsen, C. (Director). (1994). *From one prison* [Videotape/DVD]. United States: Human Rights Watch.

Jacobsen, C. (Director). (1997). *Clemency* [Videotape/DVD]. United States: University of Michigan.

Jacobsen, C. (Director). (2000). *Segregation unit* [Videotape/DVD]. United States: Amnesty International.

Jacobsen, C. (2008). Creative politics and women's criminalization in the United States. *Signs: Journal of Women in Culture and Society, 33*(2), 462–470.

Kupers, T. A. (2010). The role of misogyny and homophobia in prison sexual abuse. *UCLA Women's Law Journal, 18*, 107–130.

Lerner, R. L. (2006). The worldwide popular revolt against proportionality in self-defense law. *Journal of Law, Economics & Policy, 331*, 2.

Louisell, P. C. (2003). Unfair parole board interpretation of lifer law. *Michigan Criminal Law Annual Journal, 1*(1), 29–30.

Love, M. C. (2010). The twilight of the pardon power. *Journal of Criminal Law and Criminology, 100*, 1169, 1175–1195.

Lyon, A. D., Hughes, E., & Thomas, J. (2001). *People v. Juanita Thomas*: A battered women's journey to freedom. *Women & Criminal Justice, 13*(1), 27–63.

Maguigan, H. (1991). Battered women and self-defense: Myths and misconceptions in current reform proposals. *University of Pennsylvania Law Review, 140*(2), 379–486.

Mahoney, M. R. (1991). Legal images of battered women: Redefining the issue of separation. *Michigan Law Review, 90*(1), 1–94.

McColgan, A. (1993). In defence of battered women who kill. *Oxford Journal of Legal Studies, 13*(4), 508–529.

Nourse, V. F. (2001). Self-defense and subjectivity. *University of Chicago Law Review, 68*, 1235–1308.

Neal et al. v. Michigan Department of Corrections et al. (1997). 454 Mich. 886; 562 NW2d 201.

Nunn et al. v. Michigan Department of Corrections et al. (1993). 96-CV-71416-DT.

Pearl, J. (1987). The highest paying customers: American cities and the cost of prostitution control. *Hastings Law Journal, 38*(4), 769–800.

People v. Juanita Thomas. (1983). 126 Mich. App. 611; 337 NW2d 598.

People v. Lekisha Danielle Hines. (2011). 2011 Mich. App. 6.

People v. Nancy Seaman. (2007). 480 Mich. 888, 738 NW2d 736.

People v. Quiana Kenisha Lovett. (2012) Mich. 855; 820 NW2d 802.

Quester, N. (2007). Refusing to remove an obstacle to the remedy: The Supreme Court's decision in *Town of Castle Rock v. Gonzales* continues to deny domestic violence victims meaningful recourse. *Akron Law Review, 40*, 391–434.

Ramsey, C. B. (2010). Provoking change: Comparative insights on feminist homicide law reform. *Journal of Criminal Law & Criminology, 100*(1), 33–108.

Rozenberg, J. (2010, September 10). Battered women who kill to be main beneficiaries as homicide law changes, *The Guardian*. Retrieved from http://www.guardian.co.uk/law/2010/sep/30/murder-law-reform

Schneider, E. M. (2000). *Battered women & feminist lawmaking*. New Haven, CT: Yale University Press.

Sigritz, B. (2007). *State expenditure report fiscal year 2006*. National Association of State Budget Officers. Retrieved from http://www.nasbo.org/sites/default/files/ER_2006.pdf

Smart, C. (1989). *Feminism and the power of law*. London, UK: Routledge.

Snell, T. L. (1994) *Women in prison*. Washington, DC: Bureau of Justice Statistics.

State of Michigan Journal of the House of Representatives, 95th Legislature, Regular Session, No. 90. (2010). Retrieved from http://www.legislature.mi.gov/(S(w1rjm3nkjs1iuhzsbd5qes3c))/documents/2009-2010/Journal/House/pdf/2010-HJ-11-04-090.pdf

Sudbury, J. (2002). Celling Black bodies: Black women in the global prison industrial complex. *Feminist Review, 80*, 57–74.

Trent, C. (2006). *Street level prostitution and drug abuse in the city of Detroit*. Detroit, IL: Detroit Department of Health and Wellness Promotion.

United Nations Commission on Human Rights. (1996). *Report of the Human Rights Committee*. New York, NY: Author.

U.S. Department of Justice. (1996). *The validity and use of evidence concerning battering and its effects in criminal trials*. Retrieved from https://www.ncjrs.gov/pdffiles/batter.pdf

Walker, L. (1979). *The battered woman*. New York, NY: Harper and Row.

Whitcomb v. Sizemore et al. (1996). Michigan Civil Case 06-638722CK.

CHAPTER 5

"Why Study if I Can Be in Somebody's Video?"

Challenging the Hypersexualization of Young Black Girls in the United States

TONISHA TAYLOR

I have this one prayer I say all the time, every night, for my ass to swell up. . . . Yes that's my number one prayer, to give me a big ass. The titties is all right, but the ass is kinda flat. The bitch is wide, but it ain't got no weight on it! I see the brothers know what I mean when I say some weight on it. I want me one of them call-a-call asses, you know. I want an ass so big that when I'm walking through the club, a man could just take his drink and lay it up on my ass, and I don't even know it's there. I'm just moving' on through the club and shit; knocking drinks off the tables and shit, movin' tablecloths over and shit. I want me a big ol' ign'ant ass. The kind of ass you just frown up, you be like, dayum! I want an ass so big that if I'm on top, he roll me over, I'm still on top. It's a wrap around ass.
—Sommore, as cited in Parasecoli (2007, p. 120)

In the film *Queens of Comedy* Black comedienne Sommore offers this provocative, over-the-top depiction of her ideal "booty." Cultural scholar Fabio Parasecoli (2007), who studies issues of race and gender in media, notes that the Black comediennes in *Queens of Comedy* use the rhythm, language, and postures of rappers and male comedians in ways that seem misogynist, objectifying, and self-deprecating, despite claims of self-affirmation. Beneath the humor lie

101

serious questions about the ways Black girls receive, interpret, and internalize hypersexualized messages about bodies and behaviors. There has been considerable research and media discussion about the hypersexualized activities of and subsequent outcomes for young Black girls. A range of published research highlights the correlation of overly sexualized behavior among young Black women with negative self-esteem, premarital sex, unplanned pregnancy, and sexually transmitted diseases (Brown, 2006; Hobson, 2003; Keyes, 2000; West, 1995). However, data is limited regarding the macrolevel construction, marketing, and globalized circulation of these racialized and sexualized media messages in diverse venues (e.g., television, print ads, music, and the Internet). There is also a lack of focus on the microlevel in terms of the everyday internalizations of media messages these young girls receive. In this chapter I draw on critical race feminism and culturally relevant pedagogy (CRP) to address both of these questions. I briefly explore the circulation of these images in historical and contemporary contexts and consider some of the current research addressing the effects of these images and messages on the self-esteem and identity formation of young Black girls in the United States. I provide examples of practices and programs geared to help young girls develop critical media literacy so they can deconstruct and challenge these images. I present my experience in facilitating a consciousness-raising group with young Black women at Sisterlink, a Harlem-based program that works primarily with Black women ages 18–35 as a demonstration of how CRP can be used in a group setting.

I came into young adulthood in Brooklyn, New York, during the late 1990s. At that time female rappers Lil' Kim and Foxy Brown dominated the hip-hop scene with a message that was much different from their predecessors, Queen Latifah and MC Lyte. Shouts of "Ladies first!" and "Who you calling a bitch?" quickly morphed into "I'm a throw shade if I can't get paid/blow you up to your girl like the Army grenade" (Lil' Kim, 1996, track 6) and "My sex drive all night like a trucker" (Foxy Brown, 1997, track 12). I proudly sang along with the latter lyrics, taking pride in my sexual liberty and ability to choose my sexual partners without concern about the larger context, much like the two women I fiercely idolized.

Nearly a decade later, as I have settled into a career as a social worker and an educator, I have found faults in my prior logic. After years of reexamining patriarchal standards through a feminist lens, I began to adopt a new outlook.

While co-opting the sexual freedom purported by the likes of Lil' Kim and Foxy Brown, I found that this stance still called attention to a willingness to be objectified and subjugated by men. This led to an intense reflection on whether exchanging sexual favors for clothes, money, or just a good time was worth it. I believe that at the time I lost the sense of the true value of my self-worth, which I equated with my ability to obtain tangible goods. Since the explosion of social media and reality shows, there have been many instances of young Black women who have been caught in compromising situations and have been heavily vilified for it. These occurrences, juxtaposed with the sentiments of some of my former students when this subject was discussed, led me to examine the issue of the hypersexualization of Black women in a broader context.

Black Girls, Hypersexualization, and Globalization

The widespread connotation of Black women as hypersexualized beings is not a new phenomenon. In the 19th century, according to Sander Gilman (1985a), the Black female was often portrayed by White male observers as possessing not only a "primitive" sexual appetite, but also the external signs of this temperament—"primitive" genitalia (p. 213). The White Western colonizing gaze became fixated on the Black female body, subjecting her to endless pseudoscientific scrutiny that was at once objectifying, sexualizing, and pathologizing (Gilman, 1985b). Correlating with this time period was the "discovery" of Sarah Baartman, most commonly known at the time as the "Hottentot Venus." *Hottentot*, which now has offensive connotations, was the name 17th-century White European colonizers gave to the Khoisan people of southwestern Africa; Venus refers to the Roman goddess of love. Baartman possessed a body type with large buttocks common to Khoisan women but deemed unusual and a subject of prurient interest to the White colonists. Baartman, who had been enslaved by Dutch colonizers near Capetown, was taken from her Khoisan people in South Africa and brought to Europe, where she was promised wealth for being placed on exhibit (Crais & Scully, 2008). In Europe Baartman's body (with great emphasis on her buttocks and elongated labia) was stigmatized as an illness called steatopygia. This stigmatization served as a marker of pathology and of difference between African and European women, differentiating the undesirable from the acceptable in society (Gilman, 1985b). Baartman was soon relegated to performing in circus acts, and as Hobson (2003) states:

Thomson notes that Baartman's London show was framed within a context of freakery, in which other "freak shows" on Piccadilly Circus existed alongside hers. She asserts that "absolutely no distinction existed between this African woman, whose body shape was typical of her group, and the conjoined twins, congenital amputees, or dwarfs who also fall outside the narrow, culturally constructed borders that distinguish the normal from the abnormal." (p. 90)

Sadly, Baartman met a tragic end at the early age of 26. She died ill and poor, though her journey was far from over. Her body was dissected by the surgeon general of France for observation. Her genitalia and brain were preserved and examined, as well as her skeleton and a mold casting of her buttocks. Baartman's body remained on display in museums until the late 1970s, and it was not until 2002 that her remains were returned to and interred in South Africa. Although Baartman met an early demise, several other Hottentot Venuses were similarly scrutinized, displayed, and objectified.

As shown by this discussion, any ethnicity that does not fit into the ascribed idealization of the European aesthetic can be viewed as an eroticized and often pathologized *other*. The Hottentot's image became the de facto representation of the presumed inferior, abnormal Black woman. Concurrently, another image surfaced—that of the Jezebel. Carolyn West (1995) describes the Jezebel as a mixed-race woman with more European features, such as thin lips, straight hair, and a slender nose. The image is rooted in Biblical references to the Phoenician princess who engaged in religious and political intrigues and associated with false prophets, thus marking her as powerful and dangerous. Jezebel differs from the Hottentot Venus because she was presumed to have an insatiable appetite for sex and used her sexuality to manipulate and seduce for her benefit (Dunn, 2008). Historically, the Jezebel image was used to justify the objectification and rape of Black women. More recently, the image has become celebrated as a sex symbol in popular culture, and many successful non-European entertainers and models have been characterized as possessing the dangerously seductive attributes and attraction of Jezebel (Beyoncé, Halle Berry, Jennifer Lopez, Nicole Scherzinger, and Shakira, to name a few).

A late 20th-century trend was the overt raunchiness of female entertainers and the creation and widespread dissemination of so-called video vixens to a mass consumer audience. Some have raised questions regarding these women's willingness to self-objectify for the benefit of money, fame, or status. Perhaps the more important questions concern (a) how these particular images have gained such popularity and (b) how these images affect the sense of identity and esteem of young girls who are regularly exposed to them.

With the pervasiveness of hip-hop, pop culture, and the subsequent rise of video vixens, internalization of what is desirable for women in the urban community occurs as early as grade school. Raunchy images, prevalent in hip-hop culture, target young women from all ethnic and racial backgrounds through their inclusion in media-hyped programs such as Music Television's *Sucker Free Countdown* and Black Entertainment Television's *106th and Park* (Henry, 2010). More often than not, it is made clear that in the music videos aired on these programs the object of desire must possess the requisite "big booty," long hair, and fair-skinned complexion (e.g., in rapper Yung L.A.'s 2010 song "Taser Gun," he states, "light skin long hair dats the beauty queen/she the kinda of girl you see up on da movie screen" [Austin, 2010]); be scantily clad; and demonstrate the ability to perform incredible sex acts. These expectations are also amplified by the young men who listen to these lyrics and then expect the women of the community not only to look like the video vixens but also to perform the sexual acts they depict on screen and in print media.

According to Townsend, Thomas, Neilands, & Jackson (2010) the Black women who engage in these hypersexualized music video performances may influence young Black girls to view the exploitation of their sexuality as a viable option. As West (1995) argues, if a young Black woman is socialized through the media to perceive her sexuality as a material asset, it may become more of a tool for negotiation and manipulation than an expression of pleasure and caring. Some writers suggest that exposure to these hypersexualized images may lead to an internalization of a self-image that overemphasizes particular physical attributes of the body. In turn, this internalized image may affect how young Black women learn to interact with men. For example, Stephens and Few (2007) attempted to gauge the perceptions of young African American adolescents in regard to sexualized images of Black female entertainers. They found that young Black girls internalize not only images from the media but also expectations of their male peers. As one participant responded, "[Boys] want the girl who will give them sex and looks good, too. Boys like girls like these and want us to be like them" (p. 57).

West (1995) contends that we are witnessing a collective decline of self-esteem in young Black women in relation to images of sexism, racism, and gender prejudice that are ubiquitous in hip-hop. The everyday consumption of cultural and interpersonal messages regarding sexual images has a direct effect on young Black girls' sexual self-identity, behaviors, and experiences (Stephens & Few, 2007, p. 252). Mass consumption of these perceptions and expectations contributes to the sociological and psychological challenges faced by young Black women coming of age in the United States in the early 21st century.

Particular trends and events in news reports illustrate some of these concerns regarding self-image. For example, an increase in illegal posterior augmentations, commonly known as "butt injections," has been reported. Many women who cannot afford the legitimate surgery (with hefty price tags ranging from $8,000 to $18,000) have reverted to subjecting themselves to illegal procedures by ill-qualified individuals in makeshift operating rooms (Lupkin, 2012). As reported by Dale (2012), individuals usually seek out this service through word of mouth, "pumping parties," or through covert blogs on the Internet. In addition, according to the report, the price for illegal procedures can cost approximately $1,000; however, the risk of death is increasingly higher than it is with a safe sterile procedure. According to the website http://www.advancedplasticsuergeysolutions.com, in a legal procedure performed by a licensed medical professional, fat is taken from an area of the individual's body (such as thighs or stomach) and injected into the buttocks. According to the Associated Press report, in an illegal procedure, synthetic materials such as caulk, industrial silicone, and hydrogel are used, and injections of these materials into the body for any purpose can have fatal consequences.

One such case occurred in February 2011 when Claudia Aderotimi, an aspiring rapper/actress of African descent from Great Britain, traveled from England to a motel in Philadelphia for a second round of illegal buttock injections after failing an audition for producers who said her buttocks needed to be bigger (Dale, 2012). The expectation of the male producers and their demands, which Aderotimi tragically tried to fulfill, reflect the centuries-old gaze of the patriarchal colonizer, at once objectifying and denigrating. For generations women have acted and reacted to the preferences and directives of men in exchange for survival, affection, financial gain, and social ascension. According to a story in the *Daily Mail*, after receiving the $1,800 silicone injection, Aderotimi complained of shortness of breath and chest pains. She was rushed to a local hospital, where she was pronounced dead. According to the preliminary autopsy report, the silicone was injected directly into her bloodstream and subsequently induced a heart attack (Bates, Fernandez, & Bains, 2011).

Although little or no data exists to support the popularity of buttock enhancements among young Black women, a subtler psychological and sociological approach is being undertaken by others. For example, in February 2012 rapper Too Short was asked to give "fatherly advice" to young boys about how to "turn girls out" in a video for *XXL Magazine* that went viral (Ramsey, 2012). Using explicit language and details, he advised the young boys to "push her up against the wall, take your finger and put a little spit on it and you stick your finger in her underwear and you rub it on there and watch what happens." The video has since been removed, and Too Short later apologized for his words. Unfortunately, this message, coupled with incidents of young Black girls being videotaped engaging in explicitly sexual activity in locations such as school halls and playgrounds can have a significantly damaging effect on what are already fragile egos of these young girls. As Gina McCauley (2012), founder of the Black woman's advocacy blog "What About Our Daughters," states in her online article, "Misogyny and sexual violence committed against young Black girls is normalized in far too many Black communities." What compounds the severity of this issue is the global stage on which these events take place. The widespread circulation, reproduction, and consumption of these images through global media sources serve to reinforce distorted norms of appearance and actions.

In light of the historical context and the power of contemporary media that serve to augment the image of Black girls as hypersexualized, it is imperative that social service workers be adequately prepared to address these issues. Insights from critical race/feminist theory and critical cultural pedagogy are instructive and are discussed in more detail in the following section. First, it is essential that social workers gain a more critical understanding of these images and their rootedness in histories of misogyny and racism shaped by colonialism. Too often, social workers resort to individual behavioral explanations and interventions that fail to grasp the historical, cultural, political, and economic context and complexity of the issue. Social workers also need to develop critical media literacy so we can better appreciate the problems faced by young girls in their contemporary community contexts. We need to be able to engage girls in deconstructing and challenging systematic practices of exoticizing and pathologizing the other and of the global circulation and marketing of these images. Using a strengths-based approach, we can recognize young Black girls as critical consumers of media who are able to question and challenge received messages rather than simply internalize them. Once we recognize young Black girls as potential critics and active agents rather than passive subjects of media, we can creatively engage them in processes of consciousness-raising and change. In the following section I offer two practice examples informed by critical race/feminist theory and critical cultural pedagogy that open possibilities for social work intervention.

Constructing an Effective Approach

Many young Black women of the hip-hop generation are fully aware of the negative global media messages portraying them as immoral, uncontrolled, aggressive, fertile, and hypersexual objects (Henry, 2010). There have been several high-profile protests against hip-hop artists who have displayed blatantly raunchy images of Black women in their videos or live concerts, such as Spelman University's rally against rapper Nelly's visit in 2004. In his now infamous video for the song "Tip Drill" the rapper swiped a credit card down the buttocks of a Black model in the video. Unfortunately, protest efforts have not been powerful enough to trigger a larger movement or to deter rappers from crafting heavily misogynistic songs and music videos. Often doubly jeopardized, Black female identity is rendered partially invisible in race and gender studies—either it is subsumed into feminist discourse that unapologetically represents White women, or it is neglected in Black histories that utterly privilege the male voice and body (Wayne, 2009). The challenge for social workers is to develop practices that build on the constitutive characteristics of what appear on the surface to be dysfunctional behaviors to develop strategies that draw out the positive dimensions of the adaptations young people make to their troubling circumstances (Munford & Sanders, 2008). Because of cultural gaps and disparities between antiquated theoretical concepts of social work and the contemporary issues facing young Black girls, especially in urban settings, new frameworks and subsequent approaches must be constructed. Continually telling young

Black girls they are under attack by oppressive forces without giving them the tools necessary to combat these forces is futile. Generic sex education classes that give redundant information about HIV/STD statistics and distribute condoms do not address the heart of the issue, which is largely rooted in myriad pervasive sociological factors, as previously noted.

Helping people empower themselves means helping them rid themselves of internalized oppression and to come to a critical understanding of the oppressive situation (Burstow, 1991). Having worked with several social service agencies in the New York metropolitan area that attempted to assist young Black women, I have noted that although tangible services (such as transportation, rental, and financial assistance) helped these women deal with barriers to their activities of daily life, efforts to reach a level of conscientiousness that allowed the young women to critically examine their life choices and circumstances were futile. This futility was not solely attributed to the clients, as the agencies themselves lacked frameworks for practitioners to use. In working with this population, an aggregation of two theories and a theoretical framework—critical race theory (CRT), critical race feminism, and CRP—offers promising results. Each concept is briefly discussed to examine the benefits of using these lenses to assist this population understand this complex nexus of micro- and macro issues of global circulation of imagery and the tensions of internalization and resistance.

CRT clearly lets people of all races know that individually and collectively their voices are heard, that they matter, and their presence and contributions are valued (Brown-Jeffy & Cooper, 2011, 73). CRT emerged in the late 1980s, stemming from the frustration of various scholars such as Derrick Bell and Patricia Williams, who felt limited by work that separated critical theory from conversations about race and racism (Yosso, 2005). According to Solorzano (1997), at least five themes form CRT's basic perspectives, research methods, and pedagogy: the centrality and intersectionality of race and racism, the challenge to dominant ideology, commitment to social justice, the centrality of experiential knowledge, and an interdisciplinary perspective. CRT can provide young Black women with a perspective on being labeled as hypersexualized by the larger public. First, returning to the pseudoscientific studies of the 19th century in which Black women's bodies were objectified, sexualized, and pathologized, CRT can be used to challenge this dominant ideology, which is still given credence. Second, young Black women can scrutinize the role that racism plays in upholding this belief system. Finally, when provided with the opportunity and encouragement to do so, these women can offer their personal experiences of grappling with this issue. For example, if a young girl was the target of street harassment from young men who labeled her a "ho" in emulation of what they have internalized from popular culture, she can share this information without fear of admonishment by other participants who have had similar experiences.

Although CRT gives immense insight into the experiences of people of color, these experiences are largely voiced through men of color, leaving women of color nearly mute. Critical race feminism, a concept that has emerged after years of work by scholars such as Venus Evans-Winters, Patricia Hill Collins, and Kimberle Crenshaw, serves to bridge this gap by examining the intersections of race, class, and gender, with great emphasis on how the latter has important effects. Critical race feminism offers multiple possibilities for the amelioration of Black female education and quality of life (Evans-Winters & Esposito, 2010). As explained by Evans-Winters and Esposito, critical race feminism is beneficial to the examination of how Black girls are affected by stating that the experiences (and perspectives) of women of color are different from the experiences of men of color and those of White women. The acknowledgment of this differentiation is crucial, because whereas Black men are applauded for studlike behavior in popular culture, Black women are denounced for similar behavior. It is common for a Black male rapper to brag about having sexual relations with multiple women, but Black women are labeled with derogatory slurs for the same practice. Similarly, White women have been upheld for centuries as the epitome of femininity according to social constructs, whereas Black women were (and are) seen as the opposite. Critical race feminism also examines the intersections of race, class, and gender within the system of White male patriarchy and racist oppression while asserting that there are multiple identities and forms of consciousness of women of color.

CRP serves as a framework for raising awareness in young people while assisting them in developing cultural competence and achieving academic success. CRP provides individuals with the tools necessary to critically analyze their environment, which in turn leads to self-empowerment and ridding themselves of internalized oppression. This approach is deeply rooted in the social justice movement in education, which was largely influenced by Paulo Freire. CRP, like CRT, recognizes the value of the life experiences of marginalized groups in understanding and making meaning of the world (Brown-Jeffy & Cooper, 2011). As defined by Gloria Ladson-Billings (1995), CRP rests on three criteria or propositions: students must (a) experience academic success, (b) develop and maintain cultural competence, and (c) develop a critical consciousness through which they challenge the current status quo of the social order. From this concept, Brown-Jeffy and Cooper constructed a conceptual framework of CRP that entails the following five themes: (1) identity and achievement, (2) equity and excellence, (3) developmental appropriateness, (4) teaching the whole child, and (5) student–teacher relationships. The first two themes hinge on identifying the student and teacher, which lays the groundwork for the inclusion of multicultural content students need to thrive. By using relevant and appropriate content the third theme prepares students to apply newly acquired knowledge beyond the classroom setting. The fourth and fifth themes address the student-in-environment dynamic, which calls on the educator to continually cultivate the students' awareness while allowing them to develop autonomously. This innovative framework offers a very practical approach that can be used not only in an academic setting but also in a social services agency. Education and social work are not mutually exclusive entities, as they are both cultivators of change agents. In the following section I demonstrate how the CRP approach was used to engage young Black women in critical consciousness-raising at Sisterlink, a social services agency in Harlem.

Use of CRP in a Group Setting

Sisterlink is a community-based program that operates under Northern Manhattan Perinatal Partnership, Inc. The program functions mainly as a referral source for high-risk pregnant women ages 18 to 35 and their families. Sisterlink also provides individual case management services and conducts weekly group meetings that offer a support system to its participants. During group meetings women are offered time to share any issues that are affecting them or to discuss social issues in a leisure environment; some members of the larger group formed a book club.

I was invited to sit in on one of the group meetings, which consisted of six women between the ages of 19 and 33 who resided in the neighborhood. Five of the women were of either African American or Afro-Caribbean descent.

The other woman, the program director, was of Caucasian and Jewish descent and was a lifelong resident of the Harlem neighborhood where the agency is located. During this group meeting the participants were examining photos that I brought in of popular Black female artists. The intent of this session was two pronged: First, I wanted to ascertain the women's viewpoints in regard to questions surrounding Black women's body images and representations of them in the larger society; and second, I wanted to rouse awareness of the implications of these images and their effect on young Black girls on micro- and macro levels.

As a group we examined 10 images of sexually provocative Black female entertainers in popular culture at different points in time, from the 19th century to the present day. After reviewing these images, the reactions from the young women were insightful, comical, and at times painful. They were representative of the dichotomy faced by Black girls: "At the end of the day, sex sells," as stated by one participant. This sentiment was supported by another participant, who added, "If doing this will ante up my bank account, I'm with it. I'll just see a therapist after." The program director posed an interesting question for the group: "Why study whatever if somebody told me I can sing and go on *American Idol*," to which a participant responded, "Or that I can look good and I can be in somebody's video?" The participant said she knew of several young Black women who prioritized their physical attributes as a means to obtain income over academic or vocational pursuits. This message has been conveyed to young Black women on a broader scale with the success of reality shows in which the characters are not traditionally employed (or employed at all), yet are enjoying the material goods enjoyed by someone who earns a six- to seven-figure annual salary.

This exercise addressed a majority of the CRP themes by presenting specific relevant content that resonated with the group and supplying a critical lens for examining not only the images but also the oppressive forces that augment the objectification of this particular population. Each participant was able to identify herself and the contexts in which she has dealt with attitudes and behaviors of others in regard to their beliefs about Black women and hypersexualization. Many recounted tales of street harassment, attempted molestation, and verbal abuse for rebuffing unwanted advances. The warm environment that I provided encouraged them to bring this type of communication to the forefront, and the young women were able to empathize with one another as well as build or strengthen bonds that transcended Sisterlink. Strengthened bonds, paired with a raised consciousness, can be successful results of this type of practice.

The Power of the Group

Although an oppressed group's experiences may put its members in a position to see things differently, their lack of control over the apparatuses of society that sustain ideological hegemony makes the articulation of their self-defined standpoint difficult (Hill-Collins, 1989, p. 749). This marginalization heightens the importance of group work among an oppressed group, in this case, young Black women. CRP can play a significant role in creating a context in which labeling young Black women as hypersexualized by the dominant culture can be critically discussed and in which inequitable power relations are interrogated and contested (Daniel, 2011).

One of the many benefits of working with groups in social work practice is the innovation that springs forth as a result of novel ideas based on different perspectives. Group work allows participants the autonomy to explore the many facets of their environment while in a safe setting where boundaries are respected. This process enables participants to share in an emotionally loaded space in which they can work together to seek insight into their respective issues and support one another toward adopting new behaviors, attitudes, and coping methods for obstacles they face. Many people tend to believe they suffer through experiences that are solely unique to them. As demonstrated by my participation with the group at Sisterlink, group work can assist in moving beyond that narrative to spark critical consciousness, create a foundation for resistance and new positive narratives, and encourage a community among all participants.

Conclusion

Even with Michelle Obama and Oprah Winfrey exalted as role models and endearing figures in American society, the video vixen still holds sway over many young Black girls. This begs a few questions, such as those posed by Gan, Zillman, and Mitrook (1997): Are the popular female Black rappers (and vixens) then heroes that bring desirable culture change—positive female sexual openness, in particular? Or are they, as has been feared, promoters of sexual servitude, which plays into the hands of men? Are they role models who encourage promiscuity among female teens? Or are their energetic performances sexually titillating aesthetic marvels that evoke fleeting thrills but fail to exert any lasting perceptual or dispositional influence? Though these questions can spark ongoing debates, the certainty is that there are overall effects on the psyche of young Black girls that stem from the stigma of hypersexualization. Issues revolving around mental and physical health, self-esteem, and interpersonal relationships can be rooted in how a girl perceives herself and can help determine which environmental influences she allows in her life. The incorporation of CRT, critical race feminism, and CRP by a knowledgeable, astute social worker who works with Black girls to conduct an honest, albeit painful, analysis into this issue will prove to be a beneficial tool not only for sound decision making but for a healthier way of living.

Discussion Questions and Activities

1. Consider your ethnic background and that of the population you work with. What is the larger society's opinion of that population? Is it favorable or unfavorable? How so?

2. What effect does this opinion have on you or the population you work with? Is there pressure to conform or rebuke society's largely held belief? Where does this pressure stem from?

3. Rapper Too Short's "fatherly advice" to young boys is reflective of the language and attitude rooted in misogyny. What other types of messages (subtle or overt) are being conveyed to youths by influential figures in popular culture?

4. As a practitioner, reflect on the images that were conveyed to you as a youth from popular culture.
   a. What were the images?
   b. Were they positive or negative?
   c. Did you internalize these images?
   d. How would you address your younger self now that you are equipped with a better understanding of the implication of these images?

5. Conduct an activity similar to the one used to engage the participants at Sisterlink. Have participants bring in images that encode either devaluaing or empowering messages about young women. Have the participants critically deconstruct the images as they ascertain the glaring and hidden messages.

6. Similarly, have participants bring in lyrics to their favorite songs and conduct the same type of deconstruction process.

7. Work in small groups (two to four people) to track the global circulation of a form of media (print, video, audio).

   a. Where did it originate?

   b. How is it funded (was there a major company backing it?)

   c. Where does it primarily appear?

   d. Why is it important to be aware of the issues raised in questions a–c?

References

Austin, L. (2010). *Taser gun*. On *Futuristic Leland* [CD] Atlanta, GA: RPS Entertainment & Grand Hustle.

Bates, D., Fernandez, C., & Bains, I. (2011, February 10). Tragic bottom implant: Girl thought having illegal injection would make her a hip hop star. *Mail Online*. Retrieved from http://www.daily mail.co.uk/news/article-1355080/Claudia-Aderotimi-thought-illegal-implant-make-hip-hop-star.html#ixzz2W6ttrJ00

Brown, R. (2006). *Black girlhood celebration: Toward a hip hop feminist pedagogy*. New York, NY: Peter Lang.

Brown-Jeffy, S., & Cooper, J. (2011). Toward a conceptual framework of culturally relevant pedagogy: An overview of the conceptual and theoretical literature. *Teacher Education Quarterly*, 38(1), 65–84.

Burstow, B. (1991). Freirian codifications and social work education. *Journal of Social Work Education*, 27, 196–207.

Crais, C., & Scully, P. (2008). *Sara Baartman and the Hottentot Venus: A ghost story and a biography*. Princeton, NJ: Princeton University Press.

Dale, M. (2012, May 16). Padge Windslowe's illegal butt injections caused lung damage, exotic dancer claims. *Associated Press*. Retrieved from http://www.huffingtonpost.com/2012/05/16/padge-windslowe-butt-implants_n_1522437.html

Daniel, C. (2011). Lessons learned: Pedagogical tensions and struggles with instruction on multiculturalism in social work education programs. *Social Work Education*, 30, 250–265.

Dunn, S. (2008). "Baad bitches" and sassy supermamas: Black power action films. Chicago, IL: University of Illinois Press.

Evans-Winters, V., & Esposito, J. (2010). Other people's daughters: Critical race feminism and Black girls' education. *Educational Foundations*, 24(1/2), 11–24.

Fernandez, C,. & Bates, D. (2011) Detectives hunt for transgender "doctor" over death of British student who had illegal bottom injection. Retrieved from http://www.dailymail.co.uk/news/article-1355605/Claudia-Aderotimi-dead-Police-hunt-transgender-doctor-injection.html

Foxy Brown. (1997). I'll be. On *Ill Na Na* [CD]. New York, NY: Def Jam.

Gan, S., Zillman, D., & Mitrook, M. (1997). Stereotyping effect of Black women's sexual rap on White audiences. *Basic and Applied Social Psychology*, 19(3), 381–399.

Gilman, S. (1985a). Black bodies, White bodies: Toward an iconography of female sexuality in late nineteenth century art, medicine and literature. *Critical Inquiry*, 12(1), 204–242.

Gilman, S. (1985b). *Difference and pathology: Stereotypes of sexuality, race, and madness.* Ithaca, NY: Cornell University Press.

Henry, W. (2010). Hip hop feminism: A standpoint to enhance the positive self-identity of Black college women. *Journal of Student Affairs Research and Practice, 47*(2), 139–156.

Hill Collins, P. (1989). The social construction of Black feminist thought. *Signs: Journal of Women in Culture and Society, 14*(4), 745–773.

Hobson, J. (2003). The "batty" politic: Toward an aesthetic of the Black female body. *Women, Art, and Aesthetics, 18*(4), 87–105.

Keyes, C. (2000). Empowering self, making choices, creating spaces: Black female identity via rap music performance. *Journal of American Folklore, 113*(449), 255–269.

Ladson-Billings, G. (2009). "Who you callin' nappy-headed?" A critical race theory look at the construction of Black women. *Race Ethnicity and Education, 12*(1), 87–99.

Lil' Kim. (1996). Crush on you. On *Hard Core* [CD]. New York, NY: Atlantic Records, Queen Bee Entertainment.

Lupkin, S. (2012). *Butt-injection death highlights underground plastic surgery growth* [Web log message]. Retrieved from http://abcnews.go.com/blogs/health/2012/09/26/butt-injection-death-highlights-underground-plastic-surgery-growth/

McCauley, G. (2012). *Bowing out of the Black community's reindeer games: XXL mag, Vanessa Satten, and Too Short* [Web log message] Retrieved from http://www.whataboutourdaughters.com/waod/2012/2/15/bowing-out-of-the-black-communitys-reindeer-gamesxxl-mag-van.html

Munford, R., & Sanders, J. (2008). Drawing out strengths and building capacity in social work with troubled young women. *Child and Family Social Work, 13*(1), 2–11.

Parasecoli, F. (2007). Bootylicious: Food and the female body in contemporary Black pop culture. *Women's Studies Quarterly 35*(1/2), 110–125.

Ramsey, D. X. (2012, February 14). Rapper Too Short, in XXL column, gives boys advice to "turn girls out.' *theGrio.* Retrieved from http://www.thegrio.com/entertainment/too-short-gives-boys-advice-to-turn-girls-out-xxl.php

Solorzano, D. (1997). Images and words that wound: Critical race theory, racial stereotyping and teacher education. *Teacher Education Quarterly, 24*(3), 5–19.

Stephens, D., & Few, A. (2007). The effects of images of African American women in hip hop on early adolescents' attitudes toward physical attractiveness and interpersonal relationships. *Sex Roles, 56*(3/4), 251–264.

Townsend, T., Thomas, A., Neilands, T., & Jackson, T. (2010). I'm no Jezebel; I am young gifted and Black: Identity, sexuality and Black girls. *Psychology of Women Quarterly, 34*(3), 273–285.

Wayne, C. (2009). "Baad" bitches and sassy supermama: Black power action films [Book review]. *Journal of International Women's Studies, 11*(2), 239–242.

West, C. (1995) Mammy, Sapphire and Jezebel: Historical images of Black women and their implications for psychotherapy. *Psychotherapy, 32*, 458–466.

Yosso, T. (2005). Who has culture capital? A critical race theory discussion of community cultural wealth. *Race Ethnicity and Education, 8*(1), 69–91.

Part 3

CRITICAL THEORY AND PRACTICE

CHAPTER 6

Pounding the Yam

HIV/AIDS-Related Knowledge and Behaviors of
Young Accra Market Women and the Intersections
of Gendered Livelihoods

TONYA E. PERRY AND JEONGAH KIM

We are womanists. I, Tonya Perry, am a womanist deeply centered in understandings consistent with an African feminist worldview. I am a daughter of
Africa—a descendent of Africans forcibly brought to America. I embody the
spirits of great sister warriors such as Queen Mother Nana Yaa Assantewa, Sojourner Truth, Harriet Tubman, Fannie Lou Hammer, and Elizabeth Ross-
Haynes. When I cry, my tears are intertwined with those of my grandmothers
and great-grandmothers as well as the multitudes of women whose names I will
never know—mothers, sisters, daughters, and aunties who laughed, loved,
played, prayed, and paid homage to ancestors—dancing around village fires—
enduring the Maafa, bondage, Jim Crow, freedom rides, scrubbing floors and
falling down on bended knees in old wooden churches, making a way out of
no way, sick and tired of being sick and tired, lifting as they climbed up on the
rough side of the mountain, moaning, mourning 'til morning, rejoicing, always
surviving specializing in the wholly impossible (see Barnes, 1983; Boahen, 2003;
Burroughs, 1909; Carlton-LaNey, 1997; Hamer, 1964; Martin & Martin,
1995; Terrell, 1898).

My womanist conscience is a reflection of my vested interest in not only
understanding the ways people's daily lives are constrained by oppression but
also my commitment to using the instrument of my being to contribute to
meaningful social change that will promote the liberation of all people. As

discussed in the introduction to this book, womanism is not a brand of feminism, rather it is

> a social change perspective rooted in Black women's and other women of color's everyday experiences and everyday methods of problem solving in everyday spaces, extended to the problem of ending all forms of oppression for all people, restoring the balance between people and the environment/nature and reconciling human life with the spiritual dimension. (Phillips, 2006, p. xx)

Operating from an African feminist worldview (Badejo, 1998; McFadden, 2008; Mikell, 1995; Oyewumi, 2003; Steady, 1987), I cannot compartmentalize the various spaces I occupy, in that I am a whole person—at once a womanist scholar/teacher/learner—committed to using my position in academia and all the various spaces I occupy to advance the liberation struggle. By stating that I am operating from an African feminist worldview, I suggest that I am African centered in terms of my perspective of the universe and my place in it. Here, I use the term *feminist* as an expression of my African-rooted sense of female agency (Oyewumi, 2003) Steady, 1987). Badejo (1998) suggests that African feminism, "embraces femininity, beauty . . . serenity, harmony and a complex matrix of power . . . complements African masculinity and defends both . . . as critical, demonstrable, and mutually obligatory" (p. 94).

Thus, I am a womanist scholar /teacher/learner operating from an African feminist worldview who is situated in what Robertson (1995) has termed the local/global nexus: the local spaces within which we influence and are reflexively influenced by the global. And so it is within this space, at this moment that I reflect on how I came to be engaged with the experiences of women of African ancestry living with and at risk of contracting HIV/AIDS.

I began my journey into understanding the ways women's lives were being transformed by HIV/AIDS more than two decades ago as a young social work intern at Charity Hospital in New Orleans. The lives of the women I encountered who were living with HIV/AIDS resonated with me. Early on it became clear to me that HIV/AIDS was not only a complex health condition but a phenomenon that is deeply rooted in the intersections of race, class, and gender. So many of those women I encountered in New Orleans, whose pre-HIV/AIDS lives were colored by poverty and violence, had shouldered HIV/AIDS as they had all their other burdens. What was especially astonishing to me was the reality that for many of the women their HIV/AIDS status was viewed as deliverance, a reason to get clean, to live healthier lives, and to exercise their power to manage their lives for themselves and for their children (Perry, Boller, & Cummings, 1990).

Early in my doctoral studies, I served as a research associate for my major professor, Durrenda Onolemhemhen, during which time I spent a transformative summer in Nigeria's Muslim north interviewing more than 100 young Hausa and Fulani women living with a condition called vesicovaginal fistula (VVF; Onolemhemhen, Perry, & Ekwempu, 2000). VVF is a highly preventable condition among women in resource-poor countries that is precipitated by obstructed and prolonged labor during which the bladder ruptures. This rupture leads to incontinence and accompanying shame and social isolation (Semere & Nour, 2008). Although VVF can be corrected through a surgical procedure, this option is limited in the resource-poor countries where the condition is most prevalent. Our findings supported Onolemhemhen's earlier work and the existing literature, indicating that VVF is associated with women whose status is extremely precarious—those whose lives are colored by poverty, lack of education, early marriage, early childbearing, and lack of access to medical care (Onolemhemhen & Ekwempu, 1999; Onolemhemhen et al., 2000; Semere & Nour, 2008; Wall, Arrowsmith, Briggs, & Lassey, 2002). This research experience further expanded my understanding of the social and cultural complexities of women's health as well as the very real consequences of gender-based oppression. In addition to illuminating the universal struggle of women to exert a sense of agency over their bodies, and hence their lives, my research experience in Nigeria demonstrated the power of narrative-based research.

I was later embraced by Ghanaian women living with HIV/AIDS who so graciously shared their lives with me and whose voices I attempted to elucidate through the power of narratives accessed via phenomenological methodology (Perry, 1998). My years of engagement with Ghanaian women living with HIV/AIDS provided me with meaningful insight into their life worlds. The essence of the lived experiences of the 20 co-researchers (research participants) whose experiences I attempted to capture was reflected in three emerging dimensions: pre-illness experiences of performing multiple roles, experiencing significant losses, and having very limited HIV/AIDS-related knowledge; core experiences of living with HIV/AIDS, including isolation, loss, pain, financial strain, and secrecy; and transformation of self, which reflected the women's loss and reconstruction of self as sick, incurable, carriers of death, cursed, and scorned (Perry, 1998).

What had begun in New Orleans nearly a decade earlier became the focus of much of my life's work—women's health—particularly sociocultural issues related to HIV/AIDS and other varied health conditions in women of African ancestry. From my years spent learning from women living with VVF in northern Nigeria and HIV/AIDS in the United States, Ghana, and South Africa, as well as from my prevention work with The Balm in Gilead, an international, faith-based, health promotion and advocacy nongovernmental organization (NGO) in Tanzania and Kenya, I have learned that deeply personal choices women make regarding intimacy are very much a reflection of larger, macroforces. These choices and the forces that influence them have extremely profound consequences for women and for those they love.

The research this chapter evolved from is linked to my need to not only understand and support Ghanaian women who are living with HIV/AIDS but to also gain critical insight into the ways HIV/AIDS knowledge and behaviors contribute to HIV risk among generalized populations. Given that I am a phenomenologist whose work has largely focused on women living with HIV/AIDS, my administration of a standardized survey to a fairly large sample of a nonclinical population represents a fairly radical departure from my modus operandi. I gladly received the enthusiastic support of my sister and colleague, Jeongah Kim, who on reviewing the raw data from this project dove into the process of data analysis. Given my closeness to the data and the subject matter, the project was greatly enhanced by Kim's sense of fresh objectivity and fluid understanding of the link between globalization and gender oppression.

I, Jeongah Kim, am a daughter of Asia and a womanist. Although Walker (1983), Hudson-Weems (1998), and Phillips (2006) support the notion that womanism is a perspective that is not confined to adoption solely by Black women, it may be difficult for others to comprehend that I self-identify as a womanist. This identification evolved in part from my acknowledged cultural heritage as a South Korean, who, like every other human being is a descendent of Africa. My daily experience of microaggressions extending from my intersectionality as being simultaneously female, Asian, of color, an immigrant, and possessing a first language other than English contribute to my *othered* status. My family was always fascinated by the richness and fullness of Africa, and we always admired the diversity of cultures subsumed in the continent. When we visited the Louvre Museum in Paris and the British Museum in London, our long-standing belief that civilization began in Africa was confirmed. We said to each other after our visit to each of these museums that we took so many things from Africa and forgot. This experience was a beginning of my academic journey to better understand issues that affect Africa and its decedents.

I started to expand my knowledge on the role of protective factors in initiating, shaping, and contributing to problem behaviors such as substance abuse in African American communities. I wrote an article (Kim, 2011) titled "Religiosity and Substance Abuse Among African Americans: The need for Systematic Research." I was chosen as one of 14 emerging leaders across the country to be trained as a future leader who could contribute to African American communities in the field of addictions. I participated in the Addiction Technology Transfer Center Leadership Institute for 6 months, during which I learned about the conceptual link between substance abuse and HIV/AIDS vulnerability. This was the beginning of my academic quest to understand risk and protective variables associated with HIV/AIDS. As my HIV/AIDS knowledge base expanded, I soon understood the disproportionate impact that HIV/AIDS has on women of African ancestry in the United States and in Africa. My understanding and appreciation of an African-centered worldview has deepened through my collaborations with my sister and colleague, Tonya Perry, who embodies a true womanist conscience.

Often health crises are precipitated by economic and political crises. The global proliferation of HIV/AIDS over the past three decades has been accompanied by considerable social and economic crises across the globe. Given the economic and political crises on the African continent during the late 1980s through the 1990s, it is not surprising that Africa has been disproportionately affected by the HIV/AIDS pandemic (Johnston-Anumonwo & Doane, 2011; Joint United Nations Program on HIV/AIDS [UNAIDS], 2012). Globally, it is estimated that about 34 million people are living with HIV/AIDS, with millions more at risk of infection (UNAIDS, 2012). Although HIV/AIDS prevention and treatment have improved, Africa bears the disproportionate burden of the HIV/AIDS epidemic. Although the continent of Africa only represents 11% of the world's population, it accounts for the majority of the world's population of people living with HIV/AIDS (69%). The highest estimate for people living with HIV/AIDS on the African continent is in the sub-Saharan region where 1 in every 20 adults is living with HIV (UNAIDS, 2012). Women and girls in sub-Saharan Africa account for 58% of the world's cumulative number of people living with HIV/AIDS; the majority of whom are between the ages of 15 and 49 (UNAIDS, 2012).

Consistent with other African nations, the transmission of HIV in Ghana is heterosexual in nature, with heterosexual intercourse accounting for about 70% of all HIV/AIDS infections (Bosu et al., 2009). In 2010 it was estimated that 230,348 Ghanaians were living with HIV, and new infections totaled 14,165, whereas in 2011 225,478 people were living with HIV, and there were 12,077 new infections. In 2011 the country's antenatal clinic HIV prevalence had risen to 2.1% from 2.0% in 2010 (Ghana AIDS Commission, 2012). Differential rates of HIV/AIDS prevalence are observed across geographic region, gender, and age strata (Ghana AIDS Commission, 2012). Although Ghana maintains a comparatively low national HIV/AIDS prevalence rate of 1.5% (with a range of .4% in the regions of Krachi and Adibo to 9.6% in Cape Coast), women have been disproportionately represented among the cumulative number of AIDS cases since the epidemic began (Adu-Oppong, Richard, Grimes, Ross, & Gladstone, 2007; Ghana AIDS Commission, 2012). It is estimated that of the 225,478 people who were living with HIV in 2011, 100,336 were males and 125,141 were females (Ghana AIDS Commission, 2012).

Certainly, Ghana's National AIDS Control Program and the Ghana AIDS Commission have done much to harness significant resources toward the prevention of HIV/AIDS among its citizens. Despite global HIV/AIDS education and prevention efforts, the literature suggests that the gap between knowledge of HIV/AIDS risk and the practice of HIV/AIDS protective behaviors persists (Anarfi & Owusu, 2011; Fetene & Dimitriadis, 2010; Ghana AIDS Commission, 2012; Takyi, 2003). This reality is most pronounced among the world's women, including Ghanaian women, for whom HIV/AIDS prevalence is disproportionate (Ghana AIDS Commission, 2012; Pro-Link, 2010). Amid the complexities of the sociobehavioral factors that contribute to HIV/AIDS incidence in Ghana, the reality is that "gender inequality leaves women with less control than men over their bodies and lives" (Pro-Link, 2010, p. 6).

Purpose of the Study

Although the link between globalization and HIV/AIDS in Ghana may not be readily apparent, a critical examination of the emergence of the epidemic against the backdrop of the nation's transformation under globalization reveals the ways these larger socioeconomic forces have affected women's private choices. It is within the context of the historically rooted positionality of Ghanaian women that we present the findings from our cross-sectional World Health Organization HIV/AIDS Prevention Indicator Survey (WHO-HIV/PREV Survey) of HIV/AIDS knowledge and behaviors among 138 young Ghanaian market women. Specifically, we critically examine the ways globalization has contributed to the disproportionate concentration of women engaged in marginal livelihoods in Ghana's informal economy, thereby influencing their HIV/AIDS-related risk.

The yam is a starchy, tuberous root that shares similarities with the American sweet potato. Throughout West Africa, yam, which may be prepared in various ways (roasted, fried, boiled), is a staple of the daily diet (Naylor, 2000). In Ghana, the traditional yam dish is called *fufu*. Women are traditionally responsible for preparing fufu for the evening meal, which involves boiling yam, plantain, and/or cassava and pounding it with a massive wooden mortar and pestle into a sticky, glutinous substance similar to stiff mashed potatoes (Naylor, 2000). Fufu is usually eaten with a soup or stew. The activity of preparing fufu—involving the labor-intensive process of pounding the yam—is very much a part of a culturally rooted, gender-based division of labor. Pounding yam is "women's work."

"Pounding the yam" is used in this chapter as a metaphor reflecting the common and familiar daily experiences of Ghanaian women—as surely as they live and breathe, they pound yam. They also regularly engage in behaviors such as sexual communication, sexual negotiation, and sexual decision making, which affects their risk of contracting HIV.

Background

GLOBALIZATION AND GENDERED LIVELIHOODS

Globalization is a complex process reflecting an intertwining of local and national economies that has social, cultural, and political consequences that affect nations, communities, and individual citizens (Gutal, 2001). Although it may be argued that globalization has led to the growth of markets, it is apparent that globalization processes have also contributed to increasing inequalities across multiple spheres (Johnston-Anumonwo & Doane, 2011). A considerable amount of literature suggests that women in particular have been differentially affected by globalization processes (Archer, 2005; Davids & Van Driel, 2009; Johnston-Anumonwo & Doane, 2011; Keddie, 2010; Kuokkanen, 2008).

Davids and Van Driel (2009) suggest that we approach our understanding of the relationship between gender and globalization within a global/local nexus. They suggest, like Muller (2003, that it is within "glocalized" (p. 330) spaces that the realities of globalization are evident in the lives of people on the ground. Thus, to understand the impact of globalization on Ghanaian women, it is necessary to have a historical perspective regarding the process of globalization and its historical emergence in a Ghana-specific context.

Gender inequality is not endemic to Ghana (Robertson, 1984). In fact, Steady (1987) and others (Duran, 2010; Oyewumi, 2003) contend that Africa is home to distinctly *feminist* ideals. Robertson (1984) and Archer (2005) assert that in Ghana, as in other parts of West Africa, gender inequality was far from the norm. Ghanaian history is replete with evidence supporting the notion that precolonially, women wielded positions of power, socially and politically. Archer (2005) further argues that existing inequalities experienced by Ghanaian women are rooted in colonialist policies that branded women as inferior and unfit to occupy positions of authority. The colonialists' refusal to recognize the traditional agency of Ghanaian women gave men distinct advantages, which included differential access to education, jobs, and property—all of which are linked to wealth accumulation. During this period, Robertson (1984) asserts that despite women's disfranchisement from the formal economy and governance under British rule, they maintained some autonomy within the vestiges of Ghana's traditional, cooperative kin mode of production and expanded trading activities. As the society shifted from a production-driven economy into a distribution-oriented one, capitalism further impinged on rural areas of the nation. At the same time the traditional authority that Ghanaian women once held was further diminished along with opportunities for active engagement in trade enterprises. As capitalism asserted itself through multinational corporations, and a male-dominated capitalist structure of authority became institutionalized, women became even more disfranchised (Robertson, 1984). Following Ghana's independence in 1957, neocolonialism was accompanied by legislation intended to increase the erosion of the economic autonomy exerted by women, particularly those who had achieved success in trading.

In the shadows of the economic crises and structural adjustments of the 1980s and 1990s, globalization and escalating debt yielded profound changes across Ghana and much of sub-Saharan Africa (Johnston-Anumonwo & Oberhauser, 2011). Johnston-Anumonwo & Doane (2011) and others (Baliamoune-Lutz, 2005; Davids & Van Driel, 2009; Muller, 2003; Oberhauser & Yeboah, 2011) assert that globalization's effects on sub-Saharan Africa have been especially deleterious. Globalization's effects have been particularly damaging for women for whom existing gender inequalities have increased substantially. In their 2009 analysis of panel data for 31 sub-Saharan African nations, Baliamoune-Lutz and McGillivray (2009) provide statistical evidence supporting the contention that increased growth and integration into world markets by sub-Saharan African nations, including Ghana, is strongly associated with growing gender inequalities in those nations.

For nearly three decades, neoliberalist reforms and accompanying structural adjustments have dominated Ghana's economic policies. Aryeetey, Harrigan, and Nissanke (2000) assert that neoliberal economic policies and structural adjustment programs have further diminished formal sector employment among Ghanaian women and thrust them into marginal livelihoods in the informal economy. Oberhauser and Yeboah (2011) report that 60% of Ghanaian males are wage earners in the formal economy, and nearly 80% of Ghanaian women are engaged in self-employment largely in the informal economy.

Although Ghana's gross domestic product (GDP) per capita ranked 171st out of 226 countries in the world in 2011 (Central Intelligence Agency, 2012), there has been a relatively small gap between developmental achievements and efforts toward gender equality in Ghana considering GDP per capita. According to the 2011 Global Gender Gap Report, Ghana ranked 70th out of 135 countries. Also, Ghana was ranked 54 out of 102 in the 2009 Social Institutions and

Gender Index (Organisation for Economic Co-operation and Development, 2012).

Thus, the paradigm shift in the social and political power of Ghanaian women that began with colonization has had lasting effects on the social status of women. The social inequalities established in the 18th century have been institutionalized. More than 200 years since Ghana's colonization by the British, and more than 50 years since its independence, historically rooted gender disparities persist (Archer, 1987; Oberhauser & Yeboah, 2011). Our discussion further suggests that the disproportionate concentration of Ghanaian women in marginalized livelihoods in the informal sector of the economy is deeply rooted in globalization and its precursors: colonization and neocolonization.

Having examined the historical roots of the current status of Ghanaian women as a function of globalization processes, we continue our examination by employing the positionality construct.

GHANAIAN WOMEN AND POSITIONALITY: THE INTERSECTION OF GENDER, SOCIAL STATUS, AND HIV/AIDS VULNERABILITY

Positionality is a construct useful in conceptualizing the dynamic interplay of variables such as education, gender, social status, and occupation and their influence on HIV/AIDS-related knowledge and behavior among Ghanaian women. Positionality, which is reflected in the multidimensional aspects of personhood as reflected in education, gender, social status, and livelihood, is a determinant of each person's relative state of power or privilege within a given cultural context (Andersen, 2004; Finn & Jacobson, 2003; Oberhauser & Yeboah, 2011). The disproportionate impact of HIV/AIDS on Ghanaian women may be linked to their sense of personhood in the context of Ghanaian society.

Issues such as education, gender, unequal power relationships, and poor economic status fuel the vulnerability of women to HIV/AIDS (Mill & Anarfi, 2002). As exemplified by the following quote, the consequences of poverty on the educational status of girls born into large families are particularly profound given Ghana's fee-based primary and secondary educational system:

> My mother brought forth many of us. Those who were attending school among us were many. They were seven so my mother and father said that they could not afford to send us [girls]to school. (Mill &Anarfi, 2002, p. 329)

Without your mother, everything of yours spoils. . . . My grandmother was finding it difficult to support us in school and we ourselves had to fight for food. There were my younger brothers and
sisters to think of and I had to trade and give some of my money to
my grandmother and that's why I had to stop school. (Mill & Anarfi
2002, p. 329)

In addition to education, social status also serves as a barrier to condom
usage. This social status is inextricably linked to the livelihood construct, which
in turn colors the nature of interpersonal interactions (Anderson, 2004). Oberhauser and Yeboah's (2011) livelihood framework provides significant insight
into understanding the ways neoliberal market reforms have contributed to the
large concentration of African women in urban centers such as Accra, who rely
on petty trading and other low-paying jobs in the informal economy to survive.

In urban centers such as Accra, most Ghanaian women, particularly those
who have not been formally educated and are unskilled, become traders or sellers (Anarfi & Owusu, 2011; Rakodi, 2002). Trading is a female occupation that
allows women to earn money and fulfill their domestic obligations of cooking,
cleaning, and catering to the needs of their children. Many petty traders and
sellers who are unable to survive on their market income become engaged in
various forms of sexual networking to supplement their meager incomes. There
have been arguments that the postcolonial period has shown an increasing trend
of female economic dependence on males, which has resulted in their compromised ability to make decisions concerning their sexuality, including decision
making regarding condom use (Anarfi & Owusu, 2011; Bhana, Morrell, Hearn,
& Molestsane, 2007; Mill & Anarfi, 2002).

Awusabo-Asare, Anarfi, and Agyman (1993) examined factors that contribute to the subordination of women in Ghanaian society and their subsequent increased vulnerability to STD/AIDS infection. Their seminal
cross-sectional, mixed-methods research provides significant insight into the
ways social mores dictate public opportunities and private choices of Ghanaian
women. They interviewed a purposive sample of 320 women from Acca, Tako-
radi, Tarkwa, and Agomanya who were thought to be at risk of contracting HIV
and other STDs from their sexual partners. This group of women included
commercial sex workers, migrant female traders, and wives or partners of

policemen, military personnel, truck drivers, and HIV-positive or AIDS-diagnosed men. They elicited information regarding women's views on their collective rights over sexual behavior as well as women's individual control over their own sexual behavior. Interestingly, Awusabo-Asare and his colleagues found that although 60% of women they interviewed said that as a general rule a woman had the right to refuse sexual relations with a promiscuous man, 50% of those women said they did not have the right to refuse sex with promiscuous partners and cited the traditional obligation of a woman to satisfy her partner. Ironically, 80% of the respondents said they would refuse to have sex with a partner known to have an STD (Awusabo-Asare et al., 1993). Fifty-seven percent of respondents in the study said they had refused sex with their partners, although 42% said they had never done so. Women reporting that they had refused sex with their partners in the past cited jealousy and attention getting as their motivation. Women who had refused sex also noted the consequences of their actions, which included physical coercion and familial admonishments to meet their partners' demands. These findings suggest that women "seem to be concerned with the health-related aspects of sex but accept the promiscuous behavior of their partners as part of the 'nature of men'" (Awusabo-Asare et al., 1993, p. 78).

Considering the strong relationship between promiscuous behavior and HIV risk, it is ironic that women would overlook the promiscuous behavior of their partners but refuse to engage in sexual relations with a man known to have HIV/AIDS or any STD; however, this trend uncovered in Awusabo-Asare and his colleague's seminal research has been affirmed by current epidemiological data and social research (Anarfi & Owusu, 2011; Ghana AIDS Commission, 2012; Smith, 2005; Tenkorang, 2012).

Tenkorang (2012) reported that although 79% of respondents in his study indicated that they could refuse sex or insist on condom use with their partners, their ability to do so was significantly related to their economic status. In other words, women with a higher economic status were more likely to refuse sex and insist on condom use with their partners than women who were less economically secure. A number of studies reported similar findings (e.g., Ankomah, 1999; Mills & Anarfi, 2002; Smith, 2005; Stadler, Delany, & Mntambo, 2008). Stadler et al. (2008) share the narratives of two young women they interviewed in their exploration of the experiences of HIV-positive South African women:

There are so many people in Diepkloof [a township in Soweto] who are ignorant and some of them hold power over other people because they have got money there are tsotsis [gangsters], they have guns and there are lots of things happening. They abuse people, especially women and children. If your boyfriend beats you no one will come and help you. And I see that as a big contribution to HIV/AIDS. . . . They abuse people, especially women and children. If your boyfriend beats you no one will come and help you. And I see that as a big contribution to HIV/AIDS. (pp. 191–192)

Shefer et al. (2008) also report content drawn from focus groups with South African women of the western cape that suggests that abuse by men is seen as a natural component of gender relations: "People that are victims are women and perpetrators are men, because they have the power, not women, and they tell themselves nobody is going to stop them from beating their wives" (p. 193).

The transactional nature of sexual arrangements is illustrated by the words of a young woman who discusses the ways material needs structure sexual decision making and freedom within relationships (Stadler et al., 2008):

I think if you have a boyfriend and he buys you expensive stuff he feels like he owns you. That's why if you want to do something he tries to stop you and he will start making decisions for you, tell you what to do, where to go. And if he finds you with anyone else you are in trouble. (p. 195)

Clearly, historically rooted gender inequality is at the center of the HIV/AIDS epidemic (Bhana et al., 2007). The positionality of Ghanaian women as reflected in education, gender, social status, and livelihood contributes to their diminished capacity to make empowered choices regarding HIV/AIDS-related behavior. Be they sex workers, market women, mothers, sisters, or daughters, the harsh reality is that Ghanaian women demonstrate an increased vulnerability to HIV infection. As HIV/AIDS continues to devastate the lives of Ghanaian women, the need for greater insight into their HIV/AIDS-related knowledge and behaviors becomes more urgent.

Methods

SETTING

Accra, the capital of Ghana, is an urban center with a population of about 2 million. It is Ghana's largest city and serves as the country's administrative, communications, and economic center. Makola Market, one of the largest markets in West Africa, is the major site of trade and commerce in Accra. It is located in the center of the city and serves as the hub of activity where the masses of Ghanaian women engage in daily activities. Many of the women found in the market sell various goods and services, ranging from petty items such as ice water to more high-priced goods such as ornate fabrics and Western clothing. In addition to the variety of traders who spend their working hours in the market, thousands of women regularly pass through to shop for daily staples (Pellow, 1977; Solomon, 2006). Pellow offers a descriptive picture of market women, which although documented decades earlier, clearly captures the essence of the rhythm of market women:

> Market women stay at their stalls the entire day. While there, they can do their own marketing and cooking, as well as take a nap in the afternoon when business is slow. Traders who do not sell in a stall in the market have some choice as to their hours and location. If one's compound is on a thoroughfare or well-traveled road, a table can easily be set up right out front. In this case, a child or neighbor can be left to keep an eye on the business while the seller takes care of household duties . . . the work schedule of many hawkers is constrained by their stock-in-trade. The porridge, doughnut, and rice sellers are situated by 6:00 a.m. . . . bread sellers come out in the early evening and sit beside a kerosene lamp. . . . Those who sell prepared foods early in the day must spend the previous afternoon or evening assembling ingredients, or get up early to do so. . . . After the long work day comes a new set of chores: putting together a meal, cleaning up, bathing children and putting them to bed. (pp. 142–143)

Bowers (2007) offers the following description of the Makola Market in Accra:

> Accra's frenzied Makola market is in the heart of the city; thousands of traders mingle with shoppers, taxis and tro-tros, or local minibuses.

For several blocks, narrow paths of broken pavement and dirt wind through scores of tiny container shops selling everything from colorful printed fabric to air conditioners and live chickens. (p. 2)

PROCEDURES

The World Health Organization HIV/AIDS Prevention Indicator Survey: Knowledge, Attitudes, Sexual Behavior, Stigma (WHO-HIV/PREV Survey; UNAIDS, n.d.) was administered to a convenience sample of 138 volunteer participants recruited from the Makola Market in Accra. Those deemed eligible for participation in the study were market women and 16 years or older. In the study, a subset of the sample population consisting of 104 women between the ages of 16 and 40 is examined to illuminate the unique realities of young women of childbearing age who demonstrate the highest prevalence of HIV infection in Ghana (Akwara, Fosu, Pav, Silvia, & Ani, 2005; Dageid & Duckert, 2008).

Approval to conduct the research study was granted by the market administrators with the permission of respected "mothers of the market." Volunteer respondents were recruited for participation in the study as they passed through the market or sat in their stalls selling their goods. After being briefed on the nature of the study and completing the informed verbal and written consent process, volunteer participants were administered the survey, which took about 20 minutes to complete. The researcher and trained research assistants administered the survey via face-to-face interviews in discrete areas of the market. The constant hum of the market served as a natural sound screen lending additional privacy. Volunteer participants were provided with light refreshments after completing the survey. Following administration of all surveys, the researcher provided HIV/AIDS education to market workers and patrons, which included basic information regarding HIV transmission, HIV risk and protective behaviors, identification and discussion of common myths associated with HIV/AIDS, and promotion of HIV testing.

The WHO-HIV/PREV Survey (UNAIDS, n.d.) was developed by UNAIDS to provide standardized measures of knowledge, attitudes, sexual behavior, and stigma across international populations. The survey has been normed for use with adult populations age 15 to 49 and elicits information regarding demographic variables, HIV/AIDS-knowledge and attitudes, risk and protective behaviors, and sexual negotiation. The survey consists of the following seven major sections: Background Characteristics; Marriage and Cohabitating Partnerships; Sexual History and Behavior; Sexually Transmitted Diseases; Knowledge About HIV/AIDS and Level of Exposure to Interventions; Attitudes Toward People Living With HIV/AIDS, Gender, and Counseling; and Childbearing and Antenatal Care.

DATA ANALYSIS

Demographic factors were explored to examine the individual contributions of variables to behaviors such as condom use. Data regarding HIV/AIDS knowledge and sexual risk and protective behaviors were analyzed by age and education to explore the interplay of these factors. As defined by the National Institute of Allergy and Infectious Diseases (NAID, 2007), HIV risk behaviors include those behaviors that expose a person to transmission of HIV via the lining of the vagina, vulva, penis, rectum, or mouth. Risk behaviors include sharing needles or syringes and having sexual contact, including oral sexual contact, with an infected person without using a condom and having unprotected sexual contact with someone whose HIV status is unknown (NAID, 2007). Protective behaviors include sexual abstinence, use of male latex condoms or female polyurethane condoms during oral, anal, or vaginal sexual contact.

Also examined was the relationship between HIV/AIDS knowledge and sexual risk behavior. Risky behavior was measured by condom usage, and to measure HIV/AIDS knowledge, a composite variable was created as multiple measures of a construct resulting in greater measurement reliability. HIV/AIDS knowledge was measured by responses to 10 questions related to the transmission of HIV/AIDS that have been delineated in the literature as indicators of HIV/AIDS knowledge. These questions are listed in Table 6.1

Participants who scored below the mean were classified as having insufficient knowledge, and those who scored above the mean were classified as having sufficient knowledge. Cronbach's alpha was used to evaluate the reliability of measures, as it is considered conservative, and to provide information about internal consistency (Bloom, Fischer, & Orme, 1995). Cronbach's alpha for reliability was .79 for HIV/AIDS prevention knowledge, which is consistent with previous findings on the reliability of the HIV/AIDS prevention indicators (Fatusi & Blum, 2008). The validity of the composite measure of HIV/AIDS prevention knowledge in the present study appears to be appropriate, as cor-

TABLE 6.1
SUMMARY OF PARTICIPANTS' GENERAL HIV/AIDS KNOWLEDGE

	YES		NO	
AIDS KNOWLEDGE	N	%	Y	%
Can a person who looks healthy be infected with the AIDS virus?	29	28	72	70
Can people reduce their chances of getting AIDS by using condoms correctly every time they have sex?	79	78	14	14
Can a person get infected with the AIDS virus through mosquito bites?	29	28	69	66
Can people reduce their chances of getting the AIDS virus by having one sex partner who has no other partners?	81	78	17	16
Can a person get infected with the AIDS virus by sharing a meal with a person who has HIV or AIDS?	81	80	15	14
Can people get AIDS because of witchcraft?	42	40	50	48
Can the AIDS virus be transmitted from a mother to child?	85	82	13	13
Can the AIDS virus be transmitted from a mother to child during pregnancy or at delivery?	82	79	11	11
Can the AIDS virus be transmitted from a mother to child through breast milk?	73	70	20	19
Is there any way to avoid transmission to the baby?	63	60	18	17

relations between measures indicate a good level of convergent validity. Women's communication with their partners is measured by one indicator: "During the past 4 weeks have you discussed the AIDS virus with anyone?" (UNAIDS, n.d.). Although there are some missing variables, it does not appear to be a major concern as no pattern is observed. Data were analyzed using SPSS software. Descriptive statistics were used to analyze demographic variables. The relationships between HIV/AIDS knowledge and condom use were examined by using chi-square. A significance level of 0.05 was used for the analysis.

Findings

An overview of participant characteristics is followed by a summary of data relevant to HIV/AIDS awareness and knowledge, condom use and HIV/AIDS-related communication, and the relationship between HIV/AIDS knowledge and behavior.

BACKGROUND CHARACTERISTICS

Participants' sociodemographic characteristics are displayed in Table 6.2. The mean age of participants was 29 with a range of 16 to 40 years. In terms of nationhood, 98.6% of the respondents were Ghanaian born, with 1.4% of the sample reporting that they were born in another country. The participants' ethnolinguistic affiliations are reflected in three major groupings: Ga, consisting of 47% of the respondents; Akan, consisting of 29.7% of the respondents; and Ewe, consisting of 14.5% of the participants. In addition to affiliations with the Ga, Akan, and Ewe ethnolinguistic groups, 2.9% of the respondents indicated affiliation with other Ghanaian groupings, whereas 1.4% of the respondents were identified as having Nigerian nationhood and an ethnolinguistic designation of Hausa.

Most participants (96%) had heard about HIV/AIDS. Among the 104 women, 96% were sexually active, and the mean age at their first time of sexual intercourse was 18 years. Sixty-six percent had their first sexual intercourse before the age of 18. Sixty-nine percent of the respondents described themselves as being married or in a cohabitating partnership. In the present study 45% of the respondents reported finishing primary school, and an additional 33% reported completion of secondary school. Only 9% of respondents reported having any postsecondary education. As previously indicated in the inclusion criteria, all the respondents were occupationally classified as market women, which includes women who work in the informal sector of the economy as sellers, traders, and hawkers of various commodities. It should be noted that there is socioeconomic variation among market women, including ordinary traders and sellers of goods as well as a small minority of women who have access to the necessary capital to operate extensive enterprises. Although data regarding actual earnings was not elicited by the survey, the occupational designation of *market woman* is operationalized in the current study as a woman who is a petty trader of goods and services, connoting low-income status (Robertson, 1995; Solomon, 2005).

HIV/AIDS AWARENESS AND KNOWLEDGE

Television (80%) and radio (70%) were the most common ways for participants to receive information about AIDS. Data regarding knowledge of HIV prevention methods is summarized in Table 6.3. Eighty-six percent of respondents an-

TABLE 6.2
SOCIODEMOGRAPHIC CHARACTERISTICS

VARIABLES	FREQUENCY (%)	MEAN	SD	RANGE
Age	104	29	6.4	16–40
Education				
No education	6			
Primary	45	6.7	4.5	0–22
Secondary	33			
Higher	9			
Marital/cohabitation status				
Married/cohabitated	69	1.3	.47	1–2
Not married/cohabitated	33			

Note. The educational system in Ghana is made up of 6 years of primary school, 3 years of junior secondary school (which forms 9 years of basic education), followed by 3 years of senior secondary school. This constitutes 12 years of pretertiary education (Embassy of the Republic of Ghana, 2013).

TABLE 6.3
PARTICIPANTS' KNOWLEDGE OF HIV PREVENTION METHODS

WAYS TO PROTECT AGAINST AIDS	FREQUENCY	%
Condom use	44	42
Fewer partners	5	5
Both partners have no other partners	18	17
No casual sex	8	8
No sex at all	18	17
Avoid injections with contaminated needles	1	1
Avoid blood transfusion	2	2

swered affirmatively when asked if people could do anything to avoid getting infected with HIV. Respondents' knowledge in the area of protection against getting AIDS was low. Only 42% indicated condom use as a method of HIV prevention. No respondent chose all the prevention methods. Most of them identified one or two prevention methods.

A summary of data regarding general HIV/AIDS knowledge is presented in Table 6.1. Knowledge regarding transmission modes was moderate. Respondents were aware that HIV/AIDS transmission can be avoided by condom use (78%) and one sexual partner (78%). Eighty-two percent were aware that AIDS can be transmitted from mother to child. However, there were some misconceptions regarding nontransmittable routes. Eighty percent believed that HIV could be transmitted by sharing meals. Some respondents believed that HIV could be transmitted by mosquitoes (28%) or witchcraft (40%).

CONDOM USE AND HIV/AIDS-RELATED COMMUNICATION

Only 18% of women reported that they used a condom the first time they had sex. An equal percentage of women (18%) responded that they used condoms the last time they had sex. In the past 12 months, all respondents except five reported having one sexual partner. Only 14% reported having a dialogue about HIV/AIDS with their partner.

RELATIONSHIP BETWEEN HIV/AIDS KNOWLEDGE AND BEHAVIOR

Chi-square analyses were computed to examine a relationship between knowledge and behavior. The first chi-square examined whether there was a relationship between the AIDS knowledge composite score and condom use; there were no differences in the knowledge score by condom use (χ^2=2.54, df=1, p<0.11). Although 76% of respondents reported that they knew condom use can prevent HIV transmission, 82% of respondents reported they did not use condoms the last time they had sexual intercourse. There were no differences in the knowledge score by age (χ^2=.21, df=1, p<0.64) or education level (χ^2=1.43, df=1, p<0.23).

Limitations of the Study

Limitations of this study in terms of measurement and interpretation should be noted. The use of a convenience sample of voluntary respondents recruited from a single market in Accra limits the generalizability of the findings. An additional limitation of the study is related to the use of the WHO-HIV/PREV Survey, a self-report measure that elicits information regarding highly sensitive, highly personal information related to sexuality and the highly stigmatized topic of HIV/AIDS. The use of a self-report measure may limit the reliability of the data. Social desirability bias may have affected the reporting of sexual behaviors. Additionally, the survey does not elicit narratives, which would contextualize responses provided by participants. Although the quantitative data elicited by the WHO-HIV/PREV Surveys is useful in understanding HIV/AIDS-related knowledge and behaviors of the participants, the data would be greatly enriched by the incorporation of respondent narratives. Despite noted limitations of the study, the findings lend insight into the HIV/AIDS-related knowledge and behaviors of a population that is highly vulnerable to HIV transmission. Further research regarding the dynamic interplay of HIV/AIDS knowledge and behaviors among this population is needed.

Discussion

The findings indicate that although Ghanaian market women demonstrate moderate HIV/AIDS-related knowledge, this knowledge is not being translated into the practice of HIV/AIDS risk protective behaviors. To gain meaningful insight into the social and structural issues that contribute to the increased vulnerability of Ghanaian women to HIV contraction, the findings of the current study are examined and discussed here in the context of the existing literature. Consistent with previous findings and current research (Akwara et al., 2005; Anarfi & Antwi, 1995; Anarfi, Appiah, & Awusabo-Asare, 1995; Ghana AIDS Commission, 2012; Mill & Anarfi, 2002; Smith, 2005), the respondents in the present study demonstrated a high level of HIV/AIDS awareness, reporting they had heard of HIV/AIDS either through radio (70%) or television (80%). This finding may be because of extensive HIV/AIDS campaigns administered by Ghana's Ministry of Health through the National AIDS Control Program. Mill and Anarfi (2000) reported that respondents demonstrated a high level of HIV/AIDS awareness; however, they also demonstrated a low level of HIV/AIDS knowledge, with only 42% of respondents identifying condom usage as an HIV/AIDS prevention method. This finding indicates that increased awareness of HIV/AIDS has not been translated into practical knowledge that will protect women from contracting HIV. This continuing reality has been acknowledged by the Ghana AIDS Commission (2012) and Pro-Link (2012).

The data in the present study illustrate significant discrepancies between HIV knowledge and the practice of HIV-related protective behaviors. Interestingly, a mere 18% of women used condoms the first time and the last time they had sex. Consistent with preexisting research examining the relationship between HIV knowledge and condom usage, Ghanaian market women's HIV knowledge did not positively affect the level of condom usage (Anarfi, 1997; Anarfi & Antwi, 1995; Bosompra, 2001; Ghana AIDS Commission, 2012; Neequaye, Neequaye, & Biggar, 1991; Owuamanam, 1995; Tenkorang, 2012). Although Ghanaian women know that condom usage may protect them from HIV transmission, it appears that barriers exist to practicing regular condom usage with their partners. Previous studies have identified several factors that may contribute to low condom usage among general populations. According to Callegari and colleagues (2008), low rates of condom usage are contributing to the escalation of HIV/AIDS prevalence rates among married women. These factors include lack of access, lack of HIV/AIDS education, male resistance, various cultural issues such as the high value placed on fertility and the negative association of condom use (Kibungu et al., 2008; Mill & Anarfi, 2002). However, the phenomenon of low condom usage among women is different and far more complicated. The complexities of this situation may be a reflection of the host of variables associated with the positionality of Ghanaian women, which include personhood as reflected in low educational attainment and social status, lack of HIV/AIDS-related communication, and lack of partner negotiation (Anarfi & Owusu, 2011; Andersen, 2004; Finn & Jacobson 2003; Mill & Anarfi, 2002; Tenkorang, 2012).

It appears that personhood as reflected in gender and socioeconomic status may affect a woman's ability to communicate regarding HIV/AIDS. Not surprisingly, in the present study a mere 14% of respondents reported having a dialogue about HIV/AIDS with their partners. This situation can be problematic, because without communication about HIV/AIDS, negotiation with partners about condom usage will not occur without a greater balance of power, as illustrated in the following:

My father's relatives were not helping us. My mother too had no money. . . . But my boyfriend was able to provide all that I needed. Anytime that I bought food, I didn't buy fish but he always bought fish for me and gave me money so that I was always free. . . . That's why I took a boyfriend. (Reneé, as quoted in Mill & Anarfi 2002, p. 330).

When I sold ice water and deducted my transport from the profit, I realized that I was left with nothing. So I realized selling ice water was not profitable. And so, I was forced to pick another boyfriend. (Faith, as quoted in Mill & Anarfi 2002, p. 330)

When queried about the factors that most significantly influenced their sexual relations, women interviewed by Awusabo-Asare and colleagues (1993) noted that economic dependence had the strongest level of influence, followed by children's well-being, access to partner's resources, children's right to father's property, sustenance of the relationship, fear of losing partners, familial pressure, and culture/tradition.

Our findings suggest that women's control over their sexuality is severely limited by their positionality. These findings are consistent with the literature, which suggests that although Ghanaian women are aware that condom usage may protect them from HIV transmission, issues such as personhood—as reflected in low educational attainment, occupation, and low social status as well as a lack of HIV/AIDS-related communication and lack of partner negotiation—may serve as barriers to condom usage with their partners (Anarfi & Owusu, 2011; Ghana AIDS Commission, 2012; Tenkorang, 2012). According to summary research published by the Max Planck Institute for Demographic Research, a complex mélange of factors decrease a woman's ability to protect her from HIV infection, among them being financial dependence on men (Smith, 2005). This dependence may compromise a woman's ability to leave an unfaithful partner or insist on condom use.

Implications and Conclusions

"For decades, we have known that the best way for Africa to thrive is to ensure that it's women have the freedom, power and knowledge to make decisions affecting their own lives" (Annan, 2002, p. 1).

If we examine the findings through an African feminist lens, we see that the ability of Ghanaian women to exercise agency over their bodies is being compromised by their displacement as low wage earners in the informal economy. This displacement is historically rooted in the processes of colonization, neocolonization, globalization, neoliberalism, and accompanying structural adjustments that led to existing gender inequalities.

The HIV/AIDS epidemic's escalating impact on Africa's women is very much a reflection of profound gender and class-based inequalities (Perry, Davis-Maye, & Onolemhemhen, 2007). Although the study's small sample size limits the generalizability of the findings, the preponderance of the literature suggests that broad macrolevel issues, such as culture, gender, poverty, education, and livelihood, may contribute to microlevel realities affecting a woman's ability to protect herself from HIV/AIDS. Any serious discussions regarding HIV prevention strategies must acknowledge the role of these broad contextual issues in fueling the epidemic.

According to a report from the Joint United Nations Programme on AIDS (2005):

> Many HIV strategies assume an idealized world in which everyone is equal and free to make empowered choices, and can opt to abstain from sex, stay faithful to one's partner or use condoms consistently [if at all]. In reality, women and girls face a range of HIV-related risk factors that men do not—many of which are embedded in the social relations and economic realities of their societies. These factors are not easily dislodged or altered, but until they are, efforts to contain and reverse the AIDS epidemic are unlikely to achieve sustained success. (pp. 3–4)

Certainly, efforts to reduce HIV incidence rates must focus on prevention interventions that target individual behavior change, but it is clear that for such efforts to truly make a difference we must address the interplay of gender, socioeconomic inequality, and HIV vulnerability (Faria, 2008). Findings from this study are consistent with the existing literature (e.g., Anarfi & Owusu, 2011; Ghana AIDS Commission, 2012; Mills & Anarfi, 2002; Madlala, 2004; Pro-Link, 2010; Perry et al., 2007), which supports the contention that the ability of a woman to protect herself from HIV is a reflection of her ability to provide for herself and attend to the needs of her children.

The contributions that such broad, macrolevel issues make to vulnerability to HIV/AIDS among Ghanaian women and other sisters across the globe are undeniable. At the core of the pandemic are issues such as unequal access to education; limited access to wealth-generating livelihoods, which contribute to women's vulnerability; and a diminished capacity to control what does and does not happen to their bodies (Adu-Oppong et al., 2007; Lindgren, Rankin, & Rankin, 2005).

In the context of the historically rooted structural dynamics underlying the vulnerability of Ghanaian women to HIV/AIDS, the findings suggest a number of implications relative to practice, policy, and research: (a) Programming targeting the economic empowerment of women should be supported and should address literacy, vocational education, and localized methods of income generation; (b) existing programming aimed at HIV/AIDS prevention, which is often targeted at commercial sex workers, should be expanded to provide women-centered education and greater outreach to the masses of Ghanaian women living in rural and urban areas with the highest prevalence rates; (c) HIV/AIDS educators are encouraged to provide prevention programs in market settings, as the market is an ideal venue for engaging a captive audience of a broad cross-section of women in need of HIV/AIDS education and sexual negotiation skills; (d) women-centered HIV/AIDS prevention programming, which incorporates peer outreach, education, and support, would build on the strengths of sisterhood and foster open communication, exchange of ideas, and knowledge regarding sexuality and HIV/AIDS protective behaviors; (e) male-to-male HIV/AIDS peer education regarding the value of monogamy and condom use should be implemented; (f) continued support of microenterprise programs that engender the economic empowerment of women should be integrated into the existing national control prevention strategy, such as those in Agomanya and other parts of Ghana as well as in the United States and South Africa that have shown success (Fiscian, Obeng, Goldstein, Shea, & Turner, 2009); and (g) local, national, and international women-centered, transdisciplinary HIV/AIDS research efforts exploring interrelationships of gender, health, and culture, and incorporate an appreciation of the utility of multimethod inquiry should be supported.

Finally, HIV/AIDS constituencies, such as researchers, practitioners, and policy makers, should continue to engage in activism for policy development and policy reform in the advancement of women's empowerment and freedom. To achieve serious advancements in the status of women in Ghana and other resource-challenged areas where globalization has thrust women into meager existences in the informal economy, gender-based policies and programs designed to cultivate opportunities for women to gain essential life skills and capital to enter into sustainable livelihoods must also be supported.

Until women are provided with social and economic equity, those actively engaged in HIV/AIDS-related policy making, research, and direct care are encouraged not only to lobby for the resources to support program-related initiatives but to advocate for the empowerment of women through revolutionary social change.

Discussion Questions

1. How have the processes of colonization and neocolonization in Ghana contributed to the disproportionate numbers of women who earn livelihoods in the informal sector of the economy?
2. What are the implications of livelihoods in the informal sector for Ghanaian women and others who are in resource-challenged countries?
3. What is the link between economic status and HIV/AIDS vulnerability among Ghanaian women?

References

Adu-Oppong, A., Richard, M., Grimes, M. W., Ross, J., & Gladstone, K. (2007). Social and behavioral determinants of consistent condom use among female commercial sex workers in Ghana. *AIDS Education and Prevention, 19*(2), 160–172.

Akwara, P., Fosu, G., Pav, G., Silvia, A., & Ani, H. (2005). *An in-depth analysis of HIV prevalence In Ghana: Further analysis of demographic and health surveys.* Retrieved from http://pdf.usaid.gov/pdf_docs/PNADD318.pdf

Anarfi, J. K. (1997). Vulnerability to sexually transmitted disease: Street children in Accra [Monograph]. *Health Transition Review, 7*, 281–306.

Anarfi, J. K., & Antwi, P. (1995). Street youth in Accra city: Sexual networking in a high risk environment and it's implications for the spread of HIV/AIDS [Monograph]. *Health Transition Review, 5*, 131–151.

Anarfi, J. K., Appiah, E., & Awusabo-Asare, K. (1995, December). *Livelihood and the risk of HIV/AIDS infection in Ghana: The case of female itinerant traders.* Paper presented at a scientific workshop on sexual networking and AIDS in Tropical Africa, Mbarara, Uganda.

Anarfi, J. K., & Owusu, Y. (2011). The making of a sexual being in Ghana: The state, religion and the influences of society as agents of sexual socialization. *Sexuality and Culture, 15*(1), 1–18.

Andersen, H. M. (2004). Villagers: differential treatment in a Ghanaian hospital. *Social Science & Medicine, 59*, 2003–2012.

Ankomah, A. (1999). Sex, love, money and AIDS: The dynamics of premarital sexual relationships in Ghana. *Sexualities, 2*(3), 291–309.

Annan, K. (2002, December 29). In Africa, AIDS Has a Woman's Face. *New York Times.* Retrieved from http://www.nytimes.com/2002/12/29/in-africa-aids-has-a-woman-s-face.html?pagewanted=2%src=pm

Archer, E. (2005). The wells are drying up: Water & women in Ghana. *Off Our Backs* (March/April), 23–27.

Aryeetey, E., Harrigan, J., & Nissanke, M. (2000). *Economic reforms in Ghana: The miracle and the mirage.* Trenton, NJ: Africa World Press.

Awusabo-Asare, K., Anarfi, J. K., & Agyman, D. (1993). Women's control over their sexuality and the spread of STDS and HIV/AIDS in Ghana [Monograph]. *Health Transition Review, 3*, 69–84.

Badejo, D. (1998). African feminism: Mythical and social power of women of African descent. *Research in African Literatures, 29*(2), 92–111.

Baliamoune-Lutz, M. (2005). Globalization, economic growth and human development: What fate awaits African women? In S. Boko, M. Baliamoune, and S. Kimuna, *Globalization, liberalization, and the role of women in African development* (pp. 13–32). Trenton, NJ: Africa World Press.

Baliamoune-Lutz, M., & McGillivaray, M. (2009). Does gender inequality reduce growth in sub-Saharan African and Arab countries? *African Development Review, 21*(2), 224–249.

Barnes, F. C. (1983). *Rough side of the mountain* [CD]. Jackson, MS: Malaco Records.

Bhana, D., Morrell, R., Hearn, J., & Molestsane, R. (2007). Power and identity: An introduction to sexualities in southern Africa. *Sexualities, 10*(2), 131–139.

Bloom, M., Fischer, J., & Orme, J. (1995). *Evaluating practice: Guidelines for the accountable professional.* Boston, MA: Allyn & Bacon.

Boahen, A. (2003). *Yaa Asantewaa and the Asante-British War of 1900–1.* Oxford, UK: James Curry.

Bosompra, K. (2001). Determinants of condom use intentions of university students in Ghana: An application of the theory of reasoned action. *Social Science & Medicine, 52,* 1057–1069.

Bosu, W., Yeboah, K., Rangalyan, G., Atuahene, K., Lowndes, C., & Stover J. (2009). *Modes of HIV transmission in West Africa: Analysis of the distribution of new HIV infections in Ghana and recommendations for prevention.* Accra, Ghana: Ghana AIDS Commission.

Bowers, E. (2007). *Ghana market women pay the daily micro man.* Retrieved from http://womensenews.org/story/the-world/070226/ghana-market-women-pay-the-daily-micro-man

Burroughs, N. (1909). *Nannie Helen Burroughs papers, 1900–1963.* Washington DC: Library of Congress. Retrieved from http://lccn.loc.gov/mm80057026

Callegari L., Harper, C. C., Van der Straten, A., Kamba, M., Chipato, T., & Padian, N. S. (2008). Consistent condom use in married Zimbabwean women after a condom intervention. *Sexually Transmitted Diseases, 35,* 624–630.

Carlton-LaNey, I. (1997). Elizabeth Ross Haynes: An African American reformer of womanist consciousness, 1908–1940. *Social Work, 42,* 573–583.

Central Intelligence Agency. (2012). *World fact book: Africa, Ghana.* Retrieved from https://www.cia.gov/library/publications/the-world-factbook/geos/gh.html

Dageid, W., & Duckert, F. (2008). Balancing between normality and social death: Black, rural, south African women coping with HIV/AIDS. *Qualitative Health Research, 18*(2), 182–195.

Davids, T., & Van Driel, F. (2009). The unhappy marriage between gender and globalization. *Third World Quarterly, 30*(5), 905–920.

Duran, J. (2010). African NGOs and womanism: Microcredit and self-help. *Journal of AfricanAmerican Studies, 14*(2), 171–180.

Embassy of the Republic of Ghana. (2013). *Education in Ghana.* Retrieved from http://www.ghanaembassy.org/index.php?page=education-in-ghana

Faria, C. (2008). Privileging prevention, gendering responsibility: An analysis of the Ghanaian campaign against HIV/AIDS. *Social & Cultural Geography, 9*(1), 41–73.

Fatusi, A., & Blum, R. (2008). Predictors of early sexual initiation among a nationally representative sample of Nigerian adolescents. *BMC Public Health, 8,* 1–14.

Fetene, G. T., & Dimitriadis, G. (2010). Globalization, public policy, and "knowledge gap": Ethiopian youth and the HIV/AIDS pandemic. *Journal of Education Policy, 25,* 425–441.

Finn, J. L., & Jacobson, M. (2003). *Just practice: A social justice approach to social work.* Peosta, IA: Eddie Bowers.

Fiscian, V., Obeng, K., Goldstein, K., Shea, J., & Turner, B. (2009). A multifaceted U.S. HIV prevention education program for girls in Ghana. *AIDS Education and Prevention, 21*(1), 67–79.

Ghana AIDS Commission. (2012). *Ghana country AIDS progress report: Reporting period January 2010–December 2011.* Retrieved from http://www.unaids.org/en/dataanalysis/knowyourresponse/countryprogressreports/2012countries/ce_GH_Narrative_Report[1].pdf

Gutal, S. (2001). Women and globalization: Some key issues. *Women's International Network News*, 27(3), 15–16.

Hamer, F. L. (2011). "I'm sick and tired of being sick and tired": Speech delivered with Malcom X at the Williams Institutional CME Church, Harlem, New York, December 20, 1964. In M. Brooks & D. Houck (Eds.), *Speeches of Fannie Lou Hamer* (pp. 57–64). Jackson: University Press of Mississippi.

Hudson-Weems, C. (1998). Africana womanism. In O. Nnaemeka (Ed.), *Sisterhood, feminisms & power: From Africa to the diaspora* (pp. 149–162). Trenton, NJ: Africa World Press.

Johnston-Anumonwo, I., & Doane, D. (2011). Globalization, economic crisis and Africa's informal economy women workers. *Singapore Journal of Tropical Geography, 32*(1), 8–21.

Johnston-Anumonwo, I. & Oberhauser, A. M. (2011). Globalization and gendered livelihoods in sub-Saharan Africa: Introduction. *Singapore Journal of Tropical Geography, 32*(1), 4–7.

Joint United Nations Programme on HIV/AIDS. (2005). *AIDS epidemic update.* Retrieved from http://data.unaids.org/pub/EPISlides/2007/2007_epiupdate_en.pdf

Joint United Nations Programme on HIV/AIDS (UNAIDS). (2012). *Global report: UNAIDS report on the global AIDS epidemic.* Retrieved from http://www.unaids.org/en/media/unaids/contentassets/documents/epidemiology/2012/gr2012/20121120_UNAIDS_Global_Report_2012_en.pdf

Joint United Nations Programme on HIV/AIDS (UNAIDS). (n.d.). *HIV/AIDS prevention indicator survey: Knowledge, attitudes, sexual behavior, stigma.* Retrieved from https://www.globalhivmeinfo.org/DigitalLibrary/Digital Library/MEASURE-UNAIDSGeneralPopulationSurvey-Individual.pdf

Keddie, A. (2010). Neo-liberalism and new configurations of global space: Possibilities, tensions and problematics for gender justice. *Journal of Gender Studies, 19*(2), 139–152.

Kibungu, J. P., Mashinda, D. K., Matamba, G. M., Mayala., P. K., Kayembe, M. A., Mapatano, A. F., ...Musema, J. P. (2008). Determinants of consistent condom use among female commercial sex workers in the democratic republic of Congo: Implications for interventions. *Sexual Transmitted Infection, 84*(3), 202–206.

Kim, J. (2011). Religiosity and substance abuse among African American: The need for systematic research. *International Journal of Arts and Sciences, 4*(17), 29–33.

Kuokkanen, R. (2008). Globalization as racialized, sexualized violence. *International Feminist Journal of Politics, 10*(2), 216–233.

Lindgren, T., Rankin, S., & Rankin W. (2005). Malawi women and HIV: Socio-cultural factors and barriers to prevention. *Women & Health, 41*(1), 69–86.

Madlala, L. (2003). Transactional sex and the pursuit of modernity. *Social Dynamics, 29*(2), 1–21.

Martin, E., & Martin, J. (1995). *Social work and the Black experience.* Washington, DC: NASW Press.

McFadden, P. (2008). Globalizing resistance: Crafting and strengthening African feminist solidarities. *Black Scholar, 38*(2/3), 19–20.

Mikell, G. (1995). African feminism: Toward a new politics of representation. *Feminist Studies, 21,* 405–425.

Mill, J., & Anarfi, J. K. (2002). HIV risk environment for Ghanaian women: Challenges to prevention. *Social Science & Medicine, 54,* 325–337.

Muller, C. (2003). Knowledge between globalization and localization: The dynamics of female spaces in Ghana. *Current Sociology, 51,* 329–346.

National Institute of Allergy and Infectious Diseases (NAID). (2007). *HIV infection and AIDS.* Retrieved from http://www.Niad.Nih.Gov/Factsheets/Hivinf.htm

Naylor, R. (2000). *Ghana: An Oxfam country profile.* Boston, MA: Oxfam.

Neequaye, A. R., Neequaye, J. E., & Biggar, R. (1991). Factors that could influence the spread of AIDS in Ghana, West Africa: Knowledge of AIDS, sexual behavior, prostitution, and traditional medical practices. *Journal of Acquired Immunodeficiency Syndrome, 4*, 914–919.

Oberhauser, A., & Yeboah, M. (2011). Heavy burdens: Gendered livelihood strategies of porters in Accra, Ghana. *Singapore Journal of Tropical Geography, 32*(1), 22–37.

Organisation for Economic Co-operation and Development. (2012). *Social Institutions and gender index: Ghana*. Retrieved from http://genderindex.org/country/ghana

Onolemhemhen, D., & Ekwempu, C. C. (1999). An investigation of sociomedical risk factors associated with fistula in northern Nigeria. *Women & Health, 28*(3), 103–116.

Onolemhemhen, D., Perry, T. E., & Ekwempu, C. C. (2000). A study of socio-cultural and anthropometric risk factors associated with vesico-vaginal fistula among Hausa women of Northern Nigeria. *Ghana Medical Journal, 34*(1), 9–14.

Owuamanam, D. (1995). Sexual networking among youths. *Journal of Health Transition Review, 5*, 57–66

Oyewumi, O. (2003). Feminism, sisterhood, and other foreign relations. In O. Oyeronke (Ed.), *African women and feminism: Reflecting on the politics of sisterhood* (pp. 1–24). Trenton, NJ: Africa World Press.

Pellow, D. (1977). *Women in Accra: Options for autonomy*. Algonac, MI: Reference Publications.

Perry, T. (1998). *The lived experiences of Ghanaian women with HIV/AIDS: A phenomenological study* (Unpublished doctoral dissertation). The University of Alabama School of Social Work, Tuscaloosa, AL.

Perry, T., Boller, K., & Cummings, N. (1990). *The needs of HIV-infected post-partum minority females 1990* (Unpublished group master's thesis). Tulane University School of Social Work, New Orleans, LA.

Perry, T. E., Davis-Maye, D., & Onolemhemhen, D. (2007). Faith, spirituality, fatalism and hope: Ghanaian women coping in the face of HIV/AIDS. *Journal of HIV/AIDS and Social Services, 6*(4), 37–58.

Phillips, L. (2006). Womanism: On its own. In L. Phillips (Ed.), *The womanist reader: The first quarter century of womanist thought* (pp. xix-iv). New York, NY: Routledge.

Pro-Link. (2010). *Addressing the gender related aspects of HIV and AIDS in the Greater Accra, Ashanti and Eastern regions of Ghana year one final report (June 2009–May 2010)*. Retrieved from http://www.ghanaids.gov.gh/gac/docs/GENDER Programme Report Project to Address Gender Related Aspects of HIV Prolink.pdf

Rakodi, C. (2002). Economic development, urbanization and poverty. In C. Rakodi & T. Lloyd-Jones (Eds.), *Urban livelihoods: A people-centred approach to reducing poverty*. London, UK: Earthscan.

Robertson, C. (1984). *Sharing the same bowl: A socioeconomic history of women and class in Accra, Ghana*. Ann Arbor, MI: University of Michigan Press.

Robertson, R. (1995). Glocalization: Time-space and homogeneity-heterogeneity. In M. Featherstone, S. Lash, & R. Robertson (Eds.), *Global modernities* (pp. 25–44). Thousand Oaks, CA: SAGE.

Semere, L., & Nour, N. (2008). Obstetric fistula: Living with incontinence and shame. *Reviews in Obstetric Gynecology, 4*, 193–197.

Shefer, T., Crawford, M., Strebel, A., Simbayi, L., Dwadwa-Henda, N., Cloete, A., . . . Kalichman, S. C. (2008). Gender, power and resistance to change among two communities in the western cape, South Africa. *Feminism & Psychology, 18*(2), 157–182.

Smith, K. (2005). Why are they worried?Cconcern about HIV/AIDS in rural Malawi. *Demographic Research, 1*, 9. Retrieved from http://www.Demographic-Research.Org/Special/1/9/S1-9.Pdf

Solomon, C. (2006). The role of women in economic transformation: Market women in Sierra Leone. *Conflict, Security & Development, 6*, 411–423.

Stadler, J., Delany, S., & Mntambo, M. (2008). Women's perceptions and experiences of HIV prevention trials in Soweto, South Africa. *Social Science & Medicine, 66*(1), 189–200.

Steady, F. C. (1987) African feminism: A worldwide perspective. In R. Terborg-Penn (Ed.), Women in Africa and the African diaspora (pp. 18–19]). Washington, DC: Howard University Press.

Terrell, M. C. (1898). *The progress of colored women: An address delivered before the National American Women's Suffrage Association, at the Columbia Theater*. Washington, DC: Smith Bros.

Takyi, B. (2003). Religion and women's health in Ghana: Insights into HIV/AIDS preventive and protective behavior. *Social Science & Medicine, 56*, 1221–1234.

Tenkorang, E. (2012). Negotiating safer sex among married women in Ghana. *Archives of Sexual Behavior, 41*, 1353–1362.

Walker, A. (1983). *In search of our mothers' gardens*. New York, NY: Harcourt Brace Jovanovich.

Wall, L., Arrowsmith, S., Briggs, N., & Lassey, A. (2002). *Urinary incontinence in the developing world: The obstetric fistula*. Retrieved from http://www.fistulafoundation.org

CHAPTER 7

Chicana Feminisms, Intersectionality, and Social Work

Crossing Borders, Building Bridges

LETICIA VILLARREAL SOSA AND ALI MOORE

The feminist movement in the United States has transformed the way knowledge is acquired, developed, interpreted, and used. This movement has influenced a strong tradition of feminist scholarship in social work. Feminist scholars propose understanding the role of women and gender from a sociopolitical context as well as focusing on larger issues of social justice in regard to class, race, and homophobia (Flynn Saulnier, 2000; Hurtado, 1996). Despite advances, the current literature does not adequately address the intersectionality of identity or the historical and socioeconomic context of Chicanas in the United States. With the exception of a few studies or articles (e.g., Bryson & Lawrence-Webb, 2001; Miranda, 2002), little work in the field of social work addresses ethnicity and racial identity from a dynamic perspective that would account for the borderlands existence of Chicanas in the United States. As Bryson and Lawrence-Webb (2001) state, although there has been an effort to be more inclusive in social work, the reality is that the *other* continues to be marginalized, and this must be stated and acknowledged within the profession. One merely has to look at numbers of Chicanas and Chicanos, to see that at the very least, numerically, we are marginalized (Ortiz, Hernández, Fitch, Francis, & Aranda, 2004). This lack of representation among faculty ranks and practitioners slows the process of incorporating marginalized perspectives into social work's knowledge base. Theories grounded in the lived experiences of Chicanas and Chicanos can provide social work with a framework for creation of knowledge and work with men and women encountering intersections of race, class, and gender in an increasingly globalized world.

Our Journey

Because writing from a Chicana feminist perspective is personal, it seems fitting and necessary to begin with our own narratives about how we came to live, practice, and write using a Chicana feminist consciousness.

LETICIA VILLARREAL SOSA

My own lived experience certainly informed my research and practice as a social worker. I am a dark-skinned Mexican woman born in the United States of Mexican immigrant parents. I was raised in a predominately White suburb but traveled yearly to Mexico. I grew up speaking Spanish at home, but because my school world shamed my knowledge of Spanish, I often pretended that I did not speak Spanish. I felt lost in my borderlands existence. I did not know there was a way to frame and talk about my lived experience until I was a sophomore in college and heard Gloria Anzaldúa, a Chicana lesbian feminist, speak. My personal journey from that time bears witness to the power of this experience:

> She gave me the vocabulary to understand and articulate my own experience. Gloria talked about the dominant culture creating a checklist of who we are and how we are named. I felt as though I did not fit into any of these predetermined categories, but I felt pressured to choose one identity. Gloria said that we needed to take control of our identities and name ourselves. She described us as being a bridge. . . . I was overwhelmed and wanted to embrace her for giving me the gift of her words. (Villarreal Sosa, personal journal, April 26, 1991)

This was a defining moment for my scholarship and for my personal journey as a Chicana feminist. Although Anzaldúa's writing is grounded in the Mexican/Chicana experience, many themes are universal to any marginalized group learning to live among and negotiate physical and psychological borders. As I worked across borders in Cuba, Azerbaijan, Guatemala, and Mexico, I realized that many of us struggle with the themes Anzaldúa and other Chicana feminists describe.

In Azerbaijan, women struggle with feeling a sense of pride in their cultural experience and history while working to challenge gender oppression in their country. Azerbaijan is also experiencing its own cultural and political borderlands because of the continued influence of Russian culture as part of the former Soviet Union, because part of its land is occupied by Armenia, and because of its proximity to Turkey and Iran. In Cuba it was believed that fighting a class system would eliminate other forms of oppression. Now Cuban feminists are discussing issues of intersectionality and pushing Cuban society to recognize that although there is less economic inequality, issues with race, homophobia, and gender inequality continue. The Cuban experience demonstrates how relatively easy it is to create policy and legislative change regarding the role of women but how much more difficult it is to change everyday individual beliefs, attitudes, and behaviors. As a Chicana feminist, I felt a tremendous sense of solidarity with the Cuban people. Our struggles for social justice as Chicanas and Chicanos in the United States were parallel to the struggles of the Cuban people prior to the revolution for education, economic justice, and access to health care. Poor women and indigenous women in Mexico and Guatemala are facing serious concerns about increasing levels of violence, femicides, and impunity toward the perpetrators of this violence (Sampaio, 2004). At the same time, many women in Mexico and Guatemala are actively involved in the struggle for human rights, challenging the violence and fighting for rights as indigenous people.

In all these geographic locations, my own Chicana feminist perspective has informed the way I understand social problems and has given me an appreciation for how individuals work to resist oppression on political, economic, and cultural levels. I have gained a much better appreciation for what it is to have a sense of solidarity with others' struggles and the parallels with our own struggles as Chicanas and Chicanos in the United States. As Castillo (1994) states, "While it is crucial for us to grapple with issues of racism, it is equally crucial to realize that the root of that racism is in a historical, worldwide mindset of conquest" (p. 11). As Chicanas, we have to be grounded in the context of the U.S. economic system, its relationship to Mexico, the transnational labor force that many of us are a part of or born into, and the continued neocolonial relationship to the United States (Castillo, 1994). As we think about going from deconstructing and dismantling to building and constructing our own theory, we "move from focusing on what has been done to us (victimhood) to a more extensive level of agency" (Anzaldúa, 2002, p. 2). The logical next step as we face a period of intensifying globalization, which has only benefited the few and exacerbated existing inequalities, is to theorize how Chicana feminisms can inform transnational feminisms and help build global solidarity.

ALI MOORE

Just as the profession of social work can be described as one that encompasses multiple personal and professional intersecting ecological factors, my journey as a Chicana feminist has proven to be more than just an academic approach or a politically correct (or incorrect) opinion fit for coffee shop debates. I have found it is an approach, a theory, a guiding force, that has provided the language to better understand and respond to my lived experiences as a woman, international social worker, activist, mother, and international traveler. Most recently and profoundly, my Chicana feminist beliefs have served as the guiding force toward integrating and defining a more transnational feminism that could be used to create solidarity among other oppressed and marginalized groups (including men) through my master's thesis research and my move to Dar es Salaam, Tanzania.

Having volunteered in Tanzania for 9 months in 2008, working on HIV prevention with children, youths, and communities, I felt acutely aware of the effects gender inequality has on preventable health issues and outcomes. Unfortunately, at that time, my feminist lens had been predominately shaped by the White women's liberation movement that had focused on homogenizing, excluding, and blaming men for the social inequality they experienced in society. Additionally, having worked at a domestic violence shelter for women in the United States, I had been pulled further in the direction of wanting to work on female empowerment by focusing solely on liberating women from victimhood as the sole intervention toward achieving gender equality.

Working from this perspective, in my personal and professional life, I felt limited, conflicted, mistrustful, and frustrated as I worked very hard to prove myself to be powerful, intelligent, and worthy of equality with men. But what is equality and what men was I striving to be equal to? Apparently, I wasn't alone in this limited understanding of feminism. bell hooks (2000) argues that many White women have defined women's liberation in terms of obtaining class equality and privilege with White men; however, because they have often neglected to acknowledge their own White privilege and dismissed intersectionality, this perspective of women's liberation has promoted such messages as "all men are the enemy" (p. 69).

In relation to my international work, how could I possibly develop interventions that would effectively address patriarchy in a country not my own, challenged with historic and current elements of colonialism, racism, slavery, and neoliberal economic policies that further marginalize people of both genders without addressing contextual privilege and my own positionality as a mzungu (White) American young female with a White father and Chicana mother? For starters, it required putting my own ego away, opening my ears, and being honest with myself about personal and professional limitations because of the intersections of my own identity (and perceived identity) and privilege.

As part of my master's research and personal journey, I became immersed in literature written by feminist women of color, such as bell hooks, Cherríe Moraga, Gloria Anzaldúa, and Aída Hurtado, who put forward a postmodern perspective of identity formation that is reflective of the intersectionality of all social influences, such as "nationality, language, race and ethnicity, skin color, or other social or physical characteristics that are meaningful in particular social contexts" (Hurtado & Sinha, 2008, p. 339). From this perspective, the feminist focus shifts from fighting just sexism or classism to oppression at large. Additionally, in regard to addressing patriarchy, this perspective moves away from viewing men only as the oppressors and women only as the oppressed by eliciting a strengths-based belief that the socially constructed identities of masculinity and femininity can be transformed for the benefit of all (Hurtado & Sinha, 2008; Valentine, 2007). As I continued my work in Tanzania, the lessons learned from Chicana feminists and other women of color feminists became a part of my everyday work in addressing gender equality and empowerment in Tanzania.

In this chapter we describe Chicana feminisms, provide examples of how these perspectives informed our work, and offer implications of Chicana feminisms in a globalized context for social work, contributing to a more unified transnational feminist approach.

Chicana Feminisms

Chicana activism on behalf of women has a long history (e.g., Ruiz & Sánchez Korrol, 2005), which is largely undocumented (Castillo, 1994; Hurtado, 2003b). Most of the current Chicana feminist writing was born from the 1960s social movements in the United States. (Hurtado, 2003b; Roth, 2007). Chicana feminists were typically part of one of the progressive social movements of this time, such as the Chicano movement, women's movement, and antiwar movement, and they actively challenged oppression based on sexuality, gender, and class within these movements (Castillo, 1994; Hurtado, 2003b; Martínez, 1989).

Because Chicana feminists have not emphasized reaching consensus and have been willing to challenge oppression within other social movements, we use the term *Chicana feminisms*, acknowledging that Chicana feminists embraced their internal diversity earlier than other groups (Hurtado, 2003b). Chicana feminists write from their position as women, lesbians, members of a racial and ethnic group, and as members of a working-class group leading to different lived experiences of womanhood (Hurtado, 2003b; Sandoval, 1991). In defining feminisms in an inclusive manner that accounts for multiple experiences based on these intersections of identity, Chicana feminists have maintained solidarity with other third world feminist movements, White women's movements, Chicano movements, socialist movements, and revolutionary movements in Latin America (Castillo, 1994; Hurtado, 2003b; Sandoval, 2000). Solidarity is a political and ethical goal for Chicana feminists and is grounded in difference, rather than a vague assumption of sisterhood. However, the fundamental analysis of how power and privilege affects Chicanas is an approach that is shared with other women (Russo & Vaz, 2001). Solidarity can be created with other women of color facing similar conditions and with White feminists who have a social justice agenda.

A Chicana feminist consciousness is rooted in concepts of borders (geopolitical and psychological), and therefore cannot avoid addressing issues of globalization such as migration and a transnational existence. Chicana feminists have emphasized constructing and reconstructing affirming theoretical spaces and language that simultaneously reject colonialism and the consequences of patriarchal capitalism such as racism, sexism, and homophobia (Hurtado, 2003b; Pérez, 1991). Furthermore, when Chicana feminists speak of White women, they are speaking of White feminists in North America as well as Mexico, Latin America, and Europe. As Castillo (1994) states:

Very, very, very few dark women from poor or working class backgrounds who have taken up the pen have ever been published anywhere to date. . . . To enter into the ongoing international debate of women's issues poor, working women of color have had to rely on their representation by light-skinned or European descended women who identify with their ethnicity and/or nationality. (p. 4)

Thus, Chicana feminists have had to claim their own language and theoretical spaces that acknowledge their unique position, which includes other social identities such as gender, class, and race. In the following sections we further discuss Chicana feminisms, including the process of creating a space for Chicana feminist theorizing, the relationship to other feminisms, social identity theory, intersectionality, and borderlands.

Claiming Language and Culture

According to Hurtado (2003b), Chicana feminists claiming a *lengua*, or tongue, has multiple meanings. For many Chicanas, this is a literal attempt to reclaim Spanish and confront the trauma of language repression in the schools. Anzaldúa (1987) recalls being hit on the knuckles with a ruler for speaking Spanish at recess. In addition, because children of Mexican origin were not clearly Black or White, schools used language as a justification for de jure segregation (Gándara & Contreras, 2009; Hernández, 2002). In the context of schooling, language has been one of the main civil rights struggles for Latino students, and use of Spanish in the school has been controversial because it is used as a means to express group identity (Gándara & Contreras, 2009). The experiences for many Chicanas of either language loss or shame shaped the understanding of all discourse as political (Hurtado, 2003b): "In a consciously political act, what Gloria Anzaldúa calls 'linguistic terrorism,' I will not italicize Spanish words or phrases unless they are italicized in direct quotations" (p. 173). The use of Spanish by Chicana feminists was a way of not only asserting the value of Mexican identity and language, but to also create feminisms that accounted for the unique experiences of Chicanas.

Chicanas also recognized how important discourse, or lengua, is in shaping subjectivity (Hurtado, 2003b). Creating our own language or discourse is an important part of decolonizing ourselves and constructing our own identities. In doing so, we reclaim our everyday spaces as sources of theorizing. We pay attention to the way the women in our lives have found ways to survive and subvert patriarchy and oppression (Hurtado, 2003b; Villenas, Godinez, Delgado Bernal, & Elenes, 2006). These conversations occur in everyday life, in our homes, often at the kitchen table.

Creating space was equally important. As Chicana feminism developed, Chicano movement values were adopted but sometimes transformed. Chicana feminists were seeking a *sitio*, or a "space" within a nationalist movement (Roth, 2007). Chicana feminists also incorporated work by other feminist theorists particularly around the complexities of oppression and the emphasis on liberation (Hurtado, 2003b). Chicana feminists share a common concern with hybrid identities and multiple subjectivities with a focus on creating a theoretical space for alternative epistemologies (e.g., Anzaldúa, 1987; Castillo, 1994; Hurtado, 2003b). Hurtado (2003b) refers to this process as *relational dovetailing*. In other words, advances in feminist theory dovetail into one another, building our knowledge of women's oppression.

In creating this space, Chicana feminists are in a position of critiquing and embracing their culture. Chicana feminists recognize that some aspects of Mexican culture can be harmful to women similar to any patriarchal culture (Vazquez, 2002). However, being grounded in one's community and the positive aspects of the culture, such as an emphasis on emotional and social support within families, can provide protection and strength when dealing with racism in the larger society (Anzaldúa, 1987; Hurtado, 2003b; Villarreal Sosa, 2011). As different forms of Chicana feminism have evolved, some would now say that a Chicana is in fact a "countryless woman" (Castillo, 1994, p. 24). In other words, Chicana women and other non-White women are not represented by any country; rather they serve as a multinational and global workforce and continue to need to create their own space outside nationalist politics.

Social Identity

One area that has received some attention in psychology and social work is the negotiation and intersections of social identity among Latinas (Hurtado, 2003b, Hurtado & Cervantez, 2009; Villarreal Sosa, 2011). As a part of this work Chicana and Latina feminists have challenged assimilation and acculturation frameworks and instead proposed the more contemporary approach of social identity theory (Hurtado, 2003b).

Social identity is a framework that describes identity as fluid and context dependent. According to Hurtado, Rodriguez, Gurin, and Beals (1993), social identity is a complex phenomenon shaped by social and cultural factors and the assimilation or rejection of these factors. Social identity captures the relationship between the self-concept resulting from membership in a social group and the emotional significance attached to that membership (Tajfel, 1978). Therefore, a social identity framework helps us understand that as the social context shapes social identity, one's social identity offers a framework for negotiation and giving meaning to the social environment.

Also important here is to distinguish between personal identity and social identity to develop interventions that take into account Latinas' social identity, particularly stigmatized identities such as those based on class, race, gender, ethnicity, or sexuality (Hurtado & Cervantez, 2009). Personal identity is thought to derive from intrapsychic influences shaped within the family and tends to underestimate the effect of social context and structure in shaping individual characteristics (Hurtado & Cervantez, 2009). Individuals who occupy different social locations express meaning in distinct ways and develop meanings related to their position in the social structure. Social identity theory allows for an understanding of the subjective importance of these categorizations and how these processes might influence behavior depending on the context (e.g., racial identity in the school setting or gender in the home context).

This perspective fits well with Chicana feminist theory, emphasizing the history of Mexicans in the United States, language, culture, and a borderlands perspective on identity. A social identity perspective honors and recognizes the psychological work involved in achieving a positive sense of self when one's social identity is stigmatized in our society. In addition, an approach that recognizes and names various forms of oppression and accounts for historical and current context can lead to new approaches and interventions, such as redefining therapy from an individual approach to a collective or social approach.

Borders

"The Borderlands are physically present wherever two or more cultures edge each other, where people of different races occupy the same territory, where under, lower, middle and upper classes touch, where the space between two individuals shrinks with intimacy" (Anzaldúa, 1987).

Borderlands theory is premised on the physical border between Texas and the U.S. Southwest and Mexico, and the psychological, sexual, linguistic, and spiritual borders that function in Anzaldúa's existence as a lesbian, Chicana, Tejana, working-class academic (Anzaldúa, 1987). Many Chicana feminists have embraced borderlands theory as a way to expand our understanding of intersectionality (Hurtado & Cervantez, 2009). In addition, the geographical location of the borderlands was a metaphor for theorizing about the oppression and subordination from an ethnically specific *mestiza* consciousness (Hurtado & Cervantez, 2009). A *mestiza* conscioiusness refers to cultural and racial hybridity, grounded in the Spanish and Indian roots of people of Mexican ancestry (Beltran, 2004).

Anzaldúa (1987) undermines rigid boundaries, creates a new theoretical home for Chicanas and others experiencing a bordered identity, and refuses to fit into one academic discipline. This is intended to be a space that undermines rigid boundaries and allows for agency and ambiguity to exist (Beltran, 2004). Anzaldúa creates a new mestiza consciousness capable of crossing borders, living with ambiguities, and oppositional consciousness (Beltran, 2004; Hurtado & Cervantes, 2009). Because of their geographic reality of borders, collective history of internal colonization, and continued experiences with internalized borders, Chicanas and Chicanos have intimate experience and knowledge of borders and how to live in those borders as they accept, reject, or create new categories.

Not only did Anzaldúa (1987) create a new theoretical space for an identity characterized by fluidity, multiplicity, and contradiction, but she also created a theoretical space that was "accessible and emotionally gripping" (Beltran, 2004, p. 597) in a way that other feminist theorists were not able to accomplish. Furthermore, Anzaldúa draws on a history among Mexicans grounded in the recognition of hybridity and mestizaje. In Anzaldúa's (1987) poem, "To live in the Borderlands means you," she states that to survive this borderlands existence, one must live without borders and allow multiple subject positions to emerge.

A borderlands perspective complements social identity theory by providing the lived experience related to the psychological work needed to deal with the burden of a stigmatized identity and the conflict between a Chicana's own meaning of that identity and the negative meanings imposed by society. In fact, many Chicanas and Latinas deal with this conflict in creative ways, often leading to a commitment to social justice (Hurtado, 2003b). Although Anzaldúa's

Borderlands/La Frontera has become a widely cited and influential text (Beltran, 2004), it has not made its way into social work theorizing about Mexican-origin populations, our theories of human development and the social environment, nor our understanding of the globalized context. This perspective could inform our understanding of any group living in psychological or physical borders and subsequently shape our practice and policy.

Intersectionality

While I have more in common with a Mexican man than a white woman, I have much more in common with an Algerian woman than I do with a Mexican man. This opinion, I'm sure chagrins women who sincerely believe our female physiology unequivocally binds all women throughout the world, despite the compounded social prejudices that daily affect us all in different ways. Although women everywhere experience life differently from men everywhere, white women are members of a race that has proclaimed itself globally superior for hundreds of years. (Castillo, 1994, p. 23–24)

Early Chicana feminists were directly concerned with issues related to their status as women who were non-White, culturally different, with varying citizenship status, and from a working-class background (Castillo, 1994). At the time African American women also challenged White feminist comparisons of sexism to racism because this did not account for the experience of being Black and a woman (Castillo, 1994; Hill Collins, 1991, 2000). Publications such as *This Bridge Called My Back* (Moraga & Anzaldúa, 1981) provided powerful testimonies by women of color about the intersections of oppression and challenged the condescension by White women toward poor, culturally different women of color. Anzaldúa's (1987) groundbreaking and influential book, *Borderlands/La Frontera*, laid the foundation for the concept of intersectionality by describing Chicana oppression because of gender, race, ethnicity, class, and sexuality (Hurtado & Cervantez, 2009).

A sophisticated understanding of intersectionality involves a context-based analysis that addresses intersecting social identities based on gender, race, class, sexuality, immigration status, and others (Hurtado, 1996). Intersectionality theorists such as Hill Collins (1991, 2000) state that inequality cannot be explained nor challenged if only one dimension of oppression is addressed. Addressing intersectionality allows for connecting issues of oppression on a macrolevel and helps us understand how individuals negotiate intersecting social identities on a microlevel (Hill Collins, 2000). Others refuse to "rank" oppressions and argue that the intersection of various identities affects the experience of oppression (Moraga, 1981). An intersectionality perspective also informs and problematizes a human rights paradigm applied to women worldwide (Fregoso, 2003). For example, understanding the femicides in Guatemala or Cuidad Juarez, Mexico, requires not only a gender analysis but one that would address the fact that the victims are primarily young, working class or poor, and indigenous or dark skinned instead of privileged White Mexican or Guatemalan women.

The Incorporation of Men

Incorporating Latino men in feminist analysis and scholarship is a necessary part of coalition building for Latina feminists. Understanding patriarchy within a specific culture can provide a much more nuanced and complicated understanding of masculinity than is typically found in White feminist writings (Hurtado & Cervantez, 2009). Using a Chicana feminist perspective, Chicano men's vulnerabilities are considered as well as their position of privilege as men. Chicana feminist research on Latino men by Hurtado and Sinha (2006) found that men experience privilege in the family, such as fewer responsibilities for household chores or more freedom. However, Hurtado and Sinha also found that Latino men are more likely to experience harassment by the police, feel less close to their parents, and have fewer close friends compared to Latinas. This combination of fewer rules at home with more experiences of negative categorization by police or school potentially leads to less educational success or other forms of marginalization (Hurtado & Cervantez, 2009; Hurtado & Sinha, 2006; Villarreal Sosa, 2011). A Chicana feminist perspective must also emphasize the deconstruction of masculinities and allows for multiple masculinities (Hurtado & Sinha, 2006; Hurtado & Sinha, 2008).

Reflexive Practice

Chicana feminism calls for reflexive practice in our work and our research (Hurtado & Cervantez, 2009). Reflexivity suggests that no one is exempt from contributing to oppression, even if in limited ways, and becomes essential in gaining a deeper understanding of another's perspective and necessary for coalition building (Hurtado & Cervantez, 2009; Pérez, 1991). Anzaldúa (1987) describes this as a mestiza consciousness that can simultaneously embrace and reject, perceive multiple realities at once, and incorporate indigenous Aztec beliefs that bypass linear ways of thinking. Chicana feminist scholars conduct research that attempts to build inclusivity and continued self-reflexivity into the process. In this way, it is possible to create a more accurate and respectful scholarship than has been conducted in the past.

The following sections contain two case studies that show how both authors incorporated the principles of Chicana feminisms into their own scholarship and practice. The first case study describes Leticia Villarreal Sosa's research with a Mexican community in Chicago, and in the second case study Ali Moore describes her practice and her research with a group of young men and women in Tanzania.

Case Studies
LETICIA VILLARREAL SOSA: BORDER IDENTITIES IN CHICAGO
I followed a group of 32 Mexican-origin youths in Chicago from 1997 to 1999 as they moved from eighth grade to high school. During the course of the study, I conducted nine in-depth qualitative interviews with each student, collected information from teachers, and interviewed parents (Villarreal Sosa, 2011). My theoretical framework incorporated social identity theory to help understand the negotiation students had to do in response to the anti-immigrant sentiment of the time as well as the legacy of the historical context of oppression and colonization. Because I felt that current educational theories had not adequately addressed the experiences of Mexican-origin youths in the schools, I used the Chicana feminist concepts of borderlands, the emphasis on intersectionality, as well as the attention to historical context to address the unique position and experiences of Mexican-origin youths. Finally, because of the particular struggles of young Latino men and the lack of feminist attention to Latino men, I felt it was critical to include adolescent boys as well as girls in the study.

My research methodology was grounded in what Hurtado (2003a) calls an *endarkened epistemology*. This approach includes challenging dominant research methods and what is considered data. For example, this approach necessitates not claiming one discipline but rather dovetailing in and out of theoretical approaches to construct a theory that can account for the lived experiences of those who are marginalized and often excluded from knowledge production (Hurtado, 2003a). Although Chicana feminisms are primarily found in the humanities, I could not accurately represent or understand the experiences of my students without using the knowledge from Chicana feminists as a grounding framework. In fact, Chicana poetry was a form of data and a part of the theoretical framework. I also had to be aware of various voices in my own writing reflecting my own social position. I employed the scholarly, university-trained, ethnographer voice and the border-crossing ethnographer voice situated in my experience as a woman, descendent of Mexican immigrants to the United States, and first-generation university student from a working-class background.

From this research I developed a model (see Figure 7.1) to conceptualize how key variables are linked to social identity and academic performance grounded within a borderlands and social identity theoretical framework. This model is intended to be an interactive process with all variables working simultaneously to have an effect on each other.

In this model I begin with the historical context of colonization leading to the construction of Mexicans as racially inferior, described by Anzaldúa (1987) and other Chicana feminists (e.g., Castillo, 1994; Elenes, 1997, 2001). The educational experiences of Mexican Americans are also included in this historical context. Mexican Americans have a history of being treated as intellectually inferior, segregated, and devalued in the school system and have been defined as intellectually inferior (Donato, 1997). This history of conquest also created a border, which continued to hold geographic and practical meaning as individuals were suddenly incorporated into the United States, and as migration and border crossing continues to be a part of the Mexican experience. Mexican-origin youths in this study experienced a borderlands existence psychologically, culturally, and sometimes physically as they traveled between borders with their families.

Second, I have included the current sociopolitical context drawn from student interviews. I included those issues that were relevant to students at the time of the study. Students felt attacked as Mexican-origin youths because of the anti-immigration laws and rhetoric they experienced. As one 10th-grade student, Anna, born in the United States stated:

> I don't think they should even call them immigration laws. I think
> they're laws against just Mexicans because I don't see them saying any-

FIGURE 1
SOCIAL IDENTITY AND BORDERLANDS

Social Identity Processes and Academic Performance

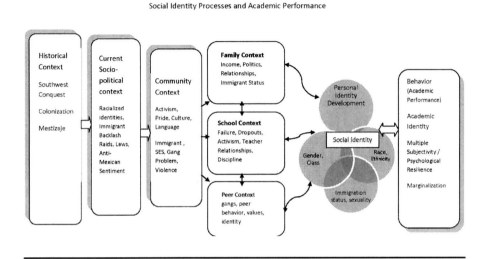

thing about people from other parts of the world coming here saying you're the one that, you know it's always the Mexicans, Mexicans.

Students brought these issues and concerns into the school context and had to negotiate the meaning of these attacks as it related to their own Mexican identities. In addition, the student interviews make clear that their Mexican identities were more than just an ethnicity but also a racial identification. Students had to negotiate intersections of identity related to gender, class, color, and immigration status and perceived a lack of outrage about the injustice Mexicans experienced. Sergio, a U.S.-born 10th grade student, makes this point about the 1996 videotaped beating of two undocumented Mexican immigrants by California sheriff's deputies:

I don't know if you noticed that everybody [in the] Rodney King riot, everybody got united because they beat some guy and they weren't going to take it. Look at the Mexicans at the border. They got beat up for no reason, they had it on videotape and everything, for who knows what. I don't even know what's going on about that. Nobody really speaks about that.

This model not only seeks to present the challenges students face coming from a history of oppression and colonization, and current experiences of oppression, but also the strengths of students' identity and survival. Students were proud of their parents' struggles and were proud of being Mexican. In the face of discrimination and marginalization, students retreated to their Mexican identities as a way of providing the necessary psychological strength to cope with the negative circumstances. In the following, Janette talks about the reasons she considers herself Mexican:

> I consider myself Mexican even though I was born here. I wish so much that I would be born in Mexico. I consider myself one hundred percent Mexican just because my parents are from there. I love my country [Mexico] so much. It's like I'd rather be born there than here. Over there, yeah, it's hard, but here, what's the point of being born here if you got your brown skin. Brown hair. They don't care if you were born here.

Academically, the students negotiated fragile academic identity in a context that constructed their academic identities as at risk. In other words, those who succeeded were framed as successful in spite of their culture. Yet my findings suggest that those students who were the most distanced and alienated from their Mexican identity were the ones who had the most difficulty. The students who were well-connected to their Mexican identity could draw from their cultural resources such as family and a positive construction of being Mexican to cope with their negative school experiences.

This model was developed considering the Chicana feminist theoretical work that honors the intersectionality of the identities, the historical and current contexts that shape individual experience, and the strengths students can draw from their cultural contexts. This model could also be used as a tool to be adapted to a particular group and its unique historical and current circumstances and constructions of group members' social identity.

ALI MOORE: GENDER EMPOWERMENT IN DAR ES SALAAM, TANZANIA

In the Tanzanian context men and boys are expected to take on the dominant role of financial provider and decision maker in the home because of socially and historically constructed ideas of masculinity (Gupta, 2000; Peacock, Stemple, Sawires, & Coates, 2009; Silberschmidt, 2001). Unfortunately, because of racial and economic oppression, illustrated in the historical context of colonialism and poverty, Tanzanian men are frequently unable to uphold this role. Therefore, they may seek out other ways of feeling in control and dominant over their environment, potentially leading to gender-based violence, alcohol abuse, and infidelity (hooks, 2000; Lary, Maman, Katebalila, McCauley & Mbwambo, 2004). Solely relying on women to become empowered and liberate themselves from the negative effects of gender inequality not only runs contrary to the realities of patriarchy and oppression but is also shortsighted by not addressing the responsibility of men and boys in transforming gender inequality.

This attention to constructions of masculinity is especially important to consider when creating interventions to effectively address reproductive health and HIV in Tanzania, which is why I used this approach in my work with People in the Fight Against AIDS in Tanzania (WAMATA), an organization founded by a Tanzanian female social worker who wanted to address the increased need for support services to those infected with HIV and their caregivers, who were (and remain) predominately women. Although WAMATA has grown and operates 19 branches throughout Tanzania, my master's of social work practicum and research specifically focused on this program in the port city of Dar es Salaam from January to April 2011.

Previous social workers had noticed consistently low participation rates among the young women and girls who were involved in WAMATA-sponsored youth activities at the Dar es Salaam location (i.e., youth support groups and community outreach groups). Identifying this as an area that needed to be addressed, a monthly women's empowerment group was created. However, this group did not produce an increase in the number of young women involved in other co-ed youth activities, nor did it help increase the participation rate among the women who did attend the co-ed group activities. Men had not been equally sensitized to concepts regarding gender equality, women's rights, and empowerment. Therefore, they continued to dominate co-ed activities and discussions, discouraging the participation of women.

An assessment of the organization uncovered the need for interventions that focus on changing the gendered attitudes and beliefs of men in regard to relationships, power, gender roles, and sex to assist with HIV prevention (Bujra

& Mokake, 2000). This need for a shift in focus was adamantly expressed by the women members of WAMATA when they were quoted saying, "We know these things, please help us to make our men know" (Bujra & Mokake, 2000, p. 170). This statement reflects the burden placed on women by focusing only on female empowerment while they remain in an unchanged environment where the men have not been sensitized.

After a long process of discussion with previous interns, the acting director of WAMATA, and female participants who insisted that their voices needed to be heard by the men, it was decided that a co-ed empowerment workshop (emphasizing consciousness-raising and the practice of new behaviors) would be offered for the WAMATA youths. Additionally, I would evaluate this process of transforming the socially constructed definitions, beliefs, attitudes, behaviors, and practices associated with masculinity and femininity in their Tanzanian context. I selected the One Man Can: Working With Men and Boys to Reduce the Spread and Impact of HIV and AIDS curriculum developed by Sonke Gender Justice Network (a nonprofit organization in South Africa that promotes gender equality) because of its incorporation of intersectionality, its relevance in the African context, and its proven effectiveness in engaging men and changing their beliefs (Peacock, Stemple, Sawires, & Coates, 2009).

Participants were recruited from WAMATA's existing co-ed youth group ranging from ages 15 to 35. On average, about 60 male and 30 female youths attended each weekly session. Despite the lower percentage of women, they were the most vocal about the importance of a co-ed group. For 8 consecutive weeks, three Tanzanian cofacilitators (two male and one female) and I implemented 2-hour workshop sessions about gender, power, and health; gender and violence; gender, HIV, and AIDS; healthy relationships; and taking action for change.

As I developed this project, I continued deepening my knowledge of third world feminism, in particular Chicana feminisms. I incorporated what I learned from the literature on deconstructing masculinities (Hurtado & Sinha, 2006, 2008), the emphasis on my own positionality, the need for a reflexive approach (Sandoval, 2000), and dovetailing in and out of relevant feminist theories (Hurtado, 2003b). As Villarreal Sosa (2011) had done in her work with Mexican-origin youths, I too considered the historical context of colonization and its effects on the construction of masculinity, the current political contexts, and intersectionality of the youths.

In regard to my role it was especially important that I address as many aspects of my positionality and privilege as possible and plan around the inherent limitations caused by those factors. For example, even though I am able to communicate in Swahili, I felt that the perceived power and privilege associated with my White skin, nationality, and native English tongue made it important that I recruit and collaborate with Tanzanian social work students as cofacilitators for the workshops, providing the constant cultural and lingual modifications necessary to keep the curriculum relevant and responsive.

This meant I had to regularly meet with the Tanzanian cofacilitators to discuss the material and its relevance to the Tanzanian youths as well as the group responses to the social identities of the facilitators. I also believed it was important to have a gender balance among facilitators and for the other facilitators to be Tanzanian so they could model the equality that would be presented in the activities. By doing so, the youths and facilitators guided the process of challenging their own cultural practices of oppression while constructing positive identities reflective of a more socially conscious, responsible, and equitable (especially gender equitable) youth culture in Tanzania (Hurtado, 2003b; Sandoval, 2000).

Not only did the results of the evaluative data demonstrate the effectiveness of the curriculum and a Chicana feminist approach toward implementation, the workshop also promoted a sort of kitchen table feminism by challenging participants to become agents of change (Moore, 2011). Kitchen table feminism refers to the conversations that Chicanas or other third world feminists have at home with their mothers, sisters, aunts, and other family members. This is the theory building that happens in the flesh from lived experiences and the process of challenging cultural norms that are oppressive. One 25-year-old Tanzanian male wrote on his posttest evaluation, "Yes, I have used it [the lessons] by educating my friends together with my brothers who are not lucky enough to come . . . about the equality that everyone deserves and equal responsibilities for all."

This process of validating other forms of oppression, via discussions of intersectionality, assists in promoting empathy for the lived gendered experiences of individuals, an emotion necessary to elicit when soliciting solidarity for the promotion of this paradigm shift and the personal and societal transformation of gender norms. As demonstrated in this case study, the Chicana feminist perspective of reflexivity, inclusion of men, and understanding of my own positionality were the largest components that guided my practice and research in Tanzania.

Implications for a Globalized Context

Although the 20th century was a time of maturing of feminist ideas and movements, we have also seen the rise of colonization through capitalism and the devastating consequences of a neoliberal economic global policy. In addition, even though feminist ideas have developed and matured, the backlash to feminist ideas has grown through ethnic, nationalist, or religious fundamentalist movements and nations (Talpade Mohanty, 2004). Sandoval (2000) asserts that U.S. third world feminist women used oppositional practices in the "first essentially 'postmodern' resistance movements of the twentieth century" (p. 2) with the potential for creating spaces to develop an understanding and resistance in a globalized context. According to Sandoval, U.S. third world feminists provided an oppositional consciousness capable of forming solidarity between social justice movements in the United States and global movements toward decolonization.

Extending Chicana Feminisms

Chandra Talpade Mohanty (2004) extends the notion of borders to encompass the notion of the sense of urgency as well as an "internationalist commitment" already present in feminist praxis (p. 1). Like Anzaldúa (1987) in the southwestern United States, Talpade Mohanty, in her own context growing up in Mumbai, is grounded in the acute awareness of "borders, boundaries, and traces of British colonialism on the one hand, and of the unbounded promise of decolonization on the other" (p. 1). The work by Anzaldúa on the concept of borders, both an awareness of them and developing the ability to transcend them, has implications for the global context. Talpade Mohanty describes feminism without borders as "feminism without silences and exclusions in order to draw attention to the tension between the simultaneous plurality and narrowness of borders and the emancipatory potential of crossing through, with, and over these borders in our everyday lives" (p. 2). As Hurtado and Cervantez (2009) assert, borderlands theory can be used to describe anyone caught between contradictory social systems or experiencing social dislocation.

As we think about several concepts in Chicana feminisms, one consideration that can be extended to other groups is the special emphasis on historical trajectories of groups and the particular history of colonization (Hurtado & Cervantez, 2009). Finally, another extension of Chicana feminist theory as well as other forms of feminisms is to make them applicable to the lives of everyday women who may not have access to these labels or frameworks to help them understand their actions. Hurtado's (2003b) work demonstrates that often low-income, immigrant women live their lives in a way that exhibit feminist characteristics such as individual agency, fighting patriarchal control, seeking economic independence, and forming solidarity with other women. Hurtado suggests that we must keep our definitions of feminism flexible enough to be inclusive of the range of experiences of women. This would be a feminism that would privilege the lived experience of women whose definition of womanhood may vary by culture, language, class, or other social identities.

Conclusion

Feminist scholarship needs to have a vision for transformation and strategies to accomplish this vision. Although many women of color feminists have critiqued the development of an armchair or academic feminism, in social work we can continue to develop a feminism grounded in community, partnership, and lived experiences. We have the unique responsibility and opportunity to continue to develop these ideas, practice these principles, and learn from others in our work. Everyday practice grounded in a feminist, antiracist, and anticapitalist approach is just as important as our participation in organized political movements and the continued development of creative and scholarly work.

> To be a citizen in a democracy is to recognize one's partiality—that each perspective is simultaneously limited and in flux. Moreover, such partiality and changeableness means that political agreement is always fragile and contingent. And that while we arrive with radically different experiences, through dialogue and contestation, we can forge a shared vision of the world. This is the promise that democratic theorists have seen in Anzaldúa's theory of mestiza subjectivity. (Beltran, 2004, p. 606)

As social workers, we can all identify with and embrace the definitions and practice of Chicana feminism. Chicana feminism is interdisciplinary and intentionally incorporates the social and historical contexts. The challenge for us in social work is first of all to make sure that the knowledge developed by Chicanas and others "at the margins" is brought into the center of social work education. Second, we must challenge ourselves in our work to design interventions based on the principles of Chicana feminisms, particularly for the growing Latino immigrant population. As the preceding excerpt from Beltran (2004) suggests, through dialogue we can forge a new vision of the world while being grounded in our differences.

Discussion Questions and Activities

1. Describe your own social location and matrix of oppression. Create a list of your various social identities (e.g., race, sex, gender, sexual orientation, class, ability, religion, age, immigration status). Decide whether you consider each social identity a privileged social group, a targeted or stigmatized social group, or a border social group (which changes from privilege to stigmatized depending on the context). Which social group status was the most difficult to identify? Which were easiest to identify? How does the intersection of these various identities shape your experience of gender?

2. Consider the model in Figure 7.1. How might this model be adapted for a different ethnic or racial group? What might be some of the differences in outcomes or behavior based on the different historical and current social context? How might you adapt and use this model for practice in your own community?

3. How does considering borderlands theory inform the way you work with Latinos? What are the implications of borderlands theory for understanding issues of identity among Latinos? How might borderlands theory help build solidarity with others in other global contexts?

References

Anzaldúa, G. (1987). Borderlands/la frontera: The new mestiza. San Francisco, CA: Spinsters/Aunt Lute.

Anzaldúa, G. (2002). Preface: (Un)natural bridges, (un)safe spaces. In G. E. Anzaldúa & A. Keating (Eds.), This bridge we call home: Radical visions for transformation (pp. 1–5). New York, NY: Routledge.

Beltran, C. (2004). Patrolling borders: Hybrids, hierarchies and the challenge of mestizaje. Political Research Quarterly, 57(4), 595–607.

Bryson, B. J., & Lawrence-Webb, C. (2001). Social work practice and profession: The utility of Black feminist thought. *Race, Gender, and Class, 7*(4), 7–17.

Bujra, J., & Mokake, S. (2000). AIDS activism in Dar es Salaam: Many struggles, a single goal. In C. Baylies & J. Bujra (Eds.), *AIDS, sexuality and gender in Africa: Collective strategies and struggles in Tanzania and Zambia* (pp. 154–174). London, UK: Routledge.

Castillo, A. (1994). *Massacre of the dreamers: Essays on xicanisma.* Albuquerque, NM: University of New Mexico Press.

Donato, R. (1997). *The other struggle for equal schools: Mexican Americans during the civil rights era.* Albany, NY: SUNY Press.

Elenes, A. C. (1997). Reclaiming the borderlands: Chicana/o identity, difference, and critical pedagogy. *Educational Theory, 47*(3), 359–376.

Elenes, A. C. (2001). Transformando fronteras: Chicana feminist transformative pedagogies. *Qualitative Studies in Education, 14*(5), 689–702.

Flynn Saulnier, C. (2000). Incorporating feminist theory into social work practice: Group work examples. *Social Work with Groups, 23*(1), 5–29.

Fregoso, R. L. (2003). *MeXicana encounters: The making of social identities on the borderlands.* Berkeley, CA: University of California Press.

Gándara, P., & Contreras, F. (2009). *The Latino educational crisis: The consequences of failed social policies.* Cambridge, MA: Harvard University Press.

Gupta, G. (2000). Gender, sexuality, and HIV/AIDS: The what, the why, and the how. *Canadian HIV/AIDS Policy Law Review, 5*(4), 86–93. Retrieved from http://www.ncbi.nlm.nih.gov/pubmed/11833180

Hernández, R. (2002). *The silent minority: Mexican Americans in the Chicago public schools, 1970–2001* (Doctoral dissertation). Available from ProQuest Dissertations and Theses database. (UMI No. 3056420).

Hill Collins, P. (1991). *Black feminist thought.* New York, NY: Routledge.

Hill Collins, P. (2000). *Black feminist thought: Knowledge, consciousness, and the politics of empowerment* (2nd ed.). New York, NY: Routledge.

hooks, b. (2000). *Feminist theory: From margin to center.* Cambridge, MA: South End Press.

Hurtado, A. (1996). *The color of privilege: Three blasphemies on race and feminism.* Ann Arbor: University of Michigan Press.

Hurtado, A. (2003a). Theory in the flesh: Toward an endarkened epistemology. *Qualitative Studies in Education, 16*(2), 215–225.

Hurtado, A. (2003b). *Voicing Chicana feminism: Young women speak out on sexuality and identity.* New York, NY: New York University Press.

Hurtado, A., & Cervantez, K. (2009). A view from within and from without: The development of Latina feminist psychology. In F. A. Villarruel, G. Carlo, J. M. Grau, M. Azmitia, N. J. Cabrera, & T. J. Tahin (Eds.), *Handbook of U.S. Latino psychology: Developmental and community-based perspectives* (pp. 171–190). Thousand Oaks, CA: SAGE.

Hurtado, A., Rodriguez, J., Gurn, P., & Beals, J. (1993). The impact of Mexican descendants' social identity on the ethnic socialization of children. In M. Bernal & G. Knight (Eds.), *Ethnic identity: Formation and transmission among Hispanics and other minorities* (pp. 131–162). Albany, NY: SUNY Press.

Hurtado, A., & Sinha, M. (2006). Differences and similarities: Latina and Latino doctoral students navigating the gender divide. In J. Castellanos, A. M. Gloria, & M. Kamimura (Eds.), *The Latino pathway to the Ph.D.: Abriendo caminos* (pp. 149–168). Sterling, VA: Stylus.

Hurtado, A., & Sinha, M. (2008). More than men: Latino feminist masculinities and intersectionality. *Sex Roles, 59*(5/6), 337–339. doi: 10.1007/s11199-008-9405-7

Lary, H., Maman, S., Katebalila, M., McCauley, A., & Mbwambo, J. (2004). Exploring the association between HIV and violence: Young people's experiences with infidelity, violence and forced sex in Dar es Salaam, Tanzania. *International Family Planning Perspectives, 30*(4), 200–206. Retrieved from http://ezproxy.dom.edu/login?url=http://search.ebscohost.com/login.aspx?direct=true&db=aph&AN=15397173&site=ehost-live

Martínez, E. (1989). That old (White) male magic. *Z Magazine, 27*(8), 48–52.

Miranda, G. (2002). *Mixed feelings: Stories of race, kinship, and identity among biracial adoptees* (Doctoral dissertation). Available from ProQuest Dissertations and Theses database. (UMI No. 3072790).

Moore, A. (2011). *Gender empowerment in Dar es Salaam, Tanzania: An evaluation of a male-focused empowerment intervention* (Unpublished master's thesis). Dominican University, River Forest, IL.

Moraga, C. (1981). La Guera. In C. Moraga & G. Anzaldúa, *This bridge called my back: Writings by radical women of color* (pp. 29–34).Watertown, MA: Persephone Press.

Moraga, C., & Anzaldúa, G. (Eds.). (1981). *This bridge called my back: Writings by radical women of color*. Watertown, MA: Persephone Press.

Ortiz, L. A., Hernúndez, S. H., Fitch, D., Francis, E. A., & Aranda, M. (2004). *Latinos in social work education: Demographics and strategies for change: A strategic paper*. Alexandria, VA: Council on Social Work Education.

Peacock, D., Stemple, L., Sawires, S., & Coates, T. (2009). Men, HIV/AIDS, and human rights. *Journal of Acquired Immune Deficiency Syndromes, 51*(3), S119–S125. doi: 10.1097/QAI.0b013e3181 aafd8a.

Pérez, E. (1991). Sexuality and discourse: Notes from a Chicana survivor. In C. Trujillo (Ed.), *Chicana lesbians: The girls our mothers warned us about* (pp. 159–84). Berkeley, CA: Third Woman Press.

Roth, B. (2007). A dialogical view of the emergence of Chicana feminist discourse. *Critical Sociology, 33*(4), 709–730.

Ruiz, V. L., & Sánchez Korrol, V. (Eds.). (2005). *Latina legacies: Identity, biography, and community*. New York, NY: Oxford University Press.

Russo, N. F., & Vaz, K. (2001). Addressing diversity in the decade of behavior: Focus on women of color. *Psychology of Women Quarterly, 25*(4), 280–294.

Sampaio, A. (2004). Transnational feminisms in a new global matrix. International *Feminist Journal of Politics, 6*(2), 181–206. doi: 10.1080/1461674042000211290.

Sandoval, C. (1991). U.S. third world feminism: The theory and method of oppositional consciousness in the postmodern world. *Genders, 10*, 1–24.

Sandoval, C. (2000). *Methodology of the oppressed*. Minneapolis, MN: University of Minnesota Press.

Silberschmidt, M. (2001). Disempowerment of men in rural and urban East Africa: Implications for male identity and sexual behavior. *World Development, 29*(4), 657–671.

Tajfel, H. (1978). *Differentiation between social groups: Studies in the social psychology of intergroup relations*. London, UK: Academic Press.

Talpade Mohanty, C. (2004). *Feminism without borders: Decolonizing theory, practicing solidarity*. Durham, NC: Duke University Press.

Valentine, G. (2007). Theorizing and researching intersectionality: A challenge for feminist geography. *Professional Geographer, 59*(1), 10–21. doi: 10.1111/j.1467-9272.2007.00587.x.

Vazquez, M. J. T. (2002). Complexities of the Latina experience: A tribute to Martha Bernal. *American Psychologist, 57*(11), 880–888.

Villarreal Sosa, L. (2011). *Mexican origin students in the borderlands: The construction of social identity in the school context* (Doctoral dissertation). Available from ProQuest Dissertations and Theses database. (UMI no. 3472970).

Villenas, S. A., Godinez, F. E., Delgado Bernal, D., & Elenes, A. (2006). Chicanas/Latinas building bridges. In D. Delgado Bernal, C. A. Elenes, F. E. Godinez, & S. Villenas (Eds.), *Chicana/Latina education in everyday life: Feminista perspectives on pedagogy ad epistemology* (Kindle edition, section 3). New York, NY: SUNY Press.

Part 4

POLICIES AND PRACTICE

CHAPTER 8

Globalization and Gender Policy in South Korea

A Global Feminist Perspective

JEONGAH KIM

I vividly recall images I saw as a child of thousands of South Korean women working in dark blue uniforms in factories. These images were projected and reinforced through various forms of mass media, including television and print. Although the South Korean general public was aware of the remarkable contribution female factory workers were making to the nation's economic growth, the society, influenced by Confucianism, expected mothers and sisters to sacrifice their lives for their families and for the nation. It is true that female workers were constantly complimented by the society for making an important contribution to South Korea's development, but their contributions were always viewed as being what was expected of them as women. It is also safe to say that in many ways current South Korean society continues to take women's contributions and sacrifices for granted.

My parents, in particular my father, were always sad for these female workers. When there was news coverage praising them for their sacrifices and contributions, my father used to say, "We should treat them better. They are somebody's daughters, and we should not take advantage of them by sugarcoating this. They should at least get paid more." Although he had a genuine respect for South Korean Confucius culture, he did not agree with Confucianism's ideology (or the abuse of Confucianism, as it was rightly argued that gender inequality is far from original Confucius teachings) regarding women as it did not grant women equal status with men.

My father wanted me to be a woman leader who makes a difference in the world. Although we were a middle-class family, my father invested in his dreams for me by sending me to an all-girl private elementary school that was traditionally open to girls from the wealthiest South Korean families. The explicit mission of the school was raising future women leaders. My father always told me that I should be able to take care of myself if I want to help other people. He taught me the importance of navigating the delicate balance between independence and interdependence. My father was the first true social worker and feminist I ever met. In realizing the dreams of my father, I have chosen social work, the profession that is committed to the pursuit of social justice. It is my sincere desire that this chapter serves as one small step in illuminating the status of women's equality in South Korea to support them in assuming their rightful place in society.

Gender has been one of the most persistent indicators of inequality across all societies. Although a body of evidence indicates that the gap in certain areas such as health outcomes and educational attainment has shrunk to 10%, there is still on average a 41% gap between women and men in terms of economic participation and an 81% gap in terms of political empowerment (World Economic Forum, 2011). The influence of globalization has generated new challenges and problems for women around the globe. The benefits of globalization have been unevenly distributed within and between countries. Globalization has not helped the majority of women in newly developed nations such as South Korea (Heyzer, 2002). Furthermore, gender inequality has not decreased with economic growth in South Korea (World Bank, 2011).

Globalization is a crucial concept for explaining the complexities of modern society; however, it has yet to be fully recognized in the social work profession as being central to approaching social work practice, research, and policy development in a dynamic world. Globalization is considered by many in the profession to be far too complex and too abstract an idea to connect to systems of welfare and practices of social workers here in the United States. More and more, however, inside and outside the profession, it has become evident that what happens in one part of the world often affects what happens in other parts of world, with implications across systems levels (Saulnier, 1996). This reality is consistent with a system's perspectives so central to the profession. As market-oriented globalization focuses on markets rather than people, inequalities and injustices abound. To competently navigate in this complex environment, social workers need to be keenly aware of the globalization process and its implications for the lives of people throughout the globe.

This chapter explores the gendered effects of globalization in South Korea and the nation's policy responses to gender-linked risks and precariousness from a global feminist perspective. I summarize the waves of globalization Korea has experienced since the beginning of the 20th century and consider their effects on women's lives. I then turn to a more detailed analysis of gender-equality legislation in South Korea that has been enacted over the past two decades, including the Equal Employment Opportunity Act (EEOA) (1987), amended by the Act on Equal Employment and Support for Work-Family Reconciliation (2009); Women's Development Act (WDA, 1995); Gender Discrimination Prevention and Relief Act (GDPRA) (1999); the Act on Fostering and Supporting Women Scientists and Technicians (AFSWST, 2008); and the Act on Promotion of Economic Activities of Career-Interrupted Women (APEACIW, 2010). I draw on Beverly McPhail's (2003) work on feminist policy analysis to pose three critical questions of each of these statutes:

1. Are feminist values and ideals integrated into the law?
2. Does the law take into account the contexts of women's lives and lived experiences now and in the past?
3. Does the law promote and achieve gender equality?

I conclude with reflections on the relevance of feminist policy analysis informed by a global feminist perspective for social work and questions for discussion.

The fact that income growth in South Korea has not led to increased gender equality suggests that gender equality is multifaceted and requires a coordinated approach. Understanding the dynamics of the interplay among globalization, culture, gender, and policy may offer significant guidance toward implementing transformative strategies aimed at realizing gender equality. An examination of South Korean gender policies in the context of globalization has significant implications for social work practice, policy, and research.

Globalization and Its Effects on South Korean Women

Globalization is not new to South Korea; it has been at the very root of unrealistic pressures and responsibilities ascribed to South Korean women. The globalization process in South Korea can be roughly grouped into three waves.

Japanese colonialism (1910–1945) led the first wave with colonial powers imposing harsh political and economic control over South Korean women. The second wave of globalization occurred under the principle of growth first, redistribute later, which has been to the detriment of women. The third and latest wave, fueled by advanced technologies and telecommunications, recognizes the importance of women's labor force participation. Declining birth rates, combined with an aging population, have forced South Korea to expand its view of the role of women in society.

South Korea provides a natural laboratory to examine gender equality in the context of liberal economic globalization and the interplay of various aspects of globalization. South Korean women have been differentially positioned in relation to the labor market because of demands and pressures imposed by neoliberal globalization. In addition, it is my contention that culturally determined gender ideologies rooted in a Confucianist worldview put women consistently at a disadvantage. Gender inequality has been a particular problem for women in South Korea because of Confucianism's sustained influence across multiple spheres of South Korean society. Inglehart, Norris, and Welzel (2002) found that nations with Confucian traditions are less likely to hold more gender-equal attitudes. Substantive particularities of the culture in question should be included for a better understanding of the gendered issues of South Korea. Operating in South Korea are the twin pressures of an internal cultural system (Confucianism) and an external economic system (neoliberal globalization).

South Korea's Three Waves of Globalization

In the first wave of globalization Korea was colonized, as was the case in other less economically developed countries. Colonization by Japan in 1910 resulted in Korea's loss of independence and sovereignty. The colonization of Korea by Japan for 36 years had a particularly devastating impact on women, in part linked to their forced sexual servitude in Japanese military brothels. Although the full extent of the sexual slavery imposed on South Korean women has not been fully disclosed by the Japanese government, about 200,000 Asian women from all the areas Japan occupied were kidnapped or falsely recruited to serve as comforters (sex slaves) for Japanese soldiers (Amnesty International, 2008; Hicks, 1995; Jung, 2001). Eighty percent of these Asian women were unmarried Korean girls and young women from 11 to 27 years old. Each woman was forced to sexually serve an average of 30 to 50 soldiers a day (Chung, 2010; Kwon, 1994).

The sexual degradation of South Korean women was denied by the South Korean and Japanese governments until it was revealed in the early 1990s following the testimonies of 200 brave survivors of the Japanese comforter camps (Min, 2003). South Korean feminist leaders supported these survivors in coming forward and raising their voices. In the context of South Korean culture, which is heavily influenced by Confucianism and the concept of shame, the survivors' statements of their exploitation were significant. In summary, the first wave of globalization in Korea was punctuated by colonialism and the sexual degradation of women.

Compared to the first wave of globalization in Korea, the second wave, which occurred mostly between the 1960s and 1980s, can be considered somewhat benign, at least in terms of direct infliction of physical and psychological harm to women. The nation's early and wide-ranging economic growth, of which women were a critical element, is considered to be a product of the second wave of economic globalization. It would not be an exaggeration to say that everything in Korea during this second wave was aimed at maximizing national wealth through an export-driven economy.

The growth in demand for South Korean exports in the early 1960s was met by a female-intensive workforce. Decades of women's labor for menial wages literally built the various competitive industries that continue to fuel South Korea's modern economy. In only one generation, South Korea made the transition from a predominantly agricultural society into an industrialized urban society with unprecedented improvements in the standard of living (Chun, Doyal, Payne, Il-Cho, & Kim, 2006; Organisation for Economic Co-operation and Development [OECD], 2012). Without a doubt, economic globalization contributed to South Korea's improved standard of living and increasing job opportunities.

Although it may be argued that South Korea is one of the greatest economic success stories in modern history, much of that success was greatly undermined by the financial crisis of 1997 (Haggard, 2000), which resulted in South Korea entering the most serious period of economic hardship since the Korean War in the 1950s. This economic crisis in the late 1990s coincided with the advent of the third globalization wave.

This crisis left Korea under the control of the International Monetary Fund (IMF), which imposed strict austerity measures to ensure prompt payments on debt. Although the original intention of the IMF may be viewed as contributing to the general financial stability of the country, its involvement has been deemed by many critics as having undermined national sovereignty and legitimating neocolonial domination (Stiglitz, 2003). Korea was required by IMF to cut government spending and raise interest rates, which created a double burden that contributed to escalating economic distress and poverty. Many considered the third wave of globalization as a convergence of colonialism (the first wave) and an expansion of global capital (the second wave) that continued as a third wave but in a different package (Kim, 2005).

The 1997 financial crisis also contributed to women dropping out of the labor force at greater rates than men and to women becoming discouraged workers (Kim & Voos, 2007). As jobs became scarcer, South Korean women were among the first to be laid off and could not compete with men, who, according to widespread gender norms (i.e., male breadwinner bias) were perceived to be the legitimate job holders (Elson & Cagatay, 2000). Ultimately, the 1997 economic crisis resulted in the systematic exclusion of women from the South Korean job market.

However, by 2001 the employment rate of women had almost fully rebounded (Kim & Voos, 2007). Some may attribute this recovery to being indicative of Adam Smith's (1976) "invisible hand of the market place," (p. 184) which suggests that economic imbalances are self-correcting. This, however, may not be the case as it relates to women's participation in the South Korean economy. In the face of declining real wages, inflation, and cutbacks in public services and subsidies, more and more women have had to enter the workplace to ensure the survival of their families (Pearson, 1999). Although increasing numbers of South Korean women are entering the labor market, these women are often confined to seasonal or temporary positions with very poor salaries.

Thus, throughout all three waves of globalization in South Korea, female workers were absorbed or released depending on the needs of the society. The South Korean experience offers valuable insights into the contentious nature of the process of globalization and its gendered patterns. An examination of the effects of globalization on the women of South Korea provides insight into the risks and problems generated or exacerbated by gendered globalization with its up-and-down cycles. Although women were broadly recognized for the contributions they were making toward the economic growth of South Korea, they did not receive what they had earned and deserved: full and equal access to and participation in all facets of the labor market. The next section examines South Korea's policy responses to its three waves of globalization.

South Korea's Policy Responses to Globalization

Korea's gender policies have been immensely affected by the trend of globalization. One of the popular definitions of globalization has focused on economic perspectives such as "increasing interdependence of national economies in trade, finance, and macroeconomic policy (Gilpin & Gilpin, 1987, p. 389). Although globalization is not a singular concept and has been defined in several different ways (e.g., Castells, 1996; Gilpin & Gilpin, 1987; Harvey, 1989; Kobrin, 1997; Larsson, 2001; Nikitin & Elliott, 2000), this definition best captures the nature of globalization in South Korea. In the case of South Korea and elsewhere, the economic thrust of globalization is inseparable from social, cultural, and political dimensions of development.

Although South Korean economic policies are based on free market economics and economic liberalization, the economy has also been characterized by active and strong governmental intervention, which is justified by Confucianism. Globalization in South Korea can be characterized by two interlocking features that have negatively affected the status of women: economic liberalization and Confucianism (Kong, 2005; Mi, 2009), even though this may not have been the original intent. It is not off target to say that Korea's gendered policies were tailored to the nation's interests and needs in meeting the challenges of globalization. South Korea's gendered responses can be viewed in light of the three waves of globalization.

The first wave of South Korean globalization can literally be equated with imperialism as Korea faced the encroaching forces of Japanese imperialism from 1910 to 1945. Although little is known about female workers during this period, South Korean females were characterized as victims of imperialism and capitalism, cheap labor, and sex slaves (Ladino, 2009). The policy responses to gender inequality in the first wave were simply nonexistent. It is no surprise that no legislation was enacted to support women's equality during this time, as Korea was colonized and unable to serve and protect its citizens. After South

Korea became an independent nation, the constitution was adopted in 1948, providing the grounds for gender equality that "All citizens shall be equal before the law, and there shall be no discrimination in political, economic, social or cultural life on account of sex, religion or social status" (South Korean Const., art. 10).

During the second wave of globalization the EEOA (1987) was considered as a first attempt at granting equality for men and women in normative, systemic, and procedural domains. The EEOA is the first act that acknowledged the importance of work for women's economic empowerment and stated that its purpose is to achieve gender equality in compliance with the idea of equality in the constitution by ensuring equal opportunity and treatment for men and women in employment.

In response to the 1995 Beijing Declaration and Platform for Action at the fourth World Conference on Women the WDA was enacted in 1995 to promote gender equality and foster women's development in all areas of South Korean society, including the political, economic, and social realms. The WDA provides legal grounds for women and men to share as equals in dividing up familial responsibilities.

Even more than a decade into the third wave of globalization in South Korea, women's status in the labor market has not improved. After the severe global financial crisis of 1997, a large body of legislation dedicated to gender equality in South Korea was enacted. During this third wave of globalization, the South Korean government began to recognize and understand the implications of gender equality for the economic and social development of the nation. However, the continuous lack of improved status among women in the labor market is in part because of the terms of South Korea's agreement with the IMF to slash public expenditures and eliminate many governmental jobs and benefits, which disproportionately affected women. Women were the first to lose jobs and the last to be rehired, thus contributing to their financial vulnerability.

In 1999 the GDPRA was passed to make gender equality a lived reality. Article 1 of the GDPRA states that the primary legislative purpose of the act is "to prevent gender discrimination in employment, education, and the provision and utilization of goods, facilities, and services and in the enforcement of laws and policies and to realize gender equality in every sector of society by protecting the interests and enforcing the rights of victims."

Clauses in Article 39 state that a person becomes liable to the imposition of administrative fines in the event that corrective actions have not been followed. An oversight committee was set up to monitor implementation of the act and to provide remedies. This act bestows the Ministry of Gender Equality and Family, a quasi-judicial body, the authority to take decisive action to investigate gender discrimination cases and to prescribe corrective sanctions if a party involved has not implemented the stated corrective actions.

Following South Korea's 3-year arrangement with the IMF, the information technology industry has played a key role in the process of economic recovery (Chadwick, 2004). The government makes efforts to strengthen women's vocational competency in science and technology, as the level of women's participation in science and technology is very low compared to that of men. Responding to new patterns of technological practices, the South Korean government recognizes the importance of gender equality as a key component of sustainable economic development because of a correlation between the highest levels of inequality and lowest levels of per capita income (International Labour Organization, 2005).

Led by South Korea's Ministry of Information and Communications, efforts have been made for women to become familiar with up-to-date information technology, and more than four million women have benefited from technology-related government-sponsored workshops (United Nations, 2005). Also, the government enacted the AFSWST in 2002 to support women in science and engineering fields. Article 8 of the AFSWST states, "The State and local governments shall devise and promote preferential policies in their assistance of research expenses, etc. for the colleges of science and technology fields, etc. that maintain adequate percentage of female students who enter such colleges pursuant to the provisions of section (1)."

Also, the South Korean government designed a 5-year female resources development plan in 2006 called Dynamic Women of Korea 2010. Through a joint effort of 14 government agencies including the Ministry of Gender Equality and Family, the Ministry of Finance and Economy, the Ministry of Education and Human Resources Development, and the Ministry of Labor, the government established a goal to create 600,000 new jobs for women by 2010. The thrust of this initiative was to focus on increasing employment of women who have been unable to continue their careers because of marriage, childbirth, or child rearing (Ministry of Gender Equality and Family, 2006).

Following the Dynamic Women of Korea 2010 plan, the second master 5-year plan for women's resource development, Dynamic Women Korea 2015, was launched as the government's attempt to advance the status of women and promote gender equality. This plan aims at increasing labor force participation of women by 55% until 2015 and focuses on the reemployment of women (Ministry of Gender Equality and Family, 2010).

Along with this initiative, many previous acts were amended in an effort to improve gender inequality. The Equal Employment Opportunity Act was amended and became the Act on Equal Employment and Support for Work-Family Reconciliation in 2009. The purpose of this law is (a) to provide for women to balance work and family without taking a career break, (b) to promote reemployment of women who were displaced from careers, (c) to reduce women's working hours for family responsibilities, (d) to increase women's job marketability, and (e) to ensure discrimination-free and gender-friendly work environments.

The APEACIW was passed in 2010 to reduce the impact of career breaks on women. According to Rose and Hartman (2004), women's annual earnings drop by 30% after an interrupted career. Article 1 of this act states that its purpose is "to contribute to the sustainable growth of the national economy as well as to the financial self-support and self-realization of women through the promotion of economic activities of career-interrupted women." This act established an infrastructure to support women's reemployment and includes a primary center and 98 regional centers and offices (Minister of Gender Equality and Family, 2011). This piece of legislation represents substantial efforts toward enhanced gender policy, as it acknowledges the economic disadvantages of women whose careers have been interrupted.

In sum, South Korean gender policies comprise various provisions concerning access to employment, eradication of gender-based discrimination, maternity protection, development of women's ability, women's social participation, and an increase in women's welfare. However, the actual effects of laws on South Korean women's lives is still up for more discussion, which is taken up later beginning on p. 191.

Global Feminism

Before we examine South Korean gender policy in more detail, it is important to introduce the feminist theoretical lens that guides my analysis. I use global feminism as a conceptual framework to explore the nature of South Korean gender policies. Further, I contend that a global feminist perspective could inform social work efforts toward gender equality in diverse cultural contexts. Hartsock (1979) defines global feminism as "a mode of analysis, a method of approaching life and politics, a way of asking questions and searching for answers" (p. 35). A global feminist lens operationalizes *global* as "a reference to the planetary scale of feminist collaboration for peace, justice, and women's rights," (Porter, 2007, p. 44).

As noted in the introduction to this volume, feminist theoretical perspectives have historically provided a strong framework to defend gender equality in various circumstances. Feminist scholars have largely been concerned with the gendered effects of globalization (e.g., women's marginalization, the gendered division of labor, the exploitative nature of economic liberalization, the augmentation of the double burden; Cheng, 1999; Hippert, 2002; Jagger, 2001; Pande, 2000). There are various points of view with several ideological theories and opinions on gendered globalization among feminists and, consequently, varied feminist approaches toward achieving gender equality in this globalized world.

Some of these approaches are grounded in a strongly relativist ideology emphasizing the uniqueness of particular contexts and histories, whereas others take a more universalist stance, making the case for common cause among women throughout the world. Examination of these diverse, complex, and often contested perspectives is beyond the scope of this chapter. It is my contention that a global feminist perspective, in line with social work values, emphasizes the universality of women's rights as human rights while also recognizing the importance of particular cultural and political histories in shaping ideas about gender, rights, and capacities; public policies regarding gender equality; and women's everyday lives.

Those who embrace a strong cultural relativist stance might argue that standards of gender equality bound to the value of basic human rights represent an imposition of Western values that deny the sanctity of cultural heritage and national sovereignty. As a woman from a third world country, to me, sovereignty of nations appears to be a utopian ideal, because sovereignty implies there is no higher power among nations. However, we all know too well that is not the case in an increasingly capitalized global world. As much as I do believe in the sovereignty of nations and as much as I respect tradition, a nation with less economic power may not have the option of resisting global trends of opening its borders to different ideas and influences. Less economically developed countries of the world have to learn and adapt as soon as possible to maintain their identity. That may be the only choice we may have in this impersonal globalized world.

Clearly, Korea learned this lesson the hard way; the nation's 36 years of colonization is a historical scar of this reality. Until the end of the 19th century, Korea was a "hermit nation" that was closed to Western goods, ideas, people, and culture (Kim, 2005, p. xx). In part because of its policy of seclusion, Korea was not colonized by Western countries. Ironically, however, Korea was colonized by an Eastern country, Japan, a nation that drew heavily from a Western model of economic development. Korea once considered all Westerners as uncultivated, uncultured barbarians. This extreme position combined with isolationist policies resulted in 36 years of colonization by Japan, an Eastern culture with a Confucius tradition. Many Koreans, like my grandparents, who lived during Japanese colonization may have taken the position that we accept Western cultures and avoid colonization at all costs. In other words, many South Koreans would prefer national sovereignty to cultural tradition if they had only had those two options.

The colonization by an Eastern culture did not make things any easier for Korea. Following colonization, we were not able to preserve our own cultural traditions despite the fact that we were colonized by a nation that shares a similar Confucian collectivist cultural tradition. We were not allowed to learn Korean languages at school, and we were forced to change our Korean names to Japanese names.

It is important to remember that each nation is a reflection of multiple cultural, political, and historical influences originating within and beyond its borders. In South Korea, for example, our ancestors fiercely defended Confucius and Buddhist traditions and fought against foreigners and Western influences in particular. However, they depended on Confucianism and Buddhism as our own basis for the traditions and beliefs that shape social and cultural life. Ironically, these two religions also originated in two foreign countries, China and India. In a strict sense, they were not ours either.

A global feminist perspective attends to these questions of context and to the cultural, political, and historical influences that shape ideologies of gender, women's experiences, and the ways struggles for gender equality and women's rights play out. I have also found it instructive as a perspective for critical policy analysis and action. Global feminism is a vehicle for us to be teachers and learners as we seek to understand gender-bound issues of global concern. Global feminism "requires that we learn from each other and develop a global perspective," thereby expanding "our understandings of feminism" and making "changes in our work, as we respond to the ideas and challenges of women with different perspectives" (Bunch, 1987, p. 192).

I believe the best theoretical lenses are those that are situationally dependent regarding strategies and situationally independent regarding principles. This is what a global feminist perspective provides. It remains true to the ultimate feminist goal of women's equality and liberation and yet gives us the flexibility to broaden feminist goals dependent on the realities of various cultures. Critical reflection through global feminist lenses can highlight how South Koreans construct and negotiate complex meanings of gender equality in cultural and economic contexts that are reflexively influenced by the process of globalization.

Specifically, there are three major reasons why I examine South Korean gender policies from a global feminist perspective. First, global feminist theory allows us to consider the philosophical and ideological bases of gender equality. An understanding of the ideological basis of the issue is critical in forming a real understanding of South Korean gender policies because all policies are value laden. This perspective provides a good starting point, as society's interpretation of social problems and strategies of change would be different depending on its way of viewing the world.

Recognition of the significant impact of ideological forces (often manifested in culture and economic approach) on policy development can provide important insights into the reality of gender inequality in Korea because Confucianism has been a prominent part of the lives of South Koreans and affects every aspect of our daily lives. Also, because South Korean gender policies are inextricably connected with ideologies of globalization, and South Korean women's experiences are grounded in the globalized cultural and economic structures of society, the global feminist perspective can provide a verifiable frame of reference for engaging in meaningful dialogue regarding globalization and gender equality.

The global feminist perspective is useful for South Korea in illuminating the significance of the global economy as well as local culture ideology regarding women's status. Global feminists acknowledge that women's survival and the struggle for substantive justice significantly depends on the global economy and ideology in the era of neoliberal globalization. They recognize that economic justice is foundational for other types of social justice.

My second reason is that a global feminist analysis of globalization and its effect on gender can address the predominant subordination of women as a problem and promote women's equality as an inalienable human right. Global feminism argues that women's rights are universal human rights that surpass geographical borders (Minda, 2010). A global feminist perspective is a vehicle social workers can use to understand the local environment and approach social problems from a social justice perspective. My third reason is that global feminists understand that the world is becoming increasingly interconnected and interdependent along a number of dimensions. They recognize interdependencies and interconnections among nations that "decisions taken in one territorial state often impact the lives of women outside [it], as do the actions of supranational and international organizations, both governmental and non-governmental" (Fraser, 2009). A global feminist perspective allows us to understand the interconnectedness of economic and ideological forces and their reciprocal influence on each other. This sense of interconnectedness can lead nations into universal responsibility toward each other's rights and those of their citizens on a different level.

In sum, a global feminist perspective recognizes that problems and issues in society are ideologically driven and interconnected. Also, although understanding notions of gender as being culturally produced and highly variable, the global feminist perspective's emphasis on human rights may shed light on what is universally and truly valuable and important for South Korean women in an ever-shrinking world.

Reflection on South Korean Gender Policies

A global feminist perspective provides a sound analytic framework for explaining how South Korea has developed gender polices in a globalized context. It also provides a basis for further examination and discussion regarding the observable realities regarding gender policy development and implementation in South Korea. The policy analysis presented here is guided by a question-and-answer format informed by McPhail's feminist policy analysis model (McPhail, 2003). I employ a question-and-answer format because it models the approach I use in teaching social policy to social work students. One of the best ways of learning something is by asking questions. This approach can avoid unnecessarily complicating the issue, give sufficient priority to the core issue, and enable us to examine the relevant issues in an engaging and nonintimidating way.

Based on her extensive review of existing literature, McPhail (2003) compiled 13 constructs to be asked in conducting a feminist policy analysis. Under these constructs, she developed a number of guiding questions to examine each element in a policy analysis. Because of space constraints and a good deal of overlap among these constructs, I have collapsed her 13-construct model into three constructs central to a global feminist perspective. The selected questions have relevance to the underlying emphasis of a global feminist perspective regarding gender equality: that is, the role of values and ideologies and a human rights perspective. The three main questions are: (1) "Do feminist values undergird the policy?; . . . (2) Does the policy take into account the . . . contexts of women's lives and lived experiences both now and in the past? [and] (3) Does the policy achieve gender equality?" (McPhail, 2003, pp. 55–56). In addition to these questions, supplemental questions were included for the purpose of clarifying answers.

VALUES

Policy making is complex and heavily value laden. Understanding values is a critical precursor to understanding all types of policies, as values are a set of lenses lending a specific perspective regarding policies and their implementation. The first and foremost question in examining gender policy is, Do feminist values undergird the policy? This complex question begs the subsequent question: What is a feminist value? Although there is no consensus among feminists regarding what constitutes a feminist value, Brandwein (1986) provides a comprehensive list that is instructive here. According to Brandwein, feminist values include elimination of false dichotomies; the reconceptualization of power; valuing process equally with product; renaming or redefining reality consistent with women's reality; acknowledging that the personal is political; holism; nonhierarchical relationships; acceptance of a spiritual dimension; valuing diversity; collectivity and the importance of connections or webs of relationships; commitment to social justice; and respect of the inherent dignity and worth of all people.

Now we turn to the question of whether feminist values undergird South Korea's gender policies. From the perspective of global feminism, which highlights a value-conscious and human rights–based approach, South Korea integrated the value of human rights into its gender policies. Article 2 of the GDPRA (1999) clearly states that "gender discrimination" is defined as all forms of differentiation, exclusion, or limitation, made without any justifiable reason on the basis of one's sex, in the recognition, enjoyment or exercise of basic *human rights* [emphasis added] in any political, economic, social, and cultural sectors."

Despite significant room for improvement, South Korea has made progress in terms of recognizing gender equality as an integral part of human rights in a Confucian-influenced culture. Also, South Korea infused human dignity, "the 'ultimate value' that gives coherence to human rights," (Hasson, 2003, p. 83) into gender policies. Article 2 of the WDA (1995) emphasized "the promotion of equality between men and women, protection of motherhood, eradication of gender-based discrimination mindset and development of women's ability, based upon *the dignity of individuals*" [emphasis added]. This human rights approach may provide South Korean women with a nonnegotiable foundation for any discussion of gender equality within South Korea's traditionally authoritarian and patriarchal culture.

The value manifested in the slogan of global feminism, "Women's rights are human rights," is essential because marginalized minority groups in underdeveloped nations need the protection of universal standards to ensure justice (Grewal, 1999). Also, universality exists among many women's concerns, regardless of geographical place, as Rubin (1975) aptly demonstrates in her well-known phrase that there is an "endless variety and monotonous similarity" (p. 160) of women's oppression in various places.

Attention to questions of values provides the opportunity to consider the possibilities for common ground between Confucian values and those of global feminism. The two are not necessarily irreconcilable. In fact, Confucian approaches and global feminist perspectives can go a long way together toward having a gender-equal society (Li, 1994). For example, the self-denying morality of Confucian ethics may be used to support South Korean gender policies that advance women's equality as a reflection of morally acceptable values consistent with a global feminist perspective.

South Korean gender policies are good examples of the myth of value-free policy. This is even truer for gender policies. South Korean gender policies, at least in terms of their legislative intent, can be viewed as an attempt to harmonize feminist values and Confucianist values to promote gender equality. For example, APEACIW (2010), and the Framework Act on Women's Development (2008) not only support the development of healthy families but also promote gender equality.

Understanding the value orientation of South Korea's gender policies is essential in gaining an understanding of women's status in South Korea and other newly developed nations. We need to continue to engage in dialogue regarding the best possible policy approaches to achieving gender equality. The ideal policy approaches would be those that avoid casting women as victims of culture and that cultivate an intellectual climate respectful of women and culture so that women may physically and emotionally experience gender equality in the everyday realities of their lives.

CONTEXTS

In this section we consider South Korean gender policies in the contexts of globalization and Confucianism. Globalization is more than just a popular buzzword of this millennium. It is a process that has an effect on the lives of the world's most vulnerable populations in very meaningful ways. The world's women are particularly vulnerable to experiencing the deleterious effects of globalization. A significant body of literature considers how neoliberal globalization has affected women negatively and resulted in the outright feminization of poverty and gender inequality (Peterson & Runyan 1993; Pettman 1996). South Korea is not an exception. Women's issues cannot be fully understood in isolation from the larger context in and through which globalization-related policies have emerged.

Accordingly, as noted in the introduction to this book, gender inequality in the context of globalization has been driven by neoliberal economic policies that place the masses of the world's women at a disadvantage (Molyneux & Razavi, 2006; Streeten 2001). Thus, it is important to ask whether the policy takes into account the contexts of women's lives and experiences.

South Korean gender policies were developed in the contexts of economic liberalization and Confucianism as they relate to women's roles. These dual influences remain strong in South Korea, which has been widely acknowledged as an exemplar of economic liberalization and Confucianism (Jones, 1993; Kong, 2005). South Korean gender policies are also good examples of the myth of context-free policy.

South Korean gender polices have been updated to reflect economic trends and changes in the market for the nation's need for economic growth. The relationship between changes in global economic trends and changes in South Korean gender polices are positively correlated. For example, the latest act on gender equality, the APEACIW (2010), clearly states that one of the main purposes of the legislation is "to contribute to the sustainable growth of the national economy" (Art. 1). The government's active involvement in gender policy development stemmed from its recognition that equality between women and men is a required condition for the sustained economic development of the nation. South Korean gender policies tend to be confined within the limits of neoliberalism and Confucianism, doing little to tackle the broader structural aspects of gender inequality.

Also, although South Korea has demonstrated a fairly strong record of gender equality legislation beginning with the Equal Employment Opportunity Act of 1987, there is a consensus that the country is still deeply entrenched in more than a thousand years of Confucian culture (Won & Pascall, 2004). Under the veil of Confucianism (or the abuse of Confucianism; as previously noted, gender inequality is far from original Confucius teachings) in South Korea the sacrifices of women are considered to be acceptable and desirable.

For example, the WDA states that its purpose is for "for the realization of healthy family and the development of the State and local governments" (Art. 2). Two coequal goals of this act could be considered a problem because of the implication that the inherent dignity and worth of women are conditional, depending on women's contribution to society. However, under the influence of

Confucianism, these tendencies can go undetected, as the Confucian tradition of filial piety to the nation has been an integral part of South Korean culture. Another example is the APEACIW (2010), which also established two goals: the growth of the national economy and the financial self-support and self-realization of women.

Although South Korea has developed Confucian-based public policies that do not focus on women, the nation also developed gender laws that challenge Confucian cultural contexts that predispose wives to be solely responsible for all aspects of family life. For example, the WDA includes the establishment of a tangible set of woman-focused policies (Art. 7) that include the women's development fund (Art. 9) and the women's organization (Art. 32), which specifies the responsibilities of the government to adopt interim affirmative action for prompting gender equality, protecting maternity, eliminating gender discrimination, and promoting the development of women's ability (Art. 2; United Nations, n.d.).

Equality is a loaded and highly contested concept, particularly in a nation such as South Korea. One of the most important but difficult tasks is developing and implementing a workable and fair definition of gender equality. Although the International Labor Organization (2005) defines gender equality as "equal rights, opportunities, and treatment of women and men, girls and boys in all spheres of life" (p. 3), there is no consensus in the academic literature regarding the construct of equality.

However, some consensus exists among feminist scholars that gender equality may require both preferential and equal treatment of women. "True equality means treating everyone differently in order to treat them the same. . . . Gender equality does not lie in either ignoring or glorifying innate differences between men and women" (Roberts, 1994, p. 3). The United States has adopted, or has leaned toward, an equality approach (indicated by challenges to Affirmative Action), based on an assumption that equality is achieved through equal treatment. On the other hand, South Korea provides some special treatment for women. For example, women are given exemptions to mandatory military service. Also, AFAWS (2002) has legitimated special treatment for women by stating, "The state and local governments shall devise and promote preferential policies in their assistance of research expenses, etc. for the colleges of science and technology fields, etc. that maintain adequate percentage of female students" (Art.

8). One of the major departures of this legislation from previous acts is the provision for preferential treatment for female college students majoring in science and engineering.

Although the difference between feminist and Confucian values appears to be irreconcilable, the divide between them may not be as critical as it appears. The resolution of this contradiction can be found in the following observations. First, although Confucianism may have been used to justify gender inequality, we cannot judge Confucianism, whose interpretation has been abused by some people. Second, although one of Confucius' highest moral ideals may include caring (or *jen*) for women, Confucianism may have failed to provide guidance for determining a priority when, for example, filial piety to the nation and caring for women are in conflict.

As Confucianism supports a hierarchical relationship that endorses and justifies special treatment, South Korean women's gender equality can be achieved through equal and special treatment for women if applied strategically. In South Korea, special treatment can even be deemed honorable when it is accorded to someone who deserves it. Weisberg (1993) observed, "Injustice does not flow directly from recognizing differences; injustice results when those differences are transformed into social and economic deprivation" (p. 51). Thus, the Confucian emphasis on high morality may be used for the benefit of women. Confucianism can be utilized to promote gender inequality extending with its emphasis on proper relations and morality among people.

The relationship between gender equality and Confucianism has generated strong opposing opinions. Many view Confucianism as a major threat to women's rights because the principle doctrines of Confucianism, including the hierarchical order of social relations and an emphasis on obedience to authority, conflict with notions of human equality and human rights (Lee, 1995). Others argue that feminism's goal of ensuring that women are treated with respect and dignity is consistent with one of Confucius's highest moral ideals, which is caring (Jen) for women (Li, 1994).

Because notions of human dignity are rooted in some version of Confucianism (e.g., neo-Confucianism), South Korean gender polices that protect and promote human rights, including women's rights, may be formulated based on a confluence of South Korean Confucianism and a global feminist perspective (Li, 1994). Although Confucianism has the potential to contribute to the emergence of a more egalitarian South Korean society, it is important to keep in mind that this will not happen without a strategic and prolonged campaign implemented by the multiplicity of constituencies invested in realizing women's equality.

Neoliberalism and Confucianism are ingrained in South Korean gender polices. Collectively, these two contexts have played an important role in terms of the direction and mandates of South Korean gender policy development. To understand and recount South Korean gender policies, it is important to examine the manifestations of neoliberalism that function as a fundamental economic principle as well as mainstream values that lie at the root of South Korean Confucius culture.

GENDER EQUALITY

We turn now to the third question: Does the policy achieve gender equality? Gender policy in Korea has generally evolved from regulations that center on the broader platform of women's rights in general to more provisions that promote equal opportunities and equal treatment between women and men in the workplace. South Korea has been successful in making women's issues present and visible from a legal point of view. It is safe to say that a number of the gender policies render women "visible where they have been rendered invisible" (Thiele, 1986, p. 21). South Korea developed several gender polices that are focused solely on narrowing gender equality, for example, WDA (1995), GDPRA (1999), APEACIW (2010). Although the legislation itself cannot bring directed social change, the enactment of gender-focused legislation is a significant step toward the advancement of gender equality. South Korea has made outstanding progress in making gender inequality a visible social problem. Also, the South Korean constitution has been amended with a number of articles promoting gender equality in employment since its ratification in 1948. However, the implementation of a comprehensive, women-focused labor policy has been extremely slow moving.

Globalization has been justified by its alleged contributions to economic development. How then has globalization contributed to economic justice for South Korean women? About 50% of women are currently in the labor force in South Korea (Lee, Jang, & Sarkar, 2008), a situation well explained by Molyneux and Razavis's (2002) assertion that "women are not necessarily in a position to benefit from enhanced legal rights if they lack the economic means, or the access to key services such as education, to enable them to benefit in practice" (p. 132).

Although South Korea has passed a number of laws over the past two decades to support women in the workforce and to promote gender equality, a majority of female workers are still confined to temporary, part-time, or sub-contract positions (Lee, 2003). Also, there has been very little change regarding gender roles and the traditional role of women as family caregivers because of the influence of Confucius ideals. Accordingly, the double burden of work and family responsibilities is becoming increasingly heavy for women. Historically, working women have not received effective support from governmental gender policies or from the Confucian-based culture (Won & Pascall, 2004).

The early economic growth of the nation more than a half century ago has not enabled women to benefit equitably from the spoils of South Korea's sustained growth. Despite the negative effects of IMF policies on women's status in the labor market, their constant labor contributions have contributed to the sustained growth of the economy. The South Korean gross domestic product ranked 14th in the world in 2011, even after the economic crisis in 1997 (World Bank, 2011). However, there have been disturbing gaps between developmental achievements and efforts toward gender equality in South Korea.

According to data released in 2011, the World Economic Forum reported that of 135 countries, South Korea ranks 117th on economic participation and opportunity (Hausmann, Tyson, & Zahidi, 2011). At the same time, South Korea continues to be among the lowest-ranking nations in the world in terms of gender inequality. According to the Korean Women's Development Institute, the index of gender equality in South Korea was 0.594 in 2008. In a South Korean Gallup poll on gender satisfaction, only 45.8% of women said they would want to be born a woman if given the option of being born again (Shin, 2001). The gender wage gap persists at around 17% in OECD countries, ranging from 38% in South Korea to 9% in Belgium (OECD, 2009).

The enactment of gender-related laws was a necessary first step toward the nation's effort to develop gender policies that mandate more egalitarian gender roles (Sung, 2003). Although it may be argued that the current state of South Korean gender policies reflects significant progress toward achieving gender equality, implementation of the current gender policies has been severely lacking and perhaps much more of a problem than commonly acknowledged.

Overall, South Korean gender policies appear to be limited with respect to the breadth and depth of coverage, the nature of financing, and levels of benefits. Thus, deeply entrenched in Confucian ideals and neoliberal economic approaches, South Korea's gender laws may be described as being quite far from gender equality. For example, the courts have been reluctant to directly challenge the traditional Confucian ethics about women (Lee, 1995). Many of the gender policies have not been implemented in ways that are consistent with the original intentions of the legislative initiatives. One of the clearest examples of this gap between legislative intent and policy implementation is the reality that following the passage of the EEOA (1987) and the WDA (1995), many South Korean women entered the labor market but were relegated to newly created, low-wage, temporary jobs.

Although capitalist globalization has a reputation of being unfair to developing nations, globalization can be used as an impetus to achieve gender equality as a function of global responsibility. For example, South Korea developed a number of polices to follow the United Nation's response to gendered globalization by adopting the Beijing Declaration and Platform for Action in 1995. Problems do not exist independently of people recognizing the situation as problematic. To be effective in advancing the status of women in South Korea, transformative strategies must be accompanied by a meaningful cultural shift in the hearts and minds of people globally and locally.

Conclusion and Implications for Social Work

South Korea faces many issues that have led to rising gender inequality, as is the case in other developing nations. Even though South Korea has enacted new legislation and policies reflecting a more progressive gender perspective, there is still a gap between national policies regarding women and the nuanced realities of gender. It is not an exaggeration to say that economic development has become the driving force of South Korean society as well as an excuse for ignoring the nation's gender inequality. Existing gender inequality in South Korea has been shaped over time by complex cultural, political, ideological, and economic forces. It is rooted in part in the enduring influence of Confucianism and its emphasis on hierarchical relationships between men and women, and in part in the structure of the political economy in the context of neoliberal globalization. As this chapter has highlighted, a critical understanding of gender inequality must take into account the complexity of these various forces in the context of South Korea.

Clearly, a gap exists between South Korea's gender policies and actual outcomes. A global feminist perspective offers insight related to this discrepancy and provides direction for critical policy analysis and advocacy. It promotes needed attention to specific cultural, political, and historical contexts, while also remaining committed to an understanding of women's rights and human rights. A global feminist perspective, which recognizes human dignity as a universal value, provides an excellent vehicle for social work to participate in the global advocacy journey. Furthermore, the perspective's firm stance on human dignity as a universal truth is fundamentally connected to the mission of social work, which has always been concerned with "matters of right and wrong and matters of duty and obligation" for social justice (Reamer, 1998, p. 488).

For social workers to fight against social inequalities and create change in society for the lives of marginalized women, incorporation of a global feminist perspective in the design of gender polices can challenge associated problems related to the trends of neoliberalism and globalization. Concerning neoliberalism, global feminism's emphasis on economic perspectives in understanding gender equality (Enns & Sinacore, 2001) can enable us to see neoliberalism's fixation on economic growth and individual responsibility, which undermines women's status in society. Further, a global feminist perspective may support us in developing economy-conscious policies that lend sufficient consideration to existing structural constraints that perpetuate the oppression of women.

The global feminist perspective suggests that gender inequality does not happen in a vacuum but within specific contexts. Global feminism may serve as a conceptual tool for understanding social problems such as gender inequality, poverty, and the sexual exploitation of women as products of neoliberal economic globalization. In this sense, global feminism further extends social work's long standing person-in-environment approach, which maintains that "everything is connected: future to the past, the parts to the whole, the biological to the social, the inner to the outer (body, mind, etc.), personal to political, the local to the global" (van Wormer, 2002, p. 34). Social work's partnership with global feminism presents us with a major opportunity to advance the struggle for gender equality.

Discussion Questions

1. Why should women expect equality in the first place?
2. Why does the cultural/historical/political context matter in developing an understanding of globalization and its effects? Based on your reading of this chapter, what is your understanding of the relationship between Confucianism and feminism in South Korea?
3. What is the relationship between gender equality and economic development in South Korea? What is the relationship between ideology and policy development? How has Confucianism influenced the development of gender equality policies in South Korea?
4. What is your understanding of the concept of ideology? What are some examples of ways ideology intersects with and shapes social policy in the South Korean context? Where do you see examples of the intersection of ideology and public policy in your own state, province, or country? What strategies might you use to create a shift in ideology?

References

Act on Equal Employment and Support for Work-Family Reconciliation, Act No. 9795 (2009). Retrieved from http://www.moleg.go.kr/english/korLawEng?pstSeq=52977&brdSeq=33&rctPstCnt=3&searchCondition=AllButCsfCd&searchKeyword=Act+on+Equal+Employment+and+Support+for+Work-Family+Reconciliation

Act on Fostering and Supporting Women Scientists and Technicians, Act No. 8852 (2008). Retrieved from http://www.moleg.go.kr/english/korLawEng?pstSeq=52170&rctPstCnt=3&searchCondition=AllButCsfCd&searchKeyword=ACT+ON+FOSTERING+AND+SUPPORTING+WOMEN+SCIENTISTS+AND+TECHNICIANS

Act on Promotion of Economic Activities of Career-Interrupted Women, Act No. 10039 (2010). Retrieved from http://www.moleg.go.kr/english/korLawEng?rctPstCnt=3&searchCondition=AllButCsfCd&searchKeyword=Act+on+Promotion+of+Economic+Activities+of+Career-Interrupted+Women&x=0&y=0

Amnesty International. (2008). Comfort women: Waiting for justice after 62 years. Retrieved from http://www.amnesty.org/en/appeals-for-action/comfort-women-waiting-justice

Brandwein, R. A. (1986). A feminist approach to social policy. In N. Van Den Bergh & L. B. Cooper (Eds.), Feminist visions for social work (pp. 250–261). Washington, DC: National Association of Social Workers.

Bunch, C. (1987). Passionate politics: Feminist theory in action. New York, NY: St. Martin's Press.

Castells M. (1996). *The rise of the network society.* Cambridge, MA: Blackwell.

Chadwick, B. (2004). Information technology revolution in the Republic of Korea: Socio-economic development issues and policymaking challenges. In A. Mansourov (Ed.), *Bytes and bullets of Korea* (pp. 52–69). Honolulu, HI: Asia-Pacific Center for Security Studies.

Cheng, L. (1999). Globalization and women's paid labor in Asia. *International Social Science Journal,* 51(160), 217–228.

Chun, H., Doyal, P. L., Cho, S., & Kim, H. (2006). Understanding women, health, and social change: The case of South Korea. *International Journal of Health Service, 36*(3), 575–592.

Chung, H. (2010). Spirituality of trans-borders: A narrative of transformation of a South Korean sex slave. *Pastoral Psychology, 59*(4), 483–494. doi:10.1007/s11089-009-0214-x

Elson, D., & Cagatay, N. (2000). The social content of macroeconomic policies. *World Development,* 28, 1347–1364.

Enns, C. Z., & Sinacore, A. (2001). Feminist theories. In J. Worell (Ed.), *Encyclopedia of women and gender: Sex similarities and differences and the impact of society on gender* (Vol. 1, pp. 469–480). San Diego, CA: Academic Monographs.

Equal Employment Opportunity Act, Act No. 3989 (1987). Retrieved from http://www.moleg.go.kr/eng lish/korLawEng?rctPstCnt=3&searchCondition=AllButCsfCd&searchKeyword=Framework+Act+ on+Women%E2%80%99s+Development&x=18&y=12

Fraser, N. (2009). *Scales of justice: Reimagining political space in a globalizing world.* New York, NY: Columbia University Press.

Gender Discrimination Prevention and Relief Law, Act No. 5934 (1999). Retrieved from http://www. google.com/url?sa=t&rct=j&q=&esrc=s&source=web&cd=1&ved=0CDEQFjAA&url=http%3 A%2F%2Fwww.iwraw-ap.org%2Fresources%2Fdocuments%2FGE_South_Korea.doc&ei= 0NKbUZTZHljg8ASdmoHYBA&usg=AFQjCNGwVmtaW6JKOrSMusH8FKu69o1Rbw&sig2=PLB UleVeFTfApxBPcYWeww

Gilpin, R., & Gilpin, J. M. (1987). *The political economy of international relations.* Princeton, NJ: Princeton University Press.

Grewal, I. (1999). "Women's rights as human rights": Feminist practices, global feminism, and human rights regimes in transnationality. *Citizenship Studies, 3,* 337–354.

Haggard, S. (2000). *The political economy of the East Asian financial crisis.* Washington, DC: Institute for International Economics.

Hartsock, N. (1979). Feminist theory and the development of revolutionary strategy. In Z. R. Eisenstein (Ed.), *Capitalist patriarchy and the case for socialist feminism.* (pp. 56–82) New York, NY: Monthly Review Press.

Harvey, D. (1989). *The condition of postmodernity.* Oxford, UK: Blackwell.

Hasson, K. J. (2003). Religious liberty and human dignity: A tale of two declarations. *Harvard Journal of Law & Public Policy, 27*(1), 81–92.

Hausmann, R., Tyson, L., & Zahidi, S. (2011). *The global gender gap report.* Retrieved from from http://www3.weforum.org/docs/WEF_GenderGap_Report_2011.pdf

Heyzer, N. (2002). *Globalization and democratic governance: a gender perspective.* Retrieved from http://unpan1.un.org/intradoc/groups/public/documents/un/unpan006228.pdf

Hicks, G. (1995). *The comfort women: Japan's brutal regime of enforced prostitution in the Second World War.* New York, NY: Norton.

Hippert, C. (2002). Multinational corporations, the politics of the world economy, and their effects on women's health in the developing world: A review. *Health Care for Women International, 23,* 861–869.

Inglehart, R., Norris, P., & Welzel, P. (2002). Gender equality and democracy. *Comparative Sociology, 1*(3/4), 321–345.

International Labour Organization. (2005). *Women's employment: Global trends and ILO responses.* Retrieved from http://www.ilo.org/public/english/region/eurpro/moscow/areas/gender/gender3.pdf

Jagger, A. (2001). Is Globalization good for women? *Comparative Literature, 53*(4), 298–314.

Jones, C. (1993). The pacific challenge: Confucian welfare states. In C. Jones (Ed.), *New perspectives on the welfare state in Europe* (pp. 198–217). London, UK: Routledge.

Jung, J. (2001). Ilbonkun wiansojedowa pihasasil [Comfort stations and its injurious effects]. In Hankuk jngsindae munjae dachaekhyupeuihoe [Korean Council for the Women Drafted for Military Sexual Slavery] (Eds.), *Ilbonkunwianbueue chakimeulmutnunda* [*Asking about the responsibility of comfort women*] (pp. 101–118). Seoul, Korea: Pulbit.

Kim, H., & Voos, P. (2007). The South Korean economic crisis and working women. *Journal of Contemporary Asia, 37*(2), 190–208.

Kim, K. (2005). Modernization as a politico-cultural response and modernity as a cultural mixture: An alternative view of Korean modernization. *Development and Society, 34*(1), 1–24.

Kobrin, S. J. (1997). The architecture of globalization: State sovereignty in a networked global economy. In J. H. Dunning (Ed.), *Governments, globalization, and international business.* (pp. 146–171). New York, NY: Oxford University Press.

Kong, T. (2005). Labour and neo-liberal globalization in South Korea and Taiwan. *Modern Asian Studies, 39*(1), 155–188.

Kwon, H. (1994, October). *The military sexual slavery issue and Asian peace.* Paper presented at the meeting of the First East Asian Women's Forum, Tokyo, Japan. Retrieved from http://www.vcn.bc.ca/alpha/lear/KoreanWomen.htm

Ladino, J. (2009). Ianfu: No comfort for the Korean comfort woman and the impact of House Resolution 121. *Cardoso Journal of Law & Gender, 15*, 333–355.

Larsson, T. (2001). *The race to the top: The real story of globalization.* Washington, DC: Cato Institute.

Lee, B., Jang, S., & Sarkar, J. (2008). Women's labor force participation and marriage: The case of Korea. *Journal of Asian Economics, 19*(2), 138–154.

Lee, J. (2003). Taking gender seriously: Feminization of nonstandard work in Korea and Japan. Retrieved from http://unpan1.un.org/intradoc/groups/public/documents/APCITY/UNPAN020892.pdf

Lee, K. (1995). Confucian ethics, judges, and women: Divorce under the revised Korean family law. *Pacific Lim Law and Policy Journal, 4*, 479–503.

Li, C. (1994). The Confucian concept of jen and the feminist ethics of care: A comparative study. *Hypatia, 9*(1), 70–89.

McPhail, B. A. (2003). A feminist policy analysis framework: Through a gendered lens. *Social Policy Journal, 2*(2/3), 39–61.

Mi, P. (2009). Framing free trade agreements: The politics of nationalism in the anti-neoliberal globalization movement in South Korea. *Globalizations, 6*, 451–466. doi:10.1080/14747730903298694

Min, P. (2003). Korean "comfort women": The intersection of colonial power, gender, and class. *Gender & Society, 17*, 938–957.

Minda, G. (2010). Lessons from the financial meltdown: Global feminism, critical race theory, and the struggle for substantive justice. *American University Journal of Gender Social Policy and the Law, 18*, 649–684.

Ministry of Gender Equality and Family. (2006). *Dynamic Korea women 2010: 1st women resources development master plan (06–10) action plan for FY 2010.* Seoul, Korea: Author.

Ministry of Gender Equality and Family. (2010). *Dynamic Korea women 2015.* Retrieved from http://enews.mogef.go.kr/view/board/bbs/view.jsp

Ministry of Gender Equality and Family. (2011). *The Republic of Korea permanent mission to the United Nations.* Retrieved from http://www.un.org/womenwatch/daw/csw/csw55/statements/ROK.pdf

Molyneux, M., & Razavi, S. (2002). Gender justice, development, and rights. London, UK: Oxford University Press.

Molyneux, M., & Razavi, S. (2006). *Beijing plus 10: Ambivalent record on gender justice.* Geneva, Switzerland: United Nations Research Institute for Social Development.

Nikitin, P. V., & Elliott, J. E. (2000). Freedom and the market. *Forum for Social Economics, 30*(1), 1–16.

Organisation for Economic Co-operation and Development. (2009). *Country profiles: Gender equality and social indicators.* Paris, France: OECD Development Centre.

Organisation for Economic Co-operation and Development. (2012). *OECD health care quality review: Korea.* Retrieved from http://www.oecd.org/dataoecd/24/9/49818570.pdf

Pande, R. (2000). Globalization and women in the agricultural sector. *International Feminist Journal of Politics, 2,* 409–412.

Pearson, R. (1999). *Gender and economic right.* [Unpublished report]. Geneva, Switzerland: United Nations Research Institute for Social Development.

Peterson, V. S., & Runyan, A. S. (1999). *Global gender issues.* Boulder, CO: Westview.

Pettman, J. J. (1996). *Worlding women: A feminist international politics.* New York, NY: Routledge.

Porter, M. (2007). Transnational feminisms in a globalized world: Challenges, analysis, and resistance. *Feminist Studies, 33*(1), 43–63.

Reamer, F. (1998). The evolution of social work ethics. *Social Work, 43,* 488–500.

Roberts, D. E. (1994). Foreword: The meaning of gender equality in criminal law. *Journal of Criminal Law and Criminology, 85*(1), 1–14.

Rose, S., & Hartmann, H. (2004). *Still a man's labor market: The long-term earnings gap.* Washington, DC: Institute for Women's Policy Research.

Rubin, G. (1975). The traffic in women. In R. R. Reiter (Ed.), *Toward an anthropology of women.* (pp. 157–210) New York, NY: Monthly Review Press.

Saulnier, C. F. (1996). *Feminist theories and social work: Approaches and applications.* New York, NY: Haworth Press.

Shin, B. (2001). *Recent developments in Korean criminal law to protect women and children against sexual violence.* Retrieved from http://www.legalcenter.or.kr/legalcenter/board/upload/convention//up_convention_13_0.pdf

Smith, A. (1976). The theory of moral sentiments. In D.D. Raphael & A.L. Macfie (eds.). Oxford, UK: Oxford University Press.

Stiglitz, J. E. (2003). Democratizing the International Monetary Fund and the World Bank: Governance and accountability. *Governance: An International Journal of Policy, Administration, and Institutions, 16*(1), 111–139.

Streeten, P. (2001). *Globalization: Threat or opportunity?* Copenhagen, Denmark: Copenhagen Business School Press.

Sung, S. (2003). Women reconciling paid and unpaid work in a Confucian welfare state: The case of South Korea. *Social Policy and Administration, 37,* 342–360.

Thiele, B. (1986). Vanishing acts in social and political thought: Tricks of the trader. In G. Pateman & E. Grosz (Eds.), *Feminist challenges: Social and political theory* (pp. 26–33). Boston, MA: Northeastern University Press.

United Nations. (2005). *Gender Equality and empowerment of women through ICT*. Retrieved from http://www.un.org/womenwatch/daw/public/w2000-09.05-ict-e.pdf

United Nations. (n.d). *Women's Development Act*. Retrieved from http://www.un.org/esa/gopher-data/conf/fwcw/natrep/NatActPlans/korea/korea1

Van Wormer, K. (2002). Our social work imagination: How social work has not abandoned its mission. *Journal of Teaching in Social Work, 22*(3/4), 21–37.

Weisberg, D. K. (1993). *Feminist legal theory: Foundations*. Philadelphia, PA: Temple University Press.

Won, S. K., & Pascall, G. (2004). A Confucian war over childcare? Practice and policy in childcare and their implications for understanding the Korean gender regime. *Social Policy & Administration, 38*(3), 270–289. doi:10.1111/j.1467-9515.2004.00390.x

Women's Development Act, Act No. 5136 (1995). Retrieved from http://www.un.org/esa/gopher-data/conf/fwcw/natrep/NatActPlans/korea/korea1

World Bank. (2011). *World development report 2011*. Retrieved from http://data.worldbank.org/data-catalog/wdr2011

World Economic Forum. (2011). *The global gender gap report 2011*. Retrieved from http://www3.we forum.org/docs/WEF_GenderGap_Report_2011.pdf

CHAPTER 9

Immigration and Intersectionality

Key Observations From a Community-Based Project
With Newcomers in Canada's Rural-Urban Community

BHARATI SETHI AND OLENA HANKIVSKY

It was a gorgeous summer afternoon in Brantford, a rural-urban city in Grand Erie, southern Ontario in Canada, and the site of a community multicultural event. After days of constant showers and thunderstorms, the sun had found its way out of the dark clouds. The mood was festive as men, women, and children from diverse cultures across the globe mingled with each other. I (Bharati Sethi) had set up a table with information about my research project, which explored gaps in services for newcomers: immigrants and refugees who arrived in Canada in the previous 5 years. The research, which focused on Grand Erie, sought the perspectives of newcomers (men and women) and service providers across five areas: employment, education, training, health, and social support (Sethi, 2009a, 2009b). Embracing the principles of community-based participatory research, I wanted to bridge the gap between the researcher and the subject of research by putting a face on this research and engaging participants in dialogue about their experiences.

My enthusiasm turned into discomfort as I spoke with Sapna, a newcomer woman from South Asia. The conversation did not progress as my practiced interviews had in my clinical counseling class. Sapna had come to Canada under the Family Class Sponsorship policy, which allows individuals to immigrate to Canada if a close relative who is a Canadian citizen or permanent resident sponsors them. Sapna appeared to be very isolated. She disclosed that she was gay, and then she begged me to not share that information with anyone, especially from the South Asian community. She was afraid she would be deported and ostracized. I felt empathy for her as she appeared to be torn between her desire to be true to her identity and a good role model for her young son. I sensed her feelings of exhaustion in trying to adapt to a new country, repress her sexuality, and deal with her need for community acceptance. I was worried about her health, as she had indicated that she was not able to sleep through the night and appeared extremely anxious. Per the conditions of Canada's Family Class Sponsorship policy, Sapna was completely dependent on her husband for all her basic needs (food, shelter, clothing, health, and dental care) for 3 years following migration. As a "sponsored wife" she was solely her husband's responsibility and was ineligible for any government financial or social assistance such as English-language training or support through social programs (Merali, 2009, 2010). Sapna felt trapped in her marriage.

Growing up in a culture with similar values, a part of me wanted to rescue her, but I knew that I had to allow her the right of self-determination and maintain the boundaries of our relationship. After Sapna vented her feelings, I told her I was not a counselor, but I was willing to provide her with some resources in the community.

I became apprehensive as it dawned on me that some of the immigrants and refugees in this community perceived me as an expert who had the solutions to their problems. I could not escape the heavy sense of responsibility as a researcher as I watched the sun set on the horizon and the crowd disperse while I began to dismantle the display board that proudly announced my name and contact information. I was accountable to these newcomers. The deep knowledge that I did not have all the answers did not comfort me. The words of other newcomer men and women, "We have left everything behind hoping for a better life in Canada for our children," pierced my ears like needles.

At that moment I could not locate the reason for my discomfort. In retrospect—even though I could not articulate it—I knew deep within me that this research had missed an important link in their story of migration: narratives in which intersectionalities (intersections of gender, immigration status, nationality, ethnicity, culture, geography, age, and geographical location) inform women's experiences of migration.

My preceding narrative is based on my experiences as a researcher in a community-based participatory study of supports available and needed for new immigrant integration in the Grand Erie region of Canada (Sethi, 2009a, 2009b, 2010). My work is motivated by my personal and professional experiences. Similar to Sapna, I was a newcomer to Brantford from India. I know intimately the struggles that immigrant/refugee women experience postmigration to Canada. As a resident of Brantford for 16 years, a visible minority, student, social worker, and volunteer with immigrant service agencies, I am aware that in Grand Erie newcomers often cannot find the appropriate services (such as English as a second language resources and education-bridging programs) that are integral to their integration. My encounter with Sapna, an educated immigrant woman confronted with multifaced barriers resulting from her immigration status, socioeconomic status, ethnicity/race, culture, and gender, provided a powerful learning experience regarding the multiple challenges facing newcomer women in Canada, especially those in rural areas. In this chapter, we draw on theories of intersectionality and Sapna's story as a case example to address the complicated interplay of social policy and lived experience in immigrant women's lives.

In 2003 I (Olena Hankivsky) began actively to confront my complicity as a privileged White feminist in the production of gender-focused research and policy tools that are inherently racist and exclusionary. Over the past decade, drawing on the groundbreaking work of feminists of color and indigenous women who generated the scholarship on intersectionality, I have been committed to building this body of knowledge in innovated ways that is driven by my goal to be a self-reflective ally. In particular, using my position as director of the Institute for Intersectionality Research and Policy (which I founded), I strive to institutionally, intellectually, and practically support and facilitate social justice-oriented research and policy. An intersectionality framework—a theoretical and research paradigm that prioritizes the aforementioned intersections—describes the significance of intersectional analysis for understanding the lived experiences of immigrants and refugees. We argue that intersectionality illuminates the settlement and integration realities of different and often invisible or marginalized subgroups of migrants, and thus better informs policy and programs to effectively address diverse settlement and integration needs in a globalized and interdependent world.

We first provide a brief background on the Canadian immigration policy issues to create a context for the chapter. We briefly summarize the Grand Erie study, highlighting relevant themes, and paying special attention to Sapna's lived experiences. Specifically, we suggest that without the benefit of an intersectionality framework, the Grand Erie study failed to delve into the specific conditions of newcomer women's migration, such as their immigration status and how their sponsorship obligation affected their integration and masked crucial intersecting and interacting relations of domination and inequality.

We then provide an overview of intersectionality and discuss the importance of this framework for advancing multilayered understandings of immigration. Specifically, it is our opinion that research conducted through an intersectional lens would consider how immigration "as part of the interactive dynamic processes that, along with race, gender, sexual orientation, and class," shapes women's experiences of economic and social integration in the host country (Erez, Adelman, & Gregory, 2009, p. 33). In the final section, we summarize key observations from the Grand Erie study and offer helpful tools for engaging in intersectionality-informed social work practice, research, and policy analysis.

Background on Canadian Immigration Policy Issues

The forces of globalization, characterized by an increase in the economic, cultural, and political interdependence among nations, have contributed greatly to the movement of people globally and to the growth of international populations (immigrants, refugees, and other foreign-born people) in Canada, the United States, and Europe (Healy, 2008). In 2009, for instance, Canada admitted 252,200 permanent residents[1] (Chui, 2011). Currently immigrants constitute 19.8% of the total Canadian population, the highest proportion in over 60 years (Chui, 2011). International migration thus continues to be the primary engine driving Canada's population growth.

The 1967 and 2002 changes to Canada's Immigration and Refugee Protection Act (IRPA) have dramatically shifted the source of emigrating populations from European to non-European nations, since a points-based system using factors such as education level, language ability, and employment experience replaced race with skills as criteria for immigrant selection (Citizenship and Immigration Canada, [CIC], 2012a; O'Shea, 2009). This amendment to the IRPA facilitates the migration of newcomers (men and women) and their families to Canada who possess skills (education and labor market experience) that respond to Canada's labor-market needs. According to the 2006 Canadian census, an estimated 60% of international migration came from Asia; a startling number considering that four decades ago Asian immigrants made up only 6.4% of immigrants to Canada (Statistics Canada, 2008).

With each wave of migration the proportion of women migrants to Canada continues to rise. Women now account for 52% (2.6 million) of international migration to Canada (Chui & Maheux, 2011). Strikingly, the proportion of the total female population that belongs to a visible minority has grown steadily since 1981: 55% in 1981, 71% in 1991, 73% in 2001, and by 2006 this number reached 76% (Chui & Maheux, 2011). The gradual increase of females in international migration, or the "feminization of migration" (Boyd, 2006, p. 3) has brought attention to the gendered aspects of immigration and to investigating similarities and differences between migrant men and women (Healy, 2008; Migration Policy Institute, 2003). However, gendered lines of inquiry often fall into the trap of essentialization, oversimplification, and homogenization. As Hankivsky (2012a) states, "Research that focuses on differences between men and women can perpetuate false dichotomies that fail to reflect the diversity between different groups of women and men or open the possibility of examining different types of population groups" (p. 1714).

The CIC, the ministry that oversees immigration policy in Canada, defines *settlement* as the initial period of adjustment in the host country (generally the first 4 years), after which immigrants go through the process of adaptation, or midterm settlement (CIC, 2012b). The hope of the designers of Canadian multiculturalism policy is that in the long term immigrants will integrate, that is, fully participate and contribute economically and socially to the host society and to Canada (Canadian Multiculturalism Act, 1985). In regard to the settlement of newcomers, even though two thirds of Canada's foreign-born population continues to be attracted to Canada's three largest metropolitan areas, Toronto, Montréal, and Vancouver, federal regionalization policies have contributed to the dispersion of immigrants from their initial port of entry (large urban centers) to small-town communities and rural/remote areas (CIC, 2001; Frideres, 2006; Krahn, Derwing, & Abu-Laban, 2005; Sethi, 2010; Statistics Canada, 2008; Walton-Roberts, 2006). Through policies supporting regionalization of immigration, the Canadian government hopes to attract and retain immigrants in less populated provinces. Canada's smaller centers are also taking an active role in attracting immigrants to revitalize their economies, since these communities often face the risk of declining populations (Frideres, 2006; Rose

& Desmarais, 2007; Walton-Roberts, 2006). In response to the regionalization of immigration there is a trend in research, such as the Grand Erie study (Sethi, 2009a, 2009b, 2010), toward understanding diversity and immigrant settlement outside Canada's large urban centers (Frideres, 2006; Rose & Desmarais, 2007; Walton-Roberts, 2006). However, more research, such as the Grand Erie study, is needed to understand the experiences of migrants settling in Canada's small-town communities and rural areas.

The Grand Erie Study

This study was conducted in collaboration with a local newcomer task force, the Immigrant Settlement Transition Employment and Partnership (ISTEP), whose mission is to facilitate the settlement and integration of newcomers in Grand Erie (Sethi, 2009a, 2009b, 2010). In keeping with the tenets of community-based participatory research, Sethi worked with ISTEP members in all aspects of research design, implementation, and analysis and dissemination of findings. She collected data from 212 newcomer men and women and 237 service providers using multiple methods including survey questionnaires, community dialogues, meetings with ISTEP members, and a researcher's reflexive journal. Newcomer participants reported 45 different countries of origin with India (25%) and China (15%) as the top two countries of origin. Sixty-six percent of the newcomers were female and 24% were male. The majority (70%) of the respondents were young adults between the ages of 25 and 44. Most of the study respondents (65%) were married. Sixty-nine percent of the newcomers could speak English and/or French at least "fairly well," and 71% could write at least "fairly well" in English and/or French before coming to Canada. About 59% of the newcomers were employed, whereas 41% were unemployed at the time of the survey.

Initially Sethi used descriptive statistics to analyze the data. This approach to data analysis was limited in that it merely revealed differences between men's and women's experiences but failed to illuminate participants' multiple interacting social locations. Later, as she delved deeper, exploring the data through a gender-based lens, it became evident that gender was a powerful factor that shaped participants' migration experiences. Further, as she analyzed narrative responses elicited by the questionnaire and community dialogues, Sethi began to notice how the various threads of race, immigration status, socioeconomics, sexual orientation and geography (rural area), and gender were intricately woven together to create a pattern that was complex and unique to each participant, as illustrated by Sapna's story.

Key Themes from the Grand Erie Study

An analysis of the narratives elicited by the from the Grand Erie study survey and community dialogues (Sethi, 2009a, 2009b, 2010) revealed four recurrent themes: economic integration of newcomer men versus women, immigration status and women of color, newcomer health, and discrimination.

Economic integration of newcomer men and women. Sethi's (2009a, 2009b, 2010) study corroborated existing scholarship showing that a highly skilled (in terms of education, work experience, and linguistic ability) and young cohort of newcomer men and women, especially from non-European nations, were experiencing high levels of unemployment and underemployment (Boucher, 2007; Boyd, 2006; Iredale, 2005; Merali, 2009; Oxman-Martinez et al., 2005; Reitz, 2007a, 2007b; Shankar & Northcott, 2009, Zaman, 2010). Sethi also observed that newcomer men were more likely to be employed full-time and earn higher incomes than newcomer women. Her findings were also in line with Houle and Yssad (2010), who reported that the rates of nonrecognition of foreign credentials are higher for immigrant women (51%) than men (23%).

Sapna's situation is reflective of these findings. This young university-educated woman's human and social capital obtained in India was not recognized in Canada. Even though she had completed a master's of science degree and had worked in India's pharmaceutical industry, she was unemployed at the time of the survey. Since her arrival in Canada she had only been able to find occasional work in a factory. Sapna's experience parallels that of many other immigrant women. Numerous studies have shown that even though economic globalization has increased the migration of professional and skilled female workers (for example, doctors and nurses), a large majority of women perform low-skilled work in host countries (domestic service, factory work, or illegal sex work; Brickner & Straehle, 2010; Oxman-Martinez et al., 2005; Ross-Sheriff, 2011). Many educated racial and ethnic minority women, for example, are employed as live-in-caregivers[2] (LICs) in Canadian middle- to high-income households where their remuneration is not consistent with their education levels (Brickner & Straehle, 2010; Oxman-Martinez et al. 2005). In the Grand Erie study, Sethi (2009a, 2009b, 2010) encountered several LICs who spoke of oppressive employment conditions but were unable to leave because they used their earnings to support their families in their country of origin. Referring to "push-pull" factors Ross-Sheriff (2011, p. 234), convincingly argues that faced with extreme poverty, women from the South (e,g., the Philippines) are *pushed* out of their country and *pulled* toward the job opportunities created by capitalism in the North, such as Canada.

Immigration status and women of color. In the era of rapid globalization, marriage-based migration is becoming "one of the most prevalent forms of population movement from developing to developed nations, particularly for women" (Merali, 2010, p. 5). Sapna came to Canada through the Hindu tradition of arranged marriage. She was sponsored by her husband, the "principal applicant" under the Family Class Sponsorship policy. For women immigrants who migrate to Canada as dependants of principal applicants, "this dependent status fosters the growth of various layers of discrimination and inequity already embedded in the Canadian structured labour market" (Zaman, 2010, p. 3; see also Merali, 2010; Oxman-Martinez, 2005). As Sapna's case demonstrates, she was dependent on her husband for all her financial, health, and social needs for 3 years following migration. Even though we acknowledge the positive steps the government of Canada has taken in reducing the sponsorship agreement from 10 years to 3 years, this clause continues to put sponsored wives at a disadvantage. For example, Sapna was ineligible for any government-funded services such as employment training, which is obligatory for labor market integration, or services from immigration agencies (Merali, 2010). This is because under the Family Class Sponsorship policy, men as sponsors of their spouses are primarily responsible for "facilitating the women's integration and upholding the women's human rights" (Merali, 2010, p. 7–8). Not surprisingly, 6 months after arrival, only 32% of the sponsored wives in the family class were employed, compared with 54% of men (A Commitment to Training and Employment for Women, 2007).

Turning our attention to Sapna's sexual orientation, we can speculate that the culture and community in her home country did not permit her to engage in a same-sex relationship. Despite the positive changes in the 2002 IRPA policies to expand the definition of spouse or marriage partner beyond heterosexual couples (LaViolette, 2004), Sapna was trapped in her marriage. If she walked out of her marriage, thus breaking the sponsorship agreement, she could risk deportation as well as losing custody of her son. These findings indeed confirm that "immigration schemes can create 'blanket definitions' by ignoring how ethnicity and social class establish barriers for prospective applicants, in addition to existing gender inequalities" (Boucher, 2007, p. 394). Sapna did not fit the blanket definitions encoded in immigration policy. Torn between her desire to be true to her sexual identity and the need for community/family acceptance, Sapna suffered from anxiety and sleeplessness.

Health of newcomers: Healthy? Sapna's precarious situation as a newcomer was a source of distress. She lived in a rural county of Grand Erie, had a small child, did not have a drivers' license, and had no family or friends in Canada. Without a car it is very difficult to travel around the Grand Erie region. Lack of a proper transportation infrastructure, coupled with the absence of culturally sensitive and affordable child care, further isolated Sapna at home. As Sethi observed, Sapna's fearful and sad demeanor, her inability to sleep through the night, and her lack of an understanding of her legal rights were affecting her mental health. The absence of close relatives and familial support increased Sapna's risk of isolation. Moreover, Canadian immigration policy favors an individual's economic attributes over family relationships, as evident in the current 60/40 rule, which requires selection of immigrants to be 60% economic (skilled workers and business immigrants) and 40% noneconomic (family class migrants and refugees). Thus, it has become more difficult for immigrants to sponsor their parents and extended family to immigrate to Canada (McLaren & Black, 2005). McLaren & Black (2005) contend that the government has failed to account for the value of parents and grandparents to their families and the rest of society. For instance, in collectivist cultures (e.g., Chinese, Indian, African) parents and grandparents are primary child care providers.

The issues Sapna faced were common among many women newcomers who participated in the study. Sethi (2009 a, 2009b) found that other female participants were also isolated at home because of their inability to drive and the absence of affordable child care. Women often delayed getting their educational credential assessments and driver's license so that their spouses could first get settled, as demonstrated in the following comments from survey participants: "It seems that immigrant women wait for husband to get driving license, and settled and put their needs last" (from a service provider), and "First my husband needs to find job and due to lack of culturally relevant and affordable child care as I have a small child it is difficult for me to go to work" (from a newcomer).

Themes of sadness, anxiety, loss of interest in activities, and depression especially from the female participants filled the pages of the survey questionnaire. For instance, one female newcomer participant wrote: "Not happy has no job, little friends, husband works in difficult job." Perhaps having the company of a parent/grandparent at home to provide social support and help with child care could have eased these women's settlement difficulties.

Discrimination. A disturbing finding in the Grand Erie study (Sethi, 2009a, 2009b) was that discrimination against newcomer men and women was identified in every variable explored, including education and training, employment, health, and social support. Newcomers' and service providers' responses suggest that most newcomers experienced discrimination either at work, in the community, or in the neighborhood (Sethi, 2009a, 2009b). One participant wrote that she had experienced discrimination because of her dress, which included the hijab/burka. The following service provider's comment clearly highlights the assumptions that the participant made based on a newcomer's ethnic dress: "I feel very strong that those who wear turbans . . . men . . . discriminate against women of all nationalities and scare women by the way they act towards other people." Further, despite Sethi's efforts to engage newcomers of diverse sexual orientations in the study, their voices were relatively silent. Sethi's communication with some members of the gay and lesbian community reflected that members of this population feel unsafe to voice their issues in Grand Erie. In response to hate crimes directed at newcomers in Brantford, the Peace and Diversity Circle was created "to strengthen the city of Brantford in all of its diversity—and increase our capacity to end Hate Based Crime" (Peace and Diversity Forum, 2008).

Using Intersectionality to Understand the Emerging Themes of the Grand Erie Study and Their Connection to Sapna's Story

As reflection on the key themes of the Grand Erie study (Sethi, 2009a, 2009b) suggests, gender was but one dimension shaping Sapna's experiences and those of other newcomer women; a myriad of other factors (such as immigrant status, geography, and socioeconomics) interacted to affect their integration. For Sethi, a full understanding of such factors required searching for an alternative framework to position the findings, which went beyond a simple gender analysis. In her search for an explanatory paradigm, Sethi began to work with the paradigm of intersectionality.

Intersectionality's historic genesis is in feminist and critical race theory (Anzaldúa, 1987; Hill Collins, 2000; Combahee River Collective, 1977; Crenshaw, 1989; Davis, 1981; hooks, 1981; Juteau-Lee & Roberts, 1981). Although definitions and conceptions differ, according to Hankivsky (2012a) a number of identifiable tenets include the following: (a) human lives cannot be reduced to single characteristics; (b) human experiences cannot be accurately understood by prioritizing any one single factor or constellation of factors; (c) social categories such as race/ethnicity, gender, class, sexuality, and ability are socially constructed, fluid, and flexible; and (d) social locations are inseparable and shaped by the interacting and mutually constituting social processes and structures that are influenced by time and place. As Hankivsky explains, "These tenets are intended to provide the basis for . . . an avenue of enquiry where no category of oppression is automatically considered as the most damaging and where some differences are not continually highlighted to the exclusion of others" (p. 1713). An intersectionality framework thus deepens, enriches, and complicates understandings of how gender is inextricably influenced and shaped by other social processes, structures, and locations. In addition, intersectionality scholars explicitly acknowledge the simultaneous possibilities of experiencing privilege and penalty (e.g., Hill Collins, 1990) and allow for contradictions and tensions in negotiating various positions.

Although intersectionality is burgeoning across disciplines and in many fields of research, in general, it is only starting to make inroads into the field of social work (Mehrotra, 2010; Murphy, Hunt, Zajicek, Norris, & Hamilton, 2009), and in particular, "intersectionality studies of immigration are rare" (Thing, 2010, p. 814). To date, most researchers attempting to understand the varied experiences of immigration have focused on gender and migration (Boucher, 2007; Donato, Gabaccia, Holdaway, Manalansan, & Pessar, 2006; Hondagneu-Sotelo, 1994, 2003; Menjivar, 2000; Pessar, 1999). However, as Bilge and Denis (2010) have observed, a key shift is under way:

> A key characteristic of current research on gender and migration is
> the heightened awareness of the inner diversity of the category

"migrant women" (and of "migrant men" for that matter) and the increasing taking into account of the intersectionality of multiple axes of power relations (race, class, sexualities, age, nationality, religion, caste, able-bodiedness) shaping gendered experiences and migratory processes. (p. 3)

The intersectionality shift can be observed in a number of emerging studies (e.g., Berg, 2010; Berger, 2009; de Finney, 2010; Erez et al., 2009; Kynsilehto, 2011; Lu, 2008; Lundström, 2010; Lutz & Palenga-Möllenbeck, 2011; Riano, 2011; Smith & Marmo, 2011; Thing, 2010; Yakushko & Espin, 2010) that in a variety of country contexts highlight and examine a range of immigrant experiences of the "complex relationship between multiple minority statuses, points of oppressions, and lived experiences" (Asencio, 2009, p. 1). As Ovadia (2001) states,

Intersectional theorists point out that individuals are *simultaneously* situated within the systems of race, gender, and class identity and to consider any one of these systems of difference without including the others may lead to incomplete, or possibly incorrect, conclusions about similarities and differences within and among groups. (p. 342, emphasis in original)

In the context of immigration, such an understanding of how individuals are situated requires an integrative rather than additive approach, theoretically and methodologically, to understand the complexities, variations, and full dimensions of immigrant experiences and concomitant needs. A number of preliminary observations from the Grand Erie Study (Sethi, 2009a, 2009b), and specifically Sapna's story, reveal that an intersectionality perspective advances a deeper and more accurate understanding of how multiple dimensions of inequality at the micro, mezzo, and macro levels shape settlement patterns and experiences.

Key Observations From the Grand Erie Study: Contributions of Intersectionality Perspectives to Social Work and Immigration Literature

Despite social work's long history of serving the immigrant population in Canada, social work education and research has not paid sufficient attention to the challenges experienced by newcomers (Biles, Drover, Henley, Ibrahim, &

Yan, 2010, p. 6). It is urgent that the social work profession become aware of the "complex issues of global gendered migration" (Ross-Sheriff, 2010, p. 237) and how its "practice and professional environment are shaped by interdependence" (Healy, 2008, p. 4) between the local and the global. As Moosa-Mitha & Ross-Sheriff (2011) state, globalization, though not new, "has recently been pushed to the forefront of the popular imagination for several reasons: the increased pace of economic transactions between the North and the South; climate change and its effects; war and the resulting migration of refugees and internally displaced persons" (p. 105). Using an intersectionality lens in relation to the Grand Erie study (Sethi, 2009a, b; 2010) it becomes clear that simple comparisons of male and female settlement experiences cannot fully reveal the complexity of lived realities. To access newcomers' full stories of migration, it is important to demonstrate how power structures, race/ethnicity, gender, religion, nationality, sexual orientation, class, and disability simultaneously interact with one another and with other systems of dominance (e.g., immigration institute) to affect everyday experiences of the diversity of immigrant men and women (Wamala, Ahnquist, & Månsdotter, 2009).

To begin, intersectionality offers a multilevel analysis that incorporates attention to power and social processes at the micro and macro levels through which subject formation occurs (Dhamoon & Hankivsky, 2011), including that of Sapna and other participants in the study. In this way, intersectionality requires explicitly recognizing how "international migration patterns have changed as a consequence of broad social, political, economic, and environmental trends" (Ross-Sheriff, 2011, p. 233). It is expected, for example, that in the future, marriage-based migrations will dominate population movements across North-South borders (Merali, 2010). For example, India and China rank as the top source country of marriage-based migrants to Canada (Merali, 2009, 2010), and 90% of LICs working in Canada are from the Philippines (Oxman-Martinez et al., 2005). Further, as Sapna's case demonstrates, since migrants' countries of origin often have different cultural norms, human rights codes, and value systems (Merali, 2010), some women may be compelled into arranged marriages leaving them with no option but to follow their husbands to Canada as sponsored wives.

If we bring intersectionality into an analysis of Sapna's postarrival reality, it is clear that she experienced oppression at the intersections of gender, race/ethnicity, immigration status, and sexuality. As a sponsored wife with no family in Canada she was entirely dependent on her husband for her financial and emotional needs. Because of her visible minority immigrant status, her foreign educational and work experience qualifications were not recognized, which made it difficult for her to find employment to support herself and her child. Indeed, on arrival in Canada, many migrant women face many resettlement challenges such as loss of social support, nonrecognition of foreign credentials, language barriers, transportation challenges, and lack of culturally sensitive services (Merali, 2010; Sethi, 2010; Zaman, 2010). In addition, complete reliance on their spouse for basic needs—food, clothing, shelter, and health care—puts these women in vulnerable positions (Merali, 2009, 2010).

A continuing issue facing visible minority women sponsored by their husband or the principal applicant is the lack of understanding of "their basic human rights or integration rights and how these rights will be protected in the new host society" (Merali, 2010, p. 7), and thus they do not often exercise these rights. For example, amendments to the Family Class Sponsorship policy now permit marriage migrants who are being physically or emotionally abused by their sponsor or husband to break this sponsorship agreement and support themselves through collecting social assistance. Yet many women continue to suffer sponsor-inflicted abuse because they do not fully understand these changes to policy or how to ensure protection of their human rights. Moreover, as immigration policy documents are primarily in English, women with language barriers must rely on their husband or in-laws for translation. Because the government fails to "educate sponsors about each party's rights in the context of sponsorship relationship," (Merali, 2010, p. 7–8) women have been lied to about their legal rights and threatened by their spouses with deportation if they tried to leave the abusive situation. The multidimensional vulnerability the sponsorship agreements often create requires an intersectionality-informed interrogation of the relationship between visible minority immigrant women's various social locations (e.g., socioeconomics, ethnicity/race, and immigration status) and power-laden immigration policy documents, including, for example, access to services and opportunities for labor-market integration. Fortunately, Sapna was not in an abusive situation. As she was proficient in the English language she was able to adequately discuss her sexuality issues with Sethi.

Social work research with family-sponsored wives through an intersectionality lens could also address how experiences of women with English language skills *qualitatively* differ from a sponsored wife without knowledge of English. An intersectionality researcher would further inquire: How does ethnicity/race, education, or age interlock to affect an immigrant woman's vulnerability to abuse in relation to Family Class Sponsorship policies?

Sapna's narrative also raises an issue largely unaddressed in immigration scholarship—that of sexual orientation. An intersectionality perspective reveals that Sapna's postmigration experience was shaped by the interaction of sexual orientation with several other factors including culture, gender, and immigrant status. These trapped Sapna in a marriage that she did not want, leaving her with very few options to follow her heart and be true to her sexual identity. Progress has been made. Gay men and lesbians can now officially sponsor their partners to Canada, and as noted earlier, amendments to the Family Class Sponsorship laws now permit women to leave their abusive situation and break the sponsorship agreement in case of intimate partner violence. However, what does a sponsored wife do if she wants to leave her husband because of her desire to be with another woman? This question demands our attention. Reflecting on Sapna's situation and, in particular, the evolving Canadian mosaic and federal dispersion of immigrants from larger metropolitan centers to smaller rural towns, there is an urgent need for intersectionality researchers to investigate how sexuality as a social location shapes lives of visible minority women living in these communities. Although we applaud the government's positive steps in reducing the sponsorship bond between the sponsor (generally a husband) and sponsored person (primarily a woman), Sapna's lived experience clearly demonstrates the urgency to completely remove the 3-year obligation that tie marriage migrants to their spouses. Future research must seek to understand how immigrants simultaneously experience their social locations based on their immigration status, sexual orientation, and gender in relation to existing government policies and legislation (e.g., Ascencio, 2009; Berger, 2009; Thing, 2010).

We believe that using intersectionality to expand the understanding of diversity in the social category of women by examining how the integration experiences of women of color differ qualitatively from other women (e.g., European immigrants) will lead to more insightful and comprehensive knowledge of lived realities of immigrant women. Even though we have highlighted women's marginalized status in the story of skilled migration, intersectionality cautions researchers to not legitimize homogenizing discourses, including those that position all third world women's migration as a way to escape patriarchal structures in their home country (Shankar & Northcott, 2009). Scholars must be careful of "producing/re-presenting a composite, singular 'third-world woman'—an image which appears arbitrarily constructed but nevertheless carries with it the authorizing signature of western humanist discourse" (Mohanty, 1988, p. 63).

In emphasizing the possibilities of privilege and penalty, an intersectionality lens allows recognition of the fact that Sapna and other female participants radiated strength and resilience through their difficult migratory journey. Though it must have been very difficult for her, Sapna found a way to travel with a small child from a rural area of Grand Erie to the multicultural event in Brantford. Sethi (2009a) was particularly impressed with the capacity Sapna and others demonstrated to actively seek out resources that could foster economic and social integration.

Further, the findings in the Grand Erie study (Sethi, 2009a, 2009b) on discrimination point to the value of using intersectionality to interrogate the complexity of a person's nationality in his or her settlement and integration experiences. Scholars must make efforts to understand the way nationality factors into individuals', families', and communities' settlement experiences and how these markers of difference mold immigrant/refugees identity and self-concept (Abu-Ras, 2007). Zaman (2010) writes: "In terms of nationality, people of Pakistani origin and Middle-eastern origin encounter all forms of 'Muslimphobia/ Islamicphobia,' which has been identified as 'a new wave of xenophobia' in Canada" (p. 5). An intersectional approach to discrimination recognizes that people of Pakistani origin experience racism in a very different way from those of Middle-Eastern origin. An intersectional analysis does not stop here. It also raises the question: How do the discrimination experiences of various subgroups of Pakistani or Middle Eastern people distinctively differ as their nationality interacts with other markers of difference (such as race, ethnicity and gender)?

Geographical dispersal of immigrants to rural and remote spaces aimed at "increasing cultural diversity nationwide, globalizing small communities, developing local markets to rejuvenate regional economies, and easing the pressure on the capitals of immigrant Canada" (Krahn et al., 2005, p. 2) demands that the government and the host society work together to assist with newcomer integration so that immigrants' experiences of rural areas is positive. It means ensuring amenities such as a proper transportation infrastructure, culturally sensitive and affordable child care, and programs that inform immigrant women of their human rights (such as the right to be free from domestic violence; Merali, 2010). Scholars informed by the intersectionality paradigm are beginning to factor place into their studies of migration along with other social locations. Berg (2010), for instance, used an intersectional analysis to examine how class, race, gender, and the sociodemographic context of geographic areas interacted and shaped people's attitudes to immigrants. His study is important to locales such as Grand Erie, which have traditionally not experienced migration from non-European countries. Interestingly, Berg's study shows that "social space intersects with the individual characteristics of race, class, and gender in predicting immigration attitudes" (p. 296).

Intersectionality work is complicated, challenging, and rewarding. Vigilance to power hierarchies and dynamics as they unfold in the research journey and in practice is critical to intersectionality and social work scholars. In creating knowledge for practice and praxis, intersectionality professionals do not address problems at superficial levels; rather, they problematize the underlying ideologies and assumptions, prevailing status quo, discourses, and power structures that contribute to the oppression of individuals and society. It is through reflexivity (such as awareness of our private and professional selves), Hankivsky (2012b) asserts, that intersectionality largely attends to issues of power and privilege, deconstructs various "isms" (such as heterosexism, racism, and colonialism), and engages in authentic dialogue between the self and society. We see the critical contribution of reflexivity in Sethi's recognition that the Grand Erie research had missed an important link to the story of newcomers' immigration and her search for an alternate paradigm to address Sapna's and other newcomer issues. Through self-reflection on her own multiple identities—immigrant, visible minority woman, researcher, resident of Grand Erie for 16 years, and service user—often vis-à-vis the participants' varied social locations, Sethi was able to problematize the different epistemologies used in creation of evidence-based knowledge and consider "how power influences the privileging of certain knowledge traditions to the exclusion of others" (Hankivsky, 2012b, p. 10).

Given the promise and relevance of intersectionality for immigration and social work, immigration scholars and social workers would benefit from incorporating intersectional perspectives in their research, practices, and policy analyses to uncover the complexity of multiple and interlocking systems of oppression and privilege, as well as to account for those forms of social identities that are not as easily visible, such as an individual's immigration status (Erez et al., 2009). As scholars working in partnership with their local community must engage in dialogue on intersectional perspectives with key stakeholders who work with immigrant/refugee populations, they should enhance understanding of how various forms of diversity, including but not limited to gender, have an impact on these populations' migratory lives. Murphy et al. (2009) caution us: "Intersectionality and human diversity cannot be side notes to social work knowledge. These issues constitute the difference between social workers being oppressors or champions for the oppressed" (p. 47).

Doing Intersectionality: Research Tools, Policy Frameworks

Researchers, practitioners, and educators interested in using an intersectionality framework can draw on a number of different tools that have emerged in the literature. Collectively, these methods emphasize that there is no one way to *do* intersectionality-informed research. However, researchers must clearly define what they mean by intersectionality (Hankivsky, 2012b). For example, in a collaborative research project there must be clarity among team members regarding the meaning of intersectionality (Murphy et al., 2009). Hankivsky (2012a, p. 1715–1716) recommends a set of guiding questions to help navigate the complex terrain of intersectionality research:

- Who is being studied? Who is being compared to whom? Why? (Lorber, 2006)
- Who is the research for and does it advance the needs of those under study? (Hankivsky et al., 2010)
- Is the research framed within the current cultural, political, economic, societal, and/or situational context, and where possible, does it reflect the self-identified needs of affected communities? (Hankivsky & Cormier, 2009)
- Which categories are relevant or not directly relevant? Why? (Winkler & Degele, 2011)
- What is the presumed makeup of each category? (Hancock, 2007)

•Is the sample representative of the experiences of diverse groups of people for whom the issue under study is relevant? (Hankivsky & Cormier, 2009)

•Is the tool of inquiry suited to collecting micro or macro data or a combination of both? (Hankivsky & Cormier, 2009)

•How will interactions between salient categories be captured by the proposed coding strategy?

•How will interactions at individual levels of experience be linked to social institutions and broader structures and processes of power?

•What issues of domination/exploitation and resistance/agency are addressed by the research? (Hankivsky & Cormier, 2009)

•How will human commonalities and differences be recognized without resorting to essentialism, false universalism, or be obliviousness to historical and contemporary patterns of inequality? (Cole, 2008)

Moreover, a specific framework has been developed through the Institute for Intersectionality Research and Policy (Hankivsky, 2012b) directed at those who seek to develop intersectionality-informed policy analyses. This intersectionality-based policy analysis approach is informed by key guiding principles—intersecting categories, multilevel analysis power, reflexivity, time and space, social justice and equity—and 11 overarching descriptive and normative questions contained in the appendix to this chapter on p. 232. Hankivsky (2012b) asserts that the application of questions in the appendix must be

grounded in the theoretical tenets of an intersectionality research paradigm in order to realize their intended operational objectives: the destabilization of a priori primacy and stability of singular categories; the avoidance of additive lists; and the focus on the fluid and interactive nature of multi-level complex processes and systems that shape health inequities. (p. 14)

As methods for operationalizing intersectionality continue to emerge, social workers have the opportunity and responsibility to explore their relevance for research, practice, and policy.

Concluding Remarks

It is our hope this chapter will inspire social workers, immigration scholars, health practitioners, and policy makers to consider intersectionality, an important paradigm shift, to bring to light immigrant men's and women's distinctive stories. As a human rights profession, "traditional and linear approaches to social work practice, policy, research and education" (Murphy et al., 2009, p. 91) have limited ability to promote social justice and foster social change in individuals, families, and communities, locally and globally. We are firm in our position that although gender is an important consideration in newcomers' experiences, giving primacy to gender over other markers of difference cannot accurately reflect the lived experiences of marginalized populations. Scholars working with immigrant/refugee populations would benefit from incorporating intersectional perspectives in their research, practice, and policy analysis to reveal the complexity of multiple and intersecting systems of oppression and privilege, as well as to uncover their multiple social realities (Erez et al., 2009). Returning to the opening vignette and the Grand Erie study (Sethi, 2009a, 2009b), it is clear in Sapna's narrative that the stories are complex and interlocking: story of migration, survival, emotional turmoil, arranged marriage, desire for another woman, resilience, and citizenship. Only after we understand how multiple markers of difference intersect simultaneously to account for each of these stories can we truly grasp how individuals such as Sapna are either embodied or disembodied.

Discussion Questions

1. How does Sapna's story address some of the struggles experienced by differently situated women (depending on their social, political, and cultural context) immigrating to Canada? How does an intersectionality lens challenge assumptions about female and male immigrants and promote deeper understandings of their settlement experiences?

2. How would you use the intersectionality paradigm to explore policy issues (immigration and health policy) affecting Sapna?

3. How would an intersectionality theory and paradigm inform your approach to social work practice in support of the settlement and integration of recent immigrants (newcomers)?

4. How would you use an intersectionality paradigm to assess the effects of globalization on diverse groups in your own community, state, or country?

5. How would you address issues of power in your research and practice with immigrants?

Notes

1. Broadly, the three main categories of permanent residents are family class immigrants (includes close relatives or family members sponsored by a Canadian permanent resident or citizen), economic or skilled immigrants (foreign-born nationals selected for their skills and abilities to contribute to the Canadian economy), and refugees (see CIC, 2009).

2. LICs are temporary foreign workers selected as live-in nannies to work in private Canadian households to care for children, seniors, or people with disabilities. Farm workers are also on a temporary work visa for employment at Canadian farms (see CIC, 2009).

References

ACTEW. (2008). A commitment to training and employment for women. (2008). Retrieved from http://www.theconstellation.ca/img_upload/0354dceb942b6ce6abdb2535de03bf3f/Immigrant women_ACTEW_Mar07.pdf

Abu-Ras, W. (2007). Cultural beliefs and service utilization by battered Arab immigrant women. *Violence Against Women, 13*(10), 1002–1028. doi:10.1177/1077801207306019

Anzaldúa, G. (1987). *Borderlands/la frontera: The new mestiza.* San Francisco, CA: Spinsters/Aunt Lute.

Asencio, M. (2009). Migrant Puerto Rican lesbians negotiating gender, sexuality, and ethnonationality. *NWSA Journal, 21*(3), 1–23. doi: 10.1353/nwsa.0.0093

Berg, J. A. (2010). Race, class, gender, and social space: Using an intersectional approach to study immigration attitudes. *Sociological Quarterly, 51,* 278–302. doi: 10.1111/j.1533-8525.2010.01172.x

Berger, S. A. (2009). Production and reproduction of gender and sexuality in legal discourses of asylum in the United States. *Signs: Journal of Women in Culture and Society, 34*(3), 659–685. doi: 10.1086/593380

Bilge, S., & Denis, A. (2010) Introduction: Women, intersectionality and diasporas. *Journal of Intercultural Studies, 31*(1), 1–8. doi: 10.1080/07256860903487653

Biles, J., Drover, G., Henley, M., Ibrahim, H., Lundy, L., & Yan, M. (2010). Settlement of newcomers to Canada. *Canadian Social Work, 12*(1), 5–15.

Boucher, A. (2007). Skill, migration and gender in Australia and Canada: The case of gender-based analysis. *Australian Journal of Political Science, 42*(3), 383–401. doi: 10.1080/103611 40701513547

Boyd, M. (2006, June). *Gender aspects of international migration to Canada and the United States.* Paper presented at the International Symposium on Migration and Development, Turin, Italy. Retrieved from http://homes.chass.utoronto.ca/~boydmon/research_papers/immigrant_women/P08_Boyd.pdf

Brickner, R. K., & Straehle, C. (2010). The missing link: Gender, immigration policy, and the Live-in Caregiver Program in Canada. *Policy & Society, 29*(4), 309–320. doi:.org/10.1016/j.polsoc.2010.09.004

Canadian Multiculturalism Act, R.S.C., 1985, c. 24 (4th Supp). Retrieved from http://laws-lois. justice.gc.ca/eng/acts/c-18.7/

Chui, T. (2011). Immigrant women. In Statistics Canada, *Women in Canada: A gender-based statistical report* (6th edition). Ottawa, Canada: Statistics Canada. Retrieved from http://www.statcan. gc.ca/pub/89-503-x/89-503-x2010001-eng.htm

Chui, T., & Maheux, H. (2011). Visible minority women. In Statistics Canada, *Women in Canada: A gender-based statistical report* (6th edition). Ottawa, Canada: Statistics Canada. Retrieved from http://www.statcan.gc.ca/pub/89-503-x/2010001/article/11527-eng.htm

Citizenship and Immigration Canada. (2001). *Towards a more balanced geographic distribution of immigrants.* Retrieved from http://publications.gc.ca/collections/Collection/Ci51-109-2002E.pdf

Citizenship and Immigration Canada. (2009). *Canada facts and figures: Immigrant overview—permanent and temporary residents.* Retrieved from http://www.cic.gc.ca/english/resources/sta tistics/facts2009/

Citizenship and Immigration Canada. (2012 a). *Other selection factors: Skilled workers and professionals.* Retrieved from http://www.cic.gc.ca/english/immigrate/skilled/apply-factors.asp

Citizenship and Immigration Canada. (2012 b). *Annual report to Parliament on immigration.* Retrieved from http://www.cic.gc.ca/english/pdf/pub/annual-report-2012.pdf

Cole, E. (2008). Coalitions as a model for intersectionality: From practice to theory. *Sex Roles, 59*(506), 443–453.

Combahee River Collective. (1977). A Black feminist statement. In L. Nicholson (Ed.), *The second wave: A reader in feminist theory* (pp. 63–70). New York, NY: Routledge.

Crenshaw, K. (1989). Demarginalizing the intersection of race and sex: A Black feminist critique of anti-discrimination doctrine, feminist theory, and anti-racist politics. *University of Chicago Legal Forum, 1989,* 139–167.

Davis, A. Y. (1981). *Women, race, and class.* New York, NY: Random House.

de Finney, S. (2010). "We just don't know each other": Racialised girls negotiate mediated multiculturalism in a less diverse Canadian city. *Journal of Intercultural Studies, 31*(5), 471–487.

Dhamoon, R. K., & Hankivsky, O. (2011). Why the theory and practice of intersectionality matter to health research and policy. In O. Hankivsky (Ed.), *Health inequities in Canada: Intersectional frameworks and practices* (pp. 16–50). Vancouver, British Columbia, Canada: University of British Columbia Press.

Donato, K. M., Gabaccia, D., Holdaway, J., Manalansan, M., & Pessar, P. R. (2006). A glass half full? Gender in migration studies. *International Migration Review, 40*(1), 3–26.

Erez, E., Adelman, M., & Gregory, C. (2009). Intersections of immigration and domestic violence: Voices of battered immigrant women. *Feminist Criminology, 4*(1), 32–56. doi: 10.1177/1557085108325413

Frideres, J. S. (2006). Cities and immigration integration: The future of second- and third-tier centres. *Our Diverse Cities, 2,* 20–26. Retrieved from http://canada.metropolis.net/publications/Diver sity/our_diverse_cities_vol2_en.pdf

Hancock, A. (2007). When multiplication doesn't equal quick addition: Examining intersectionality as a research paradigm. *Perspectives on Politics, 5*(1), 63–79.

Hankivsky, O. (2012a). Women's health, men's health, and gender and health: Implications of intersectionality. *Social Science and Medicine, 74*(11), 1712–1720.

Hankivsky, O. (Ed.). (2012b). *An intersectionality-based policy analysis framework.* Vancouver, British Columbia, Canada: Institute for Intersectionality Research and Policy. Retrieved from http://www. sfu.ca/iirp/ibpa.html

Hankivsky, O., & Cormier, R. (2009). *Intersectionality: Moving women's health research and policy forward.* Retrieved from http://www.bccewh.bc.ca/publications-resources/documents/Intersectionaliy Movingwomenshealthresearchandpolicyforward

Hankivsky, O., Reid, C., Cormier, R., Varcoe, C., Clark, N., Benoi, C., & Brotman, S. (2010). Exploring the promises of intersectionality for advancing women's health research. *International Journal for Equity in Health, 9*(5), 1–15. doi:10.1186/1475-9276-9-5, 1-15.

Healy, L. M. (2008). *International social work: Professional action in an interdependent world.* New York, NY: Oxford University Press.

Hill Collins, P. (1990). *Black feminist thought: Knowledge, consciousness, and the politics of empowerment.* London, UK: HarperCollins Academic.

Hill Collins, P. (2000). *Black feminist thought: Knowledge, consciousness, and the politics of empowerment* (2nd ed.) New York, NY: Routledge.

Hondagneu-Sotelo, P. (1994). *Gendered transitions: Mexican experiences of immigration.* Berkeley: University of California Press.

Hondagneu-Sotelo, P. (2003). *Gender and U.S. immigration: Contemporary trends.* Berkeley: University of California Press.

hooks, b. (1981). *Ain't I a woman: Black women and feminism.* Boston, MA: South End Press.

Houle, R., & Yssaad, L. (2010). *Recognition of newcomers' foreign credentials and work experience.* Retrieved from http://www.statcan.gc.ca/pub/75-001-x/2010109/pdf/11342-eng.pdf

Iredale, R. (2005). Gender, immigration policies and accreditation: Valuing the skills of professional women migrants. *Geoforum, 36,* 155–166.

Juteau-Lee, D., & Roberts, B. (1981). Ethnicity and femininity: (D')après nos expériences. *Canadian Ethnic Studies, 13*(1), 1–23.

Krahn, H., Derwing, T., & Abu-Laban, B. (2005). The retention of newcomers in second- and third-tier cities in Canada. *International Migration Review, 39*(4), 872–894. doi: 10.1111/j.1747-7379.2005.tb00292.x

Kynsilehto, A. (2011). Negotiating intersectionality in highly educated migrant Maghrebi women's life stories. *Environment and Planning, 43*(7), 1547–1561. doi: 10.1068/a43367

LaViolette, N. (2004). Coming out to Canada: The immigration of same-sex couples under the immigration and refugee protection act. *McGill Law Journal, 49,* 969–1003. Retrieved from http://www.law.utoronto.ca/documents/globalization/Laviolette-PaperOct26.pdf

Lorber, J. (2006). Shifting paradigms and challenging categories. *Social Problems, 53*(4), 448–453.

Lu, M. (2008, August). *The politics of immigration policy formation: A comparative intersectional analysis.* Paper presented at the annual meeting of the American Political Science Association, Boston, MA.

Lundström, C. (2010). Women with class: Swedish migrant women's class positions in the USA. *Journal of Intercultural Studies, 31*(1), 49–63.

Lutz, H., & Palenga-Möllenbeck, E. (2011). Care, gender and migration: Towards a theory of transnational domestic work migration in Europe. *Journal of Contemporary European Studies, 19*(3), 349–364. doi: 10.1080/14782804.2011.610605

McLaren, A. T., & Black, T. L. (2005). *Family class and immigration in Canada: Implications for sponsored elderly women* (Working paper series No. 05-26). Vancouver, British Columbia, Canada: Vancouver Centre of Excellence, Research on Immigration and Integration in the Metropolis.

Mehrotra, G. (2010). Toward a continuum of intersectionality theorizing for feminist social work scholarship. *Affilia: Journal of Women and Social Work, 25*(4), 417–430. doi: 10.1177/0886 109910384190

Menjivar, C. (2000). *Fragmented ties: Salvadoran immigrant networks in America.* Berkeley: University of California Press.

Merali, N. (2009). Experiences of South Asian brides entering Canada after recent changes to family sponsorship policies. *Violence Against Women, 15*(3), 321–333.

Merali, N. (2010). Marriage-based migration and human rights education: Where does Canada stand? *Cultural and Pedagogical Inquiry, 1*(2), 5–21.

Migration Policy Institute. (2003). *The feminization of international migration: Issues of labor, health, and family coping strategies.* Retrieved from http://www.migrationpolicy.org/events/030702 _sum.php

Mohanty, C. (1988). Under Western eyes: Feminist scholarship and colonial discourses. *Feminist Review, 30,* 61–88.

Moosa-Mitha, M., & Ross-Sheriff, F. (2010). Transnational social work and lessons learned from transnational feminism. *Affilia: Journal of Women and Social Work, 25*(2), 105–109. doi: 10.1177/ 0886109910364366

Murphy, Y., Hunt, V., Zajicek, A. M., Norris, A. N., & Hamilton, L. (2009). *Incorporating intersectionality in social work practice, research, policy, and education.* Washington, DC: NASW Press.

O'Shea, E. (2009). *Missing the point(s): The declining fortunes of Canada's economic immigration program.* Retrieved from Transatlantic Academy website: http://www.gmfus.org/galleries/ct_publi cation_attachments/TA_OShea_CandadaEconImmigrationProgram.pdf

Ovadia, S. (2001). Race, class, and gender differences in high school seniors' values: Applying intersection theory in empirical analysis. *Social Science Quarterly, 82*(2), 340–356.

Oxman-Martinez, J., Hanley, J., Lach, L., Khanlou, N., Weerasinghe, S., & Agnew, V. (2005). Intersection of Canadian policy parameters affecting women with precarious immigration status: A baseline for understanding barriers to health. *Journal of Immigrant Health, 7*(4), 247–259.

Peace and Diversity Forum. (2008). "How would it feel to live without hate?" Retrieved from http://www.celebratediversity.ca/archive/forum-2008

Pessar, P. (1999). Engendering migration studies: The case of new immigrants in the United States. *American Behavioral Scientist, 42*(4), 577–600.

Reitz, J. G. (2007a). Immigrant employment success in Canada, part I: Individual and contextual causes. *International Migration and Integration, 8*(1), 11–36. doi 10.1007/s12134-007-0001-4

Reitz, J. G. (2007b). Immigrant employment success in Canada, part II: Understanding the decline. *International Migration and Integration, 8*(1), 37–62. doi: 10.1007/s12134-007-0002-3

Riano, Y. (2011). Drawing new boundaries of participation: experiences and strategies of economic citizenship among skilled migrant women in Switzerland. *Environment and Planning, 43,* 1530–1546.

Rose, M., & Desmarais, J. (2007). Directions to consider in favour of the regionalization of immigration. *Our Diverse Cities, 3,* 52-58. Retrieved from http://www.canada.metropolis.net/publications/... /our_diverse_cities_vol2_en.pdf

Ross-Sheriff, F. (2011). Global migration and gender. *Affilia: Journal of Women and Social Work, 26*(3) 233–238. doi:10.1177/0886109911417694

Sethi, B. (2009a). *Exploring newcomer settlement and integration supports in Brantford, and Brant-Haldimand-Norfolk Counties: Community-based participatory research* (Master's thesis, Wilfrid Laurier University, Waterloo, Ontario, Canada). Retrieved from http://www.collectionscanada .gc.ca/obj/t

Sethi, B. (2009b). *Exploring newcomer settlement and integration supports in Brantford, and Brant-Haldimand-Norfolk counties.* Retrieved from http://www.workforceplanningboard.org/files/upload/newcomer_settlement_integration_supports.pdf

Sethi, B. (2010). Building bridges: Exploring newcomer settlement and integration supports in Brantford and the counties of Brant, Haldimand and Norfolk using a community-based participatory research (CBPR). *Canadian Social Work, 12*(1), 184–191. Retrieved from http://www.caswacts.ca/sites/default/files/csw10special_e.pdf

Shankar, I., & Northcott, H. (2009). Through my son: Immigrant women bargain with patriarchy. *Women's Studies International Forum, 32*(6), 424–434.

Smith, E., & Marmo, M. (2011). Uncovering the "virginity testing" controversy in the national archives: The intersectionality of discrimination in British immigration history. *Gender & History, 23*(1), 147–165.

Statistics Canada. (2008). *Canadian demographics at a glance.* Retrieved from http://www.statcan.gc.ca/pub/91-003-x/91-003-x2007001-eng.pdf

Thing, J. (2010). Gay, Mexican and immigrant: Intersecting identities among gay men in Los Angeles. *Social Identities, 16*(6), 809–831. doi: 10.1080/13504630.2010.524787

Walton-Roberts, M. (2006). Regional immigration and dispersal: Lessons from small- and medium-sized urban centres in British Columbia. *Our Diverse Cities, 2,* 158–161. Retrieved from http://www.metropolis.net/pdfs/ODC_WaltonRoberts_e.pdf

Wamala, S., Ahnquist, J., & Månsdotter, A. (2009). How do gender, class and ethnicity interact to determine health status? *Journal of Gender Studies, 18*(2), 115–129. doi: 10.1080/09589230902812430

Winkler, G., & Degele, N. (2011). Intersectionality as multi-level analysis: Dealing with social inequality. *European Journal of Women's Studies, 18*(1), 51–66.

Yakushko, O., & Espin, O. M. (2010). The experience of immigrant and refugee women: Psychological issues. In H. Landrine & N. F. Russo (Eds.), *Handbook of diversity in feminist psychology* (pp. 535–558). New York, NY: Springer.

Zaman, H. (2010). Pakistani skilled/educated immigrant women in Canada: An exploratory study. *Pakistan Journal of Women's Studies: Alam-e-Niswan, 17*(2), 1–23.

APPENDIX

DESCRIPTIVE QUESTIONS	EXAMPLES
1. What knowledge, values, and experiences do you bring to this area of policy analysis?	a. What are your personal values, experiences, interests, beliefs, and political commitments? b. How do these personal experiences relate to societal/structural locations and processes (e.g., gender, race and ethnicity, socioeconomic status, sexuality and age; patriarchy, colonialism, capitalism, racism and heterosexism)?
2. What is the policy problem under consideration?	What assumptions (e.g., beliefs about what causes the problem and which population(s) is/are most affected) underlie this representation of the problem

continued

DESCRIPTIVE QUESTIONS (cont.)	EXAMPLES
3. How have representations of the problem come about?	a. What was the process in framing the problem this way? b. Who was involved and why was the problem defined in this way? What types of evidence were used
4. What groups are affected by the representation of the problem?	a. Who is most advantaged and who is the least advantaged by this representation? Why and how? b. Who is most advantaged and who is the least advantaged by this representation? Why and how?
5. What are the current policy responses to the problem?	a. Who has responded to the problem and how? b. Do existing responses create competition for resources and political attention among differently situated groups?

NORMATIVE/TRANSFORMATIVE QUESTIONS	EXAMPLES
6. What inequities actually exist in relation to the problem?	a. Which are the important intersecting social locations/systems? For example, how do race, ethnicity, class, sexuality, and other social locations and systems of inequality (racism, colonialism, classism, homophobia) interact in relation to this policy problem? b. What potential approaches can be used to promote discussion of the problem across differently affected groups
7. Where and how can interventions be made to improve the problem?	a. What are the logical entry points? What are the available policy levers (e.g., research/data, political champions/allies, laws/regulations/conventions, resources)? b. Who are the key influential stakeholders?
8. What are feasible short, medium and long-term solutions?	a. How can solutions be pragmatically positioned and promoted in relation to government policy priorities (e.g., budget allocations, ministerial priorities, and departmental plans)? b. How can proposed solutions be synthesized into a clear and persuasive message
9. How will proposed policy responses reduce inequities?	a. How will proposed options address intersectional inequities, promote social justice, and not reinforce stereotypes, biases or produce further inequities for some populations? b. How will the solutions interact with other existing policies?
10. How will implementation and uptake be ensured?	a. Who will be responsible (and who is best positioned) to ensure the implementation of the recommendations? b. What time frames and accountability mechanisms are identified for implementation?
11. How will you know if inequities have been reduced	a. How will you measure implementation and outcomes? b. How will affected communities be meaningfully engaged in assessing the reduction of inequities?

Note. From Hankivsky (2012b).

Part 5

FROM GRASSROOTS TO GLOBAL ACTION

CHAPTER 10

"Here's My Heart"

Globalization, Casino Women, and Courage

SUSAN CHANDLER

In 2009 Pilar Weiss, the young political director of Las Vegas's powerful, 60,000-member Culinary Union, reflected on the relationship between the union and the immigrant women at its core. "The union is a wonderful place for women to thrive and organize and find their power," she said.

> Especially immigrant women. They walked here, some came in a trunk. [Now] they're finding this leadership. Here we're always in battle mode. People take care of each other. It's not like other organizations where you go to one meeting a month. No, here it's "here's my heart." When you're in battle mode, people have commitment and they make it work. (P. Weiss, personal communication, November 16, 2006)

"Here's my heart" fairly well captures the spirit of the union housekeepers, janitors, cooks, cocktail waitresses, and kitchen workers whose lives are at the center of Jill Jones's and my decade-long study of women casino workers in the context of economic globalization. Now a book, *Casino Women: Courage in Unexpected Places* (Chandler & Jones, 2011), our study in part describes the experience of women active in Nevada's Culinary Union (Local 226 of UNITE HERE). A grassroots organizing union under the leadership of women activists like those Pilar Weiss describes, Culinary is the poster child of the "new union movement" and one of the "most aggressive and innovative unions in the United States, intensely focused on organizing and training a broad cadre of worker leaders . . . who mobilize members for organizing drives and job and political actions" (Moberg, 2001, p. 23; see also Baker, 2009; Erem, 2001; Kraft, 2010; Sherman & Voss, 2000). Over the years the union has won living wages on the Las Vegas Strip (where housekeepers' wages start at $13.00 an hour); a health plan free to union members and their families, which the *New York Times* calls "Rolls Royce health coverage" (Greenhouse, 2004); grassroots political power; opportunity for career advancement through the Culinary Academy of Las Vegas; and overall dignity for working people (Alexander, 2002; Benz, 2004). "Las Vegas is a Union Town!" a chant frequently heard in Culinary Union mobilizations, captures the compelling union consciousness that runs deep in UNITE HERE's mostly immigrant, mostly Latino membership.

Using the experiences of the immigrant women activists in our study, I explore the two-sidedness of women's work in the global economy, on the one hand, describing the grief, dislocation, hard labor, and loss of dignity that are the lot of most migrating women, and on the other, the possibility of migrating women's agency in a vast, exploitive system.

Miriam Ching Yoon Louie (2001) in *Sweatshop Warriors: Immigrant Women Workers Take on the Global Factory* writes of the "painful yet liberating transformation" of immigrant women sweatshop activists" (p. 12), who are in her estimation the "most essential actors in the struggle to improve their own lives" (Louie in McGrath & McGrath, 2002, p. 42). Frustrated that immigrant women are often "asked to speak only as victims," Louie describes a transformation

> from women exploited by subcontractors and elites to women who clearly understood where they fit into the "big picture." . . . [They] paint[ed] themselves, their coworkers, and *comadres* [women friends] into that big picture . . . as they began to dream and talk to each other about the way that they wanted to be seen, heard, understood, respected, and, yes, paid for all the sweat, blood, and tears they had shed while squeezed down at the bottom of the pyramid. (p. 13)

In a similar vein, our study (Chandler & Jones, 2011) asks, how was it that immigrant casino women activists, assigned the bottom rungs of the economic ladder, somehow discovered spaces where they could counter the enormous, repressive influences of globalization, that they began to stand up for each other, and that they became not victims of globalization, but in a genuine and unexpected sense, subjects and actors? And, finally, what can social workers concerned about globalization and its enormous inequities learn from their transformation?

The Literature

Scholars of the global economy have regularly observed globalization's two-sided impact on women (Acker, 2004; Baker, 2009; Bergeron, 2001; Chang, 2000; Ehrenreich & Hochschild, 2002; Hondagneu-Sotelo, 2001; Kingfisher, 2002; Parrenas, 2001; Salzinger, 2003; Sassen, 2001, 2002, 2004; Tiano, 1994; Ward, 1990). On the one hand, the impact is devastating, marginalizing women, compromising fragile economies, and increasing gender-based inequalities. On the other hand, some scholars argue, women on occasion have wrested some opportunity from globalization and its unprecedented exploitation of their labor. Urban scholar Saskia Sassen (2001, 2002, 2004), in particular, focuses on women in global cities. She writes that global cities attract high-tech professionals and hundreds of thousands of displaced service workers, many of whom are immigrants, women, and people of color. An unexpected consequence of globalization in Sassen's (1998) view, is that women in global worksites may "gain presence [and] emerge as subjects" (p. xxi).

Other writers, including labor scholars and activists, have also explored the concept of agency within the oppressive structures of globalization (Arriaza, 1997; Brecher, Costello, & Smith, 2000; Cobble, 2004; Collins, 2003; Figueroa, 1998; Geron, 1997; Louie, 2001; Shailor, 1998). These writers, using examples of women's activism, maintain that not only are immigrants the fastest-growing segment of the U.S. working class, they are also its hope. Figueroa (1998), for example, writes that campaigns in which immigrants are active, "almost from the very outset take a turn towards broader demands of dignity and social justice, racial and cultural tolerance, and community empowerment" (p. 88).

The Context: Nevada Gaming

Las Vegas is one of the few cities you can see from space. Home to international gaming—a trillion-dollar industry with legendary profit-making capabilities and a dominance in the state that extends far beyond casino walls—Las Vegas is visited annually by more than 50 million people who collectively spend in excess of six times more on gaming than the amount spent in the United States on all other forms of sports and entertainment combined (Denton & Morris, 2001, p. 8). Nevada's gaming industry "sits squarely in the mainstream of US power," historians Sally Denton and Roger Morris write, labeling Las Vegas as a city "in the unbroken grip of a criminal and then corporate tyranny. . . . a fount of cash, legal and illegal, for criminals, businessmen, and politicians from every continent . . . [and] a reflection of the near-complete rule of money in American life" (pp. 3, 391).

Studies of economic globalization have most often focused on portable high-tech industries like electronics and production sites like Saipan and the U.S.–Mexico border (Bonacich & Appelbaum, 2000; Hondagneu-Sotelo, 2001; Louie, 2001). But globalization also drives the fabulously capital-rich tourist and entertainment industry in global destinations like Las Vegas and Los Angeles, cities that deal in tourists and capital from all over the world and whose workforces epitomize the transmigration of labor (Geron, 1997). Expansion into Macao, China, led by billionaires Sheldon Adelson and Steve Wynn, has been especially profitable for global gaming. In 2008 Macao generated $13.5 billion in gross gaming revenue, nearly double the amount generated by the Las Vegas Strip during the same period ("Annual Gaming Revenue," 2012).

In a pattern familiar to neoliberalism and globalization, a few giants have come to dominate the gaming industry, relations among them continually changing as their owners consolidate, merge, buy, and sell. They include Harrah's Entertainment, the world's largest provider of branded casino entertainment; Wynn Resorts, headed by Steve Wynn, who more than anyone else conceived and developed Las Vegas as it is today; MGM Mirage, dominant on the Las Vegas Strip, where it controls half of the city's hotel rooms and a third of its slot machines; and the Las Vegas Sands, which is more and more identified with its highly profitable Asian base.

The coming of global giants in historian Eugene Moehring's (2002) words also "enthroned [in Nevada] a powerful elite of casino executives" (p. 79), like Steve Wynn, whose net worth in 2009 was $1.5 billion, and Sheldon Adelson, who in the same year weighed in at $3.4 billion. Both men easily made Forbes' 2009 list of billionaires, even in an economic downturn (Kroll, Miller, & Serafin, 2009). These men wield enormous influence not only in the industry but in the state as well. "When Steve Wynn picks up the telephone, most politicians jump," Don Williams, Las Vegas political consultant said, commenting on the intersection of economic and political power. "He doesn't get everything he wants, but he rarely loses" (Moehring, 2002, pp. 81–82). In an ominous turn, the world at the top increasingly distanced itself from ordinary citizens, and in a trend seen internationally, the gap between rich and poor in Nevada continued to widen, with gaming CEOs earning more before lunch than casino janitors could make in a year (Chandler, 2001).

Complete control is gaming's watchword on the casino floor and off. Thousands of ceiling-mounted eye-in-the-sky cameras are so effective they can read the serial numbers on a dollar bill and monitor the behavior of players and employees (Jones & Chandler, 2007). Outside the casino, control is even stronger. "By [the gaming industry's] contributions to politicians," Sally Denton and Roger Morris (2001) write in *The Money and the Power*, "its tax revenue to reliant public treasuries, its hold over collateral enterprise, and not least its millions spent for ceaseless lobbying that leaves nothing to chance, the industry gains and wields unique influence throughout the nation and world. No political act is accomplished without their express approval" (p. 8). In the Nevada legislature, gaming's influence is nearly total and over the years has produced tax policies in the state that have created an "all-purpose shelter for private wealth" (p. 95). The state has no personal income tax, no franchise tax, no inheritance or gift tax, and no corporate income tax. The boon for corporations, including developers and corporate mining, is monumental. Nevada's general fund, in consequence of these policies, is frequently strapped even in boom years and subject to enormous volatility. In the latest downturn, when for the first time gaming stock, by conventional wisdom recession-proof, tumbled, Nevada found its state budget the fifth hardest hit in the nation (Moehring, 2002, p. 84; McNichols & Johnson, 2010). The state's infrastructure, education system, health care, social services, and general quality of life languish at the bottom of nearly every register, a "disastrous" case of "public sector poverty and private sector affluence (Moehring, 2002, p. 84).

But of course not everything is controlled. Though Las Vegas is a global city, it is certainly an unusual one, for it is home to 60,000 union members and their families whose ability to fight together for their futures should never be underestimated.

Methodology

For the past decade, Jill Jones and I have been interviewing women casino workers—housekeepers, waitresses, laundry workers, janitors, bartenders, cocktail waitresses, dealers, and middle managers—in Las Vegas and Reno. (As a personal aside, I have had for many years a strong personal, political, and professional interest in the lives of laboring people. My own heritage is in the rural Midwest, where sometimes, not always, small farmers like my grandfather and cousins collectively stood up to the agricultural conglomerates that threatened their families' ability to survive. Later, as a young 1960s activist, I was fortunate to hear again and again stories from the union and social justice movements of the 1930s told by my wonderful left-wing in-laws. Gradually, I became much more conscious of the history of the working class and the central role it has consistently played in the fight for a better world, a worldview that I eventually brought to social work.)

The 2- to 4-hour semistructured, confidential interviews focused on the women's backgrounds, their families, their experiences at work, and their opinions about casinos' relationships with workers, their families, and the community. These individual interviews were supplemented by focus groups of former casino workers, Latino leaders, educators, and health and social service professionals who worked with casino families. The interviews and focus groups were audiotaped in their entirety and then transcribed and analyzed. Grounded theory, a method often used in qualitative studies, guided the data analysis (Lincoln & Guba, 1985; Strauss & Corbin, 1990). In grounded theory, researchers move back and forth between empirical data (e.g., the women's accounts of their work lives) and the larger, more theoretical questions. In this way, researchers strive to conceptualize theories grounded in the realities of participants' lives. In our study, individual transcripts were first analyzed for thematic content. Next, the women's interviews were compared and additional themes identified. Finally, primary themes that best reflected the women's work experience and its effect on their families and community were selected.

In addition, we talked with nearly 100 key informants—labor leaders, demographers, economists, lawyers, researchers, legislators, advocates, community activists—and over a period of 10 years visited research centers, archives, libraries, federal courts, the legislature, union halls, demonstrations, bars and coffee shops in Las Vegas and Reno, all in an attempt to unfold the context of the women's lives and the nature of the industry that dominates our state.

The Findings

The 15 immigrant union activists in our sample varied significantly in their countries of origin, their familiarity with unions and activism on arrival, and their social and economic backgrounds. Nevertheless common themes emerged from their stories that began to elucidate the question posed earlier, that is, how it was that women assigned to the lowest rungs of the economic ladder learned to stand up for themselves and others and in time became, in a certain sense, not victims of globalization but rather subjects and actors. One might describe this as a movement from dislocation, sorrow, and hard labor to growing a collective consciousness, discovery of the union, power, and to varying extents, transformation. Of course this imagined transformation is never linear nor predictive, but it does serve to frame in general terms a collective experience.

DISLOCATION, SORROW, HARD LABOR

The stories of global workers, and especially those of women, carry sorrow sufficient to fuel the planet, something we encountered again and again in our interviews. Women often spoke with tears running down their faces; memories a decade or two old felt as if they happened yesterday.

Rita Gallegos and Maria Ruiz came to Reno from El Salvador 30 years ago when they were in their late 20s. Wages, benefits, and working conditions in Reno where casinos are largely unorganized differ dramatically from those in highly unionized Las Vegas; Reno housekeepers begin at minimum wage, benefits are stingy and difficult to come by, and job security is minimal. Both women found work in downtown casinos, Rita as a waitress and Maria as a cashier. Each began by telling us about their family backgrounds. Rita, who came from "a fairly loving family of poor, hard-working people from San Salvador," was, she laughed, "very spoiled" as a child. Maria, on the other hand, was from a land-owning family: "[My father] had his own farm. We had cows, we had chickens, we had land. So I had a good life when I was a kid. We were not rich, but we never struggled for anything."

In El Salvador Rita had been a student. "I went to the University of El Salvador," she said. "I was studying to be an architect. By that time, my mother was already here in the U.S.—she used to come back and forth trying to help the family." In the late 1970s the political climate in El Salvador descended into violent clashes between the country's U.S.-trained military and nationalist liberation forces that daily threatened the lives of the Salvadoran people. Under these conditions, Rita reluctantly agreed to join her mother and brother in Los Angeles:

> When we came to the U.S. in 1980, things were getting really bad in El Salvador. And I didn't want to come. To me it was like, "What happens to me in the United States? I'm here studying, and here are my friends." It was very rough when I came. I didn't see myself in this society.

Maria, a teacher, was working on her PhD in El Salvador and was active as a member of the Human Rights Commission.

> I participated in the Commission of Truth. . . . because too many people were disappearing and we have to find out who was doing that. Of course it was the military. . . . I got in a controversy with the government and was given 24 hours to leave the country. So this is how I came to Reno. . . . And that was that. My heart, I left behind.

Nothing was easy in the United States. Rita found work in a dry-cleaning establishment and studied English:

> I remember my brother, the first thing he said, "You have to go to school to learn English." And I did. I used to go to work during the day and go to school at night in that famous school, the ESL in Los Angeles. . . . It was hard. It was rough. I never really did feel like this was home, even [though] I lived six years in L.A.

Not feeling at home was common among the immigrant women. For some of the women—Rita and Maria included—class issues were part of the alienation. In their countries of origin, these women identified as middle class, or at least as students they aspired to it, whereas in the United States they were regarded as poor immigrants. Rita described her early years in Los Angeles:

I couldn't get the opportunity to get friends or relate with people that I feel like I will fit in [with] . . . I was coming from a poor family, but I did have some education, and when I came to the United States, to me it was a kind of shock to be with another level of people. The people that I worked [with] . . . used to look at me like, "why doesn't she just adjust [to] the way we are?" It was so hard to make them to understand. . . . It was not that I was stuck up, nothing like that. It was that I didn't know [anything] about their world or the United States. It was like, "What am I going to talk to them [about]?" That's why, to me, it was [a] horrible experience.

Maria also had problems. Leaving El Salvador with her two young daughters, she traveled to Reno where she had friends. "When I came over here I have to sleep on the floor and I have to feel this cold," she said in tears. "My god, I almost died. I tried to go back—I wanted to go back. I arrived in September and hoped I could go back. [But] the next year some of my colleagues were killed [and] Monsignor Romero got killed so I knew I couldn't." (Archbishop Oscar Romero, a voice for the poor in El Salvador, was assassinated on March 24, 1980.)

Survival depended on finding work, and the work available was nearly always manual labor. In spite of the fact that she was an experienced teacher, Maria took a job as a maid in a small Reno casino.

[It was] very traumatic. . . . You get some very demanding [people], and they think because you are Hispanic, and because you are cleaning rooms, you are the worst. . . . They want extra towels, they want extra cleaning; they slip on the floor, and they say it's because the maid left some water over there. Well, it's horrible how they accuse the poor Hispanics. And they know these people can't communicate. So for me that was like a trauma.

Many, many women reported working two jobs, a necessity when wages are low, annual wage increases minimal, and promotions nearly nonexistent. Alicia Bermudez, a laundry worker who came to Reno from Mexico, told us, "I was making $4.25 [an hour]. Because I cannot live with one job [I took] another in a [casino] laundry. Was making there $5.25. Yes, I had two jobs. . . . I didn't like that, having two jobs. [It was] very hard."

Alicia also complained bitterly about the stinginess of casino management and the general disrespect for workers, especially immigrant workers:

> They're very tight . . . very cheap. They want the people to work for free. They don't care about how you feel. They don't care about employees like a human being. They think we're robots. We cannot even go to the bathroom or have lunch. The managers and supervisors, they really squish you. . . . They don't care if we are sweating blood. They're happy with that. I'm very disappointed with them—and I'm very angry.

GROWING A COLLECTIVE CONSCIOUSNESS, DISCOVERING THE UNION

In these harsh conditions, however, the women reported another consciousness arising. Because the work had a strong collective nature, and housekeepers, for example, depended on each other, the women, all impressive workers, slowly learned how to stand up for shy or fearful co-workers, shared whatever they knew with everyone, and kept working, working, working. An awareness developed among them that they as immigrants had dignity, as did the knowledge that their interests as a group were distinctly different from those of management.

Each woman's story of her initial contact with the Culinary Union was different. We talked with Geoconda Arguella Kline, a former maid, originally from Nicaragua, who is now president of the Culinary Union, and Mirna Preciado, a former waitress, originally from Mexico, and now a union staff organizer. For Geoconda, who had worked at minimum wage jobs in Miami where she first lived after leaving Nicaragua, it was the wages that first caught her attention.

> I started working as a maid at Fitzgerald's [Casino]. [It] was very hard. But you compare, I was making almost double what I was making in Miami. . . . And I saw the difference. I saw completely the difference. I saw what I could offer to my kids, the benefits, and I saw I could save money and buy my first house.

Geoconda didn't fully appreciate how important union membership was, though, until Fitzgerald's threatened to take away health benefits.

My little girl, she was born with a disease. I didn't really want to be involved, be part of the union. . . . It was, "No, I don't want to be involved because I have my kid sick and I know I can't do much." She had five surgeries. But the organizers keep coming and talking to me. And when they [said] they're going to take away the health benefits, that was something that really affect[ed] me. Because if I don't have the union, I can't take care of my kids. . . . And then I was thinking what would happen . . . and I start getting involved.

The first lesson of Geoconda's story is a basic one: Immigrant women earn more and have access to much better benefits when they are union members. They can buy homes, get good health care for their families, and work one job instead of two. They have time for their families and time to be involved in their children's education. Their physical and mental health is better. They can escape the poverty-wage work the economy assigns to the vast majority of poor immigrant women. None of this was lost on immigrant workers, who had excellent networks for communication. No Nevada worker we interviewed was unaware of the benefits of union membership, despite the strong antiunion sentiment in much of this right-to-work state.

But that was not all. In addition to securing better wages and benefits, becoming activists had changed the Latina immigrants. In interview after interview, the union women described a transformation of spirit and consciousness, an opportunity to develop themselves, to realize their humanity. There was a profound contrast between union and nonunion women; we felt it, and the women often talked about it.

Rita Gallegos, the waitress from El Salvador whose college career had been interrupted by civil conflict, described the change in herself:

I have seen myself more outspoken. No matter what, I can always fight for my rights. I have grown mentally. It was a big step in my life. Before I didn't know what was happening around me . . . go to work, come home, do my shopping—that was my life. Now I see a lot. . . . [I have had the] opportunity to meet so many different people, many different cultures. In the end we are all together—we're fighting for our life.

How and why did that change occur? What was the basis for these women to begin to speak for themselves and others?

Globalization, understandably, is generally perceived as a force quite beyond the power of individual workers to control (Hardt & Negri, 2000; Mander 1996). Immigrants in particular are often presented as little more than flotsam on the ocean of the global economy. The experience of these Latina activists, however, suggests a different image, one in which the power of corporations is not absolute, and the energy of committed workers finds a voice.

Several factors seemed to lie at the root of the changes the Latina immigrants experienced. First, work in the union gave them access to a genuine experience of collective power, a power they were part of building. Geoconda Kline spoke eloquently of this:

> When I start to organize, it was an incredible experience for me because I start to really believe in the power. . . . it was like for me this fist. We got the power. The companies can't have everything. . . . I really found this is the truth. If we get together, we can move companies.

Second, the Latina activists came to understand that workers, even immigrant workers, have rights—like the right to wear a union button, the right to be addressed in language that isn't abusive, the right to file a grievance, the right to have that grievance addressed in a timely fashion, and the right to organize during breaks. This was a critical part of becoming union activists—and a lesson that the women never failed to pass along to the people they were organizing.

Finally, the hard day-to-day work of organizing provided the opportunity for the transformation of the Latina activists to take place. In Nevada, union contracts are won by tens of thousands of hours of invisible work—knocking on doors, visiting workers after hours and on lunch breaks, carefully building committees, and planning action. The work is methodical, focused, and proceeds from strategies the union has carefully mapped out.

For Geoconda Kline and Mirna Preciado, the Frontier Strike brought them together and changed their lives. In 1991, 550 workers, Mirna among them, walked out of the Frontier, a small Las Vegas joint, in protest against the draconian wage and benefit cuts exacted by owner Margaret Elardi. The longest work stoppage in U.S. history (from September 1991 to January 1998), the

Frontier strike solidified the Culinary Union's identity and strength in Las Vegas, and for strikers it provided years of education in power and rights, grassroots organizing, national and international solidarity, and keeping on keeping on when strikers' spirits flagged and desert temperatures soared. In this strike, where Geoconda was a lead organizer and Mirna a picket captain, the two women developed their friendship, the kind of abiding friendship that comes from a long struggle together.

A decade later, Mirna and Geoconda talked about their experience. "I changed totally," Mirna said.

I was happy, because for the first time in many years—you know—I feel strong. I could do something on my own. I'm a woman from Mexico. I don't even speak good English, but I could fight for my rights. That's the beauty of when you learn about what the union is, because the person that I am right now, the woman that I am right now, it's what I learned in the union.

When we asked Mirna if she had ever had doubts as months turned into years on the picket line, she replied,

This is hard to believe [for] people who haven't been in a strike—but the longer the strike was going, the more years, the stronger you get as a union member. . . . Yes, sometimes I cry. Sometimes I argue with Geoconda. "I can't stand it no more. I wish I could go home. How long is this going to take?" Yes, many times. But I never thought to say, "I'm going back to work to the Frontier." Geoconda always used to tell me, "Mirna, we're going to win. We're going to win. Let's stick together." We keep fighting. So we won.

Discipline too was part of building power. Mirna and Geoconda exchanged memories about how Mirna changed and what Geoconda learned working with her. "I was one of the bad girls probably of the strike," Mirna began.

Geoconda knows. The first years in the strike, I'd say, "Geoconda, we're going to buy a lemonade." We used to leave the line once in a while. [But Geoconda] was always there. "Come on, let's go, Geoconda. You need a break." "No, [she would say]." We didn't understand. Later, I didn't leave the line like at the beginning. I knew the responsibility. That's what I mean, the changes—you grow.

Geoconda reflected on her own growth as an organizer and how she came to see beneath the surface of workers' complaints.

It's tough. . . . The strikers walk four or five hours. Some, they have to go to other jobs to support their families. Some days was great. Some days was not that great. But people worked through the struggles and know they're going to have their victory one day. . . . The struggle makes you see a lot of things you not see before in human beings. . . . It's a process. Summer here is pretty hot. That's when they come to us and say, "it's so hot." We know that they aren't talking only about the weather. They're talking about, "I can't take it." That's what they really wanted to submit to you. And that's why we always say, "It's not that bad." We try to [find] something. . . . You know, really pay attention to how [they] feel that day. "My family," [they say], "got a lot of pressure." [You talk, and then] they start feeling better. After a while—it's hot, but we're okay. Keeping going, be another day.

Paolo Freire (1972) in *Pedagogy of the Oppressed* speaks of *conscientization*, the growth in adult learners of an awareness of their place in history. In a final exchange Mirna and Geoconda spoke about their own historical consciousness. "That's the thing about the union," Mirna began. "It's the workers who are here [at the union hall]. Just like me. Geoconda used to be a maid. Me, somebody from Mexico who didn't speak English, who didn't know nothing. We're just workers. . . . We're just workers organizing workers from our experience."

And Geoconda, always eloquent, replied:

What makes a good organizer [is someone who] understands what [the change] is going to be. That's your goal, that change. And you speak it every day when you talk to your committee. You talk to them about rights and [the] future. And when they say it's too difficult, [you say], yes, but somebody did a more difficult thing [to get us] where we are. We're lucky. Some people got killed. Some people got tear gas for where we are right now. And you have to do it not only for you, you have to do it for the people coming. I think if you're an organizer, you understand that part. It's not only you who's doing it. Somebody did it before, and you're doing it for somebody in the future. That's the beauty of being an organizer—when you understand the movement. It's a change for the families, a change for better. It is great. It is great for me.

Lessons for Social Work

The stories of women who work in the global economy provide important lessons for social workers, who, like Geoconda Kline and Mirna Preciado, also value democracy, believe in the dignity of workers, and do not want a world in which nearly all the wealth accrues for those at the very top. Here are three of the lessons.

First, it is important for us as social workers to affirm in our literature and daily professional lives the importance of working-class people themselves, for it is still the labor of tens of thousands of low-income workers that enables the global economy to function. In this, Jane Addams and Hull House provide a strong legacy. In her essay "The Objective Value of a Social Settlement" Addams (1892/2002) described activities at Hull House undertaken on behalf of working men and women; four women's trade unions met there regularly. "Recently," Addams wrote, "twenty girls from a knitting factory who struck because they were docked for loss of time when they were working by the piece" had come directly from the factory to Hull House. They had heard, Addams reported, "that we 'stood by working people'" (p. 42). Sadly, much of the intimacy of contact that Addams describes between social work agencies and working people's lives and organizations has fallen away. All too often we work in bureaucracies and universities that feel if anything unfriendly to working people. What a tragedy this is, all the more so because a good many social work students come from working-class families and have seen their mothers and fathers labor as housekeepers and factory workers.

In this same vein, social workers must also affirm contributions working-class people have made to our democracy and to economic and social justice. In Nevada the reality is that these changes (e.g., livable wages and strong health plans for 60,000 Culinary Union members and their families) far exceed what we social workers and our organizations have been able to accomplish. And yet that is a perception one would be hard-pressed to find among social work professionals. Too often, as Miriam Louie (2001) argues, we reduce working-class people, especially women and immigrants, to victim status, whereas in truth, positive changes in our country have most often arisen from the poorest among us—those who constituted the essential bases of the civil rights, welfare rights, immigrant rights, and disability rights movements; the labor movement; and the veterans' and gay, lesbian, bisexual, and transgender movements.

Second, it is important that issues of class and working peoples' lives occupy a much stronger place in our social work curriculum. Early social workers like Jane Addams, Florence Kelley, Bertha Capen Reynolds, Mary van Kleeck, and E. Franklin Frazier paid close attention to issues of work. Somehow that has slipped out of the social work curriculum—a great loss, for working peoples' basic well-being depends on employment and livable wages. Today, questions of jobs, unions, and dismantling benefits such as Social Security are high on the public agenda. Social work must be there in the midst of the debates with our own experience and strong voices.

Finally, the women's stories call out to us to strengthen our conception of collective solutions. So much of our vision is individual. In education, including social work education, the dominant paradigm is that of individual success— completing degrees, finding well-paying jobs, and so on. But for many students, particularly those from working-class, Latino, and African American backgrounds, schooling has historically been a collective achievement, and every child's success is a success and resource for the larger community. In the professional lives of social workers, solutions too are overwhelmingly individual—50- minute hours and individual subsidies are examples. But realistically, advances such as winning higher wages or protecting health plans can only be achieved collectively. Not only that; collective action, such as what we witnessed on the Las Vegas Strip, nearly always carries with it the potential of individual and collective transformation and well-being. Studs Terkel (2003) said, "Once you become active in something, something happens to you. You get excited and suddenly you realize you count." This soaring of one's spirit, a transformation of consciousness, all of which the women activists experienced, will be familiar to many social workers who themselves have gotten excited and realized they count.

Conclusion

Casino Women ends with the words of León Gieco (2005), the Argentinean singer/songwriter who, like Bruce Springsteen, fills stadiums, in "Sólo le pido a Dios":

> The only thing I ask of God is that
> he not let me be indifferent to the suffering,
> and that when death, that dusty time, comes
> that I not be alone and empty, having not given my everything.

In Latin America, "Solo le Pido a Dios" is sung as a call for justice and against war. What is not apparent on the page but leaps out in performance is the anthem's joy, for though the pronoun is "I," behind it is an implicit "we"— you and I and a thousand others together. In the end that is what the casino women were saying—don't sit alone declining to act, for a committed life is so much more joyous than a life of self-protection and consumption, and connection with each other in struggle so much more rewarding than lives lived alone (Chandler & Jones, 2011, p. 177).

Let us as social workers stand solidly with the working people of this country and the world.

Discussion Questions and Sample Assignment

AS A CLASS PROJECT, TAKE ON AN EXPLORATION OF GLOBAL INDUSTRY AND LABOR IN YOUR CITY OR REGION.

1. What are the dominant industries (including corporate agriculture) in your area? Are they global industries with global labor forces? What is the net worth of the industries' corporate leaders?

2. What wages can working-class women, immigrant and domestic, hope to earn in these global industries? What are the conditions of labor? Be very specific.

3. Interview five or six women who work in these industries. What are their life stories?

4. How do the women support each other? Are there instances of strength and leadership in the women's ranks? The casino women we met often worked collectively to support each other. Did you find a collective consciousness among the women you interviewed?

5. Is there a way that you as social workers can support these women or expose the conditions of work where they labor?

References

Acker, J. (2004). Gender, capitalism and globalization. *Critical Sociology, 30*(1), 17–41.

Addams, J. (2002). The objective value of a social settlement. In J. B. Elshtain (Ed.), *Jane Addams Reader* (pp. 29–45). New York, NY: Basic. (Original work published 1892)

Alexander, C. (2002). Rise to power: The recent history of the culinary union in Las Vegas. In H. K. Rothman & M. Davis (Eds.), *The grit beneath the glitter: Tales from the real Las Vegas* (pp. 145–175). Berkeley, CA: University of California Press.

Annual gaming revenue. (2012). Retrieved from University of Nevada Las Vegas Center for Gaming Research website: http://gaming.unlv.edu/abstract/nvstate_revenues.html

Arriaza, G. (1997). Grace under pressure: Immigration families and the nation–state. *Social Justice, 24,* 6–15.

Baker, A. H. (2009). A woman's place is in her union. In M. Shriver (Ed.), *The Shriver report: A woman's nation changes everything* (pp. 236–237). Washington, DC: Center for American Progress.

Benz, D. (2004). Labor's ace in the hole: Casino organizing in Las Vegas. *New Political Science, 26,* 525–550.

Bergeron, S. (2001). Political economy discourses of globalization and feminist politics. *Signs: Journal of Women in Culture and Society, 26,* 983–1007.

Bonacich, E., & Appelbaum, R. P. (2000). *Behind the label: Inequality in the Los Angeles apparel industry.* Berkeley, CA: University of California Press.

Brecher, J., Costello, T., & Smith, B. (2000). *Globalization from below: The power of solidarity.* Cambridge, MA: South End Press.

Chandler, S. (2001). *Working hard, living poor: A living wage study for Nevada.* Las Vegas, NV: Progressive Leadership Alliance of Nevada.

Chandler, S., & Jones, J. (2011). *Casino women: Courage in unexpected places.* Ithaca, NY: Cornell University Press.

Chang, G. (2000). *Disposable domestics: Immigrant women workers in the global economy.* Cambridge, MA: South End Press.

Cobble, D. S. (2004). *The other women's movement: Workplace justice and social rights in modern America.* Princeton, NJ: Princeton University Press.

Collins, J. L. (2003). *Threads: Gender, labor, and power in the global apparel industry.* Chicago, IL: University of Chicago Press.

Denton, S., & Morris, R. (2001). *The money and the power: The making of Las Vegas and its hold on America, 1947–2000.* New York, NY: Knopf.

Ehrenreich, B., & Hochschild, A. R. (Eds.). (2002). *Global woman: Nannies, maids, and sex workers in the new economy.* New York, NY: Metropolitan Books.

Erem, S. (2001). *Labor pains: Inside America's new union movement.* New York, NY: Monthly Review Press.

Figueroa, H. (1998). Back to the forefront: Union organizing of immigrant workers in the nineties. In J. Mort (Ed.), *Not your father's union movement: Inside the AFL-CIO* (pp. 87–98). New York, NY: Verso.

Freire, P. (1986). *Pedagogy of the oppressed* (M. B. Ramos, Trans.). New York: Continuum. (Original work published 1970)

Geron, K. (1997). The local/global context of the L.A. Hotel-Tourism Industry. *Social Justice, 24,* 85–102.

Gieco, L. (2005). *Sólo le pido a Dios.* Argentina: EMI Music Distribution.

Greenhouse, S. (2004, January 3). Organized: Local 226, "the Culinary," makes Las Vegas the land of the living wage. *New York Times.* Retrieved from http://www.nytimes.com/2004/06/03/us/orga nized-local-226-the-culinary-makes-las-vegas-the-land-of-the-living-wage

Hardt, M., & Negri, A. (2000). *Empire.* Cambridge, MA: Harvard University Press.

Hondagneu-Sotelo, P. (2001). *Domestica: Immigrant workers cleaning and caring in the shadows of affluence.* Berkeley, CA: University of California Press.

Jones, J., & Chandler, S. (2007). Surveillance and regulation in a globalized work site: Casinos and the control of women's bodies. *Affilia: Journal of Women and Social Work, 22(2),* 150–162.

Kingfisher, C. (Ed.). (2002). *Western welfare in decline: Globalization and women's poverty.* Philadelphia, PA: University of Pennsylvania Press.

Kraft, J. P. (2010). *Vegas at odds: Labor conflict in a leisure economy, 1960–1985.* Baltimore, MD: Johns Hopkins University Press.

Kroll, L., Miller, M., & Serafin, T. (Eds.). (2009, March 11). The world's billionaires." *Forbes Magazine.* Retrieved from http://www.forbes.com/2009/03/11/worlds-richest-people-billionaires-2009-bil lionaires_land.html

Lincoln, Y. S., & Guba, E. G. (1985). *Naturalistic inquiry.* Newbury Park, CA: SAGE.

Louie, M. C. Y. (2001). *Sweatshop warriors: Immigrant women \workers take on the global factory.* Cambridge, MA: South End Press.

Mander, J. (1996). Facing the rising tide. In J. Mander & E. Goldsmith (Eds.), *The case against the global economy and for a turn toward the local* (pp. 3–19). San Francisco, CA: Sierra Club Books.

McGrath, M., & McGrath, E. (2002). Victims no more. *The Progressive 66(3),* 42–43.

McNichols, E., & Johnson, N. (2010). *Recession continues to batter state budgets: State responses could slow recovery.* Retrieved from http://www.investorsinsight.com/blogs/john_mauldins_outside_ the_box/archive/2010/08/16/recession-continues-to-batter-state-budgets-state-responses-could-slow-recovery.aspx

Moberg, D. (2001, July 16). Organization man. *The Nation,* 23–29.

Moehring, E. (2002). Growth, services, and the political economy of gambling in Las Vegas, 1970–2000." In H. K. Rothman & M. Davis (Eds.), *The grit beneath the glitter: Tales from the real Las Vegas* (pp. 73–98). Berkeley, CA: University of California Press.

Parrenas, R. S. (2001). *Servants of globalization: Women, migration, and domestic work.* Stanford, CA: Stanford University Press.

Salzinger, L. (2003). *Genders in production: Making workers in Mexico's global factories.* Berkeley, CA: University of California Press.

Sassen, S. (1998). *Globalization and its discontents.* New York, NY: New Press.

Sassen, S. (2001). The excesses of globalisation and the feminisation of survival. *Parallax, 7(1),* 100–110.

Sassen, S. (2002). Global cities and survival circuits. In B. Ehrenreich & A. R. Hochschild (Eds.), *Global woman: Nannies, maids, and sex workers in the new economy* (pp. 254–274). New York, NY: Metropolitan Books.

Sassen, S. (2004). Local actors in global politics. *Current Sociology, 52,* 649–670.

Shailor, B. (1998). A new internationalism: Advancing workers' rights in the global economy. In J. Mort (Ed.), *Not your father's union movement: Inside the AFL-CIO* (pp. 145–156). New York, NY: Verso.

Sherman, R., & Voss, K. (2000). "Organize or die": Labor's new tactics and immigrant workers." In R. Milkman (Ed.), *Organizing immigrants: The challenge for unions in contemporary California* (pp. 81–108). Ithaca, NY: Cornell University Press.

Strauss, A., & J. Corbin. (1990). *Basics of qualitative research: Grounded theory procedures and techniques.* Newbury Park, CA: SAGE.

Terkel, S. (2003). Interview. *Religion & Ethics Newsweekly.* December 19, 2003. http://www.pbs.org/wnet/religionandethics/episodes/december-19-2003/interview-studs-terkel/11022/

Tiano, S. (1994). *Patriarchy on the line: Labor, gender, and ideology in the Mexican maquila industry.* Philadelphia, PA: Temple University Press.

Ward, K. (Ed.). (1990). *Women workers and global restructuring.* Ithaca, NY: ILR Press.

CHAPTER 11

To Be Poor, Hungry, and Rural

Nicaraguan Women Resisting the Consequences of Globalization

QUENETTE WALTON AND PATRICIA O'BRIEN

Access to nutritious food is a basic human need and human right regardless of geographic or social location. Hunger negatively affects health and productivity and perpetuates poverty. This chapter explores the intersection of multiple forms of oppression, globalization, and neoliberal politics as it pertains to access to nutritious food, focusing on a Central American context through a case study of the women of Tola, Rivas, Nicaragua, and their work to develop community gardens. We also discuss how the women collectively resist oppressive forces drawing on their revolutionary history while using local strategies for developing access to nutritious food for their families.

First, we define key terms. Second, we provide background information about Nicaragua in general and Tola, Rivas, specifically. Third, we describe our situated link to this work. Fourth, we use a case study to present key areas that social work educators and practitioners must address to provide effective ways to develop solutions to the problems we've described as they pertain to sustainable food development. Fifth, we unpack some of the political history Nicaraguans have experienced to further contextualize the Tola women's lives in the case study. Finally, we discuss implications for policy, practice, and social work education.

Key Terms and Definitions

We first define the terms *gender, oppression, globalization, neoliberal politics, sustainable food development, food scarcity,* and *food desert* to enhance understanding of the case study that follows.

- Gender is the socially constructed roles, behaviors, activities, and attributes that are considered appropriate for men and women (World Health Organization, 2012).
- Oppression is the unjust treatment of marginalized individuals or communities based on perceived or actual class, race, ethnicity, gender, sexual orientation, or other categories in hierarchically ordered societies (van Wormer, 2005).
- Globalization is a process in which the increasing connectivity and interdependence of the world's markets and businesses are the major driving forces for the integration of the international economic, social, and cultural activities that affects everybody throughout the world. In this context, globalization brings about benefits and problems and can enhance and limit freedoms and human rights (International Federation of Social Workers, 2012).
- Neoliberal politics is a "set of economic policies and political strategies that rely on an ideology of the market that implements a set of policies—privatization, regional-trade—initiatives in order to integrate national economies, cultures, communication, and ideas at a historically unprecedented pace" (Lind, 2002, p. 231).
- Sustainable food development refers to food that is healthy and nutritious, meets the needs of a diverse group of people, and supports rural economies and the diversity of rural culture through an emphasis on local production (Foundation for Sustainable Development [FSD], 2007; Mary, 2008).
- Food scarcity is the outcome of the increase in food demand and the decrease in food supply from population growth, climate change, natural disasters, and the loss of land for agricultural uses (Sahley, Crosby, Nelson, & Vanderslice, 2005).
- Food desert refers to the insufficient quantity and quality of food, as well as systematically higher food prices in particular geographic areas that limit people's access to affordable and nutritious foods (Bitler & Haider, 2009).

These terms provide a context in which we explore the ways historical and ideological social structures and geopolitics intersect with multiple forms of oppression, globalization, neoliberal politics, and sustainable food development in the lives of women living in Tola, Rivas, Nicaragua.

Historical and Political Context for Contemporary Issues

History and ideology, social structures and geopolitics have collided for years to shape the everyday experiences of the Nicaraguan people. A brief summary of 20th-century Nicaragua history and the role of the United States sets the stage for our discussion (see Walker & Wade, 2011, for a full account). In 1927 Anastasio Somoza García was appointed head of Nicaragua's U.S.-trained National Guard. Somoza promised to negotiate with resistance leader Augusto Sandino and the guerrillas, but instead Sandino was betrayed, executed, and the guerrillas and their family members were massacred.

By 1936 Somoza had ousted the president in a coup and assumed the presidency. For decades, he and his sons maintained their power with a combination of ruthless suppression of the Nicaraguan people and compliance toward the United States. Somoza protected U.S. economic interests in return for U.S. military and economic support.

Followers of Sandino began organizing resistance to the Somoza regime in 1958, which led to the formation of the Frente Sandinista de Liberación Nacional (FSLN, Sandinista National Liberation Front). The FSLN gained power and support after the 1972 Managua earthquake that killed and displaced thousands of people. Somoza enriched himself in the outpouring of support that followed by putting himself in charge of distribution of aid, which sparked the desire for radical change, and Sandinista support grew. In 1975 Somoza and the Nicaraguan National Guard launched a campaign against the FSLN and imposed a state of siege, censoring the press and threatening all regime opponents with detention and torture. By the late 1970s international pressure mounted against Somoza's repressive government and human rights violations. In response to this pressure, Somoza lifted the state of siege in September 1977, a lessening of state control that enabled a massive upsurge in public protest and further political development within the FLSN despite continued brutal repression. The FLSN overcame state suppression and internal conflict, and with increasing international support, seized control of Nicaragua's government in July 1979.

From late 1979 through 1980 U.S. President Jimmy Carter's administration made efforts to work with the new Nicaraguan government. However, when Ronald Reagan took office in January 1981, the U.S. government launched a campaign to discredit and isolate the Sandinista government. All aid was suspended, and the United States covertly provided funding to support residual somicista groups to overthrow the Sandinista government (the contra war). As we discuss later in the chapter, the Sandinista ascendency brought about many cultural and agrarian reforms to lessen some of the economic harms inflicted by the Somoza regime and its allies. However, enemies within and without undermined the rebuilding of a democratic nation-state in the midst of a civil war. In 1990 the end of the Sandinista Revolution was punctuated by the election of Violeta Chamorro, the candidate for a rightist coalition of political groups.

Although there are multiple estimates of the number killed during the specific Sandanista offensive as well as the Nicaraguan Civil War, Clodfelter (2002) indicates that a total of about 55,000 armed and civilian people died. The fractured evolution of the revolution, the resistance, and rebuilding efforts cannot fully tell the story of the bloody war and its aftermath of endemic poverty, political instability, and despair. This lived experience of suffering provides the historical and political context and backdrop to understand the challenges faced by Nicaraguans in urban and rural communities.

Nicaragua and Tola, Rivas

Nicaragua is the largest country in Central America with a population of roughly 5.4 million and a population growth rate of 2.8%. It is also the second poorest country in Central America after Haiti (Seelke, 2008). The country has borders on the Caribbean Sea and the Pacific Ocean and lies between Costa Rica and Honduras. The official language of Nicaragua is Spanish. The majority of the Nicaraguan population lives along the Pacific coast because of its infrastructure (i.e., government, labor, financial, and labor) and easier access to resources such as food, medical care, and education. It is largely an agricultural country with exports such as beef, shrimp, coffee, rice, beans, sugar, vegetables, gold, and textiles (Seelke, 2008). To date, most of the farming in the country is largely for export production (Cupples, 2004; FSD, 2007; Ricker, 2004; Utting, 1992).

Although exports contribute to the economic development of Nicaragua and have reduced the scale of poverty in general, one in three Nicaraguans continues to live in extreme poverty (Seelke, 2008; World Bank, 2009). Since 1990 the international poverty line was $1 per day (Ravallion, Chen, & Sangraula, 2009), which means that an adult earning less than this amount is considered to be impoverished. Although this amount was increased to $1.25 per day in 2005 (Ravallion et al., 2009), this increase is not evident in rural Tola, Rivas. Rural Nicaraguans continue to experience the devastating effects from multinational economic accords such as the Central American Free Trade Agreement (CAFTA) and continue to be marginalized socially and economically (Cupples, 2004). For example, it is well documented that the majority of the people who suffer from extreme poverty in Nicaragua live on the Atlantic side of the country or in rural communities. The Atlantic side of the Nicaraguan infrastructure is weak and resources are limited. Nicaraguans on the Atlantic coast rely heavily on exports of wood and fish. Similarly, Nicaraguans in rural communities on the Pacific coast have weak infrastructures and have limited access to resources. Yet, given these limitations, the women in these communities are attempting to address the multiple challenges of rural poverty for them and their families. Two communities—El Limón and Las Salinas—in Tola are used as exemplars for the women's actions.

Founded in 1750, known for its beautiful beaches, and touted as one of the best places in Nicaragua to go surfing, Tola lies in a rural region 77 miles (or 124 kilometers) from the urban capital of Managua. Even though Managua is bustling, the gravity of poverty in Tola is apparent, and the daily conditions for the poorest residents are worsening. Most of the people in Tola live in extreme poverty. Living on so little per day means that people are malnourished and have inadequate and unsanitary shelter (Marmot, 2004). Although citizens of Tola are subsistence farmers, salt miners, and fishermen, Tola's municipality, with a total population of 26,736, suffers from poor infrastructure, a high rate of poverty and unemployment, and few sustainable development opportunities (FSD, 2007).

El Limón (the lemon) is about 1 hour and 15 minutes northwest of Tola. Residents of El Limón rely heavily on the land and fishing for survival. El Limón's economy is dependent on the resorts frequented by many international travelers; some El Limón residents work at the resorts as servants or guards or tend to the resorts' grounds to earn a very modest living for their families. Only those with an education are eligible to work at the resorts, but many of El Limón's residents are illiterate (FSD, 2007).

The town of Las Salinas (the salt) on the other hand, is described as one of the most organized and self-governing rural communities in Tola. Las Salinas is an agricultural community that is a major producer of salt, but many of the residents earn a living from cattle ranching.

El Limón and Las Salinas are communities with rich histories and citizens who are committed to the well-being of their community. Even though community members live in an area of viable agricultural land, access to nutritious foods is limited because of the negative effects of neoliberal politics, such as privatization, cuts in health and education spending, and the lack of access to resources for farmers (Cupples, 2004). Privatizing the trade industry and public services affects the livelihoods of people in places like Tola and creates more pressure for export production. As a result, many families struggle to maintain a healthy life and often suffer from disorders such as diabetes, high blood pressure, high cholesterol, and heart disease (FSD, 2007).

Our Situated Linkage to This Work

QUENETTE

As an African American woman who identifies as a social work feminist committed to advocating for the rights of women nationally and internationally, I have always sought out personal and professional opportunities that focus on the well-being of women. Therefore, when I received information about traveling to Tola with the Foundation for Sustainable Development (FSD) to conduct volunteer work with women, families, and their communities to build sustainable vegetable gardens, I immediately sought additional information to learn more about FSD and its Nicaraguan global service trip. Once I learned the focus and goals of the trip—to become partners with local communities to examine issues of development and employ indigenous strategies to address hunger (Abram & Cruce, 2007; FSD, 2007)—and thought about what I wanted to learn from the trip, it was easy for me to participate.

The task of building sustainable vegetable gardens quickly reminded me that I was not born with a green thumb. However, I embarked on my 2-week service trip to Tola with knowledge I gained through reading and talking with the trip organizers about sustainable food development and a passion for seeing a shift toward food sustainability locally and globally. My reality is that food scarcity and hunger affects 925 million people worldwide (World Hunger Organization, 2011), and I am living in a city where healthy and fresh food options are not available to all. Therefore, traveling to Tola created the opportunity for me to understand the effect food deserts have globally, while demonstrating how the complexities of structural problems, such as unemployment and underemployment, illiteracy, poor infrastructure, low socioeconomic indicators (FSD, 2007), and malnutrition (Cupples, 2004), erode families' well-being.

Regardless of an individual's geographic location, living without access to adequate and nutritious food is a consequence of globalization in rural communities like Tola and in large cities like Chicago. The concept of living in a food desert is the same: the lack of access to nutritious food (Gallagher, 2006). Therefore, it was with this understanding and the knowledge I gained from the women in Tola that helped me crystallize my understanding of a rural food desert and led me to think more critically about the adverse effects of globalization on the economic, social, environmental, and political powers of such communities. As a social worker and a burgeoning social work scholar, my role as a Tola volunteer allowed me to see firsthand how social workers can bear some of the responsibility for helping communities build their capacities for developing solutions. My role in Tola also provided me with the opportunity to learn about the importance of traveling abroad to explore the intersection of globalization and gender oppression and their effects on the well-being of women, children, and their families.

PATRICIA

I am a White academic feminist educator who harvests vegetables with other neighbors in my urban community garden and who also works for a just world where no one is hungry. Although I have never been to Nicaragua, I have learned from Quenette's experiences and I have visited Costa Rica and Guatemala, neighboring countries to Nicaragua, and Guatemala's situation is similar to Nicaragua's because of the immense poverty. I have taught about the effects of globalization that we discuss in this chapter in several courses at Jane Addams College of Social Work in an effort to link the global context to local issues affecting struggling residents and migrants from various Global North and Global South countries who live in Chicago.

In a context of seemingly apparent prosperity in the Global North, Chicago has multiple food deserts. This term was popularized by Gallagher (2006) from a study she conducted on access to food in Chicago neighborhoods. The study provided a statistical analysis linking food deserts (not having access to mainstream nutritious food) to more diet-related deaths. From 2010 to 2011 (the date of the latest update to the study), the Chicago food desert contracted from about 64 to 55 square miles and decreased in population by 30% (Gallagher, 2011). But the food desert problem remains widespread among a current population of nearly 400,000 (Gallagher, 2011) and is localized within Chicago, a city of massive diversity and massive segregation by race and income levels. For example, Gallagher found that African Americans have to travel twice as far to get to a mainstream grocery store to buy fresh vegetables and fruit.

Living without adequate access to healthy food in Chicago produces some of the same consequences here as it does for the people of rural Nicaragua (i.e., risk of low-weight and malnourished children, diabetes, and other nutritionally related diseases). We live in a time when food as entertainment gets the headlines that distract us from the realities of hunger that affect millions of people globally. As thinking and compassionate human beings and social workers, we must understand how and why this happens and what we can do about it.

Our composite personal and professional experiences offer social work educators, students, practitioners, and advocates insights into the ways women in rural Tola come together to address the multiple challenges their families experience because of the lack of sustainable food, gender inequalities, multiple forms of oppression, globalization, and neoliberal politics. We situate these concepts in relation to the call to prepare social workers to engage in critical thought and action related to gender oppression in the context of globalization. Further, we share our work as a way to encourage social work faculty and students to become more self-critical and resist reproducing professional imperialism as a form of neocolonialism (Abram & Cruce, 2007). It is our hope that the knowledge gained from this chapter can be used to help facilitate critical dialogue and encourage global awareness and practice with social work students, practitioners, and advocates.

Case Study

This case study illustrates how issues of gender, multiple forms of oppression, globalization, and neoliberal politics are experienced in the everyday lives of the women in Tola. Sustainable vegetable gardens serve as the context to highlight the adverse effects that gender and intersecting and multiple forms of oppression, globalization, and neoliberal politics have on Tola women's lives and their access to nutritious food. More specifically, it brings to light the suffering the women endure, the women's collective effort to advocate for a community garden, and the power we gained through our engagement in this development project.

In the first part of the case study, we provide background information about the FSD and its connection with Tola. In the second part, we illustrate how the Tola women's suffering led to the development of the community's two vegetable gardens. We conclude with describing some of the lessons learned by the women and the volunteers involved in the Nicaragua global service trip.

The Volunteer Organization: FSD

FSD is a nonprofit charitable organization located in San Francisco, founded in 1995 by Alicia Robb. FSD is a volunteer-based organization created to enhance the capacity of underserved and underresourced international community organizations that work to specifically address their communities' health, social, environmental, and economic needs.

Shaped by Robb's passion and commitment for building capacity, FSD embraces practices that empower its volunteers and international partners to work together to address human needs and basic rights for all. In this context, FSD uses a four-prong approach to support underserved communities in a collaborative and sustainable manner: capacity building, grant making, international development training programs, and giving circles. These approaches promote and support U.S. volunteers through experiential learning opportunities, such as global service trips to Argentina, Bolivia, India, Kenya, Uganda, and Nicaragua. In these countries, volunteers work with community members to address the complex and intersecting issues affecting people through hands-on collaborative efforts that focus on developing microenterprises, addressing child and maternal health, and participating in youth education and development programs.

VOLUNTEERS: TOLA BRIGADE

The volunteers for the FSD trip to Tola came from several states: California, Georgia, Illinois, Massachusetts, and Michigan. The volunteers included social workers, public health workers, architects, and lawyers, ranging in age from 21 to 55, and were from diverse racial and ethnic backgrounds. The common thread for this diverse group of individuals was their passion for development work locally and abroad. A total of 13 volunteers participated in the trip: 11 women and 2 men. The FSD staff consisted of two community members who served as the Tola program directors, two U.S. program coordinators, and two U.S. program group leaders who had extensive global service trip experience in Spanish-speaking countries.

THE SUFFERING: REASONS FOR SUSTAINABLE GARDENS

Over the years research has demonstrated the devastating effects that structural adjustment policies (Cupples, 2004) and CAFTA (Ricker, 2004) have had on rural communities like Tola. The promises such policies have failed to deliver—greater economic, social, and environmental power—fell on the shoulders of community members. Communities like Tola particularly suffered from unemployment and underemployment, illiteracy, poor infrastructure, high levels of poverty, and malnutrition (Cupples, 2004; FSD, 2007). As a result, families struggle and have been unable to adequately meet their nutritional needs. Learning about histories of suffering and struggle provided a more in-depth context for Tola's reasons for wanting sustainable vegetable gardens.

With this knowledge and the passion of the FSD's director, a few years before the Nicaragua global service trip the director began connecting with key stakeholders in the Tola community. Over time, critical relationships were built and important discussions took place with community members about their concerns. Based on the community members' concerns, FSD volunteers went to Tola to conduct a needs assessment. In collaboration with the local residents, the needs assessment identified nutrition as a major concern among community members, particularly among their children, as many of them were either malnourished or undernourished. In response the data obtained from the needs assessment, the FSD Tola Brigade was created.

As volunteers, we worked with two Children and Infant Community Organizations (CICO), one in El Limón and one in Las Salinas. CICOs are funded by the government to provide food and basic child care for children ages 0 to 6 who live in El Limón and Las Salinas. Given the results of the needs assessment, the project aimed to improve nutrition levels among young children by training parents and preschool teachers in nutritional practices and creating a community garden for the children with their mothers so they could benefit from fresh fruit and vegetables, thus addressing all three elements that contribute to food security: sufficient availability, access, and knowledge of a food's proper use and storage (World Health Organization, 2006).

The FSD (2007) has noted that rice and coffee have been the most sustainable food produced in rural Tola. However, food security continues to be a challenge, as it is difficult for nutritional food and fresh vegetables to be transported to Tola from Managua because of the ongoing problem with the expense coupled with poor roads. As a result, many women relied on food for their families that they had easier access to, most of which was unhealthy: soda, chips, cookies, and other packaged and processed food. Because of limited resources, many Tola families often relied on each other to mitigate the consequences of poverty and food scarcity.

During Quenette's stay in the Tola community, many of the discussions she had with her host family focused on the impact of poverty, unemployment, government corruption, inadequate health facilities, and limited educational opportunities on their families and their community. For instance, families often talked about how the nation's land continues to be decimated by unsustainable agriculture and land mines left during the Contra War. Additionally, families described a deep frustration with the ways that the services their community needs became more privatized and left them without any economic or political power (Lind, 2002). These discussions highlighted the need for adequate health care and painted a dire picture of the economic issues the community faced as well as emphasizing the desire Tola residents had for greater infrastructure. Despite these daily concerns, the women came together, remained strong, and advocated for the changes they needed to have healthy and sustainable food options.

The development of women's collectives, like those working to build the vegetable gardens, enabled women to share the economic burdens they endured as well as provided them with the resources they needed to combat the social and economic inequalities in their communities (Lind, 2002). Given the strong history of women's collective action in Nicaragua in general (Chinchilla, 1990), coming together provided the Tola women with the opportunity to create a connection between their daily lives and the economic changes they experienced. Thus, the women's strength and advocacy prompted the FSD staff to work with the community members before the volunteers arrived. Even with all the preparation, it was clear that the burden of the community's troubles was at the forefront of the lives of the women the volunteers got to know. The interactions and conversations Quenette had with her host family, together with the knowledge she gained about women's collectives, provided her with a greater understanding about the Contra War and its aftermath.

As soon as the volunteers arrived in Tola, the work began. We immediately became quite engaged with the community members, who welcomed us with *una fiesta* (a party). Singing, dancing, playing music, and eating allowed us to get to know the Tola community members and for them to get to know us. With many of the community members at the party, conversations immediately began about the work we were going to do together. The women of the communities informed the volunteers about their lives, their challenges, and what they hoped would result from the collaboration to build the gardens. The volunteers shared their palpable excitement about the gardens, working with the women and the community members, hosting a health fair to discuss nutrition, and learning more about the CICOs that served El Limón and Las Salinas. The CICOs, according to the community members, are where most of the parents in the community leave their children so they can go to work; they are easily accessible and centrally located.

The next day we woke with great energy and readiness to work. We toured the CICOs in El Limón and Las Salinas and the two large plots of land for the gardens. Following these tours, everyone gathered in the El Limón CICO to learn about the challenges the women and community face because of food scarcity. This discussion focused on the two-part economy (i.e., export and farming) Nicaragua was known for and the limited access rural Tola had to the goods that were leaving the country.

This discussion served as an educational opportunity for volunteers and became a turning point for more community members (i.e., men and children) to get involved with the efforts the women made; community residents and volunteers determined that the communities' needs could not rest solely on the shoulders of the women. With the privatization of services, businesses leaving Nicaragua (Edwards, 2004), and rice and coffee farmers unable to supply products at reasonable prices (Ricker, 2004), families were struggling. Therefore, everyone, including the men, had to be more active in ensuring the well-being of the community in this time of economic crisis. So in short order, the promising prospect of working with volunteers to create community gardens for the benefit of the Tola community and the CICOs and to host a nutritional health fair was welcome. Everyone became involved in preparing the beds for planting beets, peppers, zucchini, cucumbers, tomatoes, and radish seeds, which were purchased by the FSD and donated to the community women advocates who would manage the gardens.

The excitement during the gardening activities was contagious. Everyone took pride in the work we did, and the community women advocates (about 10-20 women) looked on with amazement. Having the support of the CICOs and other community members to create the community gardens was just what the Tola women needed in order to work together to develop nutritious food options for their families, along with the possibility of improving the economic health of the community because the fruits and vegetables could be sold in local markets, which would have an impact on the communities of El Limón and Las Salinas for years to come.

With the creation of the gardens, the women, their families, and community members are able to have access to sustainable vegetables. (Although everyone in the Tola community has access to the gardens, at this time there are no data on how much the gardens have actually produced.) The stress of Tola's women caused by the lack of healthy food options for their families has been mitigated since the development of the community gardens. Yet their drive, passion, and commitment to serving as change agents for their communities motivates them for their next project: the development of a library to increase literacy levels, as the country has lost ground in this area since the government implemented cutbacks in all educational programs.

Social and Economic Context and Resistance

We discuss resistance while considering the daily lives of the women of Tola to emphasize that the women, who have a legacy of activist and armed engagement with constructing a democratic nation, are not passive objects in the context of the social and economic changes that frame their daily lives of struggle. One of the specific ways the women resist is by taking the power to collaborate with others for community change, whether by growing vegetables or working to establish the library, as it challenges what Tornhill (2011) describes as the neoliberal narrative of the market being the only source for social transformation. Learning about the Nicaragua women's historic and contemporary contributions to struggle and change—direct military service, literary campaigns, and now sustainable food—served as critical background information for the service Quenette and the other volunteers were charged to perform during their time in Tola.

Literacy is a fundamental need and ticket for the few economic options there are in Tola, where uneducated women do not have access even to low-level hotel work. Many authors (see Baracco, 2004; Daniel, 2000; Randall, 1981; Walker & Wade, 2011) have discussed the importance of the 1980 literacy campaign as a defining feature of the Sandinista Revolution and a reflection of the power of the people to rebuild their nation.

After the triumph in defeating the Somoza regime in 1979 and the election of Daniel Ortega as president in 1984 (since reelected in 2006 and in 2011), the country was reportedly in physical and social ruins, and for the people to participate in the reconstruction of their country, they had to be educated. The literacy campaign recruited 50,000 young volunteers, trained them, and sent them to teach in the factories, the slums, and in the isolated areas of the countryside over a 5-month period. Daniel (2000) describes an organizational model of multiplicative and participatory learning so that the population was teaching each other what they needed to know using popular education strategies (Freire, 1972), and by so doing, becoming literate. Daniel reports that women were at the forefront of this revolution in education, which was called "the Sunrise of the People" (2000, p. 18).

Walker and Wade (2011) report that this massive literacy crusade resulted in a reduction in the illiteracy rate from over 60% to less than 13%. Randall (1981) draws on interviews with Nicaraguan women involved with the campaign and concludes that it transformed the structure of society. A longitudinal study by Epstein on the effects of the campaign found that women who learned to read and write as adults in this period had healthier children (as cited in

Daniel, 2000), likely because of their ability to access public health information regarding nutrition and wellness.

Women tended to be the ones who ran the education collectives. In his reexamination of the literacy campaign Baracco (2004) argues that it was most effective as a nation-building effort because of the engagement of the people involved in it and the approaches they used. Daniel (2000) claims that Nicaragua remains committed to the adult education program with its focus on popular education but also acknowledges that since the elections of 1990, when the revolutionary government was replaced by a conservative coalition, the economic situation for the poor majority has worsened, largely because of structural adjustment policies imposed as a condition of loans provided by the World Bank.

Along with the heavy debt schedule to repay foreign-initiated loans, public sector cuts have been particularly severe for adult education, leading to increasing rates of illiteracy. Reportedly, literacy classes have continued through the work of voluntary/community groups, often supported by nongovernmental organizations. These programs still relate reading to environment, health, and gender equality issues. One such organization is Puntos de Encuento, a feminist organization in Nicaragua that has specifically focused on building women's leadership capacities and challenging gender inequalities since 1990 (see http://www.puntos.org.ni/).

Quenette's time in Tola serves as a testament to social work's commitment to collaborative work that addresses immediate injustices while also working with the community to build capacities for long-term engagement in larger change efforts. Furthermore, this hands-on work and shared passion has the potential to cross boundaries and connect people with similar stories, experiences, and commitments.

It may be that resistance takes many different forms in the context of globalization. One form may be the necessary and daily coping with hardships that also inspires the women's passion for change. Another form the women of Tola exhibited was their focus on building leadership in their communities. Although men were also involved in construction of the community garden, the women in Tola led the way, perhaps also challenging gender norms and expectations by doing so. The volunteers were able to witness the women of Tola's strength, wisdom, and collective action in their engagement in the garden project as well as in a community health fair. The women's energy allowed them to come together, recognize the need in their community, and advocate for healthier food options for their children and families in solidarity with the FSD staff.

Also the women's collective resources (e.g., talents, hard work, voice, etc.) and efforts gave them the ability and desire to consider the crucial role they play in their community and use that power to organize and implement a project to mitigate the ill effects of poverty by ensuring access to nutritious food and challenging the effects of food insecurity. Furthermore, the women's collective resources served as direct examples of the ways Quenette and the other volunteers learned about how policy shifts have eroded some of the past gains, ultimately allowing them to bear direct witness to contemporary struggles and collective action.

The Effects of Globalization and Neoliberalism in Contemporary Nicaragua

After the election loss by Daniel Ortega, in 1990 three conservative presidents headed the government of Nicaragua: Violeta Chamorro (1990-1997), Arnoldo Alemán (1997-2002), and Enrique Bolaños (2002-2007). Montoya (2003) describes the many ways that women during the Sandinista era participated in collectives in their community-building efforts that led to many reforms. Many of these reforms were immediately scrapped under the first post-Sandinista president, Chamorro. Walker and Wade (2011) report on the increasing losses in women's rights, particularly related to contraception and abortion (and the FSLN has joined this conservative bloc). The adoption by the state of neoliberal policies was the culmination of this trio of leaders that not only dismantled the revolutionary legacy but shaped the neoliberal script that still holds sway in contemporary Nicaragua.

Tornhill (2011) provides a thoughtful analysis of how the transformation of the nation as an ideal location for transnational capital was framed and used, particularly by President Bolaños to situate Nicaragua as an underdeveloped country, and free trade development as the solution for building citizens' progress and well-being with an increasing emphasis on foreign investment especially focused on tourism and the *maquila* (primarily clothing factories) producing for such retailers as JC Penney, Walmart, and K-Mart (Mendez, 2005). When Bolaños took office, Nicaragua had the highest foreign debt per capita in Latin America and one of the world's widest income gaps (Tornhill, 2011).

Free trade had been introduced to Nicaragua on a small scale before the overthrow of Somoza. Walker and Wade (2011) characterize the three governments that followed Ortega's defeat into office as having "a religious devotion" (p. 142) to neoliberal economic principles as advocated by the United States and enforced by the International Monetary Fund and the World Bank. Neoliberal policies are argued to make trade easier by deregulation and privatization. The justification is that poorer nations will benefit from policies that enable the economy to reach a natural balance through international market demands. Following the North American Free Trade Agreement signed by the United States, Mexico, and Canada that promoted expanded free trade within North America, Nicaragua signed CAFTA in 2004.

Free trade has not been good for women in Nicaragua. Tornhill (2011) discusses the image of the docile, hardworking, and compliant woman as represented in job recruitment media. The message conveyed by these materials is that factory or tourism work ensures women of gaining a livelihood and respectability, the "ticket to progress" (p. 86). This representation of mostly young and uneducated women "happy" in their status as proud workers in the new economy overlooks the reality that the work is "poorly paid, tedious, lacking upward mobility, stressful, and often hazardous" (p. 87).

Although it is true that the people in Tola had limited healthy food options because they lacked the resources to purchase or grow food, the significance of the women's collective efforts to advocate for community gardens with the FSD staff was crucial. The women in this community adopted a grassroots empowerment approach grounded in community participation and organization in an attempt to cope with the high levels of undernourished people and unhealthy food options in their community (Cupples, 2004; Gonzalez, 2004). By doing so, they countered and resisted the docile, happy-worker image construction and complicated their position in terms of gender and class relations.

Contrary to what is often believed about international rural communities and food insecurity—ill health, malnourishment, and so forth—food insecurity is not caused exclusively by food scarcity; rather, people are undernourished and hungry because of the economic inequalities caused by the policies that shape access to nutritious food. These inequalities and oppressive structures provide the necessary context for understanding the need for effective ways social work practitioners can find solutions to the challenges of sustainable food development, globalization, and neoliberalism for the communities they serve locally or globally. To that end, we discuss policy, practice, and educational implications.

Implications for Social Work Practice, Policy, and Education

The International Federation of Social Workers' (2012) statement on social work in a globalized world states that any practice begins with "consultation with local communities and civil society organizations and the active involvement of excluded individuals and communities in the decisions that affect them." We highlight some of the planning issues and personal qualities we suggest social workers consider when they work in communities outside the Global North. First, we find Kreitzer and Wilson's (2010) solidarity model and Abram and Cruce's (2007) discussion of "reverse mission" useful models for a general approach to social work students and faculty from the Global North working with development projects in the Global South where there are evident disparities and major differences in worldviews.

Kreitzer and Wilson (2010), faculty members in social work in Canada, draw from their work in Nicaragua and Ghana to propose that international collaboration between social work practitioners and community members in non-Western countries begin by countering the hegemony of the Western-dominant social work content and identify and work from localized practice appropriate to the countries' own contexts. First, they establish the importance of "trading the troublesome concept of partnership" (p. 703) for one of solidarity. This requires students to question the usefulness of Western social work knowledge in addressing issues in their own contexts-that is, there is no *importable* social work base of knowledge for dealing with the realities of living in Tola or anywhere else in the Global South. But what then are culturally appropriate approaches to social work education and practice?

Kreitzer and Wilson (2010) suggest that the service social workers provide has to focus on "preconditions, planning, and implementation" issues and a whole set of "personal qualities and skills" (p. 711). The planning and implementation generally include an analytic process that identifies the issues, the work, and the strategies people will join together to execute. However, personal qualities and skills are very useful for even considering how individuals develop their own self-awareness and bring their best selves to this work. One quality that seems particularly important to emphasize is cultural humility, which incorporates "genuine respect for the worldview and knowledge base of our collaborators, and willingness to learn" (p. 713). Finally, all the qualities can be linked to the need for relationship building, which was reflected in Quenette's recollection of belly laughter and tears in her time with the community members of Tola.

Abram and Cruce's (2007) perspective on the reconceptualization of *reverse mission* for international social work practice also presents some important concepts that support learning from indigenous people in host countries and about conducting social work in a place like Tola. Abram and Cruce argue that it is difficult to imagine a social work career without a global dimension, and that this global dimension informs social work professionals of some of the injustices developing countries suffer from and increases social work practitioners' commitment to the broader struggle for social justice worldwide.

Additionally, such global practice places social work students in a position where they can and should learn from the people they are working with. Seeing the community members as experts helps to create collaborative relationships and enables students to critically reflect on the issues that have made people poor. Such collaborative relationships become mutually beneficial and support students as they act as allies and advocates with those who are marginalized or oppressed nationally and internationally, integrate their efforts through continued action to work toward social change, and evaluate their efforts by thinking critically about how to improve social conditions locally and globally.

From a policy perspective, there is much to recommend to social workers who are learning and working in a place like Tola. First, when social workers practice in impoverished rural communities, they may be able to develop a keener awareness about the grave conditions communities like Tola face because of economic issues, for example, structural adjustment policies (Cupples, 2004) and CAFTA (Ricker, 2004). Second, as students engage in global practice, they become aware of the economic and historical perspectives of the host country. It is essential for social work students to understand and challenge the social, racial, economic, and political forces that constrain people's well-being and shape the social policies and social services that have been created to respond to human need. Finally, students will learn how to have an effect on social change at the policy level by advocating and drawing from the voices of the most vulnerable, oppressed, and marginalized people they travel to serve.

Social work curricula are guided by the mandates of the accrediting body of social work, the Council on Social Work Education (2008), which has changed its policies and instituted core competencies regarding the knowledge base and skills for practice that social work programs must include. With these changes, the purpose of the profession has been refined, and social work professionals are expected to support the well-being of humans and their communities.

Courses that focus on topics such as globalization, at-risk populations, social and economic justice, and human behavior and the social environment are offered to students to support their interests in global social work practice and to help them learn how to address the needs of the people they will serve. Given that students and practitioners are increasingly interested in international social work practice to serve people and communities that endure persistent poverty, economic challenges, neoliberal development policies, and political and cultural crises (Lind, 2002), social work faculty will be expected to provide students with the necessary knowledge and tools to advocate for diverse and vulnerable populations.

In addition to the mandates of social work education by the Council on Social Work Education, the International Federation of Social Workers (2005) has constructed a statement that expects social work faculty, students, practitioners, and advocates to "recognize that pain and disruption in social, health and education services associated with structural adjustment policies has resulted in negative consequences for social programs and the practice of the social work profession in many parts of the world" (p. 2). This organization of social work practitioners and policymakers has challenged the profession to become more responsive to how globalization affects individuals and communities.

To date, there is some scholarship that provides conceptual ways to engage in discussions and practice about gender, multiple forms of oppression, globalization, and neoliberalism politics (Lind, 2002), and much work has been done to explore the ways these constructs intersect to affect the well-being of women in international social work practice, but more work that critically examines and analyzes these issues is needed.

Likewise, this scholarship will provide social work educators and practitioners with the necessary tools and resources to consider globalization as a feminist/womanist issue, begin to focus on the status and experiences of women, consider their vulnerabilities and resiliencies, deconstruct the various forms of oppression shaping their lives, and begin to identify the possibilities for social work action nationally and internationally. We argue that addressing these issues inside and outside traditional social work educational spaces is most likely to support solidarity efforts.

Tying It All Together

Many concerns that emerge in global social work practice revolve around power and control (Kreitzer & Wilson, 2010). To combat these challenges it is imperative for social workers to become more critical in their actions and value the historical and cultural knowledge indigenous people bring to the partnership to create change socially and economically. Thus, as our world becomes flatter (Friedman, 2005), it is incumbent on social workers in the 21st century to question and understand how economics and trade policies play a greater role in perpetuating poverty and food insecurity while, at the same time, the Global North has the resources to address malnourishment and hunger. Whether on our urban streets or the rural roads of Tola, we need to do better in advocating for and facilitating the actions that can help families and communities develop avenues for well-being and health. The effects of globalism and neoliberal policies can be integrated into practice and policy courses; we are not separate from these effects, given the realities of transnational migration and labor exploitation.

Pushing beyond voluntary efforts and grounding practitioners and policy advocates in a human rights perspective can provide social work students and educators with a foundation for ethical practice. In this context, they will be able to grapple with complex questions related to multiple forms of oppression, globalization, neoliberal politics, and sustainable food development. Practitioners and policy advocates will also be able to wrestle with issues related to "national sovereignty, cultural relativity, collective rights, the nature and extent of rights, the very right to have rights, and the myriad tensions therein" (Finn & Jacobson, 2008, p. 145). Social work students and educators will no longer be able to avoid a more thorough integration of human rights into the study and practice of social work. They will be called to intentionally make a commitment to human rights and boldly challenge the oppressive economic, political, social, and cultural structures that continue to have an impact on the lives of women locally and abroad.

Global social work has important implications for how we practice, especially because more social workers are coming into contact with citizens from all over the world. Therefore, it is critical for social workers to understand how a human rights perspective provides the context for food scarcity. It is also important for social workers to understand neoliberal policies in the context of adverse affects on an individual's and a community's health and well-being. To do so, social work programs must provide opportunities for students to develop the skills to analyze the diverse and intersecting needs of communities locally and abroad so that future practitioners can be most effective. Making a shift in the ways social work programs educate students about global social work practice can lead students toward more critical learning opportunities, consciousness-raising, and advocating for changes in one's home country and host country to challenge poverty and injustice in the world.

Discussion Questions

1. In the case study on Nicaraguan women's sustainable food development, globalization, and neoliberalism, what were the significant contributions of the social worker(s) to the women's development of the community garden? What were the significant contributions of the Nicaraguan women to the social worker(s) development of the community garden?

2. What lessons can be learned from this case study to inform practice in one's home community?

3. What are the implications of this knowledge (the case study) for social work practice with women locally and globally?

4. What linkages do you see between issues of food insecurity in rural Nicaragua and in your home community? Are there patterns you can identify that may connect issues of food security across regional and national borders?

5. What steps would you take to learn more about issues of food security and sustainability in your home community? What steps might you take to educate others about these issues?

References

Abram, F. Y., & Cruce, A. (2007). A re-conceptualization of "reverse mission" for international social work education and practice. *Social Work Education, 26* (1), 3-19.

Baracco, L. (2004). The Nicaraguan literacy crusade revisited: Teaching of literacy as a nation-building project. *Bulletin of Latin American Research, 23* (3), 339-354.

Bitler, M., & Haider, S. J. (2009, January). *An economic view of food deserts in the United States.* Paper presented at the meeting of the National Poverty Center/United States Department of Agriculture-Economic Research Service, Washington, DC.

Chinchilla, N. S. (1990). Revolutionary popular feminism in Nicaragua: Articulating class, gender, and national sovereignty. *Gender and Society, 4* (3), 370-397.

Clodfelter, M. (2002). *Warfare and armed conflicts: A statistical reference to casualty and other figures, 1500-2000* (2nd ed.). Jefferson, NC: McFarland.

Council on Social Work Education. (2008). *Educational policy and accreditation standards.* Retrieved from http://www.cswe.org/File.aspx?id=13780

Cupples, J. (2004). Rural development in El Hatillo, Nicaragua: Gender, neoliberalism, and environmental risk. *Singapore Journal of Tropical Geography, 25,* 343-357.

Daniel, P. (2000). Mujer! Women, the Nicaraguan literacy crusade and beyond. *Equal Opportunities International, 19* (2/4), 17-24.

Edwards, B. (2004). Selling free trade in Central America. *NACLA Report on the Americas, 37* (5), 8-9.

Finn, J. L., & Jacobson, M. (2008). *Just practice: A social justice approach to social work* (2nd ed.). Peosta, IA: Eddie Bowers.

Foundation for Sustainable Development. (2007). *Nicaragua: Development issues-2007.* Retrieved from http://www.fsdinternational.org/nicaragua/tola/Nicaraguacountryoverviewfinal.pdf

Freire, P. (1972). *Pedagogy of the oppressed* (M. B. Ramos, Trans.). New York, NY: Continuum

Friedman, T. L. (2005). *The world is flat.* New York, NY: Farrar, Straus and Giroux.

Gallagher, M. (2006). *Examining the impact of food deserts on public health in Chicago.* Chicago, IL: Author. Retrieved from http://www.marigallagher.com/site_media/dynamic/project_files/1_ChicagoFoodDesertReport-Full_.pdf

Gallagher, M. (2011). *The Chicago food dessert progress report.* Retrieved from http://www.marigallagher.com/site_media/dynamic/project_files/FoodDesert2011.pdf

Gonzalez, C. G. (2004). Trade liberalization, food security, and the environment: The neoliberal threat to sustainable rural development. *Transnational Law & Contemporary Problems, 14* (2), 419-498.

International Federation of Social Workers. (2012). *Globalization and the environment.* Retrieved from http://ifsw.org/policies/globalisation-and-the-environment/

Kreitzer, L., & Wilson, M. (2010). Shifting perspectives on international alliances in social work: Lessons from Ghana and Nicaragua. *International Social Work, 53* (5), 701-719.

Lind, A. (2002). Making feminist sense of neoliberalism: The institutionalization of women's struggles for survival in Ecuador and Bolivia. *Journal of Developing Societies, 18* (2/3), 228-268.

Marmot, M. (2004). *The status syndrome: How social standing affects our health and longevity.* New York, NY: Times Books.

Mary, N. L. (2008). *Social work in a sustainable world.* Chicago, IL: Lyceum.

Mendez, G. B. (2005). *From the revolution to the masquiladoras: Gender, labor, and globalization in Nicaragua.* Durham, NC: Duke University Press.

Montoya, R. (2003). House, street, collective: Revolutionary geographies and gender transformation in Nicaragua, 1979-99. *Latin America Research Review, 38* (2), 61-93.

Randall, M. (1981). *Sandino's daughters: Testimonies of Nicaraguan women in struggle.* Vancouver, British Columbia, Canada: New Star Books.

Ricker, T. (2004). Competition or massacre? Central American farmers' dismal prospects under CAFTA. *Multinational Monitor, 25* (4), 9-12.

Sahley, C., Crosby, B., Nelson, D., & Vanderslice, L. (2005). *The governance dimensions of food security in Nicaragua.* Washington, DC: U.S. Assistance for International Development. Retrieved from http://pdf.usaid.gov/pdf_docs/PNADE106.pdf

Seelke, C. R. (2008). *CRS report for Congress. Nicaragua: political situation and U.S. relations.* (Report No. RS22836). Washington, DC: Congressional Research Service and Library of Congress.

Tornhill, S. (2011). Capital visions: Scripting progress and work in Nicaraguan free-trade zones. *Latin American Perspectives, 38*(5), 74-92.

Utting, P. (1992). The political economy of food pricing and marketing reforms in Nicaragua 1984-87. *European Journal of Development Research, 4* (2), 107-131.

Van Wormer, K. (2005). Concepts for contemporary social work: Globalization, oppression, social exclusion, human rights, etc. *Social Work and Society, 3* (1), 1-10.

Walker, T. W., & Wade, C. J. (2011). *Nicaragua: Living in the shadow of the eagle* (5th ed.). Boulder, CO: Westview Press.

World Bank. (2009). *Supporting progress in Latin America's second poorest country: Nicaragua* (Issue Brief No. 51993). Washington, DC: Author.

World Health Organization. (2012). *Gender, women and health.* Retrieved from http://www.who.int/gender whatisgender/en/

World Hunger Organization. (2011). *2012 world hunger and poverty facts and statistics.* Retrieved from http://www.worldhunger.org/articles/Learn/world%20hunger%20facts%202002.htm

Part 6

PEDAGOGY AND PRACTICE

CHAPTER 12

Globalization and Gender Oppression

Reflections on Teaching and Learning

JANET L. FINN AND KARA MILESKI

On a snowy February night our class Social Work in a Global Context meets on the University of Montana-Missoula campus. It is the week before Valentine's Day, and our topic for the evening is the plight of flower workers in Colombia. We have read Cynthia Mellon's (2007) article, "Roses, Thorns, and Seven Dollars a Day: Women Workers in Colombia's Export Flower Industry," that describes the gendered nature of the work, the labor and sexual exploitation of workers, and the toxic working conditions. We have learned that the export-oriented production of roses and carnations is promoted by the World Bank and the Andean Free Trade Agreement, even though it supplants local food production.

We draw on our collective knowledge of popular education strategies and pose "But why?" questions, challenging ourselves to greater critical consciousness regarding the connection between the flower workers' struggles and the discount prices on Valentine's Day bouquets in local stores. We view a short video featuring flower worker Stella Orjuela describing a day in her life, and we learn about the solidarity work of the U.S. Labor Education in the Americas Project (USLEAP, 2011), which offers strategies for education and direct action. Armed with fact sheets, talking points, and a tool kit for action in support of flower workers and economic justice, class members break into groups to discuss key issues and develop plans for concrete local and U.S.-focused action. One group decides to take up the cause as its semester project. A few students wistfully bemoan the fact that a gift of flowers on Valentine's Day will never be the same. At 9:00 p.m. we wrap up our class for the week and face the cold. Thus concludes one encounter with gender oppression and globalization. Is it a valuable encounter? What did we learn about gender oppression and globalization? Did we disrupt or reinforce assumptions about "us" and "them"? Will our learning be a catalyst for change?

In this chapter we explore some of the challenges and possibilities of addressing questions of globalization and gender oppression in social work teaching and learning. We explore ways we can come to a deeper understanding of the globalizing forces shaping women's experiences, the policies and practices affecting women's everyday lives, and the possibilities for transformative social work education and action. In an effort to further our understanding of gendered forms of oppression in the context of globalization and to consider the implications for social work education, we engaged in an ongoing teaching-and-learning dialogue, identifying ways to render these powerful and complex issues meaningful in the classroom.

We began our conversations as professor (Janet) and master's of social work (MSW) student (Kara) and continued them over time. We became co-learners as we talked about our preparedness, perceptions, hopes, and concerns in grappling with the phenomenon of globalization and its relationship to gender oppression. Drawing from our conversations and the directions our mutual teaching–learning experience took, this chapter represents our attempt to respond to several key questions: What can we learn through dialogue about the teaching–learning process that might inform and transform social work education and practice? How can we best address the intersection of globalization and gender oppression without one theme eclipsing the other? How do we recognize and address our own positions within systems of oppression as we teach and learn about globalization and gender oppression from the relatively privileged position of a U.S. university? How might sparks of critical consciousness light fires of advocacy and action to challenge oppressive consequences of globalization in women's lives?

We drew inspiration from feminist scholars in and beyond the arena of social work who have been engaged in a range of projects that address the intersection of globalization and gender oppression and the consequences in women's lives (see, for example, Cabezas, Reese, & Waller, 2007; Chang, 2000; Enloe, 2000, 2004; Hondagneu-Sotelo, 2001; Mohanty, 2003). These scholars and activists consider neoliberalism, the economic logic behind globalization that privileges the expansion of the free market at the expense of state support of social services, education, and health care, as a feminist issue. They challenge the idea that globalization is gender neutral. They highlight the intersections of gender inequality, racism, poverty, violence, economic and cultural imperialism, and other forms of oppression in the lives of vulnerable women. And they show how women's everyday experiences are shaped by ideologies and consequences of globalization. Critical feminist scholars have also argued that the pressing issues of survival confronting so many women, their families, and communities cannot be understood or addressed without a grasp of the larger historical, political, economic, and social forces that shape local experience and the challenges for social justice (Anderson, 2000; Cabezas et al., 2007, p. 8; Collins, Falcon, Lodhia, & Talcott, 2010; Enloe, 2007; Ferree & Tripp, 2006; Hill Collins, 2000; Mies, 1998; Mohanty, 1991; Nicholson, 2006; Ramirez, Dominguez, & Morais, 2005; Riley, Mohanty, & Pratt, 2008; Sparr, 1994; Stoever, 2007; Waller & Marcos, 2005; Wright, 2006).

Our teaching/learning process was also informed by feminist and popular education theorists who speak about the process of coming to critical consciousness through dialogue and posing questions; the intimate connection of personal, political, and historical forces in women's lives; the significance of subaltern voices; and the transformative potential of knowledge for action (see, e.g., Abrams & Moio, 2009; Boal, 1985; Delgado & Stefancic, 2001; Finn, Jacobson, & Campana, 2004; Freire, 1974, 1990; Hill Collins, 2000; hooks, 1984, 1994; Sakamoto & Pitner, 2005; Spivak, 1987; Tuhiwai Smith, 1999; Van Soest & Garcia, 2003; Weiler, 1988). We draw inspiration from popular educator Paulo Freire (1974), who stated, "The teacher-student and the student-teachers reflect simultaneously on themselves and the world without dichotomizing this reflection from action, and thus establish an authentic form of thought and action" (p. 83). This reflection-action process guided our critical dialogue and the teaching–learning experiences in the classroom.

We start by addressing the concept of positionality and locating ourselves in the story. We then draw on the five key concepts of the just practice perspective (Finn & Jacobson, 2008)—meaning, power, history, context, and possibility—as a framework for engagement with questions of globalization and gender oppression. In describing each concept, we offer examples of teaching–learning moments, activities, and opportunities and resources for critical pedagogy regarding globalization, gender oppression, and the relationship between the two.

Positionality: Locating Ourselves

The concept of positionality provides a starting point for critical education. *Positionality* refers to one's location in the social world, shaped by cultural knowledge and experience, gender identity and expression, racial/ethnic identification, social class, citizenship, sexual orientation, and other forms of identification (Hill Collins, 2000; Reed, Newman, Suarez, & Lewis, 1997). Our positionalities configure the angle and lenses through which we view the world, which, in turn, shape our actions in the world. As Reed and colleagues (1997) stated:

> Positionality implies that each and every one of us, in our varied positions and identities as privileged and oppressed, are both implicated in and negatively affected by racism, sexism, heterosexism, homophobia, classism, and other oppressive dynamics. The recognition of positionality, and of one's partial and distorted knowledge, is crucial for individuals of both dominant and subordinate groups, or we all contribute to perpetuating oppression. (p. 59)

We suggest that an exploration of positionality among participants in a teaching–learning process creates an important starting point for addressing concepts of globalization and gender oppression in the classroom and beyond. As we address positionality, questions of power, values, and difference are brought to consciousness in concrete and accessible ways. The two of us are White women of the global North, from relatively privileged backgrounds, which have shaped our experiences with gender oppression and globalization and our ability to understand their interplay. We both have advanced degrees from U.S. universities and have had opportunities to travel and live outside the United States. We bring unique histories and experiences to bear as well, which we summarize here.

JANET

I have been teaching courses in social work and women's studies that address issues of globalization for the past 15 years. I try to bring questions of culture, power, and history front and center as we struggle to make sense of the "intimate politics of globalization" (Cole & Durham, 2007, p. 19) and the forms of oppression, inequality, and violence shaping many women's lives. My own thinking about these experiences was influenced while growing up in Butte, Montana, a copper mining town whose history was powerfully shaped by a transnational mining corporation. My consciousness was transformed as I returned home to record women's stories of struggle and survival during long strikes. Their stories led me to learn about the lives of women in our sister city of Chuquicamata, a copper mining town in northern Chile. There I learned not only of women's lives in relationship to copper mining but also of their struggles and courage in the face of military state violence. I probed historical, political, and economic threads that both joined and separated us (Finn, 1998). I am committed to bringing women's stories of resistance, resilience, vulnerability, and creativity into the classroom in an effort to spark critical reflection and action.

KARA

I had experience working with refugees and resettlement programs prior to graduate school. I then worked with the local AIDS council, explored questions of social justice, and took the course Social Work in a Global Context during my first year as an MSW student. During the summer of 2008 I spent 3 weeks in Central America, including a 2-week intensive seminar in Guatemala, looking at human rights and sustainable development. These experiences have given me opportunities to question my own biases and assumptions, recognize my location within systems of oppression and domination, and develop a clearer understanding of human rights. When I went to Guatemala and heard directly from women about the trauma of war and their ongoing struggles for family and community survival I began to open up to their accounts of oppression. The process of being invited into a woman's home and learning about her everyday life, beliefs, language, and history continues to have a deep impact on me. I came to more deeply appreciate their struggles and humanity as well as my own. As I listened to personal experiences of oppression, I came to consider my own role as oppressor, recognize the role the United States has played in this oppression, and take responsibility for action. Being physically in that space played a major role in lowering my guard and allowing me to be part of a process of exploration and transformation.

Our personal experiences have been formative in shaping (and constraining) our understanding of the intersections of gender oppression and globalization and our commitment to a consciousness-raising process. We view our process of critical dialogue, wherein we start from a place of self-reflection and acknowledgment of the limits of our understanding, as a parallel process to that of the classroom, where students and teachers alike actively engage with questions of power and positionality as they grapple with the complex intersections of globalization and gender oppression.

Taking a Social Justice Approach to Teaching and Learning

To organize this discussion we draw on the Just Practice perspective (Finn & Jacobson, 2008) as a framework to guide thought and action. Just Practice offers a social justice–oriented approach to social work thought and action grounded in questions of meaning, power, history, context, and possibility. The perspective builds on these five key themes, links them with seven core processes—engagement, teaching–learning, action, accompaniment, evaluation, critical reflection, and celebration—and challenges us to consider them in relation to one another in guiding social justice–oriented practice. How do we give meaning to the experiences and conditions that shape our lives? How do structures and relations of power shape people's lives and their choices for individual and collective action? How might a historical perspective help us grasp the interplay of sociopolitical structures and human agency, the ways struggles over meaning and power have played out, and the human consequences of those struggles? What are the contexts in which those experiences and conditions occur, and how might context limit or expand courses of action? How might an appreciation of those struggles help us claim a sense of possibility for transformative social work practice? (Finn & Jacobson, 2008, p. 199)

The Just Practice perspective provides a starting place for social work teaching and learning about the relationship between globalization and gender oppression. In the following sections we address each of the five key themes of Just Practice and use them to frame personal reflection, teaching–learning moments, and opportunities and resources for dialogue and practice.

MEANING

Meaning involves how we make sense of the world and interpret our experiences in it. Humans are cultural beings, and as such we are meaning makers. Our social location and experiences in the world influence the ways we make sense of the world (Finn & Jacobson, 2008). In addressing questions of gender oppression and globalization in social work education and practice we face the twofold challenge of attempting to understand how we and others make sense of the world and our experiences and of trying to grasp the complex concepts that are central to contemporary discussions of globalization and gender oppression. Professional and popular literatures rely heavily on a number of big ideas whose meanings are too often assumed rather than explored. In struggling to grasp these complexities, students and teachers alike may find it hard to stay connected to the grounded experiences of those who live and embody the daily realities of gender oppression.

Teachers may feel a sense of urgency and responsibility to engage students in unpacking and examining big ideas that are central to contemporary debates on globalization and gender oppression. Some examples of these big ideas are the concept of globalization itself, gender as a social construction, oppression, feminism, transnationalism, and neoliberalism. The very language of these big ideas carries an intimidating weight that can leave students feeling overwhelmed, silenced, and convinced they do not know enough to be part of the conversation. The classroom needs to be a place for unpacking meanings and making concepts accessible, using participants' own language, and providing examples of how big ideas translate into the lives of real people.

Popular education methods can be used to help students create accessible definitions of these big ideas through small-group activities in the classroom. Popular education strategies draw on the direct experiences of the participants, encourage active participation in learning, and use multiple modes of teaching–learning, including artwork, skits, games, and music to create and communicate ideas. Popular education provides opportunities to "explore our multiple identities and experiences of inclusion and exclusion, oppression and privilege" (Cho, Paz y Puente, Louie, & Khokha, 2004). For example, in our dialogues we talked about the feelings students might experience in being presented with "official definitions" of the big ideas. Kara expressed the sense of being overwhelmed by the concepts. We developed a brief skit, subsequently used in the classroom, wherein a student was crouched on the ground with her head down while the teacher stood over her and read a list of big idea terms printed on a large poster board. It opened an opportunity for class members to talk about their anxieties in confronting topics that were important and intimidating and to talk about meaning and power.

Students have created and debated bottom-up definitions of big ideas and compared those to official definitions in the academic literature to illustrate their understandings of these concepts and to spark dialogue. They have developed interactive games and theater pieces to make connections between complex global forces and the lives of women in particular work settings, communities, and migration circuits. They have worked in small groups to create posters that represent globalization and gender oppression as generative themes and have then led colleagues in facilitated discussions of those themes. Meaning making thus becomes a group process in which all participants bring their collective critical thinking to bear in understanding globalization and gender oppression from the ground up.

The classroom also becomes a place to examine sanctioned ignorance resulting from the silences and omissions in our prior educational experiences. Literary critic and theorist Gayatri Spivak (1987) puts forth the concept of sanctioned ignorance to name systematic processes through which experiences of those in subordinated positions are variably silenced, marginalized, devalued, or misrepresented in dominant institutions and systems of knowledge. We do not want the classroom to be a space that reproduces and reinforces silencing, but rather a place of posing questions and of critical curiosity. Thus, no assumptions can be made about an individual's knowledge base on entering the classroom. For example, few U.S. students are familiar with the Universal Declaration of Human Rights (UDHR). Students often personalize their lack of understanding of human rights and feel a sense of embarrassment when first addressing it. As adult learners we feel we should know what human rights are, but it is rare that those of us with a mainstream U.S. education have had any systematic exposure to human rights. It is important to actively explore the meaning of human rights and the meaning of our collective lack of understanding of those rights before we can more fully explore women's rights as human rights. This exploration also opens space for those educated in national and cultural contexts outside the U.S. to speak about whether and how they have acquired knowledge of human rights.

Use of plain language versions of the UDHR and resources from the United Nation's CyberSchoolBus (http://cyberschoolbus.un.org/), developed for teaching children about human rights, can help make human rights accessible for adults as well. Participants in the discussion are able to ask why it is that attention to human rights has been marginalized in their educational experience, thereby challenging sanctioned ignorance, building an appreciation of rights, and questioning the politics of knowledge development. Further, as we challenge sanctioned ignorance we begin to demystify the process of unpacking and understanding the big ideas.

By engaging in dialogue about the UDHR and their experiences in the classroom, students may come to more deeply embrace the concepts and invest in the learning process. For example, as a teaching–learning project, one class member used a popular education approach to explore human rights, women's rights, and children's rights. She described returning home after our evening class during which women's rights and human rights were discussed and we had critically questioned the limited nature of our collective knowledge of the UDHR. The student's teenage daughter and four of her daughter's friends were at home engaged in their own study group when she arrived. She asked the girls about their understanding of human rights and found they were familiar with civil rights and reproductive rights, in a rather limited way. She asked the girls if they would like to help her with her class project and join her in a study group, and they agreed. The group met one evening a week for several weeks, using materials from the class, the CyberSchoolBus website, and other web-based resources to spark conversation. The teenagers created a series of posters addressing issues of gender and human rights, which the student brought to class as tools for further critical dialogue. The teens expressed particular interest in female children and rights to education. They also made a commitment to write to their senators and representatives calling for ratification of the UN Convention on the Rights of the Child. Their commitment to action served as a catalyst for dialogue and action in our class as well.

Understanding meanings of gender oppression in the context of globalization requires ongoing dialogue in which we can explore what we knew, what we have learned, and the contrast between these perspectives. In so doing it is important to incorporate the voices of women who tell their own stories of oppression, struggle, and action. First-person narratives of those engaged in struggles of resistance, survival, and change are important in making big ideas meaningful and concrete as they play out in everyday lives of people around the world. One woman's story can be the starting point to give meaning to history, politics, oppression, resistance, and action, and spark discussion in the classroom on the mutually shaping relationship between personal experiences and broader historical, political, and social forces. Stella Orjuela's (USLEAP, 2011) account of a day in her life as a flower worker, cited at the beginning of this chapter, provides one entry point into critical conversation about the meaning and power of globalization and gender oppression.

POWER

Questions of meaning are intimately linked to those of power. An understanding of power conceptualized by poor women activists in rural Mexico is of particular relevance for this discussion (Townsend, Zapata, Rowlands, Alberti, & Mercado, 1999). The women identified four forms of power: power over (oppression), power from within (discovery of inner strength through dialogue with other women), power with (ability to organize to challenge and change life conditions), and power to do (concrete, material actions). This framing uses the language of those experiencing oppression to open discussion and present examples of the workings of power. Further, it challenges us to consider and look beyond oppressive forms of power and explore the many ways women in vulnerable positions resist top-down power, find a common cause, draw on inner resources and the support of others, and take action even in the face of seemingly overwhelming forces working against them. Moreover, this frame is readily digestible and usable in the classroom context. For example, we have found Iris Marion Young's (1990) concept of the five faces of oppression—exploitation, marginalization, powerlessness, cultural imperialism, and violence—to be a valuable tool for analysis and consciousness-raising (see the Appendix to this chapter on p. 305). Identification of various faces of oppression is a way to name practices of power over in concrete terms. We can then look for examples of individual and collective strength and action employed to resist power over and assert one's own voice, dignity, and capacity.

As we attend to women's language and practices of power we become mindful of their "right to reality" (Gergen, 2000, p. 7; Goffman, 1974). To appreciate another's right to reality requires suspending disbelief and reining in the impulse to interpret another's experiences. It calls on us to bear witness to another's story to come to a deeper appreciation and understanding of how that person sees and responds to the globalizing forces that shape his or her life (Farmer, 2003). The concept of right to reality can be brought to life in the classroom through the use of photovoice. As described by Wang and Burris (1997), photovoice is a community-based participatory research method that involves community members in identifying, representing, and helping build community through taking photographs, critical reflection, and disseminating the results. Photography provides people with a means of accessing their worlds (Wang, Burris, & Xiang, 1996) and providing others with windows into their worlds. Photovoice is a potentially empowering process. As people take cameras into their own hands, they are able to document their realities, tell their own stories, and spark consciousness and dialogue with others.

As a popular education strategy, photovoice provides teachers and students with a way to engage in critical dialogue about complex issues. The film *Maquilopolis* (Funari & de la Torre, 2006) provides an insightful example of the power of photovoice to address questions of globalization and gender oppression. The cameras that filmed *Maquilopolis* were in the hands of four women *maquiladora* (manufacturing facility) workers in Mexico as they document their efforts to hold corporate and state players accountable for human rights and social and environmental justice. The film is both process and product of participatory action research using photovoice, wherein women living the consequences of globalization and gender oppression claim their right to reality, offer incisive political critique, and model possibilities for action. The film demonstrates not only the power of transnational corporate forces over the lives of poor working women but also the women's power within, power with, and power to do as they organize to question the conditions of their lives, investigate root causes of their economic and health problems, and seek transformative change in themselves, their communities, and the relations of power that shape their lives.

Students can creatively assess and address ways that forces of globalization and forms of gender oppression play out in local contexts by creating their own photovoice projects. For example, students have used photovoice to capture the local practices of predatory lending companies and to communicate their own stories about the effects of economic hard times on their responsibilities as mothers, workers, students, and consumers. They have also created documentary films telling the story of the founding of the local chapter of Women in Black who stand together each week in silent, nonviolent protest of the ongoing U.S. involvement in wars. The filmmakers and activists together told a story of the effects of war, occupation, and military repression on the lives of women, of the emergence of Women in Black in Israel in 1988, and of the role of Women in Black groups in women's peace activism around the world over the past 25 years (see Enloe, 2000, 2004; Women in Black, 2012). Through these activities students document struggles and resistance locally, trace forms and mechanisms of gender oppression across borders, and make meaningful connections between local and global issues.

In the classroom context, bearing witness to another's reality may also take the form of reading testimonial literature, inviting local and international speakers to share their knowledge and experiences, and using diverse media to bring women's voices, stories, and struggles to life. For example, our campus and classroom experiences have been enriched by a long-standing connection to a social worker affiliated with the Montana Human Rights Network who has participated in solidarity work in El Salvador and Colombia and along the U.S.–Mexico border and regularly arranges speaking tours for labor, community, and human rights activists. The majority of activists who have visited the campus were women who have spoken powerfully on the intersection of globalization and gender oppression in their lives. Women have spoken very directly about their multiple responsibilities as wage earners, caregivers, and community activists and the challenges they face in negotiating these oftentimes competing demands. Through this connection we have borne witness to the power over their lives and to their power from within. We are able to engage power with and power to do as we develop and sustain solidarity efforts over time that extend beyond the bounds of the classroom and the course.

As students and teachers, we come to a deeper understanding of power and the concept of right to reality as we question our own biases and assumptions and begin to recognize our varied locations in systems of oppression and domination. Through sustained engagement with these difficult concepts and with another's reality, in the classroom and beyond, we can, as Kara suggests, come to more deeply appreciate another's struggles and humanity as well as our own. Further, through use of personal narratives and documentaries, we seek to reveal chains of complicity, that is, to make visible the patterns that connect state, corporate, military, and consumer power to grounded struggles of survival and resistance, and recognize our own roles in these systems.

However, as these chains of complicity are made visible and available for discussion, the shame of complicity may take its toll. The learning experience itself can provoke pain, denial, and resistance, and can weigh heavily on a classroom. Too often our educational practices have encouraged emotional distance from the subject of study and discouraged us from challenging and critically analyzing the systems in which we work and live. Drawing from the work of Paulo Freire (1974, 1990), the classroom can become a place for exploring the experiences that have shaped us as oppressors and as oppressed and for acknowledging the weight of the learning experience.

HISTORY

To understand present-day forms of gender oppression and the role of globalizing forces in constraining women's lives, we need a grasp of history. History is much more than a chronology of significant events. As Paulo Freire (1974, 1990) argues, history is a human creation, and ordinary people are active players in the making of history even as they are being shaped by history. History serves as a warning device, compels us to scrutinize the present, and helps us create linkages and connect themes across time. History helps us understand how power works and inspires us to act as it reminds us of possibilities for change created by ordinary people in extraordinary times (Finn & Jacobson, 2008; Zinn, 1970). What is new about globalization and its effects relative to gendered inequalities, and what is the continuation of historic patterns and practices? How have current circumstances of gendered oppression come to be constructed, justified, and naturalized? How might they be interrupted? These are key questions of history.

Our question-posing process can help us uncover the connections between women's contemporary struggles and historical forces. For example, Beverly Bell's (2001) powerful account, *Walking on Fire*, draws on the testimonies of Haitian women to show how survival itself may be a profound act of resistance.

Bell uses the term *istwa*, which melds story and history, to link Haitian women's personal experiences to larger histories of oppression and survival. The practice of *istwa* is one that classroom participants can embrace as well: bearing witness to others' stories, telling their own stories, and exposing the links in chains of complicity.

Attention to the specific historical backdrop behind particular practices of gender oppression in national, cultural, and geographic contexts helps make forms and mechanisms of oppression comprehensible and brings to light the too often invisible effects of colonialism, occupation, militarization, and imperialism in women's lives. Through critical historical analysis, students begin to locate the roots and formation of big ideas and explore the invention of our notions of global poverty, the third world, development, and globalization. Historical inquiry provides us with opportunities to explore the various ways the lives of women have been regulated by social hierarchies, gender ideologies, public policies and laws, multiple forms of violence, and exploitation of paid and unpaid labor.

History comes alive in the classroom through creative activities such as interactive museum installations. Inspired by the popular education resources of the National Network for Immigrant and Refugee Rights (Cho et al., 2004), such as the Immigration Timeline—which depicts key moments in U.S. immigration history in graphic images and archival documents—class members are engaged as researchers, identifying specific policies and practices in particular historic moments and bringing archival texts and images to class to contribute to a history timeline. Through their critical investigations, class members uncover accounts of women's action and resistance that too often go untold, locate those stories in a larger historical context, and make connections across time in the workings of and challenges to gender oppression. We have addressed such themes as immigration policies affecting women; women's labor activism; immigration and lesbian, gay, bisexual, and transgender issues; and the regulation of women's lives through shifting welfare policies. As the images are fixed on long rolls of paper and hung for public display the weight of history and the force of women's resistance and resilience in the face of globalizing forces emerges in very concrete ways.

Examples of particular histories of oppression also provide entry points for understanding critical issues such as the politics of population control, the meaning of genocide, legacies of historical trauma, and the particular ways women are subjected to racialized and sexualized practices of oppression and exploitation in the context of globalization. For example, the film *La Operacion* (García, 1982), which documents the systematic sterilization of women in Puerto Rico from the post–World War II era through the 1980s, offers a provocative exploration of the ways historical forces and transnational economic interests and political practices have collided in the bodies of poor and working-class women of color. It can set the stage for a critical analysis of ways discourses and practices regarding birth control have been conflated with population control, and as a result have violated reproductive rights and denied reproductive justice to poor women and women of color around the world (see for example, Lawrence, 2000). Participants can make the connection between histories of oppression and current practices of resistance, advocacy, and transformative action by exploring social movements for reproductive justice led by dynamic organizations such as Sistersong (http://www.sistersong.net/), a collective dedicated to reproductive justice for women of color (Luna, 2009). Through sustained attention to particular histories of oppression, participants in the learning process come to a deeper appreciation of the interlocking and mutually informing relationships among policies, images, lived experiences, and women's resistance struggles.

History also comes alive as we trace the stories and travels of particular commodities and consider the gendered forms of labor, issues of production and consumption, and the inequalities between the Global North and South that are woven into their very fabric. For example, as a classroom exercise, we have used handouts with the lyrics to "Are My Hands Clean?" (Johnson Reagon, 1985) performed by Sweet Honey and the Rock, which tells a transnational story of gender oppression bound up in the production and journey of a simple cotton blouse. The history of the blouse provides a powerful opening to explore a larger history of gender, labor, consumption, and complicity. It also sets the stage for learning about and participating in local and global fair trade efforts, where participants can trace the journey of products to producer organizations and consider local strategies to promote understanding of the relationship between consumer practices and producer livelihoods.

When we take history seriously, we honor vulnerable women as chroniclers and interpreters of their histories. As we historicize women's actions and struggles we are better able to identify and appreciate their critical analyses of their situations and the courses of individual and collective action taken in response. History can be a source of inspiration as we draw on the courage and wisdom of women who have come before us to inform our present-day activism.

CONTEXT

Looking at the context of gender oppression and globalization provides another tool for understanding women's experiences. Context can be thought of as the background or set of conditions that surround and influence particular events and experiences. Context shapes meaning and helps us make sense of people, events, and circumstances (Finn & Jacobson, 2008, p. 43). Concepts of gender and the realities of women's everyday lives are profoundly shaped by social, political, cultural, and economic contexts. A critical understanding of the contexts in which women encounter, embody, resist, and acquiesce to everyday systems and practices of oppression in the face of globalization is a necessary condition for meaningful action.

Integrating context helps us recognize and honor the ways women's everyday realities are shaped by very specific political, historical, and economic forces in particular cultural and social settings (Kenny, 2007). By grounding analyses in particular contexts of women's lives, we are able to explore the workings of globalization from below and trace patterns that connect women's everyday experiences to broader social forces and structural arrangements (Cabezas et al., 2007; Finn, 1998; Galvan, 2005; Waller & Marcos, 2005). Case studies and personal accounts powerfully demonstrate the need for critical examination of neoliberal policies and ideologies shaping the socioeconomic world context and the lives of vulnerable women (Morgen, Acker, Weigt, & Gonzales, 2006; Staudt & Campbell, 2008; Useche & Cabezas, 2007). For example, Carolina Bank Muñoz (2007) traces the connections among the exploitation of women workers at a Mexican tortilla factory; their husbands' loss of jobs as a result of the North American Free-Trade Agreement, the lack of enforcement of labor protections for Mexican workers, and the militarization of the U.S. Mexican border. She provides an incisive analysis and critique of the micropractices of gender oppression and racism on the tortilla factory floor and their inseparability from the macropractices of exploitation in the context of neoliberal globalization. She also describes women's practices of resistance crafted in the confines of their limited agency. Grounded case studies such as this provide rich food for thought in the teaching–learning process.

Women's struggles for justice and change are often grounded in contexts of family, community, caregiving, and the well-being of children (Galvan, 2005; Nicholson, 2006; Ramirez et al., 2005). Through women's stories we gain an appreciation for the spaces of women's lives and the power of women to transform these spaces into bases for collective resistance and action (Finn, 1998). We see how women have served as shock absorbers for structural adjustment policies around the globe (Sparr, 1994). For example, we witness the contradictions of transnational motherhood summed up by a Salvadoran woman working in the United States who maintains her mothering ties while physically separated from her children for over a decade as she states, "I'm here and I'm there" (Hondagneu-Sotelo & Avila, 1997). There is a rich interdisciplinary literature base to draw on that addresses these contradictions in women's lives as they globetrot South to North sacrificing daily ties to their own families and communities to serve as "maids to the world" (Mendoza Strobel, 2003, p. 46; Hondagneu-Sotelo, 2001; Hochschild & Ehrenreich, 2004). We also come to appreciate ways contexts of gender oppression are also sites of creative resistance where women craft possibilities for action from the resources at hand (Bell, 2001).

The classroom itself serves as a powerful context. As noted earlier, the classroom can serve as a space for a parallel process, recognizing that addressing power relations in the world requires addressing power relations in the learning experience. The idea of parallel process serves as a caveat and counterpractice to reproducing power-laden understandings of cultural differences that play on problematic assumptions about "us" and "them." As we have illustrated, the classroom can be a space not only for teaching but also for modeling strategies of popular education where teachers and students together engage in critical dialogue and pose questions about the realities of gender oppression in the context of globalization and the ways that our own lives are shaped by these realities.

POSSIBILITY

Possibility refers to the ability to envision alternatives and challenge fatalism. It asks us to consider what is historically possible and to move beyond the past and the present to contemplate alternatives for the future. A sense of possibility enables us to look at what has been done, what can be done, and what can exist.

Possibility draws attention to women's agency, or the capacity to act in the world as intentional, meaning-making beings, whose actions are shaped and constrained, but never fully determined by life circumstances. By what critical and creative means are forms of gender oppression being challenged? How are women taking individual and collective action to challenge and change practices of gender oppression? How are they reinventing globalization from the bottom up in the process? What critical and creative strategies emerge in the face of women's everyday struggles for survival? What can we learn from the expertise of women who have taken up these struggles?

To embrace possibility is to seize moments for transformational learning and involve classroom participants in developing lessons for practice that stem from women's grounded practice. Our thinking as teachers and learners on globalization, gender oppression, and strategies of resistance may be profoundly shaped by opportunities to bear witness to the work of women organizing collectively for change. For example, Janet had the opportunity to meet with and interview founding members of Fuerza Unida (United Force), an organization founded in San Antonio in 1990 that emerged from the struggles of women workers who lost their jobs at a Levi Strauss plant when the company moved its fabricating operations outside U.S. borders. The women formed Fuerza Unida to fight for their rights as workers and women. They launched a boycott of Levi Strauss and filed a lawsuit to reclaim benefits owed them by the company. Over the past two decades Fuerza Unida has developed into a formidable organization that contributes to meaningful change in women's lives. Its members have worked in solidarity with women in the maquiladoras of Mexico and Central America on issues of wages, benefits, and health care. And they have expanded their efforts from the factory floor to the larger community through their women's sewing cooperative, food bank, and youth projects. Fuerza Unida continues its commitment, empowering women through workshops on issues such as domestic violence, adult education, sewing classes, and advocacy for undocumented workers (Finn, 2002). Class participants read the case study, visit Fuerza Unida's website, and watch video interviews of key organizational players available on YouTube. Simple technologies enable us to bring global activists into the classroom, engage participants in discussion of strategies and tactics of community change, develop possibilities for solidarity, and articulate lessons for practice.

As we find inspiration in women's creative and critical actions, we tap into a wellspring of possibilities for our own transformative practice. Class participants can bear witness to women's struggles and strengths in diverse, creative ways. We can develop individual and collective forms of action and accompaniment to support women's everyday struggles for justice, rights, dignity, and equality. The classroom experience can provide a base for the development of what Abrams, Slosar, and Walls (2005) refers to as "reverse mission." The authors critically examine the top-down colonizing and missionizing models that have characterized much of the history of intervention abroad. They call on social workers to consider the possibilities of reverse mission, wherein our responsibility is to bear witness to others' realities and listen to and learn from their expertise regarding what constitutes problems and solutions. Our energies, then, can be directed to creating change in policies and practices in the United States and in the social and economic policies and practices of agencies and institutions whose actions have profound effects on the everyday lives of vulnerable women, men, and children around the world.

We have sought to incorporate possibilities for critical thought and action throughout this discussion. We hope this chapter serves as a catalyst for dialogue with readers and as a base for crafting and extending connections with a global community of activists engaged in the struggles for women's rights and empowerment. Perhaps, through sustained reflection and action, we can play a part in transforming the vision of globalization into one that honors and promotes gender and racial equality, social justice, and human rights.

Perhaps, as Kara suggested in one of our early dialogues, we who enjoy positions of relative privilege can think of ourselves as "oppressors in recovery," as we also identify our personal experiences with gender oppression and globalization. In doing so, we bring possibilities for healing and recovery into the classroom. Processes of healing can be connected to processes of transformation through a teaching–learning experience that embraces witnessing, testifying, and acting. Witnessing involves learning from another's story, honoring one's right to reality, and coming through critical dialogue to a deeper grasp of oppression, its consequences, and the roles we play. Testifying entails sharing what we know with a broader audience. Our critical reflection and dialogue on our new knowledge then serves as a catalyst for our change-oriented action (Farmer,

2003). Together we spark critical consciousness and light fires of advocacy and action to challenge oppressive consequences of globalization in women's lives.

Teaching–Learning Activities

We include a brief sampling of teaching–learning activities to promote critical dialogue and action regarding gender oppression and globalization in and beyond the classroom.

- Popular Education on the Meaning and Power of Language: As a class, compile a list of big ideas you find hard to understand and digest in learning about globalization and gender oppression. Create small groups, with each group assigned two or three big ideas. Each small group, using popular education approaches, develops a short skit, poster, story, song, or other interactive strategy to teach the class about the concepts in accessible language that creates an opportunity for posing "But Why?" questions. Over the course of several class meetings, the small groups take turns starting the session by engaging the class in popular education teaching–learning exercises they have developed.

- Power and Possibility: Visit the USLEAP website and read the report "Gendered Injustice: The Struggle of Women Flower Workers in Colombia" (http://www.usleap.org/files/USLEAPGenderedInjustice.pdf). As a group, view the short video "A Day in the Life of a Flower Worker," also accessible through the USLEAP website. Working in small groups, identify examples of the forms of power that intersect in the lives of flower workers; review the flower workers' campaign initiatives, organizing tool kit, and action plans; select three concrete actions you could participate in, and consider their strengths and limitations; and present your power analysis, action plans, and assessments of strengths and limitations to the class. As a large group, consider what actions you might individually or collective want to take. What actions are most consistent with social work values? What actions might challenge you personally? What actions focus on the nexus of gender oppression and globalization? Provide ongoing opportunities, perhaps through use of a course website, for follow up reports related to the issues and to actions taken.

- From Faces of Oppression to Forces of Resistance and Change: As a group, view the film *La Operacion* (García, 1982), which recounts the history of sterilization practices targeting Puerto Rican women. Create five groups, with each group focusing on one of the five faces of oppression identified by Iris Marion Young (1990; see Appendix, p. 305). In a small-group discussion identify concrete examples from the film that illustrate the workings of the group's face of oppression, then present the examples to the class as part of full-group discussion on the faces of oppression. Over the course of a week, each of the small groups undertakes a brief action research project, with members identifying other concrete examples of sterilization policies and practices targeting poor women, especially poor women of color, in the United States as well as in other national and political contexts affected by U.S. funding, policies, and organizations. Groups are encouraged to search websites, locate published articles, and identify specific public policies, historic and contemporary, that address practices of sterilization. Participants bring their findings to class and as a full group participate in the construction of a timeline of policies, events, and practices. There is likely to be considerable overlap among participants regarding some data as well as unique individual discoveries. As a group, critically reflect on the findings in light of the five faces of oppression as well as forms of resistance and action. Identify possible threads that may connect to larger issues of globalization. Visit the Sistersong website (http://www.sistersong.net) to learn about the organization's work on reproductive justice and view Part One of founder Loretta Ross's presentation, "Reproductive Justice 101" (http://www.youtube.com/watch?v=JRcT_NMa6aI).

•How does the concept challenge and expand ideas of reproductive rights? How does it address the intersection of gender oppression and globalization? Identify concrete strategies for solidarity, alliance, and action with the movement for reproductive justice.

References

Abrams, L., & Moio, J. (2009). Critical race theory and the cultural competence dilemma in social work education. *Journal of Social Work Education, 45*, 245–262.

Abrams, F., Slosar, J., & Walls, R. (2005). Reverse mission: A model for international social work education and transformative intra-national practice. *International Social Work, 48*(2), 161–176.

Anderson, B. (2000). *Doing the dirty work? The global politics of domestic labor.* New York, NY: Zed Books.

Bell, B. (2001) *Walking on fire. Haitian women's stories of survival and resistance.* Ithaca, NY: Cornell University Press.

Boal, A. (1985). *Theatre of the oppressed.* New York, NY: Routledge.

Cabezas, A., Reese, E., & Waller, M. (2007). *The wages of empire: Neoliberal policies, repression, and women's poverty.* Boulder, CO: Paradigm.

Chang, G. (2000). *Disposable domestics: Immigrant women workers in the global economy.* Boston: South End Press.

Cho, E., Paz y Puente, F. Louie, M., & Khokha, S. (2004). *Bridges: Building a race and immigration dialogue in a global economy.* Oakland, CA: National Network for Immigrant and Refugee Rights.

Cole, J., & Durham, D. (2007). *Generations and globalization: Youth, age, and family in the new world economy.* Bloomington, IN: Indiana University Press.

Collins, D., Falcon, S., Lodhia, S., & Talcott, M. (2010). New directions in feminism and human rights. *International Feminist Journal of Politics, 12*(3/4): 298–318.

Delgado, R., & Stephancic, J. (2001). *Critical race theory: An introduction.* New York, NY: New York University Press.

Enloe, C. (2000). *Maneuvers: The international politics of militarizing women's lives.* Berkeley, CA: University of California Press.

Enloe, C. (2004). *The curious feminist: Searching for women in the new age of empire.* Berkeley, CA: University of California Press.

Enloe, C. (2007). *Globalization and militarism: Feminists make the link.* Berkeley, CA: University of California Press.

Farmer, P. (2003). *Pathologies of power: Health, human rights, and the new war on the poor.* Berkeley, CA: University of California Press.

Ferree, M., & Tripp, A. (2006). *Global feminism: Transnational women's activism, organizing, and human rights.* New York, NY: New York University Press.

Finn, J. (1998). *Tracing the veins: Of copper, culture, and community from Butte to Chuquicamata.* Berkeley, CA: University of California Press.

Finn, J. (2002). Fuerza Unida, *Affilia, Journal of Women and Social Work, 17,* 497–500.

Finn, J., & Jacobson, M. (2008). *Just practice: A social justice approach to social work.* Peosta, IA: Eddie Bowers.

Finn, J., Jacobson, M., & Campana, J. (2004). Participatory research, popular education, and popular theatre. In C. Garvin, L. Gutiérrez, & M. Galinsky (Eds.), *Handbook of social work with groups* (pp. 326–343). New York, NY: Guilford Press.

Freire, P. (1974). *Pedagogy of the oppressed* (M. B. Ramos, Trans.). New York, NY: Continuum.

Freire, P. (1990). A critical understanding of social work. *Journal of Progressive Human Services, 1*(1), 3–9.

Funari, V., & de la Torre, S. (Producers, directors). (2006). *Maquilopolis: City of factories.* United States: Independent Television Service.

Galvan, R. T. (2005). Transnational communities en la lucha: Campesinas and grassroots organizations "globalizing from below." *Journal of Latinos and Education, 41*(1), 3–20.

García, A. M. (1982). (Producer, director). *La Operacion* [Documentary film]. Puerto Rico.

Gergen, K. (2000). *The saturated self: Dilemmas of thinking in contemporary life.* New York, NY: Basic Books.

Goffman, E. (1974). *Frame analysis: An essay on the organization of experience.* London: Harper and Row.

Hill Collins, P. (2000). *Black feminist thought: Knowledge, consciousness, and the politics of empowerment*. New York, NY: Unwin Hyman.

Hochschild, A., & Ehrenreich, B. (2004). *Global woman: Nannies, maids, and sex workers in the new economy*. New York, NY: MacMillan.

Hondagneu-Sotelo, P. (2001). *Doméstica: Immigrant workers cleaning and caring in the shadows of difference*. Berkeley, CA: University of California Press.

Hondagneu-Sotelo, P., & Avila, E. (1997). "I'm here but I'm there": The meaning of Latina transnational motherhood. *Gender and Society, 11*, 548–571.

hooks, b. (1984). *Feminist theory from margin to center*. Boston, MA: South End Press.

hooks, b. (1994). *Teaching to transgress*. New York, NY: Routledge.

Johnson Reagon, B. (1985). Are my hands clean? [Recorded by Sweet Honey in the Rock]. On *Still on the journey* [CD]. Washington, DC: Songtalk Publishing.

Kenny, M. (2007). Gender, institutions, and power: A critical review. *Politics 27*(2), 91–100.

Lawrence, J. (2000). The Indian health service and the sterilization of Native American women. *American Indian Quarterly, 24*, 400–419.

Luna, Z. (2009). From right to justice: Women of color changing the face of U.S. reproductive rights organizing. *Societies Without Borders, 4*, 343–365.

Mellon, C. (2007). Roses, thorns, and seven dollars a day: Women workers in Colombia's export flower industry. In A. Cabezas, E. Reese, & M. Waller (Eds). *The wages of empire: Neoliberal policies, repressions, and women's poverty* (pp. 140–151). Boulder, CO: Paradigm Publishers.

Mendoza Strobel, L. (2003). The maid of the world. *The other side, 39*(5), 46–51.

Mies, M. (1998). *Patriarchy and accumulation on a world scale: Women in the international division of labor*. London, UK: Zed Books.

Mohanty, C. (1991). Under western eyes: Feminist scholarship and colonial discourses. In C. Mohanty, A. Russo, & L. Torres (Eds.), *Third world women and the politics of feminism* (pp. 1–47). Bloomington, IN: University of Indiana Press.

Mohanty, C. (2003). *Feminism without borders: Decolonizing theory, practicing solidarity*. Durham, NC: Duke University Press.

Morgen, S., Acker, J., Weigt, J., & Gonzales, L. (2006). Living economic restructuring at the bottom: Welfare restructuring and low-wage work. In K. Kilty and E. Segal (Eds.) *The promise of welfare reform: Political rhetoric and the reality of poverty in the twenty-first century* (pp. 81–96). Binghamton, NY: Haworth.

Muñoz, C. (2007). The tortilla behemoth: Sexualized despotism and women's resistance in a transnational Mexican tortilla factory. In A. Cabezas, E. Reese, & M. Waller (Eds). *The wages of empire: Neoliberal policies, repressions, and women's poverty* (pp. 127–139). Boulder, CO: Paradigm Publishers.

Nicholson, M. (2006). Without their children: Rethinking motherhood among transnational migrant women. *Social Text, 24*(3), 13–33.

Ramirez, C., Dominguez, M. G., & Morais, J. M. (2005). *Crossing borders: Gender, remittances, and development*. New York, NY: United Nations Entity for Gender Equality and the Empowerment of Women.

Ravallion, M., Chen, S., & Sangraula, P. (2009). Dollar a day revisited. *World Bank Economic Review, 23*(2), 163–184.

Reed, B. G., Newman, P., Suarez, Z., & Lewis, E. (1997). Interpersonal practice beyond diversity and toward social justice: The importance of critical consciousness. In C. Garvin & B. Seabury (Eds.),

Interpersonal practice in social work: Promoting competence and social justice (2nd ed., pp. 44–78). Boston, MA: Allyn & Bacon.

Riley, R., Mohanty, C., & Pratt, M. (2008). *Feminism and war: Confronting US imperialism.* London, UK: Zed Books.

Sakamoto, I., & Pitner, R. (2005). Use of critical consciousness in anti-oppressive social work practice: Disentangling power dynamics at personal and structural levels. *British Journal of Social Work, 35,* 435–452.

Sparr, P. (Ed.). (1994). *Mortgaging women's lives: Feminist critiques of structural adjustment.* London, UK: Zed Press.

Spivak, G. (1987). *In other worlds: Essays in cultural politics.* New York, NY: Metheun.

Staudt, K., & Campbell, H. (2008, Winter). The other side of the Ciudad Juarez femicide story. *ReVista: Harvard Review of Latin America,* pp. 1–2.

Stoever, J. (2007). Under Western eyes of fashion: Marie Claire's construction of global feminism. In A. Cabezas, E. Reese, & M. Waller (Eds.), *The wages of empire: Neoliberal policies, repression, and women's poverty* (pp. 40–54). Boulder, CO: Paradigm.

Townsend, J., Zapata, E., Rowlands, J., Alberti, P., & Mercado, M. (1999). *Women and power: Fighting patriarchies and poverty.* London, UK: Zed Books.

Tuhiwai Smith, L. (1999). *Decolonizing methodologies: Research and indigenous peoples.* London, UK: Zed Books.

Useche, B., & Cabezas, A. (2007). The vicious cycle of AIDS, poverty, and neoliberalism. In A. Cabezas, E. Reese, & M. Waller (Eds.). *The wages of empire: Neoliberal policies, repression, and women's poverty* (pp. 16–27). Boulder, CO: Paradigm Publishing.

U.S. Labor Education in the Americas Project. (2011). Flower workers and economic justice. Retrieved from http://www.usleap.org/usleap-campaigns/flower-workers-and-economic-justice

Van Soest, D., & Garcia, B. (2003). *Diversity education for social justice: Mastering teaching skills.* Alexandria, VA: Council on Social Work Education.

Waller, M., & Marcos, S. (Eds.) (2005). *Dialogue and difference: Feminisms challenge globalization.* New York, NY: Palgrave.

Wang, C., & Burris, M. (1997). Photovoice: Concept, methodology, and use for participatory needs assessment. *Health Education and Behavior, 24*(3), pp. 369–387.

Wang, C., Burris, M., & Xiang, Y. (1996). Chinese village women as visual anthropologists: A participatory approach to reaching policy makers. *Social Science and Medicine, 42,* 1391–1400.

Weiler, K. (1988). *Women teaching for change: Gender, class and power.* New York, NY: Bergin & Garvey.

Women in Black. (2012). A short history of Women in Black. Retrieved from http://www.womeninblack.org/en/history

Wright, M. (2006). *Disposable women and other myths of global capitalism.* New York, NY: Routledge.

Young, I. M. (1990). *Justice and the politics of difference.* Princeton, NJ: Princeton University Press.

Zinn, H. (1970). *The politics of history.* Boston, MA: Beacon Press.

Appendix[1]

IRIS MARION YOUNG: FIVE FACES OF OPPRESSION

Feminist philosopher Iris Marion Young (1990) identifies five faces of oppression to distinguish the various ways oppression manifests itself in people's everyday experience. Where do you see examples of these forms of oppression in your community? What are some ways you could interrupt and challenge these forms of oppression?

Exploitation: steady process of the transfer of the results of the labor of one group to benefit another group; denial of the social and economic value of one's paid and unpaid labor. Examples include unsafe working conditions, unfair wages, and the failure to recognize the labors of whole sectors of a society, such as women's work as caregivers.

Marginalization: creation of second-class citizens by means of social, political, and economic exclusion from full participation in society of people who are often subjected to severe material deprivation as a result.

Powerlessness: denial of access to resources and the right to participate in the decisions that affect one's life; lack of power or authority even in a mediated sense to have a meaningful voice in decisions.

Cultural imperialism: imposition of a dominant group's meaning system and worldview onto another group so that the other group's meaning systems are rendered invisible and become the other,

Violence: systematic violation, physical and structural, leveled against members of oppressed groups; unprovoked attacks, threats, reigns of terror, humiliation, often accompanied by a high degree of tolerance or indifference on the part of the dominant society.

Note

1. Adapted from Iris Marion Young (1990), Justice and the Politics of Difference as cited in Finn & Jacobson (2008, p. 40).

CHAPTER 13

Critical Consciousness in International Contexts

Teaching Globalization and Antioppression
for MSW Students

IZUMI SAKAMOTO

In her well-respected book on international social work, Lynne Healy (2008) quotes Professor Tatsuru Akimoto, formerly of Japan Women's University, who raised a thorny issue in international social work:

> He asks whether it is appropriate to call it domestic social work if a Japanese person does something in Japan while labeling the same activity international social work if it is performed in Japan by a Kenyan or an American. (pp. 9–10)

Akimoto's point effectively questions who are considered legitimate bodies to carry out international social work in a globalized context and why, which starts to uncover the power dynamics hidden in the seemingly benign label of "international social work."

This chapter is based on my experience in designing a class titled Globalization and Transnationalization: Social Work Responses Locally and Globally and teaching it from 2005 to 2010 at the University of Toronto Factor-Inwentash Faculty of Social Work.[1] I write about the challenges I have faced and classroom exercises that class members and I have used, assignments that seemed to help students, and the kinds of creativity class members have shown in dealing and grappling with some of the critical issues involved in addressing globalization and oppression in social work contexts. Although gender-based oppression was not the main focus of the course, I believe the content and pedagogy of the course would be relevant to addressing gender-based oppression. Examples are given where applicable.

To begin, I would like to share with readers how I was drawn to the topic of globalization and social work. As discussed in Chapter 12, we as teachers ask students to address positionality and questions of power, values, and differences. Thus, as I write this chapter, it is important to reflect on my own positionality and social location as a privileged person with advanced university degrees from the Global North, teaching on the topic of globalization and oppression. I was born and raised in Japan and obtained bachelor's and master's degrees in social welfare before moving to the United States to pursue my master's of social work (MSW) and PhD degrees. In the United States I was inevitably classified as an international student by the university; a resident alien by the U.S. government; and an ethnic minority, Asian woman, or woman of color by the general public; in other words, I had become the *other* in the United States. The experience of marginalization in turn highlighted my privileged citizenship, class, and educational status in Japan, which were not as obvious to me while growing up there. In MSW and PhD classes I struggled to find my own voice, as my previous experiences and knowledge seemed irrelevant to the course content for the most part, unless the topic was international issues. These experiences also led me to develop a keen interest in international social work. I felt there was a bit more room in international social work to insert my perspectives and experiences and to explore answers to my question about the extent to which social work is universally and/or locally defined.

In the mid-1990s I was part of a student group at the University of Michigan that organized a 2-day conference on international social work during which presenters offered competing views on whether Western social work models can be exported to countries in the Global South. One of the faculty members argued that he saw nothing wrong with exporting social work models and, in fact, people abroad actually request these Western/American models. In contrast, another professor presented a critical view on simply exporting Western models, and argued the importance of co-learning and challenging the uncritical imposition of hegemonic views on other countries with different political, social, and cultural backgrounds. As an organizer of this panel as well as a co-panelist critiquing the so-called export model in social work, I was thrilled to hear the second speaker's presentation. However, I was also discouraged to learn how broadly accepted this view of an export model was, because many in the audience seemed to agree with the first presenter. I wondered how it was that the status quo in knowledge transfer is so taken for granted in social work beyond the border of the nation–state. This made me wonder whether U.S.-based social work does (or does not) critically engage with questions of globalization. Grappling with this question also eventually led me to think about my positionality as Japanese, coming from one of the richer nations with a colonizing past,[2] and how my thinking might have been shaped because I possessed privileges both from my country of origin and from living in North America, while feeling minoritized at the same time in the context of also living in North America as an immigrant woman of color.

Fast-forward to the present. As a faculty member of social work in Toronto, I was fortunate to have the opportunity to develop a required MSW course focusing on globalization. To give the reader some context, Toronto boasts about being one of the most diverse cities in the world, with about half of its population foreign born. Canada has proactively facilitated immigration of skilled professionals to counterbalance the aging population and maintain economic growth. There are many similarities in the history of social work in Canada to that of the United States, although there are notable differences in its historical and political roots. For example, Canada has two official languages (English and French) and a closer relationship to England in professional knowledge development as a former colony than the United States (for more information, see Hick, 2010, and Jannissen & Luncy, 2011). Canadian schools of social work were accredited by the Council on Social Work Education in the United States until the 1970s when a Canadian equivalent organization was developed. The school I am affiliated with was established in 1914, and it is the oldest school of social work in Canada and one of the oldest in North America.

In 2004 a new MSW curriculum was developed at our school, changing from the previous method-oriented specialization structure (i.e., micro- vs. mezzo/macro practice) to specializations according to fields of practice. After much deliberation, four specializations for second-year MSW students were formulated to be taken after 1 year of generalist social work training. These included children and their families, gerontology, health and mental health, and social justice and diversity.[3] As part of the four required courses in the social justice and diversity specialization, I proposed and developed a course focusing on globalization and its implications for social work. From 2005 to 2010 I taught Globalization and Transnationalization to a range of MSW students along with a few PhD students.[4] In the following sections I present an overview of the course and discuss challenges I have faced and strategies used to address them. In this chapter the discussion on gender may not appear to be at the forefront but is framed within a larger anti-oppression framework (Sakamoto & Pitner, 2005), because I believe that complex effects of globalization and their power implications need to be understood from an intersectional lens, including interlocking oppressions and transnational identities and agencies (cf. Mehrotra, 2010).

Brief Summary of the Course Globalization and Transnationalism

The course was designed as a creative mix of learning about macro contexts (e.g., key players in globalization), practice (e.g., international social work, globalization from below,[5] social movement, social work practice with immigrants), and theory (e.g., antioppression, empowerment, transnationality) as they pertain to globalization and transnationalization, although the weight in each domain shifted from year to year.[6] A diverse range of students have taken the course, including many who did not feel they had much knowledge on the topic. A handful of students in each class had extensive backgrounds in this regard, having had antipoverty/anti-globalization activism experiences, personal experiences of transmigration, or having graduated from programs that included this topic, such as international development studies and political science focusing on international human rights.

The first couple of sessions focused on an introduction to globalization and transnationalization and how these forces may affect people's lives locally and globally. We addressed not only effects on their user populations but also on class members' own lives. For example, in an early course session the class viewed the film *Life and Debt*, directed by Stephanie Black (2001), which is somewhat dated now but has proven to be an excellent tool to engage class members. The film begins with American tourists going to Jamaica, blissfully oblivious to the lives outside their resort where globalized economic forces (such as the International Monetary Fund and free trade zones) deeply affect people's lives. Drawing on insights from the film, class members could put human faces on the realities of globalization in the Global South and grapple with key underlying concepts such as structural adjustment, free trade, neoliberal capitalism, and national debts.

Next we linked the understanding of globalization to concepts of racism, colonialism, and critical consciousness, paying special attention to indigenous ways of knowing and aboriginal peoples' experiences with their ongoing colonization in Canada. Sometimes we also identified examples in *Life and Debt* and other examples class members brought up during the discussions. Just when this course was starting in the winter semester of 2010, the catastrophic earthquake that hit Haiti on January 12 occurred, which provided ongoing examples for the class to consider. I will return shortly to how this topic was covered in class.

In our course the implications of globalization and transnationalization for social work were also discussed in the contexts and areas of international social work, social development, and transnational organizing (e.g., international nongovernmental organizations, United Nations agencies, transnational social movements) as well as domestic social work practice with immigrants and refugees, which in Toronto is very common in any area of practice.

Throughout the course we discussed concepts that underlie social work responses to globalization and transnationalization such as power, empowerment, anti-oppression, and social justice, and we identified examples of advocacy, mobilization, and social action, domestically and transnationally. Care was taken to ensure discussions were not limited to an abstract level but included the implications for us and social work, so that we did not otherize the people whose lives were affected.[7] While setting out the course contents, I also made sure students had a lot of room to explore their own interests and questions in their learning through discussions and class assignments in accordance with popular education principles (see Chapter 12), in which class members are co-learners, especially on a topic as vast as globalization. Students in the class from the winter semester of 2010 in particular showed strong initiative in leading their own learning and taking it further outside the classroom.

As mentioned previously, a catastrophic earthquake hit Haiti just after this course started for the semester in January 2010. Each day the situations in Haiti became top news, and in a course such as ours, which focuses on globalization, naturally our attention turned to the situations unfolding in and surrounding

Haiti. Class members and I circulated various sources of information about how to understand Haiti and its situation as well as what we could do as Canadians, given that racism and colonialism deeply affect Haiti historically and contemporarily. We needed to think about the privileges and resultant roles associated with being Canadians from the Global North (an example of raising critical consciousness and reflecting on power and privilege). Another faculty member, Rupaleem Bhuyan, circulated a joint statement by the Women's Health and Justice Initiative and INCITE! Women of Color Against Violence, which raised the question of how to intentionally support the long-term sustainability and self-determination of the Haitian people.[8] Drawing from various sources (e.g., newspaper articles, listserv messages, other online resources), the classroom discussions focused on issues such as why Haiti had been poor even before the earthquake hit. We learned (I must admit that I knew little about Haiti until the earthquake) that Haiti's former slaves fought against the French and that Haiti became "Latin America's first independent country and the only nation ever born out of a slave revolt" (Farmer, 2004) in 1804. However, the new republic was economically sanctioned by France, the United States, and other colonial powers, whose economic systems heavily depended on slavery, and Haiti eventually had to agree to pay a hefty fee imposed by France for depriving France of its "property" including land, equipment, and slaves. It took more than 100 years for Haiti to pay this debt, which devastated Haiti's economy (Farmer, 2004).

Class members wondered how they, too, in the Global North as Canadians or Americans might have been implicated in the economic imbalance and ongoing struggles in Haiti. Another major point of discussion focused on how in the face of catastrophe in a nation already labeled as poor, the sovereignty of that nation is undermined by the well-meaning intentions of governments, organizations, and people from richer nations. We also discussed the consequences of chaos and devastation on existing oppressions, specifically on women and girls, as numerous rape incidents were reported. Class members working independently and with faculty (Bhuyan and myself), continued to address this issue outside the classroom and organized multiple actions, including a teach-in and a few fund-raising efforts for a grassroots organization in Haiti.

These examples and reflections were in turn applied to raising critical consciousness internally in Canada, where aboriginal peoples were deprived of their sovereignty and were colonized systematically through various means. The negative legacy of colonization is still present in how the dominant society understands aboriginal peoples and how they are reflected in official statistics, such as their overrepresentation in homelessness, poverty, incarceration, child welfare involvement, and so forth.

Challenges and What Was Learned

I have many rewards in teaching this course, not the least of which are the lessons I learn from students. Globalization as a topic is simply so broad and multifaceted that I enjoy how class members take it in different directions and offer their experiences and learning to instructors and peers. On the other hand, as in any other teaching experience, teaching this course has many challenges. In this section I discuss several of these challenges and then delve into some of the strategies I have used to address them.

One of the major challenges I have faced in teaching this particular course is helping (often Canadian born, White, middle class female) class members develop critical consciousness about their privileges associated with being in the Global North and spark critical curiosity regarding what they take for granted as "good" and "universal." Some of the assumptions include that women in the Global South are oppressed by societies that are authoritative and patriarchal, and that these women want to be liberated like those in the Global North, such as North American women (this sheds light on an often unquestioned assumption that all North American women are or want to be liberated, which is a question for discussion in itself).

Another assumption is that a vast majority of people from the Global South (including children) would happily immigrate to North America (or any other Western nation), especially when their countries are struck by natural disasters and war. Of course, many people do want to emigrate from terrible situations (including parents who wish their children to have better lives), whereas many others would rather stay in their own countries if the situation permits. After the tsunami disaster in Japan on March 11, 2011, several people told me that my family in Japan should immigrate to Canada and did not seem to understand why people in Japan, including my family, wanted to stay there given its frequent earthquakes big or small. Readers may recall that after the Haiti earthquake Baptist missionaries from Idaho were charged with kidnapping 33

"orphans" under the guise of charity. All or at least most of these so-called orphans actually had families (Quinn, 2010). Media speculated whether these
kidnappers believed they were going to give the children better lives by bringing
them to the United States (Robinson, 2010). Although this was an extreme situation with resulting criminal charges, it also highlighted the kind of emotional
response that many in the Global North had in the wake of the disaster, such
as wanting to adopt innocent children from the Global South. More fundamentally, there is a strong belief that is unveiled when facing disasters that it
would be better for everyone to live in the Global North, which may be termed
as globalized "whiteness" (as defined in the following paragraph).

Of course, not all class members share these assumptions, and some actively challenge them when expressed in class. Moreover, some of our class members are immigrants themselves from the Global South who may not necessarily
share the same assumptions of their domestic peers or others who may have
been born and raised in North America but have critical views on power relations because of their different life experiences (e.g., growing up poor). Sometimes class members have lively discussions challenging views that produce
uncontested privileges, such as privileges associated with settler statuses in a
country like Canada as opposed to indigenous peoples.[9] On many occasions,
however, whiteness can go unchallenged, precisely because its dominance is difficult to question in classrooms where power differentials are often masked.
Whiteness is defined as "a form of hegemony that allows one group to use its
power to dominate a group in a position of less power" (Yee & Dumbrill, 2003,
p. 102). Others may define it as strictly limited to race-based privilege. Green
and Sonn (2005) state: "Although there is a shared understanding that whiteness
is connected with issues of power and power relations and differences between
white and non-white people, the concept of whiteness remains a highly contested concept and continues to be debated and developed within different literature" (p. 480).[10] During these occasions of uncontested whiteness surfacing,
my role as an instructor becomes not only to help class members see different
perspectives and begin to challenge their or our own taken-for-granted assumptions but also to attempt to protect other minoritized class members who may
experience spiritual and emotional distress by witnessing whiteness demonstrated by their peers, especially when these instances of whiteness are uninter-
rupted.[11] Every year, students struggle with the roles of social workers in

humanitarian aid and international development. Several have had volunteer experiences abroad, and some others want to pursue international social work after graduation. Some students, including White females, found reading the article by Narda Razack (2005) on international field placement helpful as they reflect on their own whiteness and how it privileges them, even in relation to their teacher who is a woman of color, when attempting to work as a social worker in the Global South. Although being women may make these students vulnerable in the face of gender-based oppressions, being English-speaking White women from the Global North may fit into the prototype of international aid workers, which could give them privileges.

In sum, I have found it difficult to help class members expand critical consciousness beyond the boundary of the nation–state while paying close attention to how whiteness operates within globalized contexts. Of course, I would assume that in some cases my own whiteness may be operating and I may not even notice that some class members may be feeling uncomfortable or hurt because they see my whiteness. *Critical consciousness*, a concept originally proposed by Paulo Freire (1989), is defined as the process of continuously reflecting on and examining how our own biases, assumptions, and cultural worldviews affect the ways we perceive difference and power dynamics. It also includes taking actions to correct power differentials and social injustice and to challenge oppressive structures (Pitner & Sakamoto, 2005; Sakamoto & Pitner, 2005; also see Chapter 12 of this volume). Critically examining the process of otherization (that is, making a group of people the other or systematically marginalizing them) requires decolonizing our taken-for-granted assumptions including the dominance of whiteness that is embedded historically and contemporarily within the profession of social work. Teaching a class such as this with students who bring in critical questions has helped me develop critical consciousness, and I hope that I will be able to continue on the path to keep raising critical consciousness as well.

Another challenge inherent in social work as a field is the limitation of state-sanctioned social work efforts that are often bound and defined by the border of a nation–state. Policy making that affects social work efforts often occurs at the level of the nation–state and becomes the basic infrastructure that guides thinking and practice on social concerns, such as access to health care, social support, and basic provisions for human well-being.[12] These interwoven policy and practice histories shape social work efforts in profound ways and often are taken for granted, such as the very meaning of care as a fundamental concept. It is then especially difficult to engage critically with issues in the broader context of social work within a given national, political, and cultural context.

Social work's universality and cultural/regional/country-specific nature has to be understood at the same time. For example, such basic assumptions as the eligibility of care (Who is included in the service provision and who is excluded?), appropriateness of care (What care is deemed appropriate?), and deservedness of care (Who are considered to be similar others deserving care, and who are considered to be dissimilar others not deserving of care? cf. Sakamoto, 2003) may all be dependent on where (which country/region/culture) the social work efforts take place.

Despite, or because of, these challenges, this course has provided an important context for raising critical consciousness regarding students' and our own social locations in a globalized context. For the remainder of this chapter, I focus on the issue of raising critical consciousness and share how I (and students) have tackled it through classroom activities and assignments.

Activities and Assignments

Some of the following exercises are not specific to gender-based oppression. I feel that activities to help raise critical consciousness in any way are an important foundation for students to begin to question their assumptions and biases in looking at the Global South as the other and the ways they and we may be implicated in gender-based oppression. The following are examples of such activities.

CREATING A WORLD MAP

This is an exercise I developed about 15 years ago when I was struggling to find ways to convey that there are different worldviews and that one's common sense may not be compatible with another's. In this exercise the use of a world map challenges the status quo in our knowledge.

The instructor asks class members to draw a world map on the blackboard. Usually this requires more than 10 people to draw the parts of the world they are more familiar with (e.g., usually many can draw North America better than other parts of the world) in an attempt to complete a map that they can call the world map (I have led this exercise with students over a dozen times, but to this day nobody suggested other ways of drawing; rather, I see repeatedly the common world map one sees in North America with the Atlantic Ocean in the middle). When no one else can add any new information, the instructor introduces a map, which is typically called upside down, with the South on the top of the map and the North at the bottom.[13] When asked, class members typically say that I am holding the map upside down before they quickly realize that it actually is meant to be that way. They observe how the world looks very different, so much so that they don't recognize it any more as a world map, even though the only difference is the direction of the map. I have also brought in another version of the world map from Japan in which East and Southeast Asia (including Japan) and the Pacific Ocean are at the center of the map, with the Americas to the East (right), and Eurasia and Africa to the West (left). In this map, Middle East and Far East could refer to the Americas, which I point out and engage class members in a discussion. A future activity would be for the class to brainstorm and come up with other terms that are challenged by this reorientation.

Showing these alternative ways of drawing world maps then leads to discussions on the meaning of how a world map is typically drawn, including the legacy of colonization (e.g., how the world was perceived by the dominant culture/the West), what is considered common knowledge (e.g., the prominence of Europe and North America), and implications of continued power imbalances in knowledge creation and knowledge circulation in our everyday world, including academia and professional fields such as social work (e.g., how the different ways of knowing the world, such as the South on top of the map, is not seen as a legitimized way of knowing and instead is marginalized, even though the convention to draw a map with the North on top may initially have been an arbitrary decision). This discussion can be expanded to thinking about male dominance in our societies and how dominance is constructed and reinforced in our common knowledge, and how that in turn may contribute to gender-based oppression in all forms. Although I have not done so yet, it may be helpful to bring home these messages to the students if the instructor can provide the space for them to form small groups and come up with more concrete examples of how our common sense may marginalize other ways of knowing, or by asking them to write down their ideas on sticky notes to be posted anonymously (in case they feel still shy about sharing ideas freely). The entire exercise can take between 15 to 30 minutes, depending on how much discussion an instructor would like to have using the maps as a prompt. Please note that if class members have mobility or visual impairment issues, a method other than a blackboard may be necessary as this sometimes requires people to stand up and see what's written on the board.

UNPACKING THE GLOBAL NORTH PRIVILEGES

This exercise is informed by and adapted from Peggy McIntosh's (1988) classic article, "White Privilege and Male Privilege" and aims to raise critical consciousness. I find it very helpful to apply the ideas to other, often overlapping, forms of privileges as some others have done (e.g., the social class privilege checklist from http://sap.mit.edu/content/pdf/class_privilege_checklist.pdf). In this case particularly, I engage class members in creating a list of privileges from a perspective of the Global North, having "legitimate" immigration or citizenship status and other kinds of privileges northerners may take for granted. In this activity, class members are (re)introduced to the examples from McIntosh (1988). Many class members are familiar with her work, but some have not been exposed to it or it has been a while since they last read it, therefore I have them review it first. I then ask class members to work in small groups and create different lists of privileges that are often masked by and among the residents of a richer nation of the world. Table 13.1 shows actual examples of the work student groups have done in the class. Once the list is generated, student groups can swap their work, or I put the master list on the classroom projector to engage students in discussion about the lists and the mechanisms that work to maintain privileges and render them unnoticed to those who hold them.

REFLECTIVE QUESTIONS

Systematic use of reflective questions is another approach to consciousness-raising in the classroom. Although writing reflective questions based on readings is not a new pedagogical exercise, I find it is extremely useful to have students write discussion questions based on their reflections on readings, which then can be used for discussions in the classroom. I have intentionally selected readings that reflect the interdisciplinary nature of the course and that bring diverse

TABLE 13.1

EXAMPLE OF WORK BY CLASS MEMBERS: COMPARISON OF FIRST
WORLD PRIVILEGE AND CANADIAN CITIZENSHIP PRIVILEGES

FIRST WORLD PRIVILEGE	CANADIAN CITIZENSHIP PRIVILEGE
Access to recognized universities and education	Apply for funding for education (e.g., provincial financial aid, scholarships, and standard tuitions and fees as opposed to hefty international tuitions and fees)
Ability to travel internationally with unproblematic passport	
Moving across borders to live/visit in another country	
Access to educational resources (e.g., Internet, textbooks)	Access to a full range of health care for free
Setting the world agenda on important/relevant ideas	Voting rights and right to participate in democratic process
Access to clean water and food	Freedom of speech, freedom of assembly without fear
Access and use of a dominant language of the world	Freedom of dissent and expressing difference of opinion
Unlimited access to limited resources	Relatively free from fear of the police, child welfare, education, and other dominant institutions
Access to what we want and need	
Sense of entitlement over other people in other countries (e.g., international adoptions, migrant workers)	
Freedom of religious expression	
Right to due legal process	
Setting the economic stage: finances, loans, structural adjustment, International Monetary Fund, World Bank	
Right to give or take away finances, "aid"	
Privilege to media ownership and influence	
Privilege of being referred to as first world, not third world	

Note. Power differentials exist in any given country and Canada is no exception. These privileges may be applied differently to different people living in Canada. For example, there are communities (notably people in some of the aboriginal reserves) where access to clean water is an ongoing issue. Likewise, people who are perceived as Muslims may not feel they have freedom of speech and dissent, especially after the September 11, 2001, attacks.

writers from a range of social locations to the forefront. The selection is inherently limited to articles written in English that circulate widely through journals or the Internet. I ask students to submit two to three reflective questions each week ahead of time (students are to make five research question submissions throughout the term of 10 weeks) and I then compile them into documents by themes. Often I use small groups to respond to some of these questions before coming back to the large group. The topics covered by assigned readings include key concepts of globalization and transnationalism, critical consciousness and anti-oppressive practice, colonialism and decolonization, globalization from below (e.g., Wilson & Whitmore, 2000) or transnational social movements to work with or against negative impacts of globalization, critical analysis of immigration policy and trends in Canada, international social work and international development, war and conflict, and social work with immigrants. These themes and some of the corresponding articles, along with a few documentaries I showed in class, are listed in Table 13.2.

It has been my experience that students are willing to tackle this diverse and often challenging assortment of readings, and they touch on many different issues in their reflective questions. They do not shy away from difficult questions; rather they seek opportunities to grapple with them in the context of in-class conversations. Students have contemplated the dominant roles and models of social work in globalized contexts and reflected on ways they are often laden with power differentials. For example, it is easier for social workers from North America or the West to go to Global South countries to work or develop social work curricula than vice versa. Who is seen as an effective helper and what knowledge is important have much to do with the status quo in the global world order. The students have raised important questions, such as when practicing social work, how can we think outside the box and not rely solely on models of practice that are inherently limiting? Some have suggested a more holistic approach, but others have asked whether that is enough, considering that Western theorists have already defined holistic. In response to other sets of readings, students grappled with questions regarding the extent to which social work practice as we know it can be applied in different countries with different geopolitical histories. For example, one student asked, "Can social work practices specific to working with survivors of torture be applied to work with aboriginal peoples of Canada? How about women and children (and men too) who have experienced domestic violence?"

Some of the sample themes that have come up include structural issues of North–South inequalities embedded in neoliberalism and the history of

TABLE 13.2
THEMES AND SAMPLE READINGS

THEMES	SAMPLE READINGS AND DOCUMENTARIES
Globalization: concepts and trends	*Dominelli, 1999, 2005;* Guillen, 2001; *Ife, 2001;* Nelson, 2006; *Neysmith & Chen, 2002; Ross-Sheriff, 2007;* Shiva, 2002; Steger, 2003; Sudbury, 2005
Transnationalism: concepts and trends	Kobayashi & Preston, 2007; Ong, 2003; Vertovec, 1999
Globalization from below and transnational social movements to work with/against negative impacts of globalization	Appadurai, 2002; Escobar, 2004; Freire, 1989; Klein, 2007; Roy, 2004; Starr, 2005; *Wilson & Whitmore, 2000*
Critical consciousness, and anti-oppressive social work	*Daley, 2010; Kanuha, 2000; Massaquoi, 2007; Pitner & Sakamoto, 2005; Sakamoto & Pitner, 2005*
Colonialism, decolonization, and indigenous knowledge	Lawrence & Dua, 2005; McCaskell, 1996; McGregor, 2004; Schnarch, 2004; Sharma & Wright, 2009; Smith, 2012
International social work and international field placement	*Gray, 2005; Healy, 2008; McLaughlin, 2007; Midgley,1990; N. Razack, 2005; Razack & Badwall, 2006; Wehbi, 2008; Wilson & Whitmore, 2000; White, 2006*
International aid and international development	Documents from the Internet (e.g., United Nations, Canadian International Development Agency, USAID, World Vision, OxFam, PeaceCorp, World Bank, etc.); Farmer, 2005; Kamat & Goodman (2009); Kothari, 2006; Rai, 2002; Roy, 2004
War and conflict	Afflitto, 2000; Andersen, 2000; Farwell, 2004; Pederson, 2002; Henttonene, Watts, Roberts, Kaducu, & Borchert, 2008
Immigration policy in Canada and social work with immigrants	*Addams, 1910/1990; Li, 2003; Sakamoto, 2007, 2008; Sakamoto, Ku, & Wei, 2009;* Shakir, 2005; Sharma, 2002
Media literacy	Jiwani, 2005; S. Razack, 2005; Noujaim, 2004

Note. Italics indicate articles published in social work journals or that are known to have been written by social workers or social work academics. Other authors also may be social workers or social work academics. The purpose of providing this sample list is to give readers the context of the course discussed in the chapter. Readers should note that there may be newer and more relevant readings for many of these areas (I taught this course between 2005 and 2010). In addition to assigned readings, class members were encouraged to share other relevant and thought-provoking information from media and alternative sources (e.g., social media), which they did. Some of the guest speakers suggested some of these readings (e.g., Afflitto [2000] and Andersen [2000] on Rwandan genocide).

colonialism (cf. Dominelli, 1999; Roy, 2004; Shiva, 2002), how social workers can avoid the appropriation of indigenous knowledge or practices in their appreciation and possible usage of them and better understand antiracism efforts in relation to aboriginal peoples (cf. Lawrence & Dua, 2005; Sharma & Wright, 2009; Smith, 2012), the goals of social work with immigrants and the extent to which social workers' facilitation of immigrant acculturation is desired (cf. Sakamoto, 2008), and in relation to the article on the effects of structural adjustment on gender relations (Neysmith & Chen, 2002), the feasibility and effectiveness of creating a unified global voice representing labor struggles and resistance movements when our social locations are very different (cf. Rai, 2002).

Although many readings point to the negative, depressing realities of globalization and histories of oppression globally, students are also introduced to works that address the possibilities of resistance, collective action, and change from below. Students have consistently shown keen interest in the idea of globalization from below and different forms of resistance, such as grassroots efforts of organizing in Haiti before and after the earthquake to address gender-based violence. They have also responded with a healthy dose of skepticism, questioning whether international solidarity among exploited peoples is really enough to make any kind of change in the world. As one student commented in his reflective question,

> Since the few superpowers of the world put un-reigned powers into the hands of corporations and people who care only about their own profit, and not about the well-being of people. Perhaps a new system is quietly on the rise, and if so, will a clash between that system and the old Third World system occur? What does a clash really look like when all the true power is invested in the hands of so few?

Another important perspective is an idea of utopia, which was promoted by feminists decades earlier (for a list of feminist utopian novels, see, for example, http://feministsf.org/). One student asked,

> If there were no more prisons, no more hunger, no more police brutality, no more sexual violence, no more oppression, what would our world look like? And what would each of us look like? What are our relationships to critical reimagining? What can this process tell us about our work, and ourselves?

Another focused on the vision for our society and the roles of citizens in a democracy: "How can we as citizens ensure that our governments are truly accountable to us? What mechanisms would ensure that we have real choice in our democracies?" I have also invited them to come up with their vision of a feminist, anti-oppressive utopian society. Although many students liked the idea of imagining such a society, they also found it very difficult to come up with concrete and broad enough visions that they would like to include, unless they already subscribed to certain political ideologies such as anarchism.

Receiving these questions each week, classifying them by emerging themes, and hearing what students discuss in response to them have been a fun part of my teaching activities. Students too generally enjoyed small discussions and subsequent large-group discussions as one of their most favorite activities of this class. The major drawback, however, is that we have limited classroom time, so only a handful questions are selected for discussions. As part of the exercise of taking action and effecting change in whatever way we can, I adopted a class blog that my colleague (Bhuyan) developed the previous year, so students can choose to post questions and answer them in the public domain, an option some students took up enthusiastically while others decided not to participate in (http://socialworkresponses.wordpress.com/).

ARTS-BASED ASSIGNMENTS

Because knowledge that is legitimized in the Western education system tends to privilege positivistic, logical, dualist thinking, I have used arts-based final assignments as ways for students to explore and honor different ways of knowing. In the dominant ways of teaching in higher education in North America, our head (intellect/mind) is too often cut off from the rest of our body, rendering us only able to access partial (although widely encouraged and acceptable) knowledge/understandings of a given topic. Art-based assignments are helpful in providing students more room to explore different ways of knowing and styles of expressions, which may offer a more holistic understanding of the topic, including spiritual and emotional aspects (the rest of the body in addition to our head) of synthesizing and presenting information.

Students have made use of diverse artistic media for this assignment, including multimedia, collages, paintings, music, quilts, and videos. In one class two students created a collage titled "Occupation" for which they interviewed people entering our social work building and the building next door (another university building that houses the Ontario Institute for Studies in Education, known for its progressive reputation), asking them "What do you think about the situation at the parkette [small park]?" Several homeless people, many of them aboriginal, were using the parkette that faces a busy main street next to our building. It is a well-established fact that aboriginal peoples, the original residents of this land, have been colonized, their lands taken away, and that to this day they are overrepresented among the homeless in Canada. The students wanted to ask what people thought about the parkette situation because a group of homeless aboriginal people are visibly present in a university space, which is built on aboriginal ancestral land. The various responses to the students' question were placed in the collage, juxtaposed with quotes from Frantz Fanon (1952/2008) and other thinkers on antiracism and anticolonialism. The students also incorporated dual interpretations of the word *occupation*—the occupation of the parkette by the group of homeless aboriginal people and the occupation of aboriginal ancestral land by settlers—non-aboriginal people, White or otherwise. Most people who use university space, including myself, are nonaboriginal; aboriginal peoples make up only 4% of the Canadian population and are underrepresented in privileged places of higher education such as our university.

In another project three students created a quilt incorporating children's stories about their immigration. The students gave small squares to newcomer children, who drew and wrote on the squares about their experiences, which ranged from stories of exclusion and a sense of loss to those of happiness and the celebration of friends and families. Students who chose this option as opposed to a more standard final paper assignment often confessed that this was far more work than writing a paper; however, they also said they enjoyed the challenge and felt their understanding of the topic was expanded and they were able to creatively engage with it.

CRITIQUING POPULAR IMAGES

As discussed earlier, raising critical consciousness is an ongoing process that requires a multifaceted approach and should result in critical action. The following is an activity led by one of the student groups in a class session to increase media literacy, which leads to taking action. They showed a YouTube video of a TV ad for a feminine sanitary product (beinggirlHERO, 2007), and asked the class to discuss the ideas suggested by the ad. The video's caption states:

Girls living in sub-Saharan Africa can miss up to four days of school each month because they lack the basic necessity of sanitary protection and other resources to manage their periods. To help give girls in this part of the world a better chance at an education and to raise awareness of this issue, [brand and product names] are joining forces with HERO@ an awareness building and fundraising initiative of the United Nations Association to launch the Protecting Futures program (beinggirlHERO, 2007).

In the video, a 13-year-old girl in a rural area in sub-Saharan Africa cannot attend school because she is having her period, while her male peer joyfully runs to the school. With this company's donation to girls' education, she is now able to attend school every day just as boys do. The students discussed what they thought about this initiative, whether it is a commendable example of corporate social responsibility or inappropriate use of the image of a South African girl to sell the company's products, or both. The students debated whether they were likely to purchase the products or if they were more likely to be suspicious of the company's motives. After the discussion, the presenting group suggested the class write a letter to this company stating why this ad is controversial, calling attention to the prevalent (mis)use of images from the Global South suggesting that these girls can only "shine" (the word used in the video) with help from Western aid efforts such as from this company. They discussed how similar projects could be implemented and carried out and what messages would be conveyed to the public. The template letter was shared with the class, and many students participated in sending in the letter together with the group that presented this activity to the class. Initiatives like this help class members think about how we are bombarded with particular images of the Global South that suggest the North's economic and moral superiority over the South and that people in the South can only thrive with the benevolent help of the North.

Synthesizing the Learnings

In the final weeks of the course class members and I synthesized the knowledge we had gained as much as possible. I present here a summary list of keywords and strategies that help me in my ongoing work of raising critical consciousness in relation to globalized oppression and in supporting action for change, however small. The main objectives are (a) raising critical consciousness; (b) critical examination of available knowledge, decolonizing the knowledge base (Green & Sonn, 2005; Smith, 2012); and (c) taking action. To further develop these objectives, I also propose a list of keywords that students and I think are important to take away with us from class:

- Collaboration/partnership/mutual learning (Freire, 1989)
- Accompaniment (Wilson & Whitmore, 2000; keeping someone or a group of people company who are taking charge of an oppressive situation, as opposed to taking over the situation and acting on behalf of those taking charge)
- Witness (instead of trying to help, being there and bearing witness to the ongoing injustice/oppression is sometimes important)
- Avoiding the race to innocence (Fellows & Razack, 1998; some try to claim innocence in being implicated in other people's oppression just because of their own oppressive status)
- Transformative disruption (Massaquoi, 2007; a disruptive, hurtful, or embarrassing event that highlights one's own social locations may lead to transformative change in oneself)
- Choosing the battle
- Self-care

Conclusion

In this chapter I discuss my experiences of developing and teaching an MSW course on globalization and transnationality in the context of social work. Although the class is not without problems (e.g., sometimes topics are too diverse, not all the readings are discussed in class, different class members have different starting points on understanding the topic, which may affect their learning), most class members responded positively and seemed to take initiative in expanding their learning horizons. Class members' final class evaluations reflected how most class members seemed to appreciate the different forms of discussions we had in class "to explore ideas on a broader social scale beyond the local or national," its "depth and breadth," and the facilitation styles of the instructor informed by popular education and adult education. Class members also generally liked the readings (e.g., "readings were well chosen and informative"; "the readings selected were a great resource for transforming knowledge [and] developing questions for the readings helped develop critical thinking skills"), and they liked the "good mixture of guest speakers, videos, readings, discussions and assignments." Some thought that "class discussion stimulated desire for activism!" Some students who were familiar with international issues thought the content was redundant, but for others, the content was new, including some basic understandings. As an improvement, some students suggested narrowing the focus more, as the course covered a broad range of subject matter.

As discussed earlier, although I struggled to dig deeper and help class members recognize and take ownership of their own privileges (which they had, to differing degrees in differing dimensions), every year I was also encouraged and inspired by the creativity and engagement class members have shown in working with the topics. Going from the common ground of continuously raising critical consciousness from an anti-oppressive, feminist perspective, class members took the initiative to pursue different topics for their own final assignments, including globalized gender-based oppression, such as the meanings of hijab bans, war rape, trafficking in girls and women, and domestic violence in immigrant communities. I have used some of the exercises and readings to transfer the pedagogical approach to highlight globalized forms of oppression in the other courses I teach. It is my hope that this chapter will give others some ideas for their own teaching and learning in their own settings.

Teaching-Learning Activities

The following is an example of a teaching-learning activity that provides an opportunity for class members to work in small groups and engage their peers on one of the topics covered in class.

CREATING A WORLD MAP

This exercise sheds light on the fact that there are different worldviews, and one person's common sense may not be compatible with another's. In the following exercise, the use of the world map challenges the status quo in our knowledge.

1. The instructor asks for a volunteer or two to draw a world map on the blackboard. The drawing can be partial, and the instructor should emphasize that it is rare for one person to be able to draw the whole map of the world.

2. Ask for more volunteers to complete the world map as much as possible.

3. After several (sometimes 10 or more) rounds, the map is usually more or less complete with some parts often missing (e.g., the instructor can ask, "Where is Sri Lanka? Balkan Peninsula? Korea? Indonesia? New Zealand? How big is the Indian subcontinent?" etc.)

4. Then the instructor pulls out a different version of the world map. As previously noted, the one I usually use is called "What's up? South! World Map" with the South at the top of the map.

5. The instructor stays silent until somebody says something. Often somebody would say that the map is upside down, until others realize that this is the way this particular map is intended to be.

6. I also provide the Japanese version of the world map in which North and South are situated the same as they are in the traditional map, but the center of the world is the Pacific Ocean and Japan, with the Americas on the right (East), and China, Europe, and Africa on the left (West).

7. This leads to a discussion on different worldviews, the privilege the Global North has in defining knowledge and what is right or wrong, and whether the North's being at the top or bottom on a map is a purely arbitrary decision. The class also discusses how the dominant want to see themselves on the top, which also questions the scientific (or everyday) knowledge we take for granted; but are there different ways of looking at things? What is your reaction when your common sense is challenged? If so, how do we notice that they are there? What are the ways of disrupting our common sense, which may be marginalizing other ways of knowing the world?

Useful readings. The notion of "transformative disruption" is illustrated by Notisha Massaquoi (2007) who describes her own experiences as a social worker. How does it feel when one's (professional) common sense is challenged and what can one do in response? The introduction in Linda Tuhiwai Smith's (2012) book *Decolonizing Methodologies: Research and Indigenous Peoples* articulates indigenous peoples' experiences of their knowledge and their whole beings as subjugated and appropriated.

WORLD CAFÉ

"As a conversational process, the World Café is an innovative yet simple methodology for hosting conversations about questions that matter" (http://www.theworldcafe.com).

In various kinds of social justice work (e.g., community organizing, advocacy, program development, collaboration, fund-raising, grant writing, lobbying, social action, and also clinical work), we as social workers are often expected to talk to a broad audience and make a brief yet strong argument about the issue we care about in an attempt to engage people with the issue. As an exercise, we draw from and use a modified technique of World Café in Week 10.[14] During the World Café session each group will have a chance to rotate through different group "stations" (not including their own) and engage in a small-group discussion (It is preferable for the instructor to give these instructions out loud in front of the class).

The case study and three questions are due on the day students make their presentations in the World Café. There will be one grade for all members of each group. Sometimes group members contribute unequally to the final product. If this becomes an issue for the group, and if negotiating a fair workload distribution among members turns out to be difficult, the group should let the instructor know as soon as possible so this can be addressed.

Class members organize into teams of four to five students, according to the topics they are interested in. Each team will be tasked with a theme from Weeks 2 to 9, in which they have to accomplish the following tasks:

1. Post a news article (or video or any other relevant material) to the course website (accessible to course members only) or blog (publicly available; http://socialworkresponses.wordpress.com/) that the group feels relates significantly to the class readings from that week. Students are to come to class ready to present the article and their team's analysis.

2. Students create three questions that integrate the news article and class readings from that week to present to other groups for discussion on the day of the World Café.

3. Students create a case study that integrates the issues presented in the article with the concepts and theories from the corresponding readings from the syllabus. The case study should be between 200 and 300 words. This can be used to stimulate discussions. During the World Café class,

each group will have a chance to rotate through different group stations and engage in a small-group discussion.

Note: In the class of 2010, groups showed creativity and much preparation, which resulted in lively discussions in each station. For example, one group showed a clip from the movie *Avatar* and provided an analogy of social workers doing international work while visiting another planet, which then led to discussions on the roles of social workers in international social work. Another focused on a sharing-circle-style story in which group members shared their own stories, highlighting their experiences relating to decolonization and critical consciousness, which then led to open discussions with the participants. A topic related to gender-based oppression included reflections on girl/child soldiers, and using the format of a board game, highlighted how globalized oppression keeps pulling the soldiers back to yet another terrible situation, making it very difficult to change the situations they are in.

Class members liked the activity so much and wanted to visit all the stations, even though they were only able to visit a limited number during the class period. Thus, we changed the class schedule and added another week of World Café so that class members could visit most of the stations to learn from other groups' activities and share their own with more peers. More examples and information on the World Café topics from winter 2010 and some of the feedback from peers can be found in the course blog at http://socialworkresponses.wordpress.com/ (look for the tag World Café).

Notes

1. The ideas presented here were also deepened by my interactions with students and colleagues. Further, my practice and thinking were supported and enhanced by working with my colleagues on the Globalization and Gender-Based Oppression Task Group of the Council of the Roles and Status of Women in Social Work Education (aka, Women's Council) of the Council of Social Work Education (CSWE), particularly with Janet Finn and Patricia O'Brien, with whom I have co-presented twice on this topic at CSWE's annual program meetings ("Social work educators' explorations of globalization and women's oppression: Problems and possibilities" [October, 2007]; "Gender-based oppression and globalization: Critical pedagogy and practice" [October, 2008]). On another note, this class is still taught as a required core course for 2nd-year MSW students who are specializing in social justice and diversity, but the focus has shifted more to social policy. Rupaleem Bhuyan is the current instructor for this course, while I teach other courses in the curriculum.

2. Partly through my own experience of marginalization, I have gained more understanding about how Japan's colonial legacy affected other Asian countries, including forced migration and labor of Chinese and Koreans, sexual slavery imposed by the Japanese military on Korean and other Asian women during World War II (commonly known as "comfort women"), and continued colonialism sustained by the continued denial of such an oppressive system by the Japanese government. Although many continued efforts of women who have experienced this atrocity and their supporters continue, I have written about one effort to address the issue of sexual slavery elsewhere highlighting the work of performance artist, Ito Tari (Ito, 2012; Sakamoto, forthcoming).

3. Another specialization, social work service administration, has been added to the curriculum.

4. In 2011 the teaching team of our specialization modified the boundaries of the four core courses, and now the globalization course focuses more on social policy and policy analysis, which is different from the focus of the original course.

5. "Globalization from below" is a term used to describe globalized social movements that push against the "globalization from above" from powerful international organizations that regulate the neoliberal world economy that favors corporations, such as the World Trade Organization (WTO), the International Monetary Fund, and World Bank. For example, protests against major conferences of the WTO and G8/G20 as well as transnational economic activities by poor people from the Global South may be seen as examples of globalization from below. People around the world are connecting with each other to get their voices heard. For more information, please see, for example, Brecher, Costello & Smith, 2000; Matthews, Ribeiro, & Alba Vega, 2012; Wilson & Witmore, 2000).

6. During the 6 years I taught the course, the syllabus was updated every year and was revamped more substantially at times, while some learning components remained the same. What I describe in this chapter is my aggregate experience, and may not have been presented during a single semester.

7. People are otherized when they are systematically marked as different and somehow inferior to the dominant group of people and are negatively and prevalently stereotyped, marginalized, and discriminated against in a society.

8. The Women's Health and Justice Initiative is "a radical feminist of color organization dedicated to improving the social and economic health of women of color and our communities, by challenging the use of punitive social policies, practices, and behaviors that restrict, criminalize, exploit, and police the bodies and lives of low-income and working class women of color" (http://whji.org/). INCITE! Women of Color Against Violence is "a national activist organization of radical feminists of color advancing a movement to end violence against women of color and our communities through direct action, critical dialogue and grassroots organizing" (http://www.incite-national.org/index.php?s=35). The statement referred to in the text was originally circulated on the INCITE! listserv (see http://vivir latino.com/2010/01/18/responding-to-the-situation-in-haiti-incite-womens-health-justice-initiative-statement.php).

9. For more discussions and resources on settler colonialism and power relations and their implications for dominant academic knowledge and its production, please see, for example, Lawrence & Dua (2005), Sharma & Wright (2009), and Smith (2012).

10. Teaching about racism and other forms of oppression are dealt with well in a pair of volumes that I have used over the years: Adams, Bell, and Griffin (2007) and Adams, Blumenfeld, Castaneda,

Hackman, Peters, and Zuniga (2010). There is a growing body of literature on White privilege and whiteness, including Kendall (2006).

11. People are minoritized when they are made to feel like a minority in society with limited voices and access to resources that the dominant enjoy. Terms such as *minoritized* and *racialized* suggest a dominant force is making them a minority on the basis of societal markers such as race, gender identities, sexual orientation, class background, aboriginal heritage, and so on.

12. Sometimes the sovereignty of a nation-state to determine its social policy regarding social welfare and social work efforts may be overshadowed by other countries and organizations that are economically more powerful and may fund these efforts as were seen in post-earthquake Haiti.

13. The map I use is called "What's Up? South! World Map" from ODT Maps (http://odtmaps.com/detail.asp_Q_product_id_E_WUS-36x56-LT_A_Contents=TAB3). The same company also has such maps as "U.S. as Seen From Canada" (http://odtmaps.com/detail.asp_Q_product_id_E_USfromCanada) and "Latin America as Seen From Cuba" (http://odtmaps.com/ detail.asp_Q_product_id_E_LAfromCuba).

14. This assignment was originally developed by Rida Abboud, PhD student instructor of Globalization and Transnationalism, who modified it for this course.

References

Adams, M., Bell, L. A., & Griffin, P. (2007). *Teaching for diversity and social justice* (2nd ed.). New York, NY: Routledge.

Adams, M., Blumenfeld, W. J., Castaneda, C. Hackman, H. W., Peters, M. L., & Zuniga, X. (2010). *Readings for diversity and social justice* (2nd ed.). New York, NY: Routledge.

Addams, J. (1990). *Twenty years at Hull-House (with autobiographical notes).* Chicago, IL: University of Illinois Press. (Original work published 1910)

Afflitto, F. M. (2000). Victimization, survival and the impunity of forced exile: A case study from the Rwandan genocide. *Crime, Law, & Social Change, 34,* 77–92.

Andersen, R. (2000). How multilateral development assistance triggered the conflict in Rwanda. *Third World Quarterly, 21*(3), 441–456.

Appadurai, A. (2002). Deep democracy: Urban governmentality and the horizon of politics. *Public Culture, 14*(1) 21–47.

beinggirlHERO. (2007, December 18). *Always protecting futures.* [Video file] Retrieved from http://www.youtube.com/watch?v=yNYvi7_QEbI

Black, S. (Director). (2001). *Life and debt.* [DVD] United States: New York Films.

Brecher, J., Costello, T., & Smith, B. (2000, December 4). Globalization from below: International solidarity is the key to consolidating the legacy of Seattle. *The Nation,* Session VIII, Reading 5, pp. 1–3. Retrieved from http://www.wilpf.org/docs/ccp/corp/VIII-read5%5B2%5D.pdf

Daley, A. (2010). Reflections on reflexivity and critical reflection as critical research practices. *Affilia: Journal of Women and Social Work, 25*(1), 68–82.

Dominelli, L. (1999). Neo-liberalism, social exclusion and welfare of clients in a global economy. *International Journal of Social Welfare, 8,* 14–22.

Dominelli, L. (2005). Community development across borders: Avoiding dangerous practices in a globalizing world. *International Social Work, 48,* 702–713.

Escobar, A. (2004). Beyond the third world: Imperial globality, global coloniality and anti-globalisation social movements. *Third World Quarterly, 25*(1), 207–230.

Fanon, F. (2008). *Black skin, white mask* (R. Philcox, Trans.). New York, NY: Grove Press. (Original work published 1952)

Farmer, P. (2004). Who removed Aristide? Paul Farmer reports from Haiti. *London Review of Books, 26*(8), 28–31. Retrieved from http://www.lrb.co.uk/v26/n08/paul-farmer/who-removed-aristide

Farmer, P. (2005). *Pathologies of power: Health, human rights, and new war on the poor.* Berkeley, CA: California University Press.

Farwell, N. (2004). War rape: New conceptualizations and responses. *Affilia: Journal of Women and Social Work, 19*, 389–403.

Fellows, M. L., & Razack, S. (1998). The race to innocence: Confronting hierarchical relations among women. *Journal of Gender, Race and Justice, 1*, 335–352.

Freire, P. (1989). *Pedagogy of the oppressed* (M. B. Ramos, Trans.). New York, NY: Continuum.

Gray, M. (2005). Dilemmas of international social work: Paradoxical processes in indigenization, universalism and imperialism. *International Journal of Social Welfare, 14*, 231–238.

Green, M. J., & Sonn, C. C. (2005). Examining discourses of whiteness and the potential for reconciliation. *Journal of Community & Applied Social Psychology, 15*, 478–492.

Guillen, M. F. (2001). Is globalization civilizing, destructive or feeble? A critique of five key debates in the social science literature. *Annual Review of Sociology, 27*, 235–260.

Healy, L. M. (2008). *International social work: Professional action in an interdependent world.* New York, NY: Oxford University Press.

Henttonen, M., Watts, C., Roberts, B., Kaducu, F., & Borchert, M. (2008). Health services for survivors of gender-based violence in northern Uganda: A qualitative study. *Reproductive Health Matters, 16*(31), 122–131.

Hick, S. (2010). *Social work in Canada: An introduction* (3rd ed.). Toronto, Ontario, Canada: Thompson.

Ife, J. (2001). Local and global practice: Relocating social work as a human rights profession in the new global order. *European Journal of Social Work, 4*(1), 5–15.

Ito, T. (2012). *Move: Ito Tari's performance art.* Tokyo, Japan: Inpakuto Shuppan Kai. [In Japanese & English]

Jannissen, T., & Luncy, C. (2011). *One hundred years of social work: A history of the profession in English Canada 1900–2000.* Waterloo, Ontario, Canada: Wilfrid Laurier University Press.

Jiwani, Y. (2005). "War talk" engendering terror: Race, gender and representation in the Canadian print media. *International Journal of Media and Cultural Politics, 1*(1), 15–21.

Kamat, A., & Goodman, A. (2009). As US and other wealthy nations slash aid, UN warns of "silent tsunami of hunger" in global food crisis. Retrieved from http://www.democracynow.org/2009/10/14/as_us_and_other_wealthy_nations

Kanuha, V. K. (2000). "Being" native versus "going native": Conducting social work research as an insider. *Social Work, 45*(5), 439–447.

Kendall, F. E. (2006). *Understanding White privilege: Creating pathways to authentic relationships across race.* New York, NY: Routledge.

Klein, N. (2007). *The shock doctrine: The rise of disaster capitalism.* Toronto, Canada: Knopf.

Kobayashi, A., & Preston. V. (2007). Transnationalism through the life course: Hong Kong Immigrants in Canada. *Asia Pacific Viewpoint, 48*(2), 151–167.

Kothari, U. (2006). An agenda for thinking about "race" in development. *Progress in Development Studies, 6*(1), 9–23.

Lawrence, B., & Dua, E. (2005). Decolonizing antiracism. *Social Justice, 32*(4), 120–143.

Li, P. (2003). Deconstructing Canada's discourse of immigration integration. *Journal of Immigration and Migration Issues, 4*(3), 315–333.

Matthews, G., Ribeiro, G. L., & Alba Vega, C. (2012). *Globalization from below: The world's other economy.* London, UK: Routledge.

Massaquoi, N. (2007). Crossing boundaries to radicalize social work practice. In D. Baines (Ed.), *Doing anti-oppressive practice: Building transformative politicized social work* (pp. 176–190). Halifax, Nova Scotia, Canada: Fernwood.

McCaskell, T. (1996). *A history of race/ism.* Retrieved from http://ameno.ca/docs/A%20History%20of%20Race.doc

McGregor, D. (2004). Coming full circle: Indigenous knowledge, environment, and our future. *American Indian Quarterly, 28,* 385–410.

McIntosh, P. (1988). *White privilege and male privilege: A personal account of coming to see correspondences through work in women's studies* (Working paper No. 189). Wellesley, MA: Wellesley College Center for Research on Women.

McLaughlin, A. (2007). *How to snag a job in international social work.* Retrieved from http://www.socialworker.com/home/Feature_Articles/Professional_Development_%26_Advancement/How_to_Snag_a_Job_In_International_Social_Work/

Mehrotra, G. (2010). Toward a continuum of intersectionality theorizing for feminist social work scholarship. *Affilia: Journal of Women and Social Work, 25,* 417–430.

Midgley, J. (1990). International social work: Learning from the Third World. *Social Work, 35,* 295–301.

Nelson, K. P. (2006). Shopping for children in the international marketplace. In J. J. Trenka, J. C. Oparah, & S. Y. Shin (Eds.), *Outsiders within: Writing on transracial adoption* (pp. 89–104). Cambridge, MA: South End Press.

Neysmith, S., & Chen, X. (2002). Understanding how globalization and restructuring affect women's lives: Implications for comparative policy analysis. *International Journal of Social Welfare, 11*(3), 243–253.

Noujaim, J. (2004). *Control room* [Documentary film]. United States: 2929 Entertainment.

Ong, A. (2003). *Buddha is hiding: Refugees, citizenship, and the new America.* Berkeley, CA: University of California Press.

Pedersen, D. (2002). Political violence, ethnic conflict, and contemporary wars: Broad implications for health and social well-being. *Social Science &Medicine, 55*(2), 175–190.

Pitner, R. O., & Sakamoto, I. (2005). Examining the role of critical consciousness in multicultural practice: Its promises and limitations. *American Journal of Orthopsychiatry, 75*(4), 684–694.

Quinn, B. (2010, February 4). US missionaries charged with child kidnapping in Haiti. *The Guardian.* Retrieved from http://www.guardian.co.uk/world/2010/feb/04/missionaries-charged-child-kidnapping-haiti

Rai, S. M. (2002). Global restructuring and restructuring gender relations: The politics of structural adjustment. In *Gender and the political economy of development: From nationalism to globalization* (pp. 121–158). Cambridge, MA: Polity Press.

Razack, N. (2005). "Bodies on the move": Spatialized locations, identities, and nationality in international work. *Social Justice, 32*(4), 87–104.

Razack, N., & Badwall, H. (2006). Regional perspectives ... from North America. Challenges from the North American context: Globalization and anti-oppression. *International Social Work, 49,* 661–666.

Razack, S. (2005). Geopolitics, culture clash, and gender after September 11. *Social Justice, 32*(4), 11–32.

Robinson, E. (2010, February 8). Kidnapping of Haitian children was no act of charity. *Washington Post.* Retrieved from http://www.washingtonpost.com/wp-dyn/content/article/2010/02/08/AR20 10020802729.html

Ross-Sheriff, F. (2007). Globalization as a women's issue revisited. *Affilia: Journal of Women and Social Work, 22*, 133–137.

Roy, A. (2004). Public power in the age of empire: Arundhati Roy on war, resistance and the presidency. *Democracy Now!* Retrieved from http://www.democracynow.org/2004/8/23/public_power _in_the_age_of

Sakamoto, I. (2007). A critical examination of immigrant acculturation: Toward an anti-oppressive social work model with immigrant adults in a pluralistic society. *British Journal of Social Work, 37*, 515–535.

Sakamoto, I. (2008). Transnationality and diversity: An anti-oppressive perspective. In H. G. Homfeldt, W. Schröer, & C. Schweppe (Eds.), *Soziale Arbeit und Transnationalitat: Herausforderungen eines spannungsreichen Bezugs (Transnationalisation and social work,* pp. 45–59). Weinheim, Germany: Juventa Verlag.

Sakamoto, I. (In press). The use of arts in promoting social justice. In M. Reisch (ed.) *International handbook of social justice.* New York, NY: Routledge.

Sakamoto, I., Ku, J., & Wei, Y. (2009). The deep plunge: *Luocha* and the experiences of earlier skilled immigrants from mainland China in Toronto. *Qualitative Social Work, 8*, 427–447.

Sakamoto, I., & Pitner, R. (2005). Use of critical consciousness in anti-oppressive social work practice: Disentangling power dynamics at personal and structural levels. *British Journal of Social Work, 35*, 420–437.

Schnarch, B. (2004). Ownership, control, access and possession (OCAP) or self-determination applied to research. *Journal of Aboriginal Health, 1*(1), 80–98.

Shakir, U. (2005). Dangers of a new dogma: Inclusion or else ... ! In T. Richmond & A. Saloojee (Eds.), *Social inclusion: Canadian perspectives* (pp. 203–214). Halifax, Nova Scotia, Canada: Fernwood.

Sharma, N. (2002). Immigrant and migrant workers in Canada: Labour movements, racism and the expansion of globalization. *Canadian Woman Studies, 21*(4/1), 18–25.

Sharma, N., & Wright, C. (2009). Decolonizing resistance, challenging colonial states. *Social Justice, 35*(3), 120–138.

Shiva, V. (2002) Violence of globalization. *Canadian Woman Studies, 21*(4/1), 15–16.

Smith, L. T. (2012). *Decolonizing methodologies: Research and indigenous peoples* (2nd ed.). New York, NY: Zed Books.

Starr, A. (2005). *Global revolt: A guide to the movements against globalization.* New York, NY: Zed Books.

Steger, M. B. (2003). *Globalization: A very short introduction.* New York, NY: Oxford University Press.

Sudbury, J. (2005). Celling Black bodies: Black women in the global prison industrial complex. *Feminist Review, 80*, 162–179.

Vertovec, S. (1999). Conceiving and researching transnationalism. *Ethnic and Racial Studies, 22*(2), 447–462.

Wehbi, S. (2008). Teaching international social work: A guiding framework. *Canadian Social Work Review, 25*(2), 117–132.

White, R. (2006). Opportunities and challenges for social workers crossing borders. *International Social Work, 49*, 629–640.

Wilson, M. G., & Whitmore, E. (2000). *Seeds of fire: Social development in an era of globalism.* Halifax, Nova Scotia, Canada: Fernwood.

Yee, J. Y., & Dumbrill, G. (2003). Whiteout: Looking for race in Canadian social work practice. In A. Al-Krenawi & J. R. Graham. (Eds.). *Multicultural social work in Canada: Working with diverse ethno-racial communities* (pp. 98–121). Don Mills, ON: Oxford University Press.

Epilogue

Reflection on Challenges and Opportunities for Social Work

JANET L. FINN, TONYA E. PERRY, AND SHARVARI KARANDIKAR

It is our hope that this collection of teaching–learning essays, theoretical analyses, and case studies demonstrates the fundamental significance of issues for social work at the intersection of globalization and gender oppression, and the transformative potential of critical social work thought and practice to address these issues. Contributors show how forces and effects of globalization have permeated the most local and intimate spaces of everyday lives. They demonstrate the uneven distribution of the costs and benefits of economic globalization among women around the world. And they offer concrete examples of women's bold and courageous action in the face of powerful forces working to silence, marginalize, and constrain them. In conclusion we draw together common threads among this diverse tapestry of scholarship and activism, and we reflect on lessons for social work research, education, and practice.

Globalization and Its Significance for Social Work

First, the contributors to this volume make the case individually and collectively that 21st-century social workers need to have a critical, nuanced understanding of the concepts of globalization and neoliberalism. These are not issues that are just out there, with relevance only to those engaged in certain forms of macro practice or those pursuing practice in inter- and transnational contexts. Rather, the political, economic, and cultural forces of globalization are actively redefining social identity, community, welfare, and the nature of work, including social work. It is essential that social workers attend to and engage with the complexities of globalization as they are manifested in particular local, regional, national, and transnational contexts.

Social workers need the requisite knowledge and skills to document and confront the patterns of inequality that accompany particular practices of globalization. We need the wherewithal to examine the economic effects of globalization, which includes broadening our vocabulary and conceptual base to include critical understanding of debt crises, structural adjustment programs, trade agreements, and austerity plans as issues that matter to social work. Further, we need specific knowledge of the ways these practices play out in particular regional, national, and transnational contexts. We need systematic knowledge and skills to respond to forces that render particular groups more vulnerable and marginalized than others and to those that place human dignity, rights, and basic survival in jeopardy. In Chapter 6 Perry and Kim powerfully demonstrate the importance of such grounded historical, social, and economic knowledge in their account of Ghanaian market women's agency over their bodies.

In short, social workers have the responsibility to engage with rather than shy away from the complexities of globalization. We must commit ourselves to capacity building within the profession so that issues of globalization are central rather than peripheral to social work education. Moreover, as the contributors demonstrate, in order to probe questions of the intersection of globalization and gender oppression, we need an understanding of globalization as a feminist issue.

Gender as a Social Construction

A critical understanding of gender as a social construction is also essential to grappling with issues of gender oppression in the context of globalization. By this we mean that ideologies and assumptions regarding masculinity and femininity, gender relations, and gender differences and capacities matter. They shape beliefs, social institutions, public policies, and cultural practices, and they have a direct influence on the everyday lives of women, men, and children. A critical and nuanced understanding of gender as a social construction and social process pushes us beyond the simple dichotomy of male/female or notions of gender as merely a variable to be measured. It enables us to appreciate the concept of gender as a productive force that shapes fundamental ideas about and experiences of masculinity, femininity, and androgyny in diverse social political, cultural, economic, and historical contexts.

As we come to appreciate gender as a social construction, we are better able to interrogate the ways particular ideas about gender intersect with ideologies of race and racism, inform assumptions about forms and values of labor and what counts as *work*, and shape class-based assumptions and experiences. Chandler's attention to the stories of Las Vegas casino women in Chapter 10 brings this point home. Likewise, as Sethi and Hankivsky demonstrate in Chapter 9, we are better able to examine the relationship among gender, rights of citizenship, and experiences of migration. A critical understanding of gender as a social construction is key to investigating forms and practices of power and oppression, including physical and militarized violence and violation of women's bodies and dignity. Understanding gender as a social construction helps us in understanding the contexts and circumstances that render some women especially vulnerable to the deleterious effects of globalization.

Contextualizing Knowledge

As several contributors to this volume demonstrate, social workers need to understand globalization and its effects in diverse social, political, historical, and cultural contexts. There is no single universal narrative of globalization. Manifestations of globalization and constructions of gender are mutually shaped by and shapers of particular contexts. To meaningfully consider the contemporary forces affecting women's lives, social workers need a critical understanding of particular histories of colonialism, racism, occupation, migration, conflict, and resistance that have shaped social experience over time. In Chapter 8 Kim powerfully illustrates this contextualized understanding in her examination of the waves of globalization that have shaped social policy and women's lives in Korea. In their account of sex workers in Kamathipura in Chapter 1 Karandikar and Gezinski address how forces of globalization have contributed to increased rural-urban migration, commodification of women's bodies, and vulnerability to sex trafficking. Perry and Kim show us how globalizing forces intersect with the everyday lives of Ghanaian women and constrain their choices in the process. In Chapter 4 Jacobsen draws attention to prisons as very particular sites of globalization and women's oppression. Chandler takes us inside some of the wealthiest spaces in the world, Las Vegas casinos, to show how women are taking collective action to hold global corporate power brokers accountable to workers and make claims for the rights and dignity of all women and workers in the process.

Attention to context also furthers our appreciation of the critical knowledge honed through women's everyday experiences with hardship and of the forms and practices of resistance and action women have mobilized to make claims for rights and dignity and to ensure family and community survival in the face of tremendous hardship and struggle. Further, social workers not only need to contextualize knowledge of the forces affecting those we work with, we also need to deepen our critical understanding of the ways social work practice itself is being transformed in the face of globalization. Cutbacks in state-based services, welfare budgets, and programs for basic social and economic security affect the very foundations of social work practice. Likewise, pressures to privatize services, commodify needs, and embrace profit-driven modes of practice pose fundamental challenges to the mission and value base of the profession. As we practice in the context of globalization, we are forced to grapple with these complexities.

Theoretical Perspectives and Conceptual Tools

The contributors to this volume, informed by a range of critical race, feminist, and womanist perspectives, offer important new directions for social work thought and practice. They provide theoretical insights into forms and mechanisms of oppression that shape and constrain human experience. They demonstrate the need for a solid understanding of human rights and women's rights as human rights. And they contend that an in-depth understanding of intersectionality is central to social work theory and practice.

The contributors honor women prisoners, poets, casino workers, market workers, immigrants, street workers, and rural community members as critical theorists able to reflect on the conditions of their lives and speak of the social, political, economic and historical forces that shape their everyday experiences. They demonstrate bell hooks' (1984) claim that theory is a survival skill for those living under conditions of oppression. Their accounts of struggles and resistance remind social workers that we need to attend to the structural forces that shape and constrain human experience and serve to maintain and reproduce systems of oppression.

Villarreal and Moore in Chapter 7 show how Chicana feminists' theoretical contributions to understanding social identity, language, and borderlands can open important new terrains of social work thought and practice in the context of globalization. In Chapter 5 Taylor challenges the limits of behavioral explanatory models that tend to pathologize individuals and ignore broader circumstances. Using the example of her work with young Black women, Taylor points to the possibilities of culturally relevant pedagogy to create opportunities for critical and creative group work as a resource in responding to sexualized images and pressures rendered ubiquitous through globalized media. Carnahan in Chapter 3 develops an insightful discussion of critical trauma theory as an approach to understanding and action in the face of globalized forms of violence and violation.

Kim brings a global feminist perspective to bear for critical analysis of social policy responses to forces of globalization and their effects on Korean women's lives. She helps us see that attention to universal rights claims on behalf of women and an appreciation of the cultural and historical contexts of women's experiences can be mutually informing rather than antagonistic goals of theory and practice. Taken as a whole, these contributions recognize the long-standing history and value of the theoretical contributions of women of color in understanding purportedly *new* forms and directions of globalization and gender oppression. Their contributions to understanding social identity, borderlands, intersectionality, solidarity, and transformative action are at the center of social work thought and practice here. We contend that these theoretical perspectives belong front and center for the social work profession as a whole.

Modes of Inquiry

The contributors' theoretical insights are informed by diverse modes of inquiry that push beyond the bounds of the positivist models, which have enjoyed pride of place in much of contemporary social work research. In this collection we see in-depth attention to research methods that value and validate lived experience and the expert knowledge of those who bear the everyday burdens of globalizing forces. The contributors draw on ethnographic approaches of living in communities and with residents who are experiencing the consequences of globalization. Karandikar and Gezinski employ qualitative research methods to document the daily realities and life stories of men and women working and living on the streets of Kamathipura. Jacobsen combines research and advocacy as she documents the experiences of women prisoners, recognizes the women as being victims and critics of systems and institutions that impose power over them, and engages social work students as co-learners and advocates as research melds with public policy work. Sethi demonstrates the significance of community-based participatory research that blurs the boundaries between researcher and subject in documenting the experiences of women immigrants to Canada. Carnahan reveals how poetry, performance, and other forms of artistic expression can be important subjects of research engagement. In Chapter 2 Alvarez and Alessi scrutinize the history of public policies and laws to provide readers with a foundation for understanding the historical, political, ethical, and clinical aspects of sex trafficking. Taken together, the contributors demonstrate the teaching and practice of research methods that engage those who have experienced firsthand the brunt of globalizing power, not merely as subjects of research but as research collaborators. They demonstrate the need for understanding people's histories of struggle, resistance, and success. And they show the power of a gender lens to inform inquiry at the personal, group, community, and policy levels.

The contributors to this volume take a self-reflexive approach to their theorizing, teaching, and practice. By this we mean that they engage in ongoing reflection about their own social location and identity in researching and theorizing about gender, oppression, and globalization. They acknowledge the partiality of their understanding, and they seek to remain open to personal and professional transformation as their lives and understanding are influenced by those with whom they work. For example, Finn and Mileski (Chapter 12), Sakamoto (Chapter 13), and Taylor draw on and build on the power of critical consciousness and pedagogy in the classroom and in the world. Contributors encourage social workers to participate in ongoing critical questioning regarding the uneven distribution of resources and opportunities and the continued systematic marginalization of women and girls around the world. They engage in posing questions to probe beyond superficial understandings of women's experiences, and they have crafted theoretical insights informed by the perceptions of those affected by forms and mechanisms of oppression.

Power of Voice and Narrative

These diverse modes of inquiry share a common respect for the voices, perspectives, and experiences of those who have firsthand knowledge of the deleterious effects of globalization. The contributors individually and collectively bear witness to women's accounts of and experiences with diverse forms and practices of oppression in the context of globalization. They embrace social work in its most elemental and timeless form as they listen to the stories of women's everyday lives and honor the meaning and power of those stories. Through their respectful listening they come to a deeper understanding of the trajectories of women's experiences and the processes that have shaped their critical thinking and action. Chandler, for example, traces immigrant women's movement through grief, hardship, dislocation, and loss of dignity to growing collective consciousness, discovery of union power, solidarity, and transformative action. Her account, grounded in the power of voice and narrative, broadens and deepens our understanding of the movement from vulnerability and powerlessness to strength, capacity, and empowerment.

Through careful and close listening, contributors make meaningful links between personal struggles and political issues. Sethi and Hankivsky draw on Sapna's story to illustrate the ways public policy can exacerbate personal struggles over sexual identity and economic security. Carnahan demonstrates the power of community and audience in giving voice to trauma, suggesting possibilities for social community-level processes of acknowledgment and healing as well as at the individual level. Alvarez and Alessi address the importance of careful listening to stories of vulnerability, violence, and violation in order to act more effectively in response to practices of human trafficking. Further, they demonstrate the importance of social workers' giving voice to human rights in clinical settings as well as in policy and advocacy work.

Contributors speak of the power of performance to give voice publicly to emotions, experiences, and rights claims. They demonstrate the myriad ways women embody experiences of trauma, vulnerability, oppression, marginalization, and liberation. They use women's stories of migration, labor, confinement, representation, violation, and violence to give grounded meaning to theories of intersectionality. They recognize women as experts on their own lives whose theorizing from the margins expose the tensions and contradictions of the center. Further, they demonstrate that telling one's story can be a fundamental act of resistance to patriarchal, corporate, imperial, state, and militarized forms of power.

Engaging With Power in Its Many Forms

Throughout these diverse accounts the contributors demonstrate the need for social workers to have a critical understanding of power and its many forms and manifestations. Finn and Mileski draw from the insights of rural Mexican women organizers in describing power in terms of power over others, power with others, power from within, and power to act. This framing provides a way of talking about power that goes beyond power as a force of oppression or re-pression. It encourages social workers to look for and ask about the ways people make sense of their own sources of power and of the circumstances that bring people together to take action to shift the balance of power. At the same time, this frame also challenges us as social workers to examine how we are variably implicated in systems of domination and oppression, and how we may be ben-eficiaries as well as critics of the uneven distribution of burdens and opportu-nities in the global economy.

Walton and O'Brien illustrate in Chapter 11 the power of history and community that informs women's approach to local action in rural Nicaragua. Villarreal and Moore illustrate the power of young people's critique and critical consciousness to shape theory and inform practice. Taylor demonstrates the power of young women to critically engage with and deconstruct the power of media and images. Karandikar and Gezinski document the powerful critique of the globalizing forces shaping the life circumstances of a young sex worker living on the streets of Kamathipura. Carnahan illustrates the power of per-formance and the arts as forms of individual and collective expression, as sites for naming and bearing witness to trauma and violation, and as avenues for healing, consciousness-raising, and potentially transformative action. Chandler's account of casino workers' collective efforts reveals the profound value in the power of organizing from one's experience. Further, their stories of organization point to the power of connection and solidarity in the struggle rather than going it alone. Throughout the text, readers encounter the power of women's voices and action—women developing individual and collective critical consciousness grounded in their experiences of oppression, marginalization, resistance, hope, and action.

Challenge What Is Taken to Be Self-Evident

The contributors demonstrate the need to continually examine taken-for-granted assumptions about key concepts such as gender and difference. They pose questions and probe matters that are too often ignored or assumed to be self-evident. Following the direction of critical Black, Chicana, and transnational feminist theorists, the contributors examine ways assumptions about whiteness and privilege, Euro-Western worldviews, and particular constructions of the first world and third world woman and of the Global North and Global South have contributed to particular and problem-laden understandings of difference and otherness. They challenge a missionizing model of social work education and practice that positions the third world or Global South woman as the vulnerable and uninformed victim of oppressive forces, and the first world or Global North woman as her liberated, enlightened rescuer. They resist approaches that allow women to speak only as victims and point to women's capacities to critique their circumstances and engage in individual and collective action for change. Likewise, as illustrated powerfully by Jacobsen, they demand accountability of the victimizers, including the state, and the official power brokers who codify women's inequality in law.

Through their nuanced and fine-grained analyses, the contributors help us to see and better understand the ways policies and practices shape and are shaped by dominant and often taken-for-granted assumptions about gender. They avoid what Sethi and Hankivsky address as the trap of essentialization, oversimplification, and homogenization of women's lives and experiences. Instead they grapple with the complexity and diversity of those experiences. In so doing they reveal the importance of critical deconstruction of embedded assumptions about gender, vulnerabilities, capacities, and rights. Likewise, they challenge the marginalization of class consciousness and of working-class women's experience. As Chandler powerfully demonstrates, social workers have much to learn through research and practice that documents the experiences of working-class people, affirms the significance of their contributions, and critically examines the role of low-income labor in the global economy.

The contributors also challenge the notion that critical feminist theory applies only when speaking of women's lives. Karandikar and Gesinski use feminist-informed modes of inquiry to shed light on the common ground and important differences in men's and women's experiences on the streets of Kamathipura. Villarreal and Moore demonstrate the value of Chicana feminisms and borderlands theory to illuminate the struggles of men and women, young and old alike, in the face of complex forces of globalization. Alessi and Alvarez describe the complexities of human trafficking and the intricate ways in which gender relations and ideologies shape understandings and experiences of vulnerability, agency, and exploitation. Chandler shows how the experiences of casino women shed light on critical issues facing working-class laborers, men and women alike, around the world.

Action and Advocacy

The innovative approaches to research and practice undertaken by the contributors to this volume offer important lessons for social work action and advocacy. The community work of women in rural Nicaragua, the union organizing of Las Vegas casino workers, and the ongoing efforts to seek justice for battered women in prisons point to the importance of commitment to action and advocacy over the long haul, as change does not happen overnight. Further, they demonstrate the significance of history and the struggles and efforts that have gone before in informing the forms and directions of action and advocacy today.

The contributors also demonstrate the importance of listening to the diverse voices of women and of recognizing the power of their stories and their right to reality. The actions we take in response to people's struggles depend on our understanding of those struggles. As Sethi and Hankivsky's account of learning from Sapna's story of immigration illustrates, when we look through a gendered lens and listen with respect to people's stories of their experience, we come to a deeper and more complicated understanding of policy and practice issues and possible courses of action.

Similarly, as Chandler, Jacobsen, Carnahan, and Karandikar and Gezinski show, we as social workers need to be willing to challenge dominant notions of *expertise* and open ourselves to learning from those who have borne witness to trauma and violence and from those who have found their voice to name their pain and claim experience, and speak truth to power.

Further, as Jacobsen's discussion of women in prison reveals, we need to recognize and honor the power and possibility of women's agency and their capacities to not only critique exploitative systems but also to demand change and accountability. Jacobsen and others also stress the importance of collaborative action grounded in solidarity with women, men, and children engaged in daily struggles to improve the conditions of their lives. We as social workers have much to gain when we are willing to be active learners and participants in change efforts informed by the expertise of those who know intimately the needs and strengths of their communities. We are better prepared to be critical allies when our actions are informed by and in concert with those who bear the brunt of gender oppression in the context of globalization

Opening Spaces of Possibility

We end this chapter with visions of possibility. In their chapter, Finn and Mileski suggest that as teachers and learners committed to realizing gender equality we should embrace possibility; that we

> consider what is historically possible and to move beyond the past and the present to contemplate alternatives for the future. A sense of possibility enables us to look at what has been done, what can be done, and what can exist. Possibility draws attention to women's *agency*, or the capacity to act in the world as intentional, meaning-making beings, whose actions are shaped and constrained, but never fully determined by life circumstances. (p. 297)

Embracing possibility implies that we shape a vision of the future that is contextualized by the past and present but not confined by it. Embracing possibility implies that we claim and reclaim our sense of agency to create spaces where women are affirmed and supported in exercising their human capacities to sculpt fulfilling lives grounded in the global/local nexus. It implies that we recognize and appreciate that women reflexively influence and are influenced by the complexities of the global community.

Embracing possibility begins with critical consciousness. Embracing possibility in an honest way necessitates critical consciousness. Throughout the book, the contributors have approached their subject matter by first situating themselves within the contextual landscape of their work. To engage in the transformation of existing systems of gender inequality, we must critically examine our own sense of power and privilege and the roles we play in supporting oppressive structures or dismantling them.

Embracing possibility through multiple lenses. The contributors have demonstrated the utility of various theoretical perspectives and conceptual frames in accessing, interpreting, and engaging with gender justice issues. Their theoretical influences include critical race theory, radical feminism, Chicana feminisms, African feminism, womanism, intersectionality theory, critical trauma theory, global feminism, culturally relevant pedagogy, and critical race feminism.

Embracing possibility in multiple spaces. Although the contributors have introduced an expansive array of conceptual frames useful for our work in and outside the classroom, they have also suggested a number of methodological approaches to engaging in antioppressive gender justice work across the globe. Some of the approaches are theory driven. For example, critical race theory suggests that we can stimulate the consciousness of marginalized client groups through the cultivation of counterspaces (Taylor) and activities through which they may find solace in communing with one another, describe the microaggressions they experience, and share counterstories.

Carnahan's work, which extends from critical trauma theory, exemplifies the power of performance poetry in unearthing trauma toward healing and wholeness. Other methodological approaches to antioppressive gender justice work suggested by the contributors include community organization tactics, such as the cultivation of women's collectives (Walton & O'Brien).

Embracing possibilities of inquiry. In the context of making meaning through research, the contributors employed a variety of approaches. These include community-based participatory research, narrative research, case study, grounded theory, policy analysis, and empirical methodological approaches. The diversity of methods used by the contributors points to the utility of various approaches to inquiry in conducting meaningful gender-centered research.

Embracing possibilities of critical pedagogy. Although all the contributors have offered suggested learning activities designed to actively engage students in critical examination of global gender oppression, Finn and Mileski and Sakamoto have also shared specific strategies for engaging in critically conscious pedagogy. They demonstrate the importance of creating spaces in which students are not only respected but also challenged to examine their own positionality and the ways they may become intentionally engaged in the struggle for gender justice.

Embracing possibilities for social work practice across system levels. In addition to offering pedagogical suggestions, the contributors have also provided implications for social work practice across systems levels. Carnahan suggests that we examine how our clients' mental health is a function of powerful macroinfluences such as patriarchy, poverty, and political and ideological forces that shape the configurations of their daily lives. As we work with clients, we are challenged to examine the ways their individual histories of loss, trauma, dislocation, sexual violence, intersecting oppressions, scarcity, and marginalization contribute to various mental health outcomes.

In their extensive review of the literature related to gender and governance in a global context, Shepherd and Ferguson (2011) suggest that feminist engagements with globalization may be best captured by three major themes: space, institutions, and power. Clearly, our contributors have expanded our notions regarding the spaces in which we practice social work. Whether we are in the red-light district of Mumbai, India; the fields of Tola, Rivas, Nicuagara; a casino in Las Vegas; a home in Seoul, South Korea; or a market in Accra, Ghana, we are not only challenged to interrogate our sense of place but to create spaces for those with whom we intervene that recognize and draw on the significant assets that frame their social location as we partner with them to enhance their capacities to realize their aspirations.

References

hooks, b. (1984). *Feminist theory from margin to center.* Boston, MA: South End Press.

Shepherd, L., & Ferguson, L. (2011). Gender, governance, and power: Finding the global and the local level. *Globalizations, 8*(2), 127–133.

ABOUT THE AUTHORS

EDWARD J. ALESSI, PhD, LCSW, is assistant professor at Rutgers University School of Social Work. His research and scholarly interests include lesbian, gay, bisexual, and transgender (LGBT) mental health issues, LGBT-affirmative psychotherapy, posttraumatic stress disorder, and justice-oriented clinical practice. He graduated with a PhD from the New York University Silver School of Social Work in 2010 and with an MS in Social Work from the Columbia University School of Social Work in 2001.

MARÍA BEATRIZ ALVAREZ is a clinical social worker with more than 20 years of experience in psychiatric social work with immigrant children and families. She is currently a doctoral candidate at New York University Silver School of Social Work and the interim director of social work and care coordination at Morgan Stanley Children's Hospital of New York Presbyterian in Manhattan. Her interest in social justice and immigration led her to the research of human trafficking. She has written and lectured about this topic and trained physicians and nurses in identifying and assisting trafficked persons in hospital settings.

SARAH (SAY) CARNAHAN, MA, MSW, holds a BA in women's studies from the University of Maine at Farmington and an MA in women's studies and a clinical MSW from The Ohio State University (OSU). She is currently a PhD candidate in women's, gender, and sexuality studies at OSU. Sarah has worked in clinical capacities in community mental health and, most recently, at the Ohio State counseling center. She has taught undergraduate women's, gender, and sexuality courses throughout her time at OSU. Sarah's long-term goal is to work in clinical practice while teaching in an adjunct position in women's studies or social work. Sarah's practice takes a feminist, DBT-informed approach, and she is particularly passionate about the clinical areas of trauma, women/women's issues, LGBTQIA issues, eating disorders/body image, and grief. Sarah is a member of Phi Kappa Phi honor society and the National Association of Social Workers.

SUSAN CHANDLER is associate professor of social work at the University of Nevada, Reno. A graduate of Oberlin College (BA); California State University, Sacramento (MSW); and the University of California, Berkeley (PhD), she teaches courses in social welfare policy, women's issues, community organizing, and structural oppression. Chandler's and Jill Jones's book, *Casino Women: Courage in Unexpected Places* (Cornell University Press, 2011), reporting on a 10-year study of the work lives of women in Nevada casinos, won the 2012 Oral History Association Book Prize. Chandler regularly publishes articles on history, race, and wage labor in relation to social work and in 2002 was named Nevada Social Worker of the Year for her study *Working Hard, Living Poor: A Living Wage Study for Nevada.*

JANET L. FINN is professor of social work at the University of Montana and faculty member in the International Development Studies and the Women and Gender Studies programs. She holds an MSW from Eastern Washington University and a PhD in social work and anthropology from the University of Michigan. She has authored and edited numerous books and articles about community, women, childhood, youth, social justice, and transnational issues including *Mining Childhood: Growing Up in Butte, 1900–1960* (2012); *Childhood, Youth, and Social Work in Transformation* (2009); *Just Practice: A Social Justice Approach to Social Work* (2008); and a special issue of *Children and Youth Services Review* titled "Place, Power, and Possibility: Rethinking Social Work with Children and Youth" (2013).

OLENA HANKIVSKY, PhD, is professor, School of Public Policy, and founder and director of the Institute for Intersectionality Research and Policy at Simon Fraser University in Vancouver, Canada . Hankivsky is a research chair in new perspectives in gender and health at the Canadian Institutes of Health Research and a senior scholar in population health (Michael Smith Foundation for Health Research). Research interests include gender mainstreaming, gender based analysis, and intersectionality-based analysis. Her publications have appeared in Social Science and Medicine, Canadian Public Policy, Canadian Journal of Political Science, Critical Public Health, and Critical Social Policy. Among her more recent book publications are Women's Health in Canada: Critical Perspective on Theory and Policy (University of Toronto Press, 2007), Health Inequities in Canada: Intersectional Frameworks and Practices (University of British Columbia Press, 2011), and Gender, Politics and Society in Ukraine (University of Toronto Press, 2012).

CAROL JACOBSEN is professor of art, women's studies, and human rights at the University of Michigan. Her social documentary work in film and photography draws on contemporary interviews, court files, and historical archives to investigate issues of women's criminalization and censorship. Her work has been exhibited and screened worldwide, often co-sponsored by Amnesty International, Human Rights Watch, and other nonprofits. She has received awards from the National Endowment for the Arts, Paul Robeson Foundation, Women in Film, and others. Her critical writings have appeared in the Hastings Women's Law Journal, The New York Law Review, Signs Journal, Social Text, Art in America, and other publications. Jacobsen serves as director of the Michigan Women's Justice & Clemency Project, a grassroots advocacy and public education effort for human rights and freedom for wrongly convicted women prisoners.

SHARVARI KARANDIKAR, PhD, is assistant professor at Ohio State University. She began her career practicing as a social worker for sex workers and victims of sex trafficking in Mumbai, India. During her PhD program in social work at the University of Utah, and through her work at the Tata Institute of Social Sciences in Mumbai and later at The Ohio State University, she has focused her research efforts on issues related to the female victims of sex trafficking, particularly on gender-based violence and health and mental health issues. Karandikar's current research relates to sex trafficking in Asia, egg donation, international surrogacy, and medical tourism and its effects on women.

JEONGAH KIM earned her PhD in social work from The Ohio State University. She is currently an assistant professor at the University of Alabama at

Birmingham. Kim's research interests have revolved around factors associated with substance abuse and HIV/AIDS. She has more than 20 publications in national and international journals. She was chosen as one of 14 emerging leaders by the Addiction Technology Transfer Center Network institute who can contribute to minority communities and the field of addictions as a scholar. Her current interdisciplinary research concerns health and mental health disparities. Her scholarly activities also focus on addressing challenges related to various social welfare policies unique to developing nations. Kim is dedicated to social justice and attention to spirituality in social work and related philosophical, practice, and policy concerns. She has taught human behavior and the social environment, social welfare policy, spirituality and social work, program evaluation, and human diversity in BSW and MSW programs.

LINDSAY B. GEZINSKI is assistant professor at the University of Utah. She received her PhD in social work with a graduate minor in women's, gender, and sexuality studies from The Ohio State University. Gezinski is particularly interested in the intersection of poverty, gender, and social policy from a feminist perspective. Her research focuses on the commodification of women's bodies, specifically pertaining to sex work and transnational reproductive assistance. To date, her sex work research has explored gender-based violence, health, and the history of trafficking.

KARA MILESKI is currently a doctoral student at the University of Utah's School of Social Work. Her areas of interest include community-based participatory research methods and working with individuals resettled in the United States with refugee status. Currently, she spends much of her time at the University Neighborhood Partners Hartland Partnership Center in Salt Lake City, UT, working with individuals and families living on the West Side of Salt Lake City. She completed her MSW at the University of Montana, where her focus was on an international perspective in social work.

ALI MOORE attended Pacific University in Forest Grove, OR, where she earned her BSW with a minor in peace and conflict studies. In 2008 she volunteered as a peer educator in the village of Lugalo, Tanzania, to mobilize children, youths, and community members concerning issues of sexual reproductive health, HIV/AIDS, and gender equality. Moore earned her master's in international social work from Dominican University, seeking the skills and knowledge to transform social inequalities that perpetuate and exacerbate preventable health issues. She worked with EngenderHealth in Tanzania toward the nonviolent transformation of gender inequalities in the region. Moore currently is an in-home service worker with Hogares, Inc., in New Mexico, doing family and community based social work. One of her special interests is incorporating Chicana feminism and intersectionality into research and international development work.

PATRICIA O'BRIEN is an associate professor at the University of Illinois at Chicago, Jane Addams College of Social Work, teaching community practice, practice with women, practice in corrections, and qualitative methods. Her scholarship focuses on the complex and overlapping factors that relate to women's criminalization and pathways of reentry and recovery. She was the on-site coordinator of the 2011 Unsettling Feminisms Conference from which the chapter on women and food in Nicaragua in a context of globalization emerged.

TONYA EVETTE PERRY is professor of social work at Alabama A & M University. Having taught at Howard University and Fordham University, she has more than 13 years of graduate teaching experience. Perry earned her PhD in social work from the University of Alabama, a BA in psychology from Edinboro University of Pennsylvania, and an MSW from Tulane University. A former Johns Hopkins International AIDS Research Fellow and Fulbright Scholar, Perry is a seasoned international researcher whose primary publications address sociocultural issues related to the effects of HIV/AIDS and varied health conditions of women of African ancestry and the effects of development on the status of women. Perry served as a research and training consultant for the Global Health Council and The Balm In Gilead. She currently serves as a reviewer for the *Journal of HIV/AIDS & Social Services* and holds appointments on CSWE's Council on the Role and Status of Women and the U.S. Department of Health and Human Services Region IV Health Equity Council.

IZUMI SAKAMOTO is associate professor, Factor-Inwentash Faculty of Social Work, and academic fellow, the Centre for Critical Qualitative Health Research,

University of Toronto. A former Fulbright Scholar, she received her MSW, MS (social psychology), and PhD (social work and psychology) from the University of Michigan and BA and MA from Sophia University, Japan. Sakamoto's research and teaching focus on antioppression, empowerment, globalization, community organizing, qualitative research, and decolonization of dominant knowledge through community-based and arts-informed research. As principal investigator, Sakamoto has studied equity, antioppression, and social inclusion of immigrants and ciswomen and transwomen who have experienced homelessness. Focusing on the tacit dimension of knowledge and collaborating with professional artists, she has used photography and theatrical techniques to create knowledge with research participants, which then led to various knowledge mobilization activities including reader's theatre performances, art exhibits, and videos.

BHARATI SETHI is working toward her PhD in community planning, policy, and organization at the Faculty of Social Work, Wilfrid Laurier University, Ontario, Canada. In 2012 she was nominated as one of the Top 25 Immigrants to Canada and honored as one of Laurier's 100 Alumni of Achievement. She received the Primary Health Care Fellowship, the Vanier Canada Graduate Scholarship (PhD), Ontario Women's Health Scholarship, and the Inaugural Hilary M. Weston Scholarship (MSW). Sethi came to Canada as a migrant from Mumbai, India, and entered social work out of commitment to social justice and to bring about social change. Her interests include researching issues affecting immigrants and refugees in Canada today, especially those residing in small and midsized urban–rural regions of Canada; community-based participatory research; arts-based methods; and intersectionality theory. Her dream is to advocate for more policy, programs, and actions that reduce social inequality and sustain the well-being of individuals, families, and communities.

LETICIA VILLARREAL SOSA is assistant professor at Dominican University's Graduate School of Social Work. She earned her PhD at the University of Chicago, SSA. Her prior experience includes practice as a school social worker in a variety of educational settings. Her research interests include gender, migration, immigrant integration, mental health, social identity, violence, and human rights. Recent publications include articles on effective school teams and on the role of the school social worker in the state of Louisiana and a chapter titled "Identity and Trauma in the Gang Context" for a book on Latinos and education in Chicago. She also co-authored a paper examining practices of the United Nations Commissions of Inquiry. Currently she is conducting community based participatory research at Taller de Jose, a social service agency serving primarily Latino immigrants, on conceptualizing the model of "accompaniment" and identifying psychosocial outcomes, and is working on various international projects in Azerbaijan, Ecuador, and Guatemala.

TONISHA TAYLOR earned her bachelor of arts in psychology from Medgar Evers College/City University of New York (CUNY) and her MSW from Hunter College School of Social Work/CUNY. She is also near completion of an MA in language and literacy from City College/CUNY. Originally from Brooklyn, NY, she brings a unique perspective to her roles as social worker and educator, having worked with various urban social service agencies prior to assuming responsibilities as a faculty member and administrator in academia. Taylor's social work background and subsequent interactions with students in higher education have been influential in the independent research she has conducted, which examines the dynamics of societal and cultural influences within the classroom setting.

QUENETTE L. WALTON, AM, is currently a doctoral student at the University of Illinois at Chicago, Jane Addams College of Social Work; a Diversifying Faculty in Illinois fellow; and a Council on Social Work Education Minority Fellowship Program fellow. Quenette completed her undergraduate degree in psychology at the University of Michigan, Ann Arbor, and completed her MSW at the University of Chicago, School of Social Service Administration. Her research interests focus on examining the complex interaction of race, social class, gender, and cultural context as factors in behavioral health disparities among middle-class African American women.

Index

Figures and tables are indicated by f and t following the page number.